THE GODDESSES' MIRROR

THE GODDESSES' MIRROR

Visions of the Divine from East and West

by DAVID KINSLEY

State University of New York Press

Published by
State University of New York Press, Albany

Printed in the United States of America

For information, address State University of New York Press, State University Plaza, Albany, N.Y., 12246

Library of Congress Cataloging-in-Publication Data

Kinsley, David R.
The goddesses' mirror: visions of the divine from East and West / David Kinsley.
p. cm.
Bibliography: p.
ISBN 0-88706-835-9. ISBN 0-88706-836-7 (pbk.)
1. Goddesses. 2. Women and religion. I. Title.
BL473.5.K56 1988 87-36792
291.2′11—dc 19 CIP

To Cary

CONTENTS

PREFACE

I chose the title "The Goddesses' Mirror" (suggested by my wife) because it conveys my attempt to reflect accurately a variety of female images of the divine. Then, too, the word *mirror* is derived from the Latin *mirari,* meaning "to wonder at." I hope that readers of this book will feel some of the wonder that I have felt in seeking to understand and appreciate these ten visions of the divine feminine.

The chapters on Durgā, Lakṣmī, and Sītā are slightly revised versions of material that appeared in my book *Hindu Goddesses* © 1985 The Regents of the University of California.

INTRODUCTION

Some years ago, when the USSR first began its manned space program, a story was popular that featured a *Tass* reporter's interview of the first cosmonaut upon his return to earth. With a glint of mischief in his eye and pencil poised, the reporter asked the first human space voyager: "Well, comrade, did you see God up there?" Imagine the suprise of the godless Marxist reporter when his fellow comrade replied: "Yes, I did see God up there!" Briefly left speechless, the reporter recovered his professional instincts to ask: "Well, comrade, tell us then, what did God look like?" The cosmonaut replied: "She is black!"

The humor of this story is based on people's presuppositions in Western culture about the sex and color of the divine, which are assumed to be male and white. To a great extent, these presuppositions have been inherited, and are still maintained, by the three great sister religions of the West: Judaism, Christianity, and Islam. Commenting on the sexist tendencies of Christian theology, Rosemary Ruether says: "Starting with the basic assumption that the male is the normative human person and therefore also the normative image of God, all symbols, from God-language and christology to church and ministry, are shaped by the pervasive pattern of the male as center, the female as subordinate and auxiliary."[1]

Under the continuing influence of these monotheistic traditions, goddesses tend to be associated with archaic ("primitive"), pagan, or Asiatic traditions, which to varying degrees are considered peripheral or unsophisticated about the nature of deity.

It is obvious to anyone who knows something about non-Western religious traditions, however, that in the history of humankind the divine has been perceived in female form just as often and typically as it has in male form. Indeed, it also has become obvious that even in the male-dominated traditions of Judaism and Christianity (if not Islam) important strains of female imagery exist.[2] It is also apparent to students of religion that in some streams of the Christian tradition the Virgin Mary functions in many ways like a very powerful deity.[3] In fact, the history of religions offers us a rich, diverse, and vigorous population of female deities, against which, some might say, the Judaic, Christian, and Muslim pantheons seem one-sided and dull.

Several years ago, one of my graduate students in religious studies suggested that I teach an undergraduate course on goddesses. I can remember one of my first thoughts after hearing her suggestion. "A whole course on goddesses?!" A product of the Protestant Christian tradition, and still very much under its influence, I thought the material for such a course might be somewhat thin. In a sense, the material was a bit thin. There were not at that time, and there still are not, a great number of books about the female deities that have been important in the world's religious traditions. It soon became evident to me, however, that in the history of religions the material is simply overwhelming. Goddesses are everywhere.

To a great extent, this book is a result of teaching that course on goddesses for several years. I thought that the ideal textbook for an undergraduate course on goddesses would present fairly detailed portraits of different types of goddesses from several religious traditions or cultures. Such a textbook would suggest the importance of goddesses throughout the world and also would mitigate against the tendency to stereotype goddesses as all being more or less the same. Too often it is assumed or implied that if a deity is female, her sex dominates her character. It is assumed or implied that she is associated with motherhood, fertility, and the earth, for example. Of course, many very important goddesses in many places and at many times have been associated with these realities. However, the diversity of characteristics and roles played by goddesses goes far beyond such simplification. Some goddesses have nothing to do with motherhood, fertility, or the earth. Others play traditionally male roles and often seem to take delight in violating roles that are associated with women in the cultures in which they are revered. Some goddesses, as we might expect in the male-dominated cultures in which they exist, provide paradigms for female subordination to males, but this is not always, or even typically, the case.

A brief survey of some of the most popular goddesses in the world's religions also calls into question the rather neat equations: male = culture, female = nature. Many goddesses are, of course, strongly associated with the earth itself and the mysterious powers of fertility that seem to reside in the earth. But many goddesses lack this association and instead are strongly associated with the refinements and techniques of culture and the institution of civilization in general. Other goddesses, in the course of long and illustrious histories that have spanned millenia, and whose worship spread throughout many lands, achieved positions of such eminence that they were regarded as being present in all significant natural phenomena as well as instituting and inspiring in an ongoing fashion all important aspects of civilized life.

In selecting the ten goddesses featured in this book, I tried to present some of the most common types and to give an indication of the diversity of characteristics and roles that are found among goddesses in the world's religions.[4] I also limited myself to goddesses who are fairly well known in the history of religions and who were, or still are, widely worshiped. I also chose to limit my choices to goddesses associated with the so-called high religions of the past or present. There are many goddesses in tribal religions throughout the world, but I chose not to venture into this territory in this book.

Three of the goddesses treated in this book are from the Hindu tradition (Durgā, Lakṣmī, and Sītā), while two others are from the religious tradition of ancient Greece (Athena and Aphrodite). My preference for Hindu goddesses is explained by my long-standing interest in the Hindu religious tradition, and in Hindu goddesses per se.[5] My decision to include three Hindu goddesses in this book was also influenced by the fact that, among the great living religions, Hinduism has by far the most vigorous and diverse goddess mythology and worship. My preference for Greek goddesses is explained by the importance of Greece in the history of Western civilization, the importance of Greek mythology in Western culture, and the clarity with which Athena and Aphrodite represent two distinct types of goddesses.

Goddess Worship and the Status of Women

An issue that naturally arises in the study of goddesses concerns the relationship of goddess worship to the status of women. On the analogy of the Western religious traditions that are well known to us, in which a male-imaged deity reflects a patriarchal or male-dominated society, it is often assumed that religions in which goddesses figure prominently, or in which they dominate, must reflect a society in which the status of women is high, or even a society in which women dominate. "The ruling sex, having the power to diffuse its own outlooks, tends to generalize its specific ideology. Should the trends of the subordinate sex run counter, they are likely to be suppressed all the more forcibly in proportion as the dominant sex is more overwhelming. The result is that the hegemony of male deities is usually associated with the dominance of men and the hegemony of female deities with the dominance of women."[6] It is often assumed that goddesses, especially powerful and independent ones, affirm and promote female power and creativity and that this affirmation must have positive consequences in the social realm.

It certainly would be hard to deny that powerful, independent, creative goddesses have positive effects upon women in the societies in which they are worshiped, to deny that they affirm women's nature and powers.[7] However, it is not the case that a clear relationship exists between goddess-centered mythologies and religions and female-dominated societies, or even between goddess-centered religions and egalitarian societies in which neither males nor females dominate. Many examples of patriarchal cultures are found in which goddesses are very important or central. Indeed, each of the ten goddesses discussed in this book belongs to a society in which, to a greater or lesser degree, men dominate women. This does not mean that I prefer patriarchal societies or that I prefer goddesses who have been "tampered with" by male hands and minds. It reflects, alas, the fact that almost all historical cultures that we know about, and most nonliterate traditional cultures studied by anthropologists, tend to be male dominated to some extent. It is very difficult to find examples of goddesses who belong to societies in which there is egalitarianism between the sexes or in which males are subordinate to women.

Goddesses in Prepatriarchal Cultures

But perhaps there was a time when this was not so. Perhaps in the past goddesses (or a Goddess) were central in cultures that were nonpatriarchal; perhaps there were cultures in which goddesses (or a Goddess) were firmly grounded in female religious experience and were worshiped primarily by women and female priesthoods. Very tempting evidence exists, in fact, to support such a position, and the theory in recent years has found many supporters.

Although the theory of a prepatriarchal period in the history of culture is not new,[8] a wealth of new archaeological evidence in the past century has provided scholars with a great deal more data upon which to base such a theory. In the nineteenth century, the theory was based to a great extent on myths and legends in classical cultures that spoke of a period in the past when women dominated society. Today, however, with the discovery of many civilizations from the prehistoric period, scholars are able to base their arguments on physical evidence as well as on myths and legends from classical cultures. The archaeological evidence available is vast and still growing rapidly and enables scholars to gain an increasingly detailed picture of what prehistoric cultures might have been like.

Although the scholars who have argued for the existence of a prepatriarchal culture differ about many details, they share several ideas. In brief, their position is that in prehistory cultures existed in which the worship of goddesses was central. Although evidence of male deities is present in these cultures, the number of images of females and their location in sanctuaries seem to indicate that females were central to the religion (or religions) of these cultures.

The age and extent of these cultures (or culture) are still being discussed by the scholars who advocate this position. Female figurines in considerable quantity date back to the Paleolithic period throughout Europe and the Near East and may indicate a female-centred religion dating back some thirty thousand years. However, most scholars who support this theory concentrate on the Neolithic (7000–5000 B.C.E.), Chalcolithic (5500–3500 B.C.E.), and Bronze Age (3000–1200 B.C.E.) periods in the area that Marija Gimbutas has designated Old Europe.[9] Some scholars also include the prehistoric periods of the ancient Near Eastern cultures (Egypt, Sumeria, and Palestine), while others extend the period of this female-dominated religion well into the historical period, during which time it was opposed and repressed by the new, patriarchal religions until the final triumph of Christianity around 500 C.E., which spelled the final destruction of the goddess religion.[10] Some scholars also see in the veneration of the Virgin Mary in Christianity a weak survival of this religion.[11]

The new patriarchal religions are sometimes identified with the Indo-Europeans who migrated into, or invaded, the areas dominated by goddess religions during the Bronze Age. The Indo-Europeans were nomadic warriors whose pantheon was dominated by aggressive, powerful, warrior deities.[12] Others understand the shift from prepatriarchal culture to patriarchal culture as centered in the transition from village culture to city culture. That is, the shift is understood more in terms of changes in the nature of society and economics than it is in terms of the conflict between differing and conflicting cultures.[13] As people began to concentrate in cities, as population grew, as warfare increased between cities and regions, as more complicated economic factors became central to society, and as a clearer separation between private and public realms became more important, males began to assume more and more power, which came to be reflected in religion by the increasing dominance of male deities, who not infrequently are pictured as slaying female monsters (symbolic, some scholars say, of the old Goddess or of the Goddess religion).[14] Still others tend to view a shift from prepatriarchal religion to patriarchal religion as expressing no less than a change in consciousness. The dawning of historical consciousness involved the discovery of human beings as independent agents who could affect history; a gradual drawing away from the natural world (represented by goddesses) took place, and male gods representing new realities and emphases began to take over human beings' religious consciousness.[15]

The scholars who support the theory of prepatriarchal culture in which goddess worship was central, while differing on some points, generally agree on several important characteristics of this religion and culture. They generally favor thinking of one supreme goddess who manifested herself in a variety of forms, instead of speaking of a polytheistic religion, that is, a religion that reveres several (or many) different goddesses.[16] She is "the Goddess" or "the Great Goddess" or "the Ancestress." This Goddess, although undoubtedly possessing a variety of functions and characteristics insofar as she reigned for so long and over such a large area, was primarily the mother of all life. Merlin Stone refers to her as the great Ancestress who gave birth to all human beings and all plants and animals,[17] while Gimbutas deciphers a whole series of images and motifs to argue that the Goddess of Old Europe was essentially a being "incarnating the creative principal as Source and Giver of All."[18] A central function of the Goddess was her role as mother, giver of life. Images of the Goddess pregnant, giving birth, or holding infants are not uncommon.[19] But she was not just the mother of human beings, she was the mother of all, the spirit that imbued all creation with life and vitality. She was not, in any important way, a warrior goddess, although she was associated with death.[20] Her association with death, according to Gimbutas, suggests her second major aspect, "the Taker of All," a form in which she was responsible for transformation, metamorphosis, regeneration, rebirth, and so on.[21]

This Goddess (or these goddesses) also is affirmed by these scholars to have been absolutely central to this culture (or these cultures). "It is obvious that the Goddess, not gods, dominated the old European pantheon; the goddess ruled absolutely over human, animal, and plant life. The Goddess, not gods, spontaneously generated the life-force and created the universe. As demonstrated by the thousands of figurines and temples from the Neolithic through the Copper Ages, the male god was an adjunct to the female Goddess, as consort or son."[22] While evidence of male deities exists, the sheer number of female figurines and symbols seems to imply the centrality of female deities.

The worship or religion of these goddesses (or Goddess) is said by some scholars to have been controlled or dominated by women. That is, we have in these cultures, they argue, not only a goddess-centered religion but a female-centered religion, a religion in which priestesses were active and dominant and in which the theology/mythology was based on female religious experience.[23]

Finally, it is theorized, not only was the religion of this culture goddess centered and possibly female managed, the society itself, reflecting the centrality of the Goddess, was one in which there was egalitarianism between the sexes, or in which women were more important than men. "There is absolutely no indication that Old European society was patrilinear or patriarchal. Evidence from the cemeteries does not indicate a subordinate position of women. There was no ranking along a patriarchal masculine-feminine value scale as there was in Europe after the infiltration of steppe pastoralists, who introduced the patriarchal and the patrilineal system."[24] Insofar as women embodied the Goddess's life-giving power, and insofar as the role of males in the reproductive process may not yet have been known, females were probably revered more than males and probably dominated these cultures.[25]

If this theory is true, it has some important implications for the study of religions generally, and for the study of goddesses in particular. An important implication for the history of the religions that arose in the ancient Near East and Mediterranean areas—Judaism, Christianity, and Islam—is that these religions might represent a fundamental theological reorientation that transformed the social order to a patriarchy. Put another way, these three religions, which have dominated so much of the world's religious history for the past three thousand years, might be understood as recent deviations from a goddess-dominated religion and a woman-centered culture or as representing a brief interlude in the history of religions during which goddesses have been temporarily excluded from the imaging of the divine.

Another important implication of this theory is that goddesses of later patriarchal cultures might well be, to a greater or lesser extent, diminutions or modifications of earlier prepatriarchal goddesses. A further implication follows from this. If goddesses as found in patriarchal cultures are diminutions of earlier goddesses, then it might be necessary to adopt what Elizabeth Schüssler-Fiorenza calls a "hermeneutics of suspicion" when trying to interpret these goddesses.[26] That is, we should assume that these goddesses have been portrayed and envisioned from an androcentric point of view and should therefore try to see behind some of their characteristics and functions to realities and themes that are prepatriarchal, or nonpatriarchal, and grounded in female religious experience.

The Greek goddesses, for example, who are perhaps the best known to us in the West, belong to a patriarchal culture and are part of a mythology/theology dominated by the male deity Zeus. To a great extent, these goddesses are defined by their relationships to males, especially in later classical sources.[27] According to the theory of a prepatriarchal period in which goddesses were central, it would be necessary to try to trace the roots of these goddesses to earlier versions of the divine feminine that were free from patriarchal influences. This would involve, for example, tracing Athena's history and symbolism to the Minoan civilization, and perhaps earlier, in order to discover her original or primordial character as a prehistoric bird or snake goddess;[28] similarly with Aphrodite and other Greek goddesses. In classical Greece, Aphrodite to a great extent was viewed as a goddess of sexual passion who became entangled with a variety of males and who entangled others in romantic or erotic relationships. In seeking Aphrodite's earlier, prepatriarchal nature, it perhaps would be necessary to discover her roots as a goddess associated with earth and fertility. A hermeneutics of suspicion as applied to the Greek goddesses also might seek to discover a unified, primordial vision of the divine feminine in Bronze Age Greece. Such an earlier, unified deity might be hinted at in the goddesses Gaia and Demeter, who are affirmed in classical Greek mythology to be ancient or independent.[29]

In short, this theory would oblige scholars doing research on goddesses in patriarchal cultures to be sensitive to the possibility that these goddesses have been, or are in the process of being, transformed by patriarchal biases. It would oblige scholars to be suspicious particularly of goddesses who are depicted as subservient to males. Such goddesses, according to this theory, might well be survivals of earlier goddesses who affirmed female power and creativity but who subsequently were reinterpreted to conform to patriarchal biases.

The appeal of this theory, it seems to me, is obvious. It is depressing to think that even in cultures in which goddesses are central, males tend to dominate women. It is extremely appealing, on the other hand, to affirm that there was a time when women probably were equal to men, and perhaps even regarded as superior to men, and that this period is as vast, or vaster, than the period of recorded history. How subversive of smug male arrogance to affirm that for the majority of human history goddesses were the principal objects of reverence and that women were in charge of their worship and probably in charge of society as well.

I am sympathetic to this theory, and I think the evidence in support of it, or parts of it, is considerable. However, I do have some hesitations about the extent to which we can assume this theory has been proven beyond reasonable doubt and the extent to which it should be accepted as a central interpretive approach in the study of goddesses. My hesitations about the theory can be summarized under three points.

The most serious problem with the theory of a prepatriarchal culture in which goddesses were revered as central is that the cultures in question are dead and nonliterate. This means that the reconstruction of these cultures—their religion, society, and sexual roles—depends almost entirely on physical remains alone. The primary argument in favor of viewing these prehistoric cultures as nonpatriarchal is based on the abundance of female figurines and images, which are assumed (rightly, I think) to represent goddesses (or a Goddess). Indeed, that goddesses (or a Goddess) were central to these cultures (Old European, Minoan, and others) seems absolutely clear and beyond doubt.

How conclusive is this evidence, though, for determining the relative roles of males and females? Even if women dominated the worship of these goddesses, which might be implied on the basis of burial practices in which women were buried in the sanctuaries,[30] can we assume that these cultures were nonpatriarchal? Burial evidence is also cited as proof that these cultures were matrifocal in that women, and not men, were buried in houses.[31] While it is tempting to assume a necessary and positive relationship between goddess-centred and female-controlled religion, or between matrifocal (and perhaps matrilineal) customs, on the one hand, and a high status for women or sexual egalitarianism, on the other, many examples of goddess-centered religions, sometimes involving female participation and leadership, are found as part of patriarchal cultures. Hindu India is a good example of a patriarchal culture in which goddesses are central. Hinduism knows a great variety of goddesses, many of whom are powerful and independent, some of whom dominate male deities, yet Hindu culture is patriarchal. Hinduism seems to teach that a theology/religion/mythology in which goddesses are important does not necessarily imply sexual egalitarianism. Female power, creativity, and authority in the theological sphere do not necessarily imply high female status in the social sphere. Indeed, sometimes the same text can contain an elevated goddess theology, on the one hand, and a low estimate of women's status on the other. The author of the *Devi-bhāgavata-purāṇa*, for example, a text that praises the "Great Goddess" above all other deities, despises women.[32]

My hesitation concerning the extent to which physical evidence alone can be used to identify the nature of religion and society (and their interrelationships) in prehistoric cultures is expressed by the classical scholar Sarah Pomeroy. She is attracted to the theory of a prepatriarchal culture but is hesitant to affirm its existence on the basis of archaeological data alone. In an article on prehistoric matriarchy she says: "How gratifying it would be for a feminist scholar to discover that in prehistory, a period far larger than recorded history, women were not the second sex at all. Then we could rebut all the scholars since Aristotle who have complacently been stating that women are by nature inferior."[33] Later she says: "As a serious historian I must remind myself to suppress my burning desire to prove that women long ago enjoyed a position far superior than that of women nowadays, and instead merely identify the existing evidence, evaluate the evidence, and determine what deductions and conclusions, if any, may be drawn from the evidence."[34] And what does she conclude about the prehistoric period, in this case the Bronze Age in Greece and the surrounding areas? She concludes that it is very difficult to prove what kind of society existed on the basis of material evidence alone, or on the basis of later myths about earlier periods (here she is referring to Greek myths about a time when women held power over men).

> Still, what can a responsible historian deduce about the sociology of the late Bronze Age from the material remains? Very little. The major deities are mother goddesses, and mortal women played a more significant role than men in religious matters. . . . Yet in the classical period the fact that women played a significant religious role did not improve their low political, legal, and social status. Accordingly, although the prestige of Bronze Age women in religious affairs was certainly high, no historian should therefore deduce that their prestige was likewise high in other realms. . . .
>
> . . . The archaeological evidence is inconclusive with regard to social systems and women's roles, although it does permit us to say that women were dominant in the religious sphere.[35]

A second hesitation I have in accepting the theory of a prepatriarchal culture concerns the few examples we have of cultures in which men do not dominate women. The tendency toward male dominance seems strong both in historical cultures and in nonliterate cultures that have been studied by anthropologists. While some cultures are found in which egalitarianism between the sexes seems to exist, unfortunately the vast majority of cultures betray male dominance. There are several new cross-cultural studies of the status and roles of women, and the debate is far from conclusive concerning the extent to which male dominance exists in human culture. Thus far, the evidence does not seem to support the view that women enjoy more freedom and power in cultures that approximate those of which Stone, Gimbutas, and other theorists are speaking (that is, small village cultures in which agriculture is the basis of the economy). Some anthropological research also has recently shown that no strong, positive relationship exists between matrilineal and matrifocal societies and the relative freedom and power of women,[36] or between women's economic contribution and their relative status.[37]

A final hesitation I have in subscribing to the theory of a prepatriarchal culture as a central interpretive aspect of this book on goddesses concerns the geographical extent of such a culture, or cultures. Most of the research undertaken in connection with this theory concentrates on what Gimbutas calls Old Europe (southeastern Europe, primarily) and areas of the Ancient Near East (Sumeria and Palestine). Did such a prepatriarchal culture also exist in India, China, and Japan? Are we dealing with a variety of prehistoric cultures that are discreet in time and place, or are we to say that such a shift from prepatriarchal to patriarchal culture is a universal aspect of cultural development? I do not think most scholars are willing to support the latter alternative. If prepatriarchal cultures, then, are limited to certain places and times, it would be necessary to demonstrate how such a culture impinged upon a given historical culture (for example, Chinese, Indian, Japanese) in order to assume its applicability to goddesses who belong to these later historical cultures.[38]

It is also difficult to see the immediate applicability of this theory to goddesses who have arisen late in patriarchal cultures. Kuan-yin and the Virgin Mary, for example, clearly have aspects that relate them to earlier goddesses in their respective religions and cultures, but their relationship to prehistoric goddesses belonging to a prepatriarchal culture would be exceedingly tenuous at best. In short, some of the goddesses dealt with in this book are more likely than others to be affected by this theory. In cases where this is likely (where scholars have tried to apply the theory to the goddess in question), I have indicated this to the reader.

Another important point that is tangentially raised by the theory of a shift from prepatriarchal to patriarchal culture, or another way of raising similar kinds of questions, is the distinction between elite and popular religion, which is a problem I have thought about quite a bit in the context of Hinduism. Briefly, the elite version of Hinduism (or some other tradition) is dominated by males (females being excluded from educational institutions and traditions in most cases in India). The texts, upon which we are usually forced to base our pictures of these religions (especially in the case of dead cultures), are androcentric. The elite religion tends to play down certain aspects of popular religion (which may include a strong emphasis on goddess worship) that challenge, or differ from, its elitist (and male) biases. The popular tradition (often nonliterate), on the other hand, is more revealing of the religious experience of those who are excluded from the elite (usually women) and therefore may be more centered on the worship of goddesses, whose importance may be more central for women. I have tried to be sensitive to this issue in the treatment of the goddesses dealt with in this book, but I acknowledge the great dependence on written sources that is necessary, especially in the case of past civilizations.

Two women, contemporary Indian. Yves Vequaud, *Die Kunst von Mithila* (Brussels: Weber Genf, 1977), p. 91. Courtesy of Editions sous le vent, Paris.

Part I

Goddesses of the East

Chapter ***1***

Durgā, Warrior Goddess and Cosmic Queen

Hundreds of demons were slain by the shower of weapons unleashed by the Goddess. Others were thrown to the ground, stupefied by the ringing of her bell. She bound some of her enemies and dragged them on the ground with her noose. With her sword, she split demons in half and bashed others with her mace. The onslaught of the Goddess caused terrible bloodshed among the demons and resulted in a scene of gruesome carnage. Mortally wounded victims vomited blood, while some looked like porcupines having been wounded with so many arrows. Severed arms, legs, and heads littered the battlefield. Her victims jerked in the throes of death and appeared to be performing a macabre dance of death. The battlefield was so strewn with the wreckage of the demon army, and so flooded with blood, that it was nearly impassable. As a raging fire consumes fields and forests, so the Goddess devastated the ranks of the demon army.[1]

Introduction

The goddess Durgā is one of the most formidable and popular deities of the Hindu pantheon. Her primary mythological function is to combat demons who threaten the stability of the cosmos. In this role, she is depicted as a great battle queen with many arms, each of which wields a weapon. She rides a fierce lion and is described as irresistible in battle. The demon she is most famous for defeating is Mahiṣa, the buffalo demon. Her most popular epithet is Mahiṣamardinī, the slayer of Mahiṣa, and her most common iconographic representation shows her defeating him.

At a certain point in her history, Durgā becomes associated with the god Śiva as his wife. In this role, Durgā assumes domestic characteristics and is often identified with the goddess Pārvatī. She also takes on the role of mother in her later history. At her most important festival, Durgā Pūjā, she is shown flanked by four deities identified as her children: the gods Kārttikeya and Gaṇeśa and the goddesses Sarasvatī and Lakṣmī.

It also seems clear that Durgā has, or at least had at some point in her history, a close connection with the crops or with the fertility of vegetation. During her festival, which is held at harvest time, she is associated with plants, and she also receives blood offerings, which may suggest the renourishment of her powers of fertility.

The Warrior Goddess

Although several Vedic deities play central roles as demon slayers and warriors, no goddesses are cast in this function in Vedic literature. Although the name *Durgā* is mentioned in Vedic literature,[2] no goddess resembling the warrior goddess of later Hinduism is found in these early texts.

Around the fourth century, images of Durgā slaying a buffalo begin to become common throughout India.[3] By the medieval period (after the sixth century) Durgā has become a very well-known and popularly worshiped deity. Her mythological deeds come to be told in many texts, and descriptions of and injunctions to undertake her autumnal worship are common in several late texts.[4]

Historically, Durgā's origin seems to be among the indigenous, non-Āryan cultures of India. In addition to there being no similar goddesses among the deities of the Vedic tradition, many early references to Durgā associate her with peripheral areas such as the Vindhya Moutains, tribal peoples such as the Śabaras, and non-Āryan habits such as drinking liquor and blood and eating meat.[5] Although she becomes an establishment goddess in medieval Hinduism, protecting the cosmos from the threat of demons and guarding civilization like a female version of Viṣṇu, her roots seem to be among the tribal and peasant cultures of India that eventually leavened the male-dominated Vedic pantheon with several goddesses associated with power, blood, and battle.

Several accounts of Durgā's origin are found in Hindu mythology. She is sometimes said to arise from Viṣṇu as the power that makes him sleep or as his magical, creative power. In the *Viṣṇu-purāna*, Viṣṇu enlists her aid to help delude a demon king who is threatening the infant Kṛṣṇa (5.1.93). In the *Devī-māhātmya*, she comes to the aid of the god Brahmā and ultimately of Viṣṇu himself when Brahmā invokes her to leave the slumbering Viṣṇu so that he will awaken and fight the demons Madhu and Kaitabha (chapter 1). The *Skanda-purāṇa* says that once upon a time a demon named Durga threatened the world. Śiva requested Pārvatī to slay the demon. Pārvatī then assumed the form of a warrior goddess and defeated the demon, who took the form of a buffalo. Thereafter, Pārvatī was known by the name Durgā (2.83).[6] A similiar account of her origin is found in myths relating her defeat of the demons Śumbha and Niśumbha. Durgā emerges from Pārvatī in these accounts when Pārvatī sheds her outer sheath, which takes on an identity of its own as a warrior goddess.[7]

The best-known account of Durgā's origin, however, is told in connection with her defeat of the demon Mahiṣa. After performing heroic austerities, Mahiṣa was granted the boon that he would be invincible to all opponents except a woman. He subsequently defeated the gods in battle and usurped their positions. The gods then assembled and, becoming angry at the thought of Mahiṣa's triumph and their apparent inability to do anything about it, emitted their fiery energies. This great mass of light and strength congealed into the body of a beautiful woman, whose splendor spread throughout the universe. The parts of her body were formed from the male gods. Her face was formed from Śiva, her hair from Yama, her arms from Viṣṇu, and so on. Similarly, each of the male deities from whom she had been created gave her a weapon. Śiva gave her his trident; Viṣṇu, his discus; Vayu, his bow and arrows; and so on. Equipped by the gods and supplied by the god Himalaya with a lion as her vehicle, Durgā, the embodied strength of the gods, then roared mightily, causing the earth to shake.[8]

The creation of the goddess Durgā, then, takes place in the context of a cosmic crisis of one kind or another, which has been precipitated by a demon whom the male gods are unable to subdue. She is created because the situation calls for a woman, or a superior warrior, or a peculiar power that she possesses with which the demon may be deluded, or a combination of all three. Invariably, Durgā defeats the demon handily, demonstrating both superior martial ability and superior power. On the battlefield she often creates female helpers from herself. The most famous of these are the goddess Kālī and a group of ferocious deities known as the Mātṛakās (Mothers), who usually number seven.[9] These goddesses seem to embody Durgā's fury and are wild, bloodthirsty, and particularly fierce.[10] Durgā does not create male helpers, and, to my knowledge, she does not fight with male allies. Although she is created by the male gods and does their bidding, and although she is observed and applauded by them, she (along with her female helpers and attendants) fights without direct male support against male demons, and she always wins.

Durgā's distinctive nature, and to a great extent probably her appeal, comes from the combination of world-supportive qualities and liminal characteristics that associate her with the periphery of civilized order.[11] In many respects, Durgā violates the model of the Hindu woman. She is not submissive, she is not subordinated to a male deity, she does not perform household duties, and she excels at what is traditionally a male function—fighting in battle. As an independent warrior who can hold her own against any male on the battlefield, she reverses the normal role for females and therefore stands outside normal society. Unlike the normal female, Durgā does not lend her power or *śakti*

The creation of Durgā by the gods. From C. L. Bharany collection, reproduced from *Ritual Art of India* (London: Thames & Hudson, 1985), pl. 88, courtesy of Ajit Mookerjee.

Durgā slays the buffalo demon. From C. L. Bharany collection, reproduced from *Ritual Art of India* (London: Thames & Hudson, 1985), pl. 91, courtesy of Ajit Mookerjee.

to a male consort but rather *takes* power from the male gods in order to perform her own heroic exploits.[12] They give up their inner strength, fire, and heat to create her and in doing so surrender their potency to her.

Many renditions of Durgā's mythological exploits highlight her role reversal by portraying her male antagonists as enamored of her and wanting to marry her. They have no wish to fight her at all, assume that she will be no match for them in battle, and proceed to make offers of marriage to her.[13] In some variants of the myth, Durgā explains to her antagonist and would-be suitor that her family has imposed a condition on her marriage, namely, that her husband must first defeat her in battle. The suitor is unable to do this, of course, and is annihilated in his attempt. In some forms of the myth, the goddess rejects the offer of marrige with fierce, combative language, foretelling how she will tear her would-be suitor to pieces in battle. The antagonist, however, insists upon interpreting this language as a metaphor for love play and blindly insists upon trying to overcome the goddess in battle.[14] In the Mahiṣa myth as told in the *Devī-bhāgavata-purāṇa*, for example, a long dialogue takes place between Durgā and the demon in which Mahiṣa insists that as a woman the goddess is too delicate to fight, too beautiful for anything but love play, and must come under the protection and guidance of a man in order to fulfill her proper proclivities (5.16.46–65).

Because she is unprotected by a male deity, Mahiṣa assumes that Durgā is helpless (5.12.14–30), which is the way that women are portrayed in the Hindu law books.[15] In the law books, women are said to be incapable of handling their own affairs and to be socially inconsequential without relationships with men. They are significant primarily as sisters, daughters, and mothers of males, and as wives. In nearly all forms of her mythical exploits, Durgā is portrayed as independent from male support and relationships, yet irresistibly powerful. She is beautiful and seductive in appearance, but her beauty does not serve its normal function, which is to attract a husband. It serves to entice her victims into fatal battle.

In short, as a beautiful young woman who slays demons seeking to be her lovers and who exists independent of male protection or guidance, Durgā represents a vision of the feminine that challenges the stereotyped view of women found in traditional Hindu law books. She perhaps suggests the extraordinary power that is repressed in women who are forced into submissive and socially demeaning roles. In her role reversal, she exists outside normal structures and provides a version of reality that potentially, at least, may be refreshing and socially invigorating.[16]

Durgā's liminal nature is also evident in her favorite habitats and in some of her favorite habits. In nearly all of her myths, Durgā is associated with mountains, usually the Himalayas or the Vindhyas. One of her common epithets is Vindhyavāsinī, She Who Dwells in the Vindhya Mountains. These

Durgā kills the buffalo demon, contemporary lithograph.

mountain regions are areas considered geographically peripheral to civilized society and inaccessible except through heroic efforts. The Vindhyas, in particular, are also regarded as dangerous because of the violent and hostile tribal peoples who dwell there. Indeed, Durgā is said to be worshiped by tribal groups such as the Śabaras. In this worship, furthermore, she is said to receive (and to enjoy) meat and blood, both of which are regarded by civilized Āryan society as highly polluting. In the *Devī-māhātmya*, Durgā is also described as quaffing wine during battle in her fight with Mahiṣa (3.33) and as laughing and glaring with reddened eyes under its influence. In the concluding scene of the *Devī-māhātmya*, her devotees are instructed to propitiate her with offerings of their own flesh and blood (13.8). Durgā's preference for inaccessible dwelling places, her worship by tribal peoples, her taste for intoxicating drink, meat, and blood, her ferocious behavior on the battlefield, and her preference for the flesh and blood of her devotees portray a goddess who stands outside the civilized order, whose presence is to be found only after stepping out of the orderly world into the liminal space of the mountainous regions where she dwells.

Reinforcing Durgā's tendencies to the antistructural or liminal are certain associations with negative, or at least inauspicious, qualities or powers such as sleep, hunger, and *māyā* (in the sense of delusion). In the Mahiṣa episode of the *Devī-māhātmya* she is called She Whose Form Is Sleep (5.15), She Whose Form Is Hunger (5.16), She Whose Form Is Shadow (5.17), and She Whose Form Is Thirst (5.19).

These associations are particularly emphasized in versions of the myth that tell of Durgā's aid to Brahmā and Viṣṇu against the demons Madhu and Kaitabha. In this myth, as told in the *Devī-māhātmya*, Madhu and Kaitabha are born from Viṣṇu's ear wax. They threaten to kill the god Brahmā, who in turn has been born from a lotus sprung from Viṣṇu's navel. Brahmā appeals to the goddess in the form of sleep to come forth from Viṣṇu so that he will awaken and slay the demons. Throughout the episode, the goddess is called Mahāmāyā, the power that throws people into the bondage of delusion and attachment (1.40). Indeed, Viṣṇu is successful in slaying Madhu and Kaitabha only because the goddess deludes them into offering Viṣṇu a boon; he accepts and asks that they permit him to slay them (1.73–74). She is also called Great Delusion (Mahāmohā) (1.58); Great Demoness (Mahāsurī) (1.58); Black Night, Great Night, Night of Delusion (1.59); Darkness (Tāmasī) (1.68); Force That Seizes Those of Knowledge and Leads Them to Delusion (1.42); and Cause of Bondage in the World (1.44). The entire Madhu-Kaitabha episode as told in the *Devī-māhātmya* hinges on the fact that Viṣṇu is helpless as long as he is pervaded by the goddess, whose primary effect upon him is to keep him unconscious. In this episode, then, even though she is called by many positive terms, the goddess has numbing, deluding, dark qualities. Again, her role vis-à-vis Viṣṇu seems exactly the opposite of the normal role of a goddess as a male deity's *śakti*, the power that enables the god to act in the world. In this myth, Viṣṇu is only enabled to act when the goddess *leaves* him. She does not empower, enliven, or strengthen Viṣṇu; she puts him to sleep, reducing him to powerlessness.

Counterbalancing Durgā's liminal, peripheral nature, which at times seems to threaten the world's stability and to inhibit the quest for spiritual liberation, is her role as protectress of the cosmos. Her role as the destroyer of demons who have usurped the position of the gods dominates her mythology. As a great warrior she is created by the gods and acts on their behalf. While she is often said to transcend the male gods who create her and to excel them on the battlefield, she acts for their welfare. In doing this, she acts to maintain or restore cosmic harmony and balance.

The theology underlying Durgā's appearances and exploits is clear in the *Devī-māhātmya*, the most famous text extolling her deeds. Durgā is said to underlie and pervade the cosmos; to create, maintain, and periodically destroy it according to the rhythmic sequences of Hindu cosmology (12.33–35); and to assume different forms from time to time when cosmic balance is threatened by enemies of the lesser gods (11.38–51). The *Devī-māhātmya* puts the matter succinctly: "Though she is eternal, the goddess becomes manifest over and over again to protect the world" (12.32).

The *Devī-māhātmya* itself relates three of Durgā's cosmic interventions on behalf of the gods: the battle with Madhu and Kaitabha; the battle with Mahiṣa and his army; and the battle with Śumbha and Niśumbha and their generals, Caṇḍa, Muṇḍa, and Raktabīja. The text also refers specifically to five other appearances of the goddess (11.38–51) and implies that she incarnates in many more forms (12.32). The myths that are told in detail in the *Devī-māhātmya* conform to a structure that underlines Durgā's role as the upholder of cosmic order. By being cast in traditional structure, the myths also make the point that Durgā transcends the great male gods of the Hindu pantheon, who in other texts usually have the central role in these myths.

The structure to which the demon-slaying myths of Durgā conform is found throughout Hindu mythological texts and persists despite the specific deity who is featured in the myth. In basic outline, the structure is as follows: (1) a demon gains great power through doing austerities and, being granted a boon as a reward, is made nearly invincible; (2) the demon defeats the gods and takes over their positions; (3) the gods prepare their revenge by creating a special being who can defeat the demon despite the boon, or else the lesser gods petition one of the great deities (Śiva, Viṣṇu, or a great goddess) to intervene on their behalf; (4) the battle takes place and often includes the creation of helpers by the hero or heroine; (5) the demon is defeated—either slain or made subservient to the gods; (6) the demon slayer is praised by the gods.[17] In the Madhu and Kaitabha myth and the myth of Śumbha and Niśumbha, Durgā is petitioned to help the gods, while in the Mahiṣa and Śumbha and Niśumbha myths the goddess takes a direct, active part in the battle itself, demonstrating her superior martial skills against her opponents. In the Śumbha and Niśumbha myth, she also creates helpers in the form of ferocious goddesses. In all three episodes, Durgā is collectively praised by the gods at some point in the battle or after defeating the demons.

The theology underlying Durgā's cosmic interventions, then, and the structure of the demon-slaying myths conform to well-known Hindu ideas and forms. The idea that a deity descends to the world from time to time in various forms to maintain the balance of cosmic order is a central Vaiṣṇavite theme. Ever since the time of the *Bhāgavad-gītā* (circa 200 B.C.E.), the idea that Viṣṇu descends to the world in different forms to combat disorder has been well known in the Hindu tradition. Durgā, in the *Devī-māhātmya*, is heir to this theology. In fact, in many ways Durgā is a female version of Viṣṇu. She, like him, creates, maintains, and destroys the world; intervenes on a cosmic scale whenever disorder threatens to disrupt the world in the form of certain demons; and is approached by the other gods as their savior in times of distress. This conformity to a well-known type of theology of course does not detract from Durgā's appeal, power, or prestige. On the contrary, by creating her in this familiar role, and by telling her myths according to a familiar structure, the author of the *Devī-māhātmya* underlines Durgā's supremacy and might.[18]

Durgā's role as cosmic queen is complemented by her role as a personal comforter who intervenes on behalf of her devotees. Near the end of the *Devī-māhātmya*, after the world has been restored to order, Durgā herself says that she is quick to hearken to the pleas of her devotees and that she may be called upon in times of distress to help those who worship her. She mentions specifically forest fires, wild animals, robbers, imprisonment, execution, and battle as some threats from which she will save her devotees (12.24–28). At the end of the *Devī-māhātmya*, after two of her devotees petition her, she appears before them and grants their desires. To one she returns his wealth and kingdom, and to the other she grants ultimate liberation (13.11–15). Durgā, then, is not just a powerful, transcendent force whose sole concern is maintaining the cosmic rhythms, who is moved to action only when the world itself is threatened. She is attentive to the needs of her devotees and intervenes on their behalf if asked to do so. She is a personal savior as well as a great battle queen who fights to defeat the enemies of the gods.

Durgā's distinctive nature also has to do with her identification with certain important Hindu philosophical ideas. The *Devī-māhātmya* and other texts that extol Durgā state that she is identical with or associated with *śakti*, *māyā*, and *prakṛti*. In some way, Durgā represents a dramatic illustration of these ideas, or these ideas can be discerned in her nature. *Śakti* is almost always understood to be the underlying power of the divine, the aspect of the divine that permits and provokes creative activity. *Śakti*, furthermore, is almost always understood to be a positive force. When viewed in concrete form, *śakti* is usually personified as a goddess. A common belief is that without his *śakti*, without his female counterpart, a male deity is ineffective, weak, and immobilized. Durgā's creation by the assembled male deities in the Mahiṣa episode dramatically depicts the goddess as *śakti*. Although the energy and heat that the deities contribute to her formation is called *tejas*, not *śakti*, it is clear that the male gods are contributing their strength and vigor to the goddess, who epitomizes power, action, and strength in the battle with the demon.[19] Durgā, particulary in her role as battle queen, is action and power personified and, as such, is a fitting representation of the idea of *śakti*.

Durgā as a personification of *māyā* is most clearly seen in the Madhu and Kaitabha episode, in which she deludes the demons so that Viṣṇu can slay them and in which she is repeatedly referred to as Mahāmāyā and as Viṣṇu's *māyā*. *Māyā* has negative connotations in Hindu philosophy and mythology, as does Durgā, particularly in this episode, as we noted above. *Māyā* is that which deludes individuals into thinking themselves to be the center of the world, the power that prevents individuals from seeing things as they really are. *Māyā* is that which impells individuals into self-centered, egotistical actions. *Māyā* is the sense of ego, personal identity, and individuality that clouds the underlying unity of reality and masks one's essential identity with *brahman* or some exalted being such as Viṣṇu, Śiva, or Durgā. *Māyā*, however, also may be understood as a positive, creative force not dissimilar from *śakti*. *Māyā* may be understood as the power that enables a deity to display or embody himself or herself and, therefore, the power that enables a deity to act.

When Durgā is called Māyā, or equated or associated with it, both connotations, delusion and creation, are suggested. Like Viṣṇu, Durgā creates the world through her extraordinary power but then bewitches the creatures she has created. Underlying this apparently incomprehensible "game" is the idea of divine *līlā* (sport, play, or dalliance), according to which the gods never act out of necessity, but only out of a sense of play.[20] Unlike mere mortals, the gods (in this case Durgā) act, not from pragmatic motives, but only to amuse themselves or to display themselves. The way in which Durgā's defeat of Mahiṣa is often depicted in Indian art suggests this theme. Typically, she is shown bringing a blizzard of weapons to bear on the hapless demon, who is half-emerging in his human form from the carcass of his former buffalo form. Her many arms are all in motion, and she is a perfect vision of power in action. Her face, however, is calm and shows no sign of strain. For her, this is mere sport and requires no undue exertion. It is a game for her, it is *līlā*.[21] She enters into the cosmic struggle between the lesser gods and the demons because it pleases her, not out of any sense of compulsion.

Durgā's identification with *prakṛti*, and with the earth itself, makes another theological point. *Prakṛti* is the physical world as well as the inherent rhythms within this world that impel nature to gratify and produce itself in its manifold species. *Prakṛti* is both the primordial matter from which all material things come and the living instincts and patterns that imbue the material world with its proclivities to sustain and recreate itself in individual beings. As *prakṛti*, then, Durgā is inextricably associated with the physical world, the world she creates, sustains, and protects in her various forms. Durgā's identification with the world is unambiguous. The *Devī-māhātmya* makes a point at several places to say that she *is* the world, she *is* all this (11.2–3, 5–6). As the earth itself, she conveys cosmic stability. She is the foundation of all creatures and that which nourishes all creatures. As the embodiment of the earth, she supports, protects, and mothers all beings. As Śākambharī, she provides the world with food from her own body (11.45). In her role as cosmic queen, as warrior goddess and demon slayer, Durgā protects herself, as it were, in her aspect as the earth itself. As immanent in the world, Durgā is said to be the earth itself. As transcendent, she is the heavenly queen who descends from time to time to maintain harmony on earth.

Durgā's association or identification with *śakti*, *māyā*, and *prakṛti*, then, lends to the great demon-slaying goddess an immediate, tangible dimension. As an expression of these ideas, she is identified with the creation itself. Her presence is affirmed to pervade and underlie the actual world in which people live, and her power and strength are affirmed to imbue all creatures with the will to prosper and multiply.

The Worship of Durgā

One of the most important festivals in North India is Durgā Pūjā, which is celebrated in the autumn during the month of Āśvin. The festival takes place over a period of nine days and is often called the Navarātra festival. The central image of the fesitval is Durgā slaying Mahiṣa. The iconographical details of the images are usually faithful to the scene as described in the *Devī-māhātmya* and other scriptures. Durgā has many arms, each of which bears a weapon; she stands on her lion vehicle; and she is thrusting her trident into the chest of Mahiṣa, who is in human form, half-emerged from the carcass of a slain buffalo. During the festival, it is customary to recite the *Devī-māhātmya* in its entirety several times.[22] The Durgā Pūjā festival, then asserts Durgā's central role as a battle queen and regulator of the cosmos. In part, at least, the festivities celebrate Durgā's defeat of Mahiṣa and the restoration of cosmic order.

This festival, in which Durgā is worshiped in the form of a mighty warrior goddess, seems to be, or to have been until recently, part of a pattern of worship undertaken by rulers for success in battle. The festival of Dasarā, which immediately follows Durgā Pūjā in many parts of India, was primarily an occasion on which to celebrate military might and royal power and to petition for military success in the coming year. Worship of weapons was also a part of the festival in many cases.

Durgā battling a demon, contemporary folk painting from Orissa.

Writing in the early nineteenth century, when the festival of Dasarā was still widely undertaken, the Abbé Dubois wrote of the celebrations in Mysore:

> The *Dasarā* is likewise the soldiers' feast. Princes and soldiers offer the most solemn sacrifices to the arms which are made use of in battle. Collecting all their weapons together, they call a Brahmin *purohita*, who sprinkles them with *tirtham* (holy water) and converts them into so many divinities by virtue of his *mantrams*. He then makes *puja* to them and retires. Thereupon, amidst the beat of drums, the blare of trumpets and other instruments, a ram is brought in with much pomp and sacrificed in honour of the various weapons of destruction. This ceremony is observed with the greatest solemnity throughout the whole peninsula. . . . It is known by the special name of *ayuda-puja* (sacrifice to arms), and is entirely military.[23]

Alexander Forbes, who wrote in the second half of the nineteenth century, described Dasarā among the Rajputs: "The Rajpoot chiefs, on the evening of Dussera, worship also the *Fort-Protectress*, the goddess Gudeychee. On their return from the Shumee worship into the city, they join together in bands, brandishing their spears, galloping their horses, and enacting in other ways the part of an army taking the field."[24]

Although the worship of a goddess is not always part of Dasarā celebrations, there are many indications in ritual and mythological texts that the annual (usually autumnal) worship of a warrior goddess, often specified to be Durgā, was part of festivals associated with military success. Mantras to be uttered by kings on the occasion of Dasarā, for example, sometimes invoke a goddess. In the *Dharmasindhu,* the king is to speak this prayer: "May Aparājitā [the unconquerable one] wearing a striking necklace and resplendent golden girdle and fond of doing good bestow victory on me."[25]

In the *Nirnayasindhu,* this prayer is to be said at the time of blessing weapons: "O goddess, ruling over gods! may my army divided into four sections (elephants, chariots, horsemen, and foot-soldiers) attain to the position of having no enemy left in this world and may victory come to me everywhere through your favour."[26]

An eleventh- to twelfth-century Jain text, the *Yaśatilaka* of Somadeva, mentions the worship of Aparājitā, who is also called Ambikā. She is said to give victory in war and to be present in the king's weapons.[27] The text also says that she is worshiped on the last day of Durgā Pūjā. In some *Purāṇas,* furthermore, the worship of weapons is said to be held on that day.[28] In the drama *Gauḍavaho,* King Yaśovarman undertakes a military campaign in the autumn. Shortly after beginning his march, he reaches the Vindhya Mountains and there undertakes the worship of the goddess Vindhyavāsinī (She Who Dwells in the Vindhyas), an epithet of Durgā in some texts.[29]

The worship of Durgā also came to be associated with the military success of the Pāṇḍava brothers in the *Mahābhārata* and of Rāma in the *Rāmāyaṇa.* Although the heroes' worship of her was not part of either epic tradition initially (the incidents are not found in the critical editons of either epic), a tradition has developed that insists that the worship of Durgā was necessary to the success of the heroes in both epics. Durgā is worshiped twice in the *Mahābhārata:* in Viratā-parva 6 by Yudhiṣṭhira and in Bhīṣma-parva 23 by Arjuna. In the latter case, the occasion of Durgā's praise is clear. The setting is just before the great battle that is the high point of the entire epic. Kṛṣṇa instructs Arjuna as follows: "O one having great arms, standing in the face of battle, say a hymn to Durgā for the purpose of defeating your enemies" (4.6.2). The hymn that Arjuna then offers is full of references to Durgā's military might and prowess. The goddess appears to Arjuna and promises him victory, after which the text says that anyone who hears or recites the hymn will be victorious in battle.

The placement of the second hymn to Durgā in the Virāṭa-parva is more difficult to understand. The Pāṇḍava brothers have just emerged from twelve years of exile in the forest and are about to begin a year of life in the world during which they must remain in disguise lest their enemies discover them. Before entering the city of Virāṭa and taking up their disguises, they hide their weapons in a *śami* tree near a cremation ground. Yudhiṣṭhira asks Durgā for protection from being discovered during the coming year and for later success against their enemies. She appears at the end of the hymn and grants his wishes. It seems that the hymn was placed at this point in the text because the worship of a *śami* tree on the outskirts of a town is often a part of Dasarā festivals. The author or editor of the hymn probably thought this seemed an appropriate place to insert a hymn to Durgā for military success.

The association of Durgā with Rāma's success in battle over Rāvaṇa in the *Rāmāyaṇa* tradition, although not part of Vālmīki's *Rāmāyaṇa*, has become a well-known part of the Rāma story throughout India. In the *Kālikā-purāṇa* we are told:

> In former times, the great Goddess was waked up by Brahmā when it was still night, in order to favour Rāma and to obtain the death of Rāvaṇa.
>
> On the first day of the bright half of the month of Āśvina, she gave up her sleep and went to the city of Laṅkā, where Raghu's son formerly lived.
>
> When she came there, the great goddess caused Rāma and Rāvaṇa to be engaged in battle, but Ambikā herself remained hidden. . . .
>
> Afterwards, when the seventh night had gone by, Mahāmāyā, in whom the worlds are contained, caused Rāvaṇa to be killed by Rāma on the ninth day. . . .
>
> After the hero Rāvaṇa had been killed on the ninth day, the Grandfather of the worlds (Brahmā) together with all the gods held a special worship for Durgā.
>
> Afterwards the Goddess was dismissed with *śabara*-festivals, on the tenth day; Indra on his part held a lustration of the army of the gods for the appeasement of the armies of the gods and for the sake of prosperity of the kingdom of the gods. . . .
>
> All the gods will worship her and will, on their part, lustrate the army; and in the same way all men should perform worship according to the rules.
>
> A king should hold a lustration of the army in order to strengthen his army; a performance must be made with charming women adorned with celestial ornaments; . . .
>
> After one has made a puppet of flour for Skanda and Viśākha, one should worship it in order to annihilate one's foes and for the sake of enjoying Durgā.[30]

In the *Devī-bhāgavata-purāṇa*, Rāma is despondent at the problems of reaching Laṅka, defeating Rāvaṇa, and getting back his beloved Sītā. The sage Nārada, however, advises him to call upon Durgā for help. Rāma asks how she should be worshiped, and Nārada instructs him concerning the performance of Durgā Pūjā or Navarātra. The festival, which Nārada assures Rāma will result in military success, is said to have been performed in previous ages by Indra for killing Vṛtra, by Śiva for killing the demons of the three cities, and by Viṣṇu for killing Madhu and Kaitabha (3.30.25–26). Rāma duly performs Durgā's worship, and she appears to him mounted on her lion. She asks what he wishes, and when he requests victory over Rāvaṇa she promises he will be successful (3.30). The tradition that Rāma inaugurated Durgā Pūjā to defeat Rāvaṇa is also found in the *Bṛhaddharma-purāṇa* (1.21–22) and the Bengali version of the *Rāmāyaṇa* by Kṛttivāsa (fifteenth century).[31] Bengali villagers tell of a tradition in which it was customary to worship Durgā during the spring. Rāma, however, needed the goddess's help in the autumn when he was about to invade Laṅka. So it was that he worshiped her in the month of Āśvin and inaugurated autumnal worship, which has become her most popular festival. "When Rāma . . . came into conflict with Rāvan, . . . Rāma performed the pūjā when he was in trouble, without waiting for the proper time of the annual pūjā. He did the pūjā in the autumn, and later this pūjā became the most popular ritual of the goddess."[32]

Durgā's association with military prowess and her worship for military success undoubtedly led to her being associated with the military success of both sets of epic heroes sometime in the medieval period. Her association with these great heroes, in turn, probably tended to further promote her worship by kings for success and prosperity.

Durgā's association with military might is probably also part of a tradition, most evident in recent centuries, of goddesses giving swords to certain rulers and of swords being named for goddesses. In the *Devī-purāṇa*, it is said that the goddess may be worshiped in the form of a sword (chapter 98). Śivaji, the seventeenth-century Marathi military leader, is said to have received his sword from his family deity, the goddess Bhavānī. One account of the way Śivaji obtained his sword is phrased as if Śivaji himself were speaking:

> I received that famous sword very early in my career as a token of a compact with the Chief Gowalker Sawant. It had been suggested to me on my way to the place where it was being kept that I should take it by force, but remembering that tremendous storms are sometimes raised by unnecessary trifles, I thought it better to leave it to its owner. . . . In the end the wise chief brought the sword to me as a sign of amity even when he knew that its purchase-price was not to be measured in blood. From that day onward the sword, which I reverently named after my tutelary deity *Bhavāni*, always accompanied me, its resting place when not in use generally being the altar of the goddess, to be received back from her as a visible favour from heaven, always on the *Dasara* day when starting out my campaigns.[33]

In other legends concerning Śivaji's sword, the goddess Bhavānī speaks directly to Śivaji, identifies herself with his sword, and is described as entering his sword before battle or before urging Śivaji to undertake the task of murdering his enemy, Afzalkhan.[34]

The Paṇḍyan prince Kumāra Kampaṇa (fourteenth century), before going to battle against the Muslims in the Madura area, is said to have been addressed by a goddess who appeared before him and gave him a sword. "A goddess appeared before him and after describing to him the disastrous consequences of the Musselmen invasions of the South and sad plight of the Southern country and its temples exhorted him to extirpate the invaders and restore the country to its ancient glory, presenting him at the same time with a divine sword."[35]

A sacred sword also belonged to the Rajput kingdom of Mewar. The sword was handed down from generation to generation and was placed on the altar of the goddess during Navarātra.[36] According to legend, the founder of the dynasty, Bappa, undertook austerities in the woods. Near the end of his ascetic efforts, a goddess riding a lion appeared to him. "From her hand he received the panoply of celestial fabrication, the work of Viswacarma. . . . The lance, bow, quiver, and arrows; a shield and sword . . . which the goddess girded on him with her own hand."[37]

The autumnal worship of Durgā, then, in which she is shown in full military array slaying the demon Mahiṣa in order to restore order to the cosmos, seems to have been part of a widespread cult that centered around obtaining military success. The central festival of this cult took place on Dasarā day, immediately following the Navarātra festival, and included the worship of weapons by rulers and soldiers. The worship of a goddess for military success, although not always a part of the Dasarā festival, was associated with the festival. Indeed, the two festivals, Navarātra and Dasarā, probably were often understood to be one continous festival in which the worship of Durgā and the hope of military success were inseparably linked.

Although the military overtones of Durgā Pūjā are apparent, other themes are also important during this great festival, and other facets of Durgā's character are brought out by the festival. Durgā Pūjā coincides with the autumn harvest in North India, and in certain respects it is clear that Durgā Pūjā is a harvest festival in which Durgā is propitiated as the power of plant fertility. Although Durgā Pūjā lacks clear agricultural themes as celebrated today in large cities such as Calcutta, or as celebrated by those with only tenuous ties to agriculture, enough indications remain in the festival, even in its citified versions, to discern its importance to the business of agriculture.

A central object of worship during the festival, for example, is a bundle of nine different plants, the *navapattrikā*, which is identified with Durgā herself.[38] Although the nine plants in question are not all agricultural plants, paddy and plantain are included and suggest that Durgā is associated with the crops.[39] Her association with the other plants probably is meant to generalize her identification with the power underlying all plant life. Durgā, that is, is not merely the power inherent in the growth of crops but the power inherent in all vegetation. During her worship in this form, the priest anoints Durgā with water from auspicious sources, such as the major holy rivers of India. He also anoints her with agricultural products, such as sugarcane juice[40] and sesame oil,[41] and offers to her soils that are associated with fertility, such as earth dug up by the horns of a wild boar, earth dug up by the horns of a bull, and earth from the doors of prostitutes.[42] It seems clear that one theme of the worship of Durgā is to promote the fertility of the plants incorporated into the sacred bundle and to promote the fertility of crops in general.

At another point in the ceremonies, a pot is identified with Durgā and worshiped by the priest. Edible fruit and different plants from those making up the *navapattrikā* are placed in the pot.[43] The pot, which has a rounded bottom, is then firmly set upon moist dough. On this dough are scattered five grains: rice, wheat, barley, "mas (*Phaseolus Roxburghii, Wight*)," and sesame.[44] As each grain is scattered on the dough, a priest recites the following invocation: "Om you are rice [wheat, barley, etc.], om you are life, you are the life of the gods, you are our life, you are our internal life, you are long life, you give life, om the Sun with his rays gives you the milk of life and Varuna nourishes you with water."[45] The pot, which contains Ganges water in addition to the plants, is then identified in a prayer by the priest with the source of the nectar of immortality, which the gods churned from the ocean of milk.

Durgā, then, in the form of the pot, is invoked both as the power promoting the growth of the agricultural grains and as the source of the power of life with which the gods achieved immortality. In the forms of the *navapattrikā* and the pot Durgā reveals a dimension of herself that primarily has to do with the fertility of the crops and vegetation and with the power that underlies life generally. In addition to granting freedom from troubles and bestowing wealth on those who perform worship, Durgā is also affirmed to grant agricultural produce;[46] at one point in the festival, she is addressed as She Who Appeases the Hunger of the World.[47]

Durgā's beneficial influence on crops is also suggested at the very beginning of the festival when her image is being set up. The image is placed on a low platform or table about eighteen inches high. The platform is set on damp clay, and the five above-mentioned grains are sprinkled in the clay. Although not specifically stated, the presence of the goddess appears to promote the growth of these seeds.[48] On the eighth day of the festival, furthermore, the priest worships several groups of deities while circumambulating the image of Durgā. Among these are the deities who preside over cultivated fields.[49]

Two other distinctive features of Durgā Pūjā suggest its importance as a festival affecting the fertility of the crops: the animal sacrifices and the ribald behavior that is specifically mentioned in certain religious texts as pleasing to the goddess. It is certainly the case that the sacrifice of an animal, particularly when the animal is a buffalo, suggests the reiteration of the slaying of Mahiṣa by Durgā. However, the custom of offering other animals, such as goats and sheep, and the injunctions of offering several victims during the festival suggest that other meanings are intended too. These blood sacrifices occupy a central role in Durgā Pūjā. Durgā's thirst for blood is established in various texts,[50] and this thirst is not limited to the battlefield. Her devotees are said to please

Image of Durgā at Durgā Pūjā flanked by Ganeśa, Lakṣmī, Sarasvatī, and Kārttikeya. Contemporary painted and adorned clay image, Varanasi. Author's photograph.

her with their own blood,[51] and she is said to receive blood from tribal groups who worship her.[52] Furthermore, other goddesses with whom Durgā is closely affiliated, such as Kālī, receive blood offerings in their temples daily with no reference at all to heroic deeds in battle. Blood offerings to Durgā, that is, seem to contain a logic that is quite apart from the battlefield, or at least quite apart from the myth of the goddess's slaying Mahiṣa on behalf of cosmic stability.

My suggestion is that, underlying blood sacrifices to Durgā, is the perception, perhaps only unconscious, that this great goddess who nourishes the crops and is identified with the power underlying all life needs to be reinvigorated from time to time. The perception exists that, despite her great powers, she is capable of being exhausted through continuous birth and giving of nourishment. To replenish her powers, to reinvigorate her, she is given back life in the form of animal sacrifices. The blood resupplies her, as it were, so that she may continue to give life in return. Having harvested the crops, having literally reaped the life-giving benefits of Durgā's potency, it is appropriate (perhaps necessary) to return strength and power to her in the form of the blood of sacrificial victims. This logic, and the association of blood sacrifices with harvest, is not at all uncommon in the world's religions. It is a typical ceremonial scenario in many cultures, and it seems likely that at one time, at any rate, it was important in the celebration of Durgā Pūjā.[53]

Promoting the fertility of the crops by stimulating Durgā's powers of fecundity also seems to underlie the practice during Durgā Pūjā of publicly making obscene gestures and comments. Various scriptures say that Durgā is pleased by such behavior at the autumn festival;[54] wild, boisterous activities also accompany the disposal of Durgā's image in a river or pool.[55] The close association, even the interdependence, between human sexuality and the growth of crops is clear in many cultures;[56] it is held to be auspicious and even vital to the growth of crops to have couples copulate in the fields, particularly at planting and harvest time. Again, the logic seems to be that this is a means of giving back vital powers to the spirit underlying the crops. Like blood, the sexual fluids are held to have great fertilizing powers, so to copulate in the fields is to renourish the divine beings that promote the growth of the crops. While such outright sexual activity is not part of Durgā Pūjā, the sexual license enjoined in some scriptures is certainly suggestive of this well-known theme.

Another facet of Durgā's character that emerges in Durgā Pūjā but is not stressed in the texts that cast her in the role of battle queen is her domestic role as the wife of Śiva and mother of several divine children. In North India, which is primarily patrilocal and patriarchal in matters of marriage, girls are customarily married at an early age and leave their parents' home when quite young. This is traumatic for both the girl and her family. In Bengal, at least, it is customary for daughters to return to their home villages during Durgā Pūjā. The

Brahmin priest performing worship of Durgā during Durgā Pūjā in Varanasi. Author's photograph.

arrival home of the daughters is cause for great happiness and rejoicing, while their departure after the festival is over is the occasion for painful scenes of departure. Durgā herself is cast in the role of a returning daughter during her great festival, and many devotional songs are written to welcome her home or to bid her farewell. In these songs, no mention is made whatsoever of her roles as battle queen or cosmic savior. She is identified with Pārvatī, who is the wife of Śiva and the daughter of Himalaya and his wife, Mena. In this role, Durgā is said to be the mother of four divine children: Ganeśa, Kārttikeya, Sarasvatī, and Lakṣmī.

The dominant theme in these songs of welcome and farewell seems to be the difficult life that the goddess/daughter has in her husband's home in contrast to the warm, tender treatment that she receives from her parents when she visits them. This theme undoubtedly reflects the actual situation of many Bengali girls, for whom life in their husband's village can be difficult in the extreme, particularly in the early years of their marriage when they have no seniority or children to give them respect and status in the eyes of their in-laws. Śiva is described as inattentive to his wife and unable to take care of himself because of his habit of smoking hemp and his habitual disregard for social convention.[57] The songs contrast the poverty that Durgā must endure in her husband's care with the way that she is spoiled by her parents. From the devotee's point of view, then, Durgā is seen as a returning daughter who lives a difficult life far from home. She is welcomed warmly and provided every comfort. The days of the festival are ones of intimacy between the devotee and the goddess, who is understood to have made a long journey to dwell at home with those who worship her. The clay image worshiped during Durgā Pūjā may show a mighty, many-armed goddess triumphing over a powerful demon, but many devotees cherish her as a tender daughter who has returned home on her annual visit for family succor, sympathy, and the most elaborate hospitality. This theme, then, places the devotee in the position of a family member who honors Durgā with every sort of personal attendance in order to distract her from her normal life with her mad husband, Śiva. At the end of Durgā Pūjā, when the image of the goddess is removed from its place of worship and placed on a truck or some other conveyance to be carried away for immersion, many women gather about the image to bid it farewell, and it is a commmon sight to see them actually weeping as the goddess, their daughter, leaves to return to her husband's home far away.

The sacrifice of a buffalo to Durgā is practiced in South India too. While agricultural fertility and her cosmic victory on behalf of divine order are themes in this ceremony, a quite different aspect of her character is emphasized in Tamil myths and rituals. In the *Purānas*, and in North Indian traditions, an implied sexual tension exists between Durgā and Mahiṣa, her victim. In the South, this sexual tension is heightened and becomes one of the central themes of Durgā's defeat of Mahiṣa. In the South, most myths about Durgā identify Mahiṣa as her suitor, her would-be husband. In the independence of her unmarried state, Durgā is portrayed as possessing untamed sexual energy that is dangerous, indeed, deadly, to any male who dares to approach her.[58] Her violent, combative nature needs to be tamed for the welfare of the world. Mahiṣa is unsuccessful in subduing her and is lured to his doom by her great beauty. A central point of the South Indian myths about Durgā and Mahiṣa is that any sexual association with the goddess is dangerous and that before her sexuality can be rendered safe she must be dominated by, made subservient to, defeated by, or humiliated by a male.[59] In most myths she eventually is tamed by Śiva.[60]

In contrast to the North Indian tradition of Durgā Pūjā, which stresses Durgā's character as a gentle wife and daughter in need of family tenderness, is the South Indian tradition of Durgā as a dangerous, indeed, murderous, bride, who poses a fatal threat to those who approach her sexually. This role suggests again the liminal aspect of the goddess. Unlike the weak, submissive, blushing maiden of the Hindu law books, Durgā presents a picture of determined, fierce independence, which her suitors challenge only at a great risk.

Chapter **2**

Kuan-yin, the Chinese Goddess of Mercy

A mind perfected in the four virtues,
A gold body filled with wisdom,
Fringes of dangling pearls and jade,
Scented bracelets set with lustrous treasures,
Dark hair piled smoothly in a coiled-dragon bun,
And elegant sashes lightly fluttering as phoenix quills,
Her green jade buttons
And white silk robe
Bathed in holy light;
Her velvet skirt
And golden cords
Wrapped by hallowed air,
With brows of new moon shape
And eyes like two bright stars,
Her jadelike face beams natural joy,
And her ruddy lips seem a flash of red.
Her immaculate vase overflows with nectar from year to year,
Holding sprigs of weeping willow green from age to age.
She disperses the eight woes;
She redeems the multitude;
She has great compassion;

Thus she rules on the T'ai Mountain,
And lives at the South Sea.
She saves the poor, searching for their voices,
Ever heedful and solicitous,
Ever wise and efficacious.
Her orchid heart delights in green bamboos;
Her chaste nature loves the wisteria.
She is the merciful ruler of Potalaka Mountain,
The Living Kuan-yin from the Cave of Tidal Sound.[1]

Introduction

For many centuries in China, one of the most popular deities, if not the most popular, was the Buddhist goddess Kuan-yin.[2] Writing in the early part of this century, one observer said about Kuan-yin's popularity: "In all city temples, her image occupies a prominent place, and attracts crowds of worshippers, especially of the female sex, on her principal festivals. In the household or family shrine, she is also a favourite deity. In all dangers or perils whether of body or mind, as a patron and protector of mothers, and as giver of children, she is constantly invoked, and the people in general place implicit confidence in her powerful protection."[3] Another writer says: "Until recently, shrines to Kuan Yin stood in all kinds of places throughout the length and breadth of China and in several neighboring countries as well."[4] To this day Kuan-yin is widely worshiped by overseas Chinese, and even in mainland China devotees can be found in many temples offering her worship. Although Kuan-yin has a variety of functions, and appears in many different forms, her essential character is clear and consistent throughout her history: she is the essence of mercy and compassion and is quick to answer pleas from her devotees for help.

Buddhist Background

Although disagreement exists among scholars concerning different religious strands and traditions that might have blended to form the figure of Kuan-yin in medieval Chinese religions, most agree on the fact that, in nature and function, Kuan-yin is the Chinese Buddhist form of the bodhisattva Avalokiteśvara,[5] who dominates much of Indian Sanskrit Buddhist literature. What is remarkable about this fact is that Avalokiteśvara is a male, while Kuan-yin (at least after the eleventh century) is usually a female.[6] Exactly how and when the bodhisattva Avalokiteśvara/Kuan-yin came to assume a female identity in China is not clear and is still debated among scholars. The process, however, seems to have taken place over a long period of time with several distinct stages.

At an early period Kuan-yin's characteristic of assuming a variety of forms to help people in distress was expanded to include several female forms. Such female forms are not mentioned in Sanskrit Buddhist scriptures, nor do they appear in the earliest Chinese translations of Sanskrit scriptures. In Kumārajīva's translation of the *Lotus-sūtra* from Sanskrit into Chinese in 406 C.E., he expands the number of Kuan-yin's different forms to thirty-three. (The first translation of the *Lotus-sūtra* into Chinese, by Dharmarakṣa, had not expanded the number of forms.) What is significant about the expansion of forms is that several female forms have been added to the earlier list of sixteen, which was completely male.[7] The female forms that are mentioned are: a nun, a laywoman, a woman, a housewife, an officer's wife, a Brahman woman, and a young girl.

Other early Chinese Buddhist texts featuring Kuan-yin tell stories about his earlier births in which the loving devotion of his mother inspires him to practice compassion for all creatures.[8] The first stage in Kuan-yin's sexual transformation from male to female in China, then, involves the expansion of his forms to include female forms and the inclusion of compassionate female characters as inspirational models in his previous lives.

A second stage in Kuan-yin's sexual transformation is suggested when we find examples of Kuan-yin shown iconographically as a female or when we find explicit textual references to her as a female. Writing in the year 668 C.E., the author of the *Fa-yüan chu-lin* notes that Kuan-yin appeared in female form to free a certain devotee from chains.[9] An empress who lived in the seventh century is said to have become a Buddhist nun and taken the name Kuan-yin.[10] Hsiu-lieh, who lived in the eighth century, refers to a Buddhist nun of considerable piety as one whom people call Kuan-yin.[11] In the late-ninth- or early-tenth-century Annals of T'ien-chu, Kuan-yin is said to appear as a woman in the dream of the royal prince Ch'ien Liu.[12] From the fifth to the eleventh centuries, then, Kuan-yin remains primarily a male figure but is occasionally referred to or depicted as a female.

Tibetan and Chinese Background

Around the tenth or eleventh century, Kuan-yin begins to be shown and described primarily as a female. Three factors probably combined to bring about this final sexual transformation: (1) the association of Kuan-yin with the Tibetan Buddhist goddess Tārā; (2) the association of Kuan-yin with the indigenous Chinese goddesses the Holy Mother (Sheng mu) and the goddess of the sea, Matsu; and (3) the association of Kuan-yin with the heroine Miao Shan.

In Tibetan Buddhism, the numerous Buddhas and bodhisattvas became associated with female consorts or counterparts similar to the Hindu idea of

Kuan-yin, lacquered wood, Ming Dynasty, 1624 C.E. Metropolitan Museum of Art, New York.

śaktis, or female energies. The goddess Tārā in Tibetan Buddhism is associated with Avalokiteśvara. Indeed, she is said to have been born from one of the tears that he shed while compassionately observing the sufferings of humankind.[13] Like Avalokiteśvara, Tārā's nature is the essence of compassion, and, like him, she specializes in rescuing her devotees from danger if they call on her for help. She is, in many ways, a female counterpart of Avalokiteśvara. In China, it seems, some people thought of Tārā as a form of Avalokiteśvara, one of his several embodiments or forms. This identification of Tārā with Avalokiteśvara/Kuan-yin seems particularly clear in the case of one of Kuan-yin's most famous female forms in China, Kuan-yin of the White Garments, or Kuan-yin Clad in White (Po-i ta-shih). The Chinese name for this form of Kuan-yin seems to be a direct translation of the Sanskrit Pāndaravāsinī (she who is clad in white), an epithet of White Tārā (an especially popular form of Tārā in her mild aspect in Tibetan Buddhism).[14] This female form of Kuan-yin was introduced to China sometime during the eighth century and had become very popular by the tenth century.[15]

Kuan-yin became associated with another goddess during approximately the same period, or perhaps a bit later: the indigenous Chinese goddess Pi-hsia yüan-chün, Princess of the Motley Clouds. This goddess, also known simply as Holy Mother (Sheng mu) or Madame Lady (Nai-nai niang-niang), was very popular in China, and her cult dates back to the Han period.[16] Her cult was dominated by women and was concerned primarily with obtaining children. Sheng mu is usually shown with two attendants, one of whom carries a large eye and whose function is to protect children from eye diseases. The other attendant is called the Lady Who Brings Children (Sung-tzu niang-niang) and is usually shown holding an infant in her arms. Sheng mu is also associated with or attended by other female beings who preside over the different stages of pregnancy, childbirth, nourishment, and infant diseases.

One of the most popular forms of Kuan-yin is Kuan-yin Who Brings Children. While Avalokiteśvara is said to grant children in Sanskrit texts,[17] the inspiration for this form of Kuan-yin seems to be the Chinese goddess Sheng mu. Indeed, images of Kuan-yin Who Brings Children, which depict her holding a child in her lap, are rarely found in Chinese Buddhist temples. Images or pictures of her are usually found in homes or shops, where she is worshiped primarily as one who grants children. That is, she is approached in this form more as a fertility goddess than a bodhisattva, and in this form has little obvious connection with established Buddhism.[18]

Kuan-yin is also associated with the goddess Matsu, whose name means Granny.[19] This goddess was originally popular in Fukien Province in Southeast China and was primarily worshiped by fishermen. She was known, and still is, as the goddess who protects people who venture the seas. Tales featuring Matsu often concern the miraculous rescue of sailors at sea, and she is often depicted

Kuan-yin, Ming Dynasty, Jade Buddha Temple, Shanghai.

riding in a boat. As might be expected, her temples tended to be located in coastal cities or along the large navigable rivers of China.[20] Matsu is often depicted with two attendants, Thousand-League Eyes (Ch'ien-li Yen) and Favoring-Wind Ears (Shun-feng Erh). The figures appear to be attentively peering and listening, respectively. The former may be shown shading his eyes and the latter cupping his hand behind his ear. That is, they are shown straining to perceive or hear events in the distance and represent Matsu's attentiveness to her devotees' cries for help when they are in distress.[21]

It is not uncommon to find images of Kuan-yin located in Matsu's temples and vice versa.[22] Indeed, one of Kuan-yin's prime characteristics is the dramatic rescue of her devotees when, in great difficulty, they call upon her. Like Matsu, she is known to exercise control over the sea.[23] Certain Buddhist texts say that rescuing sailors at sea is one of the eight difficulties from which Kuan-yin saves her devotees.[24] Kuan-yin, like Matsu, is also often shown standing in a boat.[25] One of the most common depictions of Kuan-yin shows her standing on a rock or on a fish in the midst of swirling waves. Sometimes a shipwrecked sailor will be shown stretching his hands toward her.[26] In a more general salvific role, Kuan-yin is known as the one who guides people to the Western Paradise of Amitābha Buddha. "The journey to this Pure Land is frequently represented by more or less crude woodcuts, which show boat-loads of Amitabha's worshippers, sailing over the bitter sea of human sorrow under the captainship of *Kwan-yin*."[27]

The Legend of Miao Shan

Sometime in the tenth or eleventh century, the legend of the princess Miao Shan became associated with Kuan-yin, and ever since that time Kuan-yin has become inextricably identified with the details and themes of this popular legend. The story itself is a dramatic and brilliant account of a young woman who combines in her character both strong Buddhist tendencies and strong traditional Chinese tendencies. While the two tendencies are put in dramatic tension with each other throughout most of the story, they are beautifully reconciled in the climax of the tale. In the figure of Miao Shan, and in the figure of Kuan-yin who is identified with Miao Shan, then, we have a lovely merging of Buddhist and Confucian virtues.

The story, which has several versions, seems to have become widely known and associated with Kuan-yin in the eleventh century, first in Southeast China, and later throughout the whole of China.[28] The story, in brief, is this:[29] Once upon a time there was a king named Miao Chuang who had three daughters, the youngest of whom was named Miao Shan. When Miao Shan was born, there were several auspicious signs. Her body possessed the marks of a noble person and indicated that she was the incarnation of a holy figure. As she grew up, she was gentle and kind and took the habit of dressing in simple clothes. After her two older sisters were married, the time of her own marriage approached. Her father began to make plans for her to wed, seeking an appropriate noble youth for her. Miao Shan, however, resisted her father's plans and asked permission to renounce the world and take up the life of a Buddhist nun. In rejecting marriage and the life of ease and luxury associated with it, Miao Shan is often portrayed as espousing strict Buddhist views. She says, for example, in one version: "Riches and honour are not there for ever, glory and splendour are like mere bubbles or illusions."[30] In another version she says: "In all the emotional entanglements of this world there is no . . . spiritual release. If close kin are united, they must inevitably be sundered and scattered."[31] In resisting her father's quite reasonable request that she marry, Miao Shan presents herself as a most rebellious Chinese daughter. Her father, in all versions, is described as very upset with her wish to renounce the world. In this respect, of course, Miao Shan's story echoes the story of the Buddha himself, whose father stubbornly resisted his wish to renounce the princely life and undertake the life of an ascetic religious seeker.

Eventually, Miao Shan is given permission by her father to join the Buddhist nuns at the nearby White Sparrow Monastery. Her father instructs the nuns, however, to treat her harshly and to try to discourage her in every way possible. He is sure that the simple, harsh life of the monastery and the menial tasks she will have to perform will change her resolve to relinquish the royal life. The nuns follow the king's wishes and force Miao Shan to perform a variety of difficult chores. Miao Shan, uncomplaining, and in some versions with the help of supernatural beings, performs all the tasks required of her and takes satisfaction in the austere life. Finding it impossible in this way to change his wayward daughter's mind, the king becomes angry and decides to kill her and destroy the monastery. In some versions, Miao Shan is described as miraculously escaping the king's wrath. She is whisked away by a spirit who establishes her in a barren place, where she leads a simple, ascetic life. In other versions, she is miraculously saved when the executioner's sword suddenly breaks in two, but she is subsequently strangled. Her body is then carried off by a spirit in the form of a tiger. In some of these versions of the tale, Miao Shan descends to the land of the dead in order to relieve the sufferings of its inhabitants. Through her purity and great compassion, she transforms hell into a paradise. She gives the hungry spirits food and drink, puts out the fires that torment them, and leads them to rebirth in Sukhāvatī, the Pure Land ruled over by the Buddha Amitābha.[32]

Following her sojourn in hell, Miao Shan is sent back to earth by the ruler of the dead lest she completely abolish his domain. She reenters her body and reanimates it. At this point in the narrative, Miao Shan undertakes a long journey to a holy place that becomes her permanent dwelling place. This location

Standing white-robed Kuan-yin, gilt bronze, late Ming to early Ch'ing Dynasty (seventeenth to eighteenth century C.E.). Asian Art Museum of San Francisco, the Avery Brundage Collection.

is usually identified as P'u-t'o-shan, a sacred island associated with an island of that name off the coast of Southeast China that is the site of Kuan-yin's most famous religious center. In some versions of the story, a spiritual helper or bodhisattva gives Miao Shan a magical peach to help in undertaking this journey.

She is told that when eaten the peach will prevent her from becoming hungry or thirsty, protect her from sickness and old age, and permit her to live for eternity. In effect, the peach bestows the nature of a deity on Miao Shan.[33]

In the meantime, as punishment for abusing or killing his daughter, Miao Shan's father is afflicted with a serious disease that resists all attempts to cure it. A Buddhist monk tells the king that his disease can only be cured with medicine that is made from the arms and eyes of a living person or, in some versions, the arms and eyes of a person completely free from anger. The king is discouraged at this news, thinking such medicine impossible to come by. But the monk assures the king that such a person, free from anger, and willing to give up arms and eyes, does exist. The king duly sends a messenger to the place where Miao Shan herself dwells asking for the precious ingredients. Upon hearing of her father's distress, Miao Shan immediately agrees to sacrifice her arms and eyes to heal her father.

The medicine cures the king, and he and his wife set out to pay homage to the noble being who has sacrificed herself on his behalf. The royal couple are stunned to discover that it is Miao Shan who has given her arms and eyes to heal her father. The king and queen embrace their daughter and weep bitterly at the memory of how harshly they had treated her. In some versions of the story the king and queen accept the Buddhist religion in gratitude to their daughter.

The story often closes with a dramatic revelation of Kuan-yin. With celestial music in the background and flowers falling from heaven, Miao Shan is transformed into Kuan-yin herself in her thousand-armed and thousand-eyed form. As she hovers in the air, heavenly hosts celebrate her great compassion in a chorus that fills the world and shakes the earth. Then Kuan-yin resumes her form as Miao Shan and dies. Her body is burned and her bones reserved as sacred relics, which are kept at her temples throughout the land.[34] Having given up her form as Miao Shan, Kuan-yin is then said to return either to her home in the Western Paradise of Amitābha Buddha or to her home on the island of Potala. In whichever place, she continues her primary role as a great goddess of mercy and compassion. "She keeps perpetually open the gate of deliverance from suffering, she points out to all the way to the highest destiny, she observes the cries of all the world in times present and past, she discerns good and evil throughout the society of men."[35]

The Goddess of Mercy and Compassion

To hear her name or see her form
Or fervantly recite her name
Delivers beings from every woe.

. . . .

Though beings oppressed by karmic woes
Endure innumerable sorrows,
Kuan Yin's miraculous perception
Enables her to purge them all.

. . . .

No matter what black evils gather—
What hell-spawned demons, savage beasts,
What ills of birth, age, sickness, death,
Kuan Yin will one by one destroy them.

. . . .

To the perfection of her merits,
To the compassion of her glance,
To the infinitude of her blessings,
Worshipping, we bow our heads![36]

There is no doubt that the central role of Kuan-yin is that of helper and savior. In this respect, she quite clearly conforms to the traditional role of the bodhisattva in Mahāyāna Buddhism. A bodhisattva is a being destined for full enlightenment and *nirvāna* who, out of compassion for the suffering of other beings, has taken a vow to postpone his or her entry into *nirvāna* in order to remain in the world to help other beings. Kuan-yin's name itself emphasizes this aspect of her nature. Kuan-yin, or Kuan-shih-yin as she is often called, is usually translated as She Who Listens to the World's Sounds.[37] That is, she is the being who is ever attentive to the cries of her devotees, who constantly surveys the world of human beings in order to help those in need. A popular form of Kuan-yin is Kuan-yin of a Thousand Arms and a Thousand Eyes. Other forms of Kuan-yin have several heads. A primary meaning of these kinds of images is Kuan-yin's attentiveness to the needs of suffering humankind. With her many arms, heads, and eyes she sees all things and is equipped to perform miraculous deeds in order to rescue those in need.[38]

The most famous Buddhist scripture that speaks of Kuan-yin's role as a dramatic savior is the twenty-fourth chapter of the *Lotus-sūtra* (the twenty-fifth chapter in Chinese translations). In China, this chapter was translated and circulated as an independent scripture known as the *Kuan-yin-sūtra*. "Devout followers of the Kuan-yin cult would recite the text daily for the purpose of receiving the 'sea of merits' as well as material benefits promised in the

Kuan-yin, Shuanglin Monastery.

text."[39] In this text, in two places, are listed a series of dangers from which Kuan-yin rescues her devotees. Prominent among these dangers are: fire, shipwreck, falling from great height, execution, imprisonment, wild animals, and natural calamities, such as lightning and floods.[40] The text asserts that if one is surrounded by fire but concentrates on the power of Kuan-yin, the fire will change to a cool lake; if one slips and falls from a high place but concentrates on Kuan-yin, one will remain suspended in midair; if one is surrounded by robbers approaching murderously but remembers Kuan-yin's saving power, they will become kind hearted and do no harm; and so on.

In addition to these dramatic dangers from which she protects her devotees, Kuan-yin is also known to assist people in the more routine needs and desires of human life. In the same chapter of the *Lotus-sūtra*, for example, we are told that a woman who desires a son will certainly have a wise and good son if she worships Kuan-yin.[41] Kuan-yin is also reputed to provide health and long life. Her power to provide these earthly blessings is symbolized in the magical peach, which she is often shown holding in her hand. In the story of Kuan-yin in the form of Miao Shan, she was given this marvelous fruit to help her make her long and arduous trip to Potala. The peach transformed the heroine into a deity by bestowing divine attributes upon her. It is well-known by Kuan-yin's devotees, however, that in her great compassion she shares these attributes with them when they call upon her.

Stories abound in China of Kuan-yin's miraculous intervention on behalf of her devotees, or simply on behalf of those in danger. In the sixteenth-century *Hsi-yu chi (The Journey to the West)*, a legendary account of the famous Chinese Buddhist monk Hsuan-tsang's (586–664 C.E.) pilgrimage to India to obtain Buddhist scriptures, Kuan-yin plays a central role as guardian and protector of the hero and his companions. On several occasions, she intervenes on their behalf to trick, subdue, and convert monsters of different sorts.[42] In the story of Miao Shan, she rescues one of the sons of the Naga king, Lung-wang, who has been sent on a mission by his father that necessitates his taking the form of a fish. While in this form, the son is captured by a fisherman and taken to a fish market. With her miraculous vision, Kuan-yin, in the form of Miao Shan, becomes aware of the son's dilemma and dispatches one of her messengers, who buys the fish and sets him free. The Naga king gives Kuan-yin a magical pearl that glows constantly and enables her to see throughout the world at the darkest times. This pearl is brought to Kuan-yin by the third daughter of the Naga king's son, a girl named Lung-nü, who becomes one of Kuan-yin's constant attendants.[43]

Another story tells of a devotee of Kuan-yin's who is about to be executed. He repeats her name one thousand times, and when the executioner's sword hits him, the sword breaks in two and does not harm him. After three swords have been thus destroyed, the hero is pardoned.[44] The conversion of a naval surgeon, Dr. Ting Fu-pao, who later became a very influential Buddhist in China, involved his miraculous deliverence by Kuan-yin. "Once when he was traveling on a small overcrowded Yangtze River steamer, it began to capsize in a storm. Everyone called on Kuan-yin to save them and Dr. Ting involuntarily joined in. Just when all seemed lost, he saw a vision of Kuan-yin standing with outstretched arms on the windward side. He struggled up toward her, followed by the other passengers. The ship was saved."[45]

Kuan-yin also acts as a savior and helper to her devotees in less dramatic, more routine and mundane ways. Perhaps her most common intervention on behalf of her devotees is in the case of those who wish children. Countless stories exist of devotees petitioning Kuan-yin to grant them children. Other stories of Kuan-yin's intervention in routine, daily tribulations of humankind include her help in allowing a scholar to pass the government examinations, in aiding a poor and sick man to become a healthy millionaire, in reuniting an entire family after it had been separated by war, and in restoring the health of the father of one of her young female devotees.[46] She is also described, ironically, as helping a studious young man keep awake in his attempts to study Buddhist scriptures.[47] These everyday appearances and interventions almost always occur in the context of devotional piety. The following story nicely illustrates this and typifies the nature of Kuan-yin's appearances. It is the story of how a young man was vowed to the monastic life by his parents.

> My parents . . . vowed me to the service of the Buddha at the time of Elder Brother's illness. He was lying at the point of death, you see, when Kuan Yin's mercy saved him. When the physician told us there was no hope, my aunt shooed him from the house and took over. Calling all the neighbours in, she ordered them to spend the night in our house, reciting the Dhāranī of Great Compassion until dawn. The harvest had been brought in safely, otherwise they might have been less docile, though my aunt is not a person one cares to cross. Towards midnight Elder Brother, who had been lying all day in a coma, startled us by raising his head and shouting weakly: "Look at that girl!" His eyes were fixed upon the rafters where, to our great astonishment, sat a fairy-like girl in long antique robes. . . . I would not say that the girl's form was very clear, only that it was too clear for anyone to suppose it to be a trick of light and shadow. Besides, she was laughing and we all heard that. In her hands was a kind of vase like the one in which Kuan Yin stores the dew of compassion, as it is called. She was playing with it like a prankish child and suddenly tipped it sharply so that some liquid fell right on my brother's head. Then she was gone and everybody burst out talking at once. What a noise! My aunt was jubilant. After taking a good look at my brother, she said there was no need to go on with what she called the cure, meaning the mantra recitation. Within a couple of days, Elder Brother was on his feet. The physician was speechless when, within less than a week, Elder Brother walked over to the neighbouring village to offer him a basket of fruit! Oh, I forgot. It was when they began to recite the mantra that my aunt persuaded my parents to vow me to the monastery as a thank-offering for their eldest son's recovery. I am glad they did. I like it here.[48]

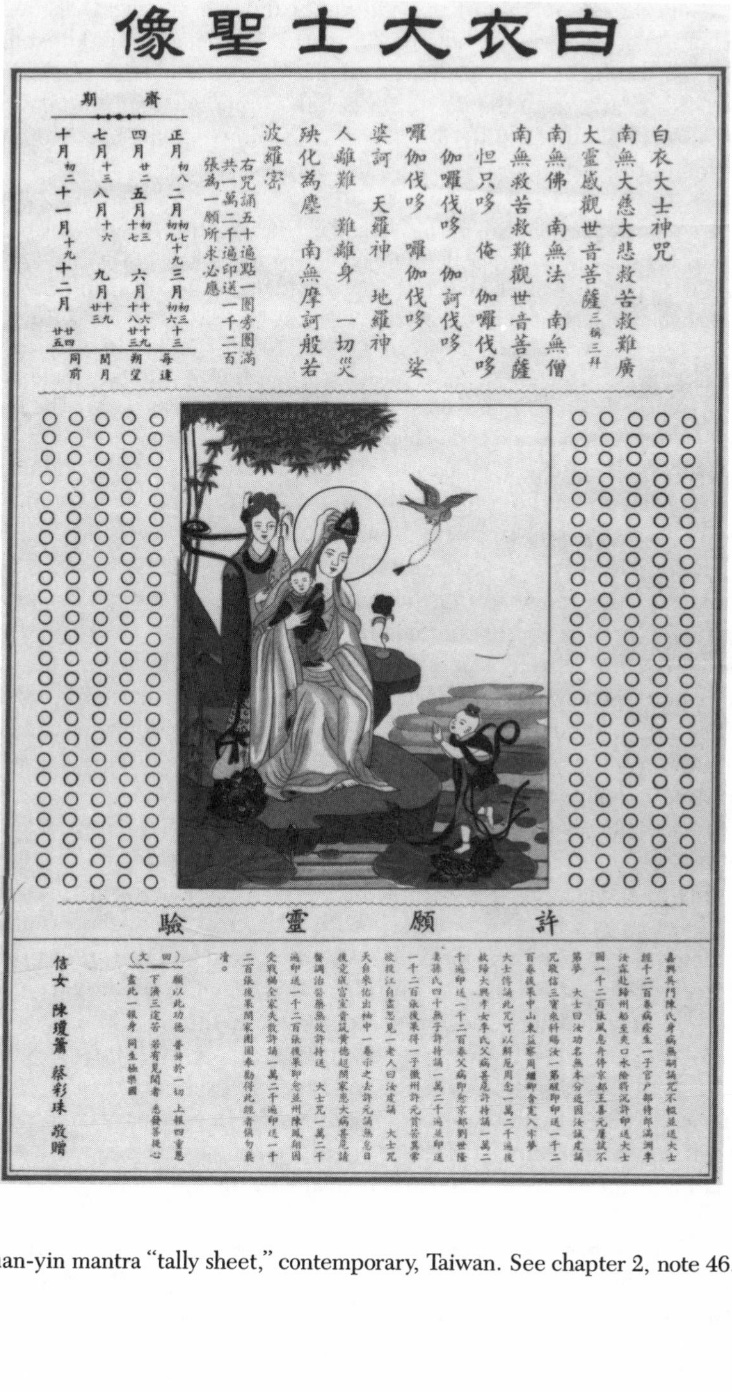

Kuan-yin mantra "tally sheet," contemporary, Taiwan. See chapter 2, note 46.

To a great extent, then, Kuan-yin's appeal lies in the fact that she hearkens to her devotees' pleas for help in *this* world. While other Buddhist figures, such as Amitābha, appeal primarily to the devotees' desire for rebirth in heaven after death, or to the desire for enlightenment and subsequent release from the world of human suffering, Kuan-yin's compassionate actions often focus on life in this world.

> It is with respect to present circumstances and tribulations that Kuan-yin played a critical role as the present savior for those in need. The mythology of Kuan-yin, from the period of its importation into China, had emphasized the bodhisattva's miraculous powers to change circumstances in this world as well as to assist the Buddha Amitābha in the next. Whereas Amitābha was centered on the "other world" of the Western Paradise, Kuan-yin, situated on Mount Poṭalaka, was much closer to the people's present concerns and needs. . . . The focal point in cult worship of Kuan-yin was to be free from suffering in this present world and to increase the "good things of life."[49]

Kuan-yin's compassionate interventions are sometimes of an educational, instructive nature and often lead to conversion. Several such examples are found in *The Journey to the West* in which Kuan-yin converts destructive demons to the path of virtue and restraint.[50] The case of the story's hero, the Monkey King (also known as Pilgrim and Wu-k'ung), is a prime example. Monkey had been imprisoned under a mountain by the Buddha because of trouble he had caused in heaven. Kuan-yin, however, releases him from bondage in order to gain his help in an important mission, a great journey from China to India to obtain sacred scriptures. Kuan-yin decides that Monkey's bravery and power will be necessary to aid and protect the monk named Tripitaka, who will undertake the long and dangerous journey. However, Kuan-yin is not willing simply to accept Monkey's word that he will in future behave himself and keep his mischievous and rambunctious nature in check. Shortly after Tripitaka has begun his pilgrimage to the West, Monkey rebels and abandons the mission. Kuan-yin contrives to equip Monkey with a magical headband by means of which Tripitaka, by saying a formula, can inflict pain and discomfort on Monkey, thereby keeping him under control. In this example, Kuan-yin's mercy is tempered with a judicious use of forcible (indeed, painful) restraint.[51]

Another example of this type of intervention is the story of King Wu chung ti, who was obsessed with sex and given to excessive drinking. So dissolute was this king that he was completely ineffective in his attempts to rule. Kuan-yin appears to him and takes away his sexual obsession and his taste for intoxicating drink. Thus sobered and restrained, the king assumes the path of virtue.[52]

A similar story from the modern period involves a young man who developed murderous intentions toward his stepmother, a petty, evil-minded woman who had originally arrived at the boy's home as a concubine. There she had belittled and hounded the young man's mother. Having decided to kill his stepmother in revenge (years after his mother had died), the young man approached her in a lonely area of a park. Sensing his intention, the stepmother invoked Kuan-yin's protection: "Save from suffering, save from harm! Bodhisattva, come!" The young man at first laughed at the incongruity of his evil stepmother reciting this pious prayer but was then seized with a bodily paralysis that prohibited him from harming the woman. Soon afterward the young man acknowledged the intervention of Kuan-yin and returned to a pious mode of life, which he had earlier abandoned. The young man also pointed out that his stepmother, from that day forward, became a much less objectionable person.[53] The story makes the point that Kuan-yin will aid even evil-minded people if they are in danger and ask her help. She will not help them in their evil actions, but she will protect them from harm if they call upon her.

In this type of intervention, Kuan-yin reveals herself as a teacher of Buddhist dharma, whose central interest is furthering the progress of various beings on their path to virtuous perfection and enlightenment, the classic concern and role of the Buddhist bodhisattva.

Comforter of the Dying and Guide and Guardian of Souls

While Kuan-yin's role as savior is often focused on this world, she also performs acts of compassion for the dead and is particularly associated with providing comfort to those who are dying. That is, in addition to alleviating suffering in this world, she acts as an intermediary between this world and the realms of the dead and as a psychopomp, one who specializes in guiding individuals in the dangerous transition from the realm of the living to the realm of the dead.

The most dramatic mythological expression of Kuan-yin's role as comforter of the dead is the account of her descent into hell in the legend of Miao Shan. In that story, Miao Shan (Kuan-yin) descends to the land of the dead in order to alleviate the torments of those in hell. Her radiant and virtuous presence puts out the fires that afflict the dead. When she begins to pray by reciting Buddhist scriptures, as she had done on earth as a Buddhist nun, the land of the dead "was suddenly transformed into a paradise; all the instruments of torture were changed into lotus-flowers, and the suffering victims enjoyed unbounded happiness."[54]

A popular Buddhist belief in some parts of Asia is that pious people, after acquiring merit, should share their merit with the souls of the dead who are suffering because of their evil deeds. Ritually, this belief is carried out by the devotee's transferring his or her merit to a container of water and then pouring the water onto the ground. Thus, the devotee's merit soaks into the earth and eventually reaches the nether world, where it alleviates the sufferings of the dead.[55] In the legend of Miao Shan's descent to the underworld, we have a dramatic representation of this Buddhist idea: a particularly meritorious being, indeed the epitome of a meritorious being, descends to hell herself, in person, to alleviate the sufferings of the dead, bringing to them, or providing them with, the positive effects of her virtuous life. Instead of sailing away to some heavenly paradise befitting her virtuous life and character, Miao Shan descends to hell to help suffering beings there.

In traditional China, there was a strong concern for relieving the sufferings of the souls of the dead, especially the souls of one's ancestors. It was assumed in traditional China that the living had the ability and the obligation to perform certain rituals that would benefit or deliver the souls of their ancestors. The Buddhist religious establishment, primarily the Buddhist monastic community, came to play an important role in meeting this concern. Even after the decline of Buddhism in the post-Sung period, the monastic community continued to play a central role in mediating between the living and the dead by means of certain rituals. "These ceremonies have been the most significant point of contact between the Buddhist Saṅgha and the community at large."[56] The most popular of these ceremonies is the Feeding of the Hungry Ghosts.

This ceremony can be performed either at private funerals and memorial services or in an elaborate, public way. When the ceremony is performed as a public event during the seventh month of the Chinese year, it aims in particular to satisfy and relieve the Orphaned Souls, those beings who for different reasons (for example, improper burial, absence of sacrificial offerings, violent death) exist in a state of constant hunger and thirst, which causes them to wander aimlessly and perpetually. The ceremony of Feeding of the Hungry Ghosts dates back to around the eighth century and since that time has become quite elaborate and diversified. In recent times, a Tantric version of the ceremony has become especially popular, and in this version of the ceremony Kuan-yin plays a central role. In the Tantric ceremony, the priest prepares a *maṇḍala*, a microcosm of the universe, and ritually enters it. Identifying himself ritually and mentally with certain Buddhas and bodhisattvas, the priest undertakes specific actions that aim at helping the souls of the dead. The dramatic high point of the ceremony takes place when the priest ritually and meditatively identifies himself with Kuan-yin. Having done this, the priest then makes certain gestures and recites certain formulas that are referred to as "the breaking open of hell." These rituals are believed to break open hell by sending forth bright rays of light. The priest (representing Kuan-yin) then recites the vow: "I vow not to attain buddhahood until Hell is empty." Then the priest (Kuan-yin) absolves the sins of the hell-dwelling souls, feeds them and gives them drink, and finally guides them out of hell to paradise.[57] In short, the priest, having identified himself with Kuan-yin, reiterates her descent into hell, her liberation of the souls dwelling there, and the transformation of hell into paradise.

The ceremony also might be understood as a ritualization of Kuan-yin's vow to continue her efforts on behalf of all those who suffer until hell itself is emptied of tormented beings.

The Resolution of Buddhist and Chinese Virtues in Kuan-yin

As mentioned earlier, part of the appeal of the Miao Shan legend concerns the way in which it portrays tensions between Buddhist and Confucian (or Chinese) ideals and then resolves those tensions in its dramatic conclusion. As a religious figure, Miao Shan (Kuan-yin) expresses clearly and strongly both Buddhist and Chinese virtues; she is an exemplar of many Buddhist virtues and ideals and of certain Chinese virtues.

Strong opposition to Buddhism arose in China because of its ideal of renunciation of the world and the concomitant emphasis on celibacy. This Buddhist ideal went against the Confucian insistence upon taking an active part in the social order and against the emphasis on filial piety, which insisted that children carry on the family tradition by marrying and begetting children. Buddhism, in its call for worldly renunciation and the celibate life, seemed, to many Chinese, alien and offensive.

In the Miao Shan legend, the young princess is consistently and forcefully depicted as an ideal Buddhist. Throughout most accounts of the legend, Miao Shan gives discourses that distill Buddhist doctrines and virtues. Several such Buddhist homilies appear in the early stages of the story when Miao Shan informs her father that she does not wish to marry but instead wishes to join the Buddhist nuns at the nearby convent. At an early point in the story, for example, Miao Shan says to her two sisters as the three disport themselves in the royal gardens:

> . . . riches and worldly glory are like a passing spring-shower, or the morning dewdrops; they last for a few moments, and then vanish for ever. Kings and rulers would fain enjoy for ages the honours which give them a privileged place among mortals, but illness brings them soon to the grave, and there all ends in dust. Where are nowadays those powerful monarchs, whose will the whole world obeyed? As for me . . . I shall deem myself happy if I can spend my life in a solitary mountain-cave, and there attend to the pursuit of perfection.[58]

In response to her father's questions concerning the type of husband she might prefer, Miao Shan replies: "Mortals here below seek a royal crown, and aspire to the joys of the married state. As for me, I wish to be a Buddhist nun. Riches and glory have no charm for me; with regard to them, my heart is as cold as an extinct ember, and I feel impelled to be more and more detached from such vain things."[59] When the king comes to visit Miao Shan after he has permitted her to spend several days in a lonely garden practicing austerities, he finds her resolve undiminished. To his request that she return to the palace and abandon her solitary life, she says: "I have already expressed to you my desire of leading a life of seclusion, and my set purpose of not getting married. During the past few days, I have enjoyed the charms of my solitary recess; I have prayed to Buddha, and kept all Buddhist observances, for the sole purpose of renouncing the world, and all worldly grandeur."[60]

Miao Shan's Buddhist sermons are met with stiff opposition from her family, particularly her father. He considers the monastic life useless and accuses those who follow such a path of being lazy and irresponsible.[61] Miao Shan's servants raise the issue of obedience to one's parents and in their comments to Miao Shan express some of the underlying Chinese suspicion of Buddhism in general and of the celibate life in particular. "We, your faithful servants, have learned from our ancestors that filial piety is the foremost of virtues, and that devotion to one's parents is much better than the itinerating and dishonourable life of Buddhist nuns. At the risk of our lives, we beg to request you to return to the palace, and give up your ideas of leading a Buddhist life."[62]

There is no doubt that in the opening scenes of the Miao Shan legend, the heroine is portrayed as single minded, rebellious, and disobedient vis-à-vis her family and her father in particular; she must have seemed an unsympathetic figure to many Chinese, who regarded respect for and obedience to one's parents as a fundamental and central virtue. Subsequent events in the story, however, reveal that Miao Shan harbors deep feelings of respect and honor for her family, especially for her father. Much of the story concerns the various persecutions that Miao Shan's father inflicts on her personally and on Buddhism generally. Through all this, however, Miao Shan herself does not criticize her father or betray anger or contempt for him. In this respect, she behaves as a virtuous Buddhist should behave. She exhibits equanimity in the face of adversity and never gives way to anger, hatred, or hostility.

The closing scenes of the story concentrate on Miao Shan's willingness to sacrifice herself unconditionally for the welfare of her father. By willingly offering her arms and eyes to provide the medicine that will cure her father, she redeems herself in the view of traditional Chinese society as an exceptionally dutiful daughter. In some versions of the story, the medicine that is prescribed as a cure for the king's illness calls for the eyes and arms of his closest kin. Thereupon the king sends a request to his two eldest daughters. They, quite understandably, decline his request. Miao Shan's subsequent willingness to sacrifice herself, then, demonstrates that she has greater reverence for her father than her two sisters, who earlier in the story were dutifully obedient to their parents in contrast to Miao Shan.[63]

What is important to emphasize in the Miao Shan story is that the heroine's Buddhist virtues and inclinations, in the end, enhance and intensify her filial piety. Far from subverting her feelings of love for her father, her Buddhist tendency toward compassion complements and increases her devotion to her father. Miao Shan's father himself acknowledges that it is his daughter's Buddhist piety and perfection that have intensified her parental affection to the point where she is willing to sacrifice her own eyes and arms in order to heal him. When the king hears a description of the person who has donated eyes and arms to provide the medicine that will heal him, in some version of the story he immediately recognizes the person as his youngest daughter and says: "It is assuredly my daughter *Miao-shen*, who has reached perfection; who else but she would have given me her own eyes and hands?"[64] A bit later in the story, after the king has gone in person to thank his daughter for her sacrifice, she asks her father if he would still prefer that she marry. He replies: "Don't mention that any more, dear daughter . . . ; I was quite wrong. If you had not reached Buddhahood, I would not be alive to-day."[65] In short, the point is made in the story of Miao Shan that the cultivation of Buddhist virtues does not subvert traditional Chinese values but enhances and deepens them.

Kuan-yin and Women

Kuan-yin is a deity who seems to be especially cherished among women. She is perceived as particularly attentive to women and their special needs and problems. "In many families . . . the women lavish their worship and affection on Kuan Yin. . . . In some places, a month after marriage the young bride receives from her parents an image of the Goddess with a censer and a pair of candlesticks. This image comes to be, for her, a centre of affectionate regard—an object to which she can turn for help, for strength and for consolation."[66]

In her form as Kuan-yin Who Brings Children, she is worshiped primarily by women. In traditional China, a woman's status was dependent upon having children, especially sons. Although the begetting of offspring was also a male concern, it is usually women who are mentioned as worshiping Kuan-yin for children. In this form, Kuan-yin is usually shown wearing a long white robe that covers her hair. She sits on a lotus flower and holds a child in her lap. A bird is sometimes shown bringing her her rosary, and she is sometimes holding a vase or a willow branch. She is flanked by two attendants.[67] Such images are much more common in homes than in Buddhist temples. Indeed, there is not much that is specifically Buddhist about Kuan-yin in this role.[68] In recent history, Kuan-yin Who Brings Children was very popular. "In nearly every house are found crudely coloured prints or even statuettes of her; in Fukien they are even given the place of honour in the family shrine, between the God of the Hearth and the God of the Place."[69] Women desiring children will offer to such images a tiny shoe. They also may make vows to Kuan-yin to abstain from certain foods until their wish is granted.[70]

Kuan-yin, in the form of Miao Shan, also came to play an important role as the exemplar of a way of life that provided Chinese women an alternative to

Kuan-yin, contemporary lithograph, Malaysia.

their traditional roles as wives and mothers. This is especially clear in certain texts belonging to a genre of popular religious tracts known as *pao-chüan*, "precious books," which date from the fourteenth century and continue to be written in Taiwan today.[71] Several of these books lament the traditional plight of women and extoll the celibate life, particularly the life of a Buddhist nun. In one such book, a Buddhist nun makes the following criticism of the married life:

> Our parents have no choice but to raise us, and when we grow up we are married to someone else. . . . When our husband's parents are angry we must hasten to please them with smiles. When our husband furiously curses us we must not answer back. . . . We taint heaven and earth when we give birth to children, and in washing filth from our bloodstained skirts we offend the river gods. . . . Once you are married to a husband you are under his control for your whole life: all your pleasures and miseries are at his discretion. When you are a man's wife you are bound to know the sufferings of childbirth, you cannot avoid the bloodstained water, and the sin of offending the sun, moon and stars. . . . If you are a wise and clever woman, you will eat vegetarian food, recite the Buddha's name and start religious cultivation at once. How favoured and honoured you will be when you migrate from a woman's body to a man's body! In your next existence you can once again follow the way to the Pure Land.[72]

In several of the precious books, women are shown submitting grudgingly to their traditional destiny and suffering in their traditional roles. Other women are depicted as heroic in their resistence to marriage. In several texts of this type, Miao Shan came to play an important role as an example of a woman who rebels against traditional injustices and seeks an alternative in the celibate, religious life. Miao Shan's heroic qualities are enhanced in this context, as she is not fleeing a particularly harsh domestic life; she is, after all, a princess, and her father has promised her a noble husband and a life of luxury and ease. Nevertheless, preferring the celibate, religious vocation of a nun, she resists marriage. "Without question Miao-shan claims a place, and a pre-eminent place, among the heroines of this specialized religious literature. Her challenge to the marriage institution is more radical and more successful than theirs: she resists even the proposal that she should take a husband."[73]

Kuan-yin, then, relates to women's concerns and problems in a variety of ways. She assists married women in giving birth and obtaining male children, which enhances their domestic status. She comforts women in their personal trials and difficulties. And by providing a model of female celibacy she provides inspiration to women who might seek an alternative to the married life.

Symbols and Attendants

Kuan-yin is often shown flanked by two attendants, a young man and a young woman. The legends concerning both figures are found in the story of

Miao Shan. The male attendant is known as Shen-ts'ai and usually stands to Kuan-yin's right. After Kuan-yin had taken her place on P'u-t'o-shan she was advised to find two attendants to care for her. After a considerable search by the god of the soil, a young Buddhist monk was chosen as a possible candidate. Both of his parents had died, and he was living a secluded life on a holy mountain in the west. When the lad was brought to Kuan-yin and questioned concerning who he was, he confessed that he was but a simple monk who had not advanced very far in perfection. He also confessed that he would very much like to stay with Kuan-yin on her island home and strive for perfection under her guidance. Kuan-yin decided to test the young man's faith in her before making a final decision. She arranged for a group of spirits to stage an attack on her island. When the spirits appeared in the form of murderous pirates, she ran to the edge of a cliff pursued by them. She then lept from the cliff into the sea. Shen-ts'ai, seeing her fall into the waves, jumped in after her in an attempt to save her. In so doing, he gave up his life for his mistress. Immediately after this, the youth was restored to life and, having proven his devotion to Kuan-yin, became her constant attendant.[74] Shen-ts'ai, then, symbolizes Buddhist devotional piety. He illustrates the attitude with which one should approach Kuan-yin (and other bodhisattvas and Buddhas). Kuan-yin's selection of Shen-ts'ai for her attendant may also suggest her partiality for those who have been abandoned or who are bereft in life. Shen-ts'ai is described as a lonely orphan, while Miao Shan is pictured as a caring parent.

Kuan-yin's female attendant, who usually stands to her left, is named Lung-nü. After Miao Shan had rescued the third son of the Naga king who had been captured in the form of a fish, the king sent his son's daughter, Lung-nü, to P'u-t'o-shan to deliver a gift to Miao Shan. The gift was a luminous pearl with which Miao Shan could read the Buddhist scriptures at night. Lung-nü was so entranced by Miao Shan (Kuan-yin) that she asked to remain and seek Buddhahood under her guidance. After testing the girl's sincerity, Miao Shan consented and accepted her as her acolyte.[75]

The magic pearl itself, which Kuan-yin is often shown holding, suggests steadfast piety. So devoted is Miao Shan that she desires to read scriptures throughout the night. The luminous pearl may also suggest Kuan-yin's watchfulness. With the pearl, she can look upon the world even at night to guard her devotees from danger.

The magical peach that Kuan-yin is shown holding was given to her before her long journey to P'u-t'o-shan so that she might not feel hunger, thirst, or fatigue. The peach also represents youthfulness and longevity or is believed to bestow these qualities on one who eats it. In Taoist legend, magical peaches were said to have grown in the garden of a mythical queen, Hsi-wang-mu. These fabulous fruits were believed to bestow immortality.[76] The peach, then, suggests Kuan-yin's power to provide her devotees with youthfulness, health, and longevity and emphasizes her willingness to aid people in this world.

Kuan-yin is often shown holding a slender vase. Sometimes she is shown pouring liquid from it. The liquid is magical water that bestows vitality and wakefulness on Kuan-yin's devotees.[77] The effect of the water on a devotee is illustrated in the legend of the parrot, which is another of Kuan-yin's attendants or symbols. In the story, the parrot goes in search of a magical peach that will revive his dying mother. The parrot is captured by a hunter who puts it in a cage. The virtuous parrot takes on the role of a teacher of Buddhist virtues by discoursing on morality during his captivity. When the parrot reaches his home, he finds his mother already dead and faints. At this point, Kuan-yin appears and pours her magical water on the parrot and his parents. The parents are reborn as human beings in their next life as a result of this divine refreshment. The parrot himself is awakened from unconsciousness and is blessed by being accepted as Kuan-yin's perpetual attendant.[78]

Several examples of the revivifying powers of Kuan-yin's magical water occur in *The Journey to the West*. At one time, Kuan-yin wagered Lao-tzu, the legendary founder of Taoism, that she could restore life to her willow branch no matter what he did to it. Lao-tzu reduced the branch to a charred twig in his brazier. Kuan-yin placed the twig in her vase, and within a day it had been restored to its previous vitality.[79] Similarly, she restores life to the cosmic ginseng fruit tree, which the hero, Monkey, had destroyed in his excessive violence. Dipping her willow branch into the vase, she sprinkled the base of the uprooted tree; shortly, a spring arose at the foot of the tree and restored life to its limbs.[80] Kuan-yin's vase, then, contains water that has great transformative and enlivening powers. She transforms beings from one state of existence to another (she changes parrots to human beings), from one state of consciousness to another (she awakens the parrot with her water), and from death into life (she restores life to the willow twig and the ginseng fruit tree).

The willow branch itself seems to be a symbol of life and longevity. The willow is one of the first trees to return to life in the spring and one of the last to give up its leaves in the fall. In *The Journey to the West*, Kuan-yin wields the willow branch as a kind of magical wand. With the branch, she deludes certain demons and produces magical effects.[81]

Finally, Kuan-yin is sometimes shown holding a rosary. In some depictions, a bird is bringing her a rosary that it clasps in its beak. This necklace may well refer to an incident in the *Lotus-sūtra* in which the bodhisattva Akṣayamati gives Avalokiteśvara (Kuan-yin) a necklace of precious pearls as a token of his admiration and devotion. Avalokiteśvara refuses to take the precious necklace at first but finally accepts it only to please his devotee, as an act of compassion toward his devotee.[82] The rosary also may suggest Kuan-yin's own

Kuan-yin, contemporary drawing, Taiwan.

piety. As Miao Shan, she is characterized as constantly reciting the Buddhist scriptures. The rosary is used in Buddhism as an aid to reciting certain mantras or texts or the names of Buddhas and bodhisattvas. As such, it is suggestive of piety.

Becoming Kuan-yin

At the popular level, Kuan-yin is considered a great goddess. She has all the marks of a goddess and is worshiped as a divine being who exists in a heavenly sphere from which she observes closely the human condition with the intention of helping suffering beings. In the Buddhist meditative tradition (as distinct from, but not necessarily opposed to, the devotional tradition), the reality of Kuan-yin as a powerful goddess, while not necessarily denied, is not emphasized. What is stressed is the idea that Kuan-yin is an aspect or dimension of each individual. The aim of Buddhist practice vis-à-vis Kuan-yin in this tradition is to become Kuan-yin. The goal is to cultivate an aspect of oneself or one's being that is beautifully expressed in the figure of Kuan-yin—an aspect that is compassionate, merciful, and selfless. The aim of Buddhist practice in this tradition is to lose oneself, or one's ego, in compassionate regard for other beings—and in this sense to become Kuan-yin herself, the very embodiment of compassion and selflessness.

In this Buddhist meditative understanding of Kuan-yin, her ability to protect beings from harm when they are in danger is said to derive from the fact that a person who cultivates Kuan-yin's qualities will act and behave in such a way that harm will naturally avoid him or her. In this interpretation, the practitioner becomes somewhat like the Taoist sages, who are immune from harm from all kinds of dangers because they attract no attention, so smoothly do they flow through the world.

> Sustained contemplation of the Bodhisattva as the embodiment of pure compassion inevitably affects the devotee's whole being. Seeking no advantages for himself, delighting to put himself out for others when urged to do so, he comes in some ways to resemble the Taoist sages of old—men so ungreedy, so easily satisfied with simple joys, so loath to take offence or put themselves forward unless pressed, so far removed from every kind of aggressive behaviour and factionalism that they were able to pass their lives in serene obscurity. Attracting no unwelcome attentions from robbers, government authorities or policemen, making no enemies, harbouring no grudges—in short, causing not the least offense to humans, animals or ghosts, they lived from day to day untroubled by savage beasts or extortioners, safe from the prisoner's manacles and strangers to the glittering horror of the executioner's sword. These were the "Immortals whom ice could not freeze nor sunbeams scorch." Calamities rarely if ever came their way.[83]

In short, according to this interpretation, Kuan-yin is a state of perfection in which one has transcended an ego-centered, selfish identity and acquired a selfless regard for all beings.

Chapter **3**

Lakṣmī, Goddess of Abundance and Luck

Her colour is like that of the inside of a lotus and she is adorned with a chained girdle. She wears a white garland and (white) clothes and is ornamented with necklace and armlets. She bears all lucky signs and has round, high and close-set breasts. Her eyes are large like a full-blown lotus and she has a smiling expression. She has locks that resemble a swarm of bees in flight. Her forehead is marked with a decorative and charming spot, her gemlike lips are (ruby) red and her teeth are like rows of pearls. Her forehead is shaped like a half-moon and her tresses are dark and curly.[1]

Introduction

From very early times, the goddess Śrī, who is also known as Lakṣmī, has been known and worshiped in the Hindu tradition. She is one of the most popular goddesses in the Hindu pantheon. She has a considerable body of mythology and is widely worshiped by Hindus of all castes throughout India to this day. Since the late epic period (circa 400 C.E.), she has been particularly associated with the god Viṣṇu as his wife or consort. In this role, she plays the part of a model Hindu wife, obediently serving her husband as lord. Throughout her history, Śrī has been associated with prosperity, well-being, royal power, and illustriousness. In many respects, she is the embodiment of these qualities, and it is commonly understood that when these qualities are evident, Śrī herself is present or reveals herself.

The Early History of Śrī-Lakṣmī

The Goddess Śrī-Lakṣmī does not appear in the earliest Vedic texts.[2] However, the term *śrī* does occur quite often in that literature, and it is clearly

Lakṣmī, late Choḷa (twelfth century C.E.). C. Sivaramamurti, *South Indian Bronzes* (New Delhi: Lalit Kala Akademi, 1963), fig. 68b. Gautam Sarabhai Collection, Ahmedabad.

the case that the meanings of the term are related to the nature of the later goddess Śrī-Lakṣmī. It is important, then, in thinking about the origins and early nature of Śrī-Lakṣmī, to look briefly at the meanings of the term in early Vedic literature.

As used in the Vedic hymns, the term *śrī* suggests beauty, luster, glory, and high rank. The term is used especially in later Vedic literature to refer to the ruling power, dominion, and majesty of kings. As such it seems to be a distinct, disembodied power that is acquired by kings in various ways. It seems to be a power associated more with the office of the king than with the king himself. At one point, *śrī* is identified with the cushion upon which the king sits. The idea is that the cushion or seat, *śrī*, ruling power, is temporarily possessed by the current owner of the seat.[3] *Śrī* also refers to riches, prosperity, and abundance in general; as such, it is something that may be acquired or possessed by anyone. In short, *śrī* refers to most auspicious qualities and suggests general well-being in terms of physical health, material prosperity, bodily beauty, and ruling majesty.

In what may be the earliest myth that speaks of Śrī as a goddess, her nature as the personification or embodiment of auspicious, particularly royal, qualities is clear.[4] She is said to have been born as a result of the austerities of the god Prajāpati. Seeing Śrī, the other gods coveted her qualities and proceeded to steal them from her. Ten qualities, or objects, are listed: food, royal power, universal sovereignty, noble rank, power, holy luster, kingdom, fortune, bounteousness, and beauty.[5] In Vedic literature, then, the goddess Śrī's origin seems to be the result of the personification of auspicious qualities, particularly those associated with royal power and riches.

The most detailed picture of Śrī-Lakṣmī in Vedic literature is found in the *Śrī-sūkta*, a hymn in praise of Śrī that is part of an appendix to the *Ṛg-veda* and probably predates Buddhism.[6] It is surely one of the earliest hymns to Śrī and associates her with certain symbols and qualities that persist throughout her history in the Hindu tradition. Not surprisingly, and in conformity with the meanings of the term *śrī* in earlier Vedic literature, Śrī is invoked to bring fame and prosperity (verse 7). She is said to be bountiful and to give abundance (5). She is said to bestow on her worshiper gold (14), cattle and horses (1), and food (10). She is asked to banish her sister Alakṣmī, "misfortune" (5, 6, 8), who appears in such inauspicious forms as need, poverty, hunger, and thirst (8). Royal qualities are suggested when she is described as seated in the middle of a chariot, possessed of the best horses, and delighted by the sounds of elephants (3). In outward appearance, she is glorious and richly ornamented. She is as radiant as gold, illustrious like the moon, and wears a necklace of gold and silver (1). She is often said to shine like the sun (6, 13) and to be lustrous like fire (4).

An important feature of Śrī in this hymn is her association with fertility, a feature that was not significantly emphasized in earlier usages of the term *śrī* in Vedic literature. In the *Śrī-sūkta*, she is described as moist (13, 14), perceptible through odor (9), abundant in harvest, and dwelling in cow dung (9). Her son is said to be Kardama, which means "mud," "mire," or "slime" (11); that is, Śrī is associated with growth and the fecundity of moist, rich soil. Her presence is affirmed to be discernable in the mysterious potency of the earth. Although her association with agricultural fertility does not play a central role in her later literary history in Hinduism, it seems clear that this aspect of Śrī remains important to this day at the village level. Villagers, particularly women, are reported to worship Śrī in the form of cow dung on certain occasions, and this form of worship is actually enjoined in the *Nīlamata-purāṇa*.[7]

The hymn to Śrī also mentions two things that come to be consistently associated with Śrī throughout her history: the lotus and the elephant. She is said to be seated on a lotus, to have the color of a lotus (4), to appear like a lotus (5), to be covered with lotuses, and to wear a garland of lotuses (14). Throughout her history, in fact, Śrī-Lakṣmī is often called Padma and Kamalā, "lotus." The popularity of the lotus in Indian art and iconography, in Buddhism as well as Hinduism, suggests a complex and multivalent meaning associated with the lotus.

As expressive of Śrī-Lakṣmī's nature, two general meanings seem apparent. First, the lotus is a symbol of fertility and life that is rooted in and takes its strength from the primordial waters.[8] The lotus symbolizes vegetative growth that has distilled the life-giving power of the waters into embodied life.[9] The lotus, and the goddess Śrī-Lakṣmī, then, represents the fully developed blossoming of organic life. At the macrocosmic level, the lotus might be taken as a symbol of the entire created world. The lotus growing from the navel of the god Viṣṇu marking the beginning of a new cosmic creation suggests the lotus as such a symbol. The frequent use of the lotus in Tantric diagrams also points to the lotus as a symbol of the entire created universe.[10] As a symbol of the world, the lotus suggests a growing, expanding world imbued with vigorous fertile power. This power is revealed in Śrī-Lakṣmī. She is the nectar or essence of creation that lends to creation its distinctive flavor and beauty. Organic life, impelled as it is by this mysterious power, flowers richly and beautifully in the creative processes of the world.

The second meaning of the lotus in relation to Śrī-Lakṣmī concerns purity and spiritual power. Rooted as it is in the mud, but blossoming above the water completely uncontaminated by the mud, the lotus represents spiritual perfection and authority. A common motif in Hindu and Buddhist iconograpy is the lotus seat. The gods and goddesses, the Buddhas and bodhisattvas, typically sit or stand upon a lotus, which suggests their spiritual authority. To be seated upon, or to be otherwise associated with, the lotus suggests that the being in question—god, Buddha, or human being—has transcended the limitations of the finite world (the mud of existence, as it were) and floats freely in a sphere of purity and spirituality. Śrī-Lakṣmī, then, suggests more than the fertilizing powers of moist soil and the mysterious powers of growth. She suggests a perfection or state of refinement that transcends the material world. She is associated not only with royal authority but with spiritual authority as well, and she therefore combines royal and priestly powers in her presence.

One of the most popular and enduring representations of Śrī-Lakṣmī shows her flanked by two elephants. The elephants shower her with water from their trunks or pour pots of water over her.[11] The elephants seem to have two related meanings. First, they most likely represent fertilizing rains. An ancient Hindu tradition says that the first elephants had wings and flew about the sky. In fact, they were clouds and showered the earth with rain wherever they went. These sky elephants, however, were cursed by a sage when they landed on a tree under which he was meditating and broke his concentration. Stripped of their wings, they henceforth had to remain earthbound. However, these earth elephants are still regarded as cousins of clouds, and their presence is supposed to attract their "white cousins," who bring fertilizing rains with them.[12] The flanking, showering elephants in images of Śrī-Lakṣmī, then, reinforce one of the central themes that we have already noted in her nature, her association with the fertility of crops and the sap of existence generally. Where Lakṣmī is, there elephants are, and where elephants are, there is produced the fertilizing potency of rain. This is one thing that the so-called Gaja-Lakṣmī images tell us.

Second, elephants suggest royal authority. Kings in ancient India kept stables of elephants, which formed their heavy artillery, as it were, in military campaigns. Kings often traveled on elephants in ceremonial processions, and in general elephants were considered an important indication of royal authority. Kings in ancient India were also believed to be responsible for rain and the fertility of the crops.[13] To ensure their beneficial influence in this area, it was probably important for them to keep several elephants for their power to bring fertilizing rains. In the king, and in the elephant, then, are brought together two central themes in the imagery of Śrī-Lakṣmī—royal authority and fertility.

Images of Śrī with elephants are probably meant to portray the act of royal consecration. The central ritual action of the Vedic royal consecration ceremony, the Rājasūya, was the *abhiṣekha* ritual, in which the king was consecrated by having auspicious waters poured over him that bestowed authority and vigor on him.[14] In these images of Lakṣmī, the elephants, themselves representatives of fertility and royal authority, bestow these qualities on Lakṣmī (insofar as they may be understood to be portraying the *abhiṣekha*), herself the source of these very qualities.[15] The elephants, furthermore, are often shown standing on lotuses,[16] the preeminent symbol of Lakṣmī. The elephants imbue Lakṣmī, then, with those very qualities that she possesses to the highest degree, and she, in turn, infuses the elephants with the same qualities. A more highly charged image denoting the increase of royal authority, fertility, and vigor would be difficult to imagine.[17]

Śrī-Lakṣmī in Later Hinduism

In the course of her history, Śrī-Lakṣmī has been associated with male deities, each of whom is significant in suggesting characteristics of the goddess. In some texts, she is associated with the god Soma. Along with several other deities, Śrī-Lakṣmī is said to attend Soma after he performs a great royal sacrifice.[18] The association of Lakṣmī with Soma is noteworthy for two reasons. First, in attending him after he has assumed the position of royal authority, she demonstrates one of her main characteristics, that of bestowing royal authority, or being present where royal authority exists. Second, Soma is well known as the lord of plants and is often identified with the fertile sap that underlies vegetative growth. In that Śrī-Lakṣmī is similarly identified, it is fitting that she and Soma should be associated in these texts. They complement and reinforce each other as symbols of the sap of existence.

In a few texts, Lakṣmī is said to be the wife of Dharma. She, along with several other goddesses, all of whom are personifications of certain auspicious qualities, is said to have been given by her father, Dakṣa, to Dharma in marriage. This association seems to represent primarily a thinly disguised "wedding" of Dharma (virtuous conduct) with Śrī-Lakṣmī (prosperity and well-being). The point of the association is apparently to teach that by behaving virtuously one obtains prosperity.[19]

A more interesting and fully developed association is between Śrī and the god Indra.[20] Several myths relate the theme of Indra's losing, acquiring, or being restored to Śrī-Lakṣmī's presence. In these myths, it is clear that what is lost, acquired, or restored in the person of Śrī is royal authority and power. Indra is traditionally known as the king of the gods, the foremost of the gods, and is typically described as a heavenly king. As such, for Śrī to be associated with him as his wife or consort is appropriate. In these myths, Śrī-Lakṣmī appears as the embodiment of royal authority, a being whose presence is essential for the effective wielding of royal power and the creation of royal prosperity.

In several myths of this genre, she is described as being persuaded to leave one ruler for another. She is said, for example, to dwell with the demons Bali and Prahlāda. While she dwells with these demons, they are demons in name only. Under her gracious presence they rule their kingdoms righteously, society operates smoothly, the lands are fertile, and the demon kings themselves shimmer with sublime inner and outer qualities. When she leaves Prahlāda, at Indra's request, the demon loses his luster and fears for his well-being.[21] Along with Śrī, the following qualities are said to depart from Prah-

Lakṣmī being showered by elephants, contemporary lithograph.

lāda: good conduct, virtuous behavior, truth, activity, and strength. With Śrī's departure, Prahlāda is left emptied of his royal might and predilections toward virtuous conduct.

The myths concerning the demon Bali make clear the same association between Lakṣmī and victorious kings. In these myths Bali defeats Indra. Lakṣmī is attracted to Bali's winning ways and bravery and joins him, along with her attendant auspicious virtues. In association with the auspicious goddess, Bali rules the three worlds with virtue, and under his rule the three worlds prosper.[22] Only when Viṣṇu, at the request of the dethroned gods, tricks Bali into surrendering the three worlds does Śrī-Lakṣmī depart from Bali, leaving him lusterless and powerless.

Śrī-Lakṣmī's presence ensures a king more than ruling power. In one of the myths associating her with Indra, we are told that when she sat down next to Indra he began to pour down rain and the crops grew abundantly. Cows gave plenty of milk, all beings enjoyed prosperity, and the earth flourished.[23] Indra is associated with fertility in Vedic texts, and festivals celebrated in his honor well into the medieval period associated him with the fertility of the crops. From the earliest Vedic texts, he is described as wielding the *vajra* (the thunderbolt) as his favorite weapon, and to the present day he is associated with bringing rain. As a couple, Śrī-Lakṣmī and Indra seem to be a clear example of a common type of divine pair in the world's religions: a female earth goddess and a male sky/rain god. Together they combine to generate the fertility necessary to all life. In this relationship, the male deity, associated with the sky, is said to fertilize the female deity with the his rain. Indra also seems to have had phallic associations in his identification with the plow, and it seems appropriate that he would become associated with a goddess representing the fertile earth.[24]

Śrī-Lakṣmī is also associated with the god Kubera in some traditions. Kubera is lord of the Yakṣas, a race of supernatural beings who frequent forests and uncivilized areas generally, and is particularly the possessor and distributor of wealth. He is the possessor and guardian of the earth's treasures in the form of gems. Śrī's relationship with Kubera is appropriate insofar as each of them is preeminently associated with prosperity and wealth.[25] Where wealth and abundance are, one or the other deity, and probably both, is certain to be found. So the two deities become associated as a couple.[26] Śrī's identification through Kubera with the Yakṣas, on the other hand, emphasizes her identity with the mysterious powers of growth and fertility.[27] Yakṣas often play the part of fertility symbols in Indian art and are associated iconographically with trees, vines, and vegetative growth. They are often shown embracing trees, leaning against trees,[28] or pouring forth vegetation from their mouths or navels.[29] To identify Śrī-Lakṣmī, the goddess who embodies the potent power of growth, with the Yakṣas is natural. She, like them, involves herself and reveals herself in the irrepressible fecundity of plant life.

Śrī-Lakṣmī's association with so many male deities, and the notorious fleetingness of good fortune, earned her a reputation for being fickle and inconsistent.[30] In one text, she is said to be so unsteady that even in a picture she moves and that if she associates with Viṣṇu it is only because she is attracted to his many different forms (*avatāras*).[31] By the late epic period (circa 400 C.E.), however, Śrī-Lakṣmī becomes consistently, and almost exclusively, associated with Viṣṇu, and as his wife she becomes characterized by steadfastness.[32] It is as if in Viṣṇu she has finally found the god she was looking for and, having found him, has remained loyal to him ever since.

Mythologically, Śrī-Lakṣmī's association with Viṣṇu comes about in the context of the churning of the milk ocean by the gods and demons, who seek the elixer of immortality (*amṛta*). In some versions of this story, Lakṣmī does not figure at all,[33] while in others she is the central focus of the myth.[34] What seems clear is that a myth concerning the churning of the ocean to obtain various valuable things existed from ancient times in India and that, at some point, Lakṣmī's origin was felt to be related to this mythological event. The interesting questions are why Lakṣmī's origin makes sense in the context of this myth and why her association with Viṣṇu comes about in later versions of the myth.

An ancient Indian tradition asserts that creation proceeds from an infinite body of primordial water, that the world or the multitude of universes of later Hinduism ultimately arise from and rest upon this limitless expanse of waters. In its unrefined state this watery world is chaotic, or at least formless and overwhelming. Creation, ordered existence, only takes place when this watery mass is somehow agitated, processed, or refined in such a way that form and growth take place. Within the watery formlessness resides the potency or essence of life, *rasa*, *amṛta*, or *soma*. When this potency is yielded up by the primordial waters, creation can proceed.[35] The churning of the ocean by the gods and demons is intended to obtain the nectar of immortality, the essence of creative power that will make the churners immortal and grant them their status as ordainers and overseers of creation. The act of churning dramatically illustrates the process of distilling the essence of the primordial waters. By churning milk, one thickens and refines it until it yields up, as it were, a richer substance, butter. Similarly, the milk ocean when churned yields up valuable essences, among them, in most later versions of the myth, the goddess Śrī-Lakṣmī.

The role or place of Śrī-Lakṣmī in this myth of creation seems fairly clear. Although the nectar of immortality is described as a separate entity that arises from the churning of the ocean, Śrī-Lakṣmī has many and obvious associations with the sap of existence that underlies or pervades all plant and animal life.

She herself represents the miraculous transformation of the formless waters into organic life.[36] The extent to which Śrī-Lakṣmī is necessary to the ongoing created order, and hence may be identified or associated with the essence of the creation, is indicated in some later variants of the myth. In these versions, Śrī-Lakṣmī disappears from the three worlds when Indra insults her. As a result, all sacrifices cease to be performed, all austerities are discontinued by the sages, all generosity ends, the sun and moon lose their brilliance, the gods lose their strength, and fire loses its heat.[37] In the absence of the goddess, the worlds become dull and lusterless and begin to wither away. Upon her return, the worlds again regain their vitality, and the society of humans and the order of the gods regain their sense of purpose and duty.

In most variants of the myth, Śrī-Lakṣmī's association with Viṣṇu is said to have taken place at the churning of the ocean. The relationship of Śrī and Viṣṇu seems appropriate in the context of the myth and at a symbolic level in several ways. During her early history, Śrī's attraction to powerful rulers among the gods (and demons) was firmly established. In the churning-of-the-ocean myth, Viṣṇu is clearly the dominant god. He oversees the entire operation and actually makes the churning possible by providing two indispensable participants: Vāsuki, the cosmic serpent that is used as the churning rope, and the cosmic tortoise, upon which the churning stick rests. Both Vāsuki and the tortoise, furthermore, are actually forms of Viṣṇu himself. When Śrī comes forth from the ocean, then, she is naturally attracted to Viṣṇu, the god who is obviously superior to the others. Conversely, Viṣṇu, as the divine overseer of the event, is the natural recipient of the treasures that result from the churning. As the master of ceremonies, as it were, Viṣṇu is entitled to the lovely goddess who emerges as a result of the efforts of the gods and demons.

Viṣṇu's royal nature is also significant in Śrī's association with him. Viṣṇu is the divine king par excellence by the medieval period. He is described as dwelling in a heavenly court, Vaikuṇṭha, and he is depicted iconographically as a mightly king. His primary role as a king is to institute and maintain cosmic and social order. This he does by means of his various *avatāras* ("descents" or incarnations), who intervene in the world from time to time to combat the forces of disorder. Viṣṇu, however, is also present wherever righteous kings rule and maintain order. He maintains order on the earth, that is, through certain human agents, namely, righteous kings.[38] We noted earlier that kings cannot rule without the authority that is bestowed by Śrī. Where she is present, royal authority waxes strong. Where she is absent, would-be rulers become weak and ineffectual. For Viṣṇu, the supreme divine king, to become associated with Śrī as her husband, then, is fitting. She follows him when he becomes part of his human agents, the righteous kings, and she bestows on these kings her royal power, prosperity, and fertility. In effect, Viṣṇu designates his human agents, and Śrī then empowers them, enabling them to be effective maintainers of Viṣṇu's cosmic scheme.

As Viṣṇu's wife, Lakṣmī loses her fickle nature. As the great cosmic king's queen, she is depicted as a model Hindu wife, loyal and submissive to her husband. In one of the most popular iconographic depictions of her, she is shown kneeling before Viṣṇu to massage his feet.[39] In her early history, Śrī-Lakṣmī was strongly associated with growth and fecundity as manifested in vegetation. There was a teeming vitality associated with her presence, a power that gave birth inexhaustibly to life. In her association with Viṣṇu, her character seems more restrained. Although she does not lose her association with fertility and growth, she seems more clearly involved in, or revealed in, the social and political order that her husband creates and oversees. When Viṣṇu assumes his various forms in order to uphold the world, she incarnates herself as his helpmate, assuming an appropriate form as his spouse or consort. She thus assists and accompanies him in his world-maintaining role. The *Viṣṇu-purāṇa* says:

> . . . as Hari [Viṣṇu] descends in the world in various shapes—so does his consort Śrī. Thus when Hari was born as a dwarf, as a son of Aditi, Lakṣmī appeared from a lotus; . . . when he was Rāghava, she was Sītā, and when he was Kṛṣṇa, she became Rukminī. In the other descents of Viṣṇu, she is his associate. If he takes a celestial form, she appears as divine; if a mortal, she becomes a mortal too, transforming her own person agreeably to whatever character it pleases Viṣṇu to put on. (1.9.142–46)[40]

Her role as a model wife typifies her more subdued nature. She is occupied in this role with household order. Indeed, she is said to cook food at the Jagannātha temple for those who come for *prasād* (food offered to a deity, then distributed to devotees).[41] In her role as an ideal wife, she exemplifies the orderliness of human society and human relations. In iconographic representations of Viṣṇu and Śrī together, she is typically shown as subservient to Viṣṇu, which is in harmony with sexual roles as described in the Hindu scriptures. She is usually shown as considerably smaller than Viṣṇu and as having only two arms instead of the four arms that she usually has when shown alone. Her position as submissive to Viṣṇu is conveyed in an image of the divine pair from Bādāmī in which Viṣṇu sits on a high stool while Lakṣmī sits on the ground and leans upon him, her right hand placed on his knee.[42]

Reflecting her increasing association with social order, several texts locate Lakṣmī's presence in righteous behavior, orderly conduct, and correct social observance. She is said, for example, to live with those who tell the truth and are generous.[43] She dwells with those who have clean bodies and are well dressed,[44] who eat with moderation, who have intercourse with their wives

Lakṣmī and Viṣṇu resting on the cosmic serpent in the midst of the universal ocean, contemporary lithograph.

regularly (something prescribed in the androcentric Hindu law books), and who cover themselves when asleep.[45] In the *Mahābhārata* she says: "I dwell in truth, gift, vow, austerity, strength and virtue" (12.218.12). Orderly social relations and traditional social virtues attract Śrī-Lakṣmī, herself a model of social decorum as Viṣṇu's wife.

In association with Viṣṇu, Lakṣmī provides a picture of marital contentment, domestic order, and satisfying cooperation and beneficial interdependence between male and female. In most iconographic representations of the pair, they are pictured as a smiling, happy couple who are often touching each other intimately. In some images, Lakṣmī is depicted seated on Viṣṇu's left thigh. Her right hand is around his neck, while his left arm encircles her waist.[46] Sometimes the two are shown holding hands,[47] and it is not unusual for them to be shown gazing into each other's eyes.

The intimacy of the two, indeed, their underlying unity, is dramatically shown in images in which they are merged into one bisexual figure, Viṣṇu constituting the right half of the figure and Lakṣmī, the left.[48] The interdependence of the two is the subject of a long passage in the *Viṣṇu-purāṇa*. There Viṣṇu is said to be speech, while Lakṣmī is meaning; he is understanding, while she is intellect; he is the creator, while she is the creation; she is the earth, he the support of the earth; she is a creeping vine, while he is the tree to which she clings; he is one with all males, and she is one with all females; he is love, and she is pleasure (1.8.15ff).[49]

Śrī-Lakṣmī in the Pāñcarātra and Śrī Vaiṣṇava Schools

Śrī-Lakṣmī's association with Viṣṇu eventually leads to her playing very important roles in the mythological and philosophical visions of the Pāñcarātra and Śrī Vaiṣṇava schools of thought and devotion. In the Pāñcarātra school, Lakṣmī comes to play the central role in the creation and evolution of the universe as the *śakti* of Viṣṇu. In the Pāñcarātra creation scenario Viṣṇu remains almost entirely inactive, relegating the creative process to Lakṣmī. After awakening Lakṣmī at the end of the night of dissolution, Viṣṇu's role in the creation of the universe is restricted to that of an inactive architect whose plan is put into effect by a builder. Lakṣmī alone acts, and the impression throughout the cosmogony is that she acts independently of Viṣṇu, although it is stated that she acts according to his wishes.[50]

The practical effect of Viṣṇu's inactive role in creation is that he becomes so aloof that Lakṣmī dominates the entire Pāñcarātra vision of the divine. In effect, she acquires the position of the supreme divine principle, the underlying reality upon which all rests, that which pervades all creation with vitality, will, and consciousness. The *Lakṣmī-tantra*, a popular Pāñcarātra text, says that Lakṣmī undertakes the entire stupendous creation of the universe with only one-billionth of herself (14.3). So transcendent is she, so beyond the ability of the mind to circumscribe her, that only a miniscule fraction of her is manifest in the creation of the universe. Elsewhere in the same text she describes herself as follows:

> Inherent in the (principle of) existence, whether manifested or unmanifested, I am at all times the inciter (potential element of all things). I manifest myself (as the creation), I ultimately dissolve myself (at the time of destruction) and I occupy myself with activity (when creation starts functioning).
>
> I alone send (the creation) forth and (again) destroy it. I absolve the sins of the good. As the (mother) earth towards all beings, I pardon them (all their sins). I mete everything out. I am the thinking process and I am contained in everything. (50.65.67)[51]

Functionally, Lakṣmī has taken over the cosmic tasks of the three great male gods of the Hindu pantheon: Brahmā, Viṣṇu, and Śiva. In the Pāñcarātra vision, creating, sustaining, and periodically destroying the universe, she completely dominates the divine, mythological landscape. She also occupies the central position as the object of devotion, the dispenser of grace, and the final bestower of liberation (50.131–32). Throughout the *Lakṣmī-tantra*, it is she, not Viṣṇu, who is described as the object of devotion, the one who grants all desires, including salvation. It is she, not Viṣṇu, whose form is described in detail and presented as the supreme object of meditation.[52]

Although Lakṣmī has been elevated functionally to a position of supreme divinity in the Pāñcarātra school and has been identified with various philosophical absolutes, she retains her nature as the goddess who both imbues creatures with illustriousness and well-being and pervades the creation as the sap of existence. At one point in the *Lakṣmī-tantra*, for example, she says of herself: "Like the fat that keeps a lamp burning I lubricate the senses of living beings with my own sap of consciousness" (50.110). Elsewhere she is said to be *prakṛti* (50.64, 96), the principle of nature in Hinduism that spontaneously creates all material reality. *Prakṛti* is the dynamic aspect of the creation that tends toward multiplication, diversification, and specificity.[53] It is an active, fertile principle that is not at all dissimilar from the sap of existence with which Lakṣmī is identified during her early history. Lakṣmī's identification throughout the Pāñcarātra system with Viṣṇu's *śakti* (power) is also a way of declaring her association with fertile power. Although the idea of *śakti* is somewhat more refined and inorganic than *rasa, soma, amṛta*, or the powers of fertility, *śakti* does suggest unambiguously the idea of vigorous, dynamic power that is associated with life and growth. Despite her promotion, therefore, it is clear that Lakṣmī retains her essential character as a dynamic, positive force that underlies growth, fertility, and prosperity.

Lakṣmī holding an oil lamp, Nayak, seventeenth century C.E., Madurai. C. Śivaramamurti, *South Indian Bronzes* (New Delhi: Lalit Akademi, 1963), fig. 96b.

In Śrī Vaiṣṇavism, a central presupposition is that Viṣṇu, the supreme deity for this school, is always accompanied by, attended by, or otherwise associated with his consort Śrī. Unlike the Pāñcarātra school, however, Śrī does not play the central cosmological role in Śrī Vaiṣṇavism. Viṣṇu is clearly the central actor on the mythological stage and is equated with the highest philosophical principles. Śrī-Lakṣmī, nevertheless, has acquired an important role among certain Śrī Vaiṣṇava theologians as the mediator between Viṣṇu and his devotees.[54]

In Śrī Vaiṣṇavism the central aim of the devotee is to cultivate and perfect one's inherent duty, which is to love the Lord, and in so loving the Lord to identify oneself with God as closely as possible. In the writings of some philosophers of the school, Lakṣmī is said to act as a mediating presence between Viṣṇu and the devotee who is requesting purity and grace. For Vedānta Deśika (1268–1368 C.E.), Lakṣmī seems indispensable in approaching Viṣṇu. She is described in his writings as a gracious mother who willingly intervenes with her often-stern husband on the devotee's behalf. "O Mother who resides on the lotus, hearken to my plea! I babble like a child; with your grace (*prasāda*) make the Lord who is your beloved listen to my [petition]."[55] Elsewhere he writes: "The mother . . . , whose nature is such that her grace is unmixed with any anger and is showered on all, does not spare any effort to make the punishing Lord be pleased with those who have committed several faults. She cools the heat of His anger, which arises because He is the father."[56]

Other Śrī Vaiṣṇava theologians share this view of Śrī as an intermediary between the sinful devotee and Viṣṇu. Periyavāccān Pillai (born 1228) describes a conversation between Śrī and Viṣṇu in which Śrī acts as a devotee's advocate. Viṣṇu speaks first: "'Since beginningless time this human has been disobeying my laws and has been the object of my anger. If I condone his faults and accept them patiently, instead of punishing him, I will be disregarding the injunctions of *Śastra*.' Śrī replies: 'But if you punish the human, instead of saving him, your quality of grace will not survive.'"[57] In the above passage, Śrī takes the side of the devotee by arguing that if Viṣṇu does not save the sinner his reputation as graceful will be threatened. Her argument plays upon Viṣṇu's own conception of himself. Elsewhere Śrī is said to resort to distracting Viṣṇu from his intention to punish a devotee by enticing him with her beauty. Maṇavāḷa Māmunikaḷ (1370–1443) says of Śrī: "She uses her beauty to entice and enslave [the Lord]. She makes eyes at Him, she lets her dress slip down a little."[58]

In Śrī Vaiṣṇavism, Śrī embodies divine compassion. While Viṣṇu, as the mighty king of heavenly Vaikuṇṭha, may seem so awesome and transcendent as to be all but unapproachable to the lowly devotee, Śrī provides an aspect of the divine that is eminently approachable. In this role as mediator, she considerably softens the Śrī Vaiṣṇava vision of the divine and allows feelings of intimacy and warmth to pervade the devotee's devotional moods toward the divine.

The Worship of Śrī-Lakṣmī

Śrī-Lakṣmī is today one of the most popular and widely venerated deities of the Hindu pantheon. Her auspicious nature and her reputation for granting fertility, luck, wealth, and well-being seem to attract devotees in every Indian village. "All of India's back country is the dominion of Lakṣmī, the goddess of the lotus. . . . She accompanies every mile traveled through central India, every visit to a temple. . . . Her likenesses are omnipresent on the walls and pillars, lintels and niches of sanctuaries, regardless of the deity of their specific dedication."[59]

She is worshiped throughout the year in a variety of festivals[60] and is the constant object of *vratas*, "religious vows," by means of which devotees ask her for a blessing in return for undertaking some act of devotion or piety on her behalf. The blessings requested from Lakṣmī by devotees vary according to the devotee and according to whether the *vrata* is undertaken during a festival in which certain kinds of blessings are traditional. The most common boons, however, have to do with marital fidelity, the longevity of one's spouse, the fertility of the crops, and the bestowal of material well-being.

The most important festival in which Lakṣmī is worshiped today (except in Bengal) is Dīpavalī (Dīvalī), which is held in the late autumn. Three important and interrelated themes are seen in this festival: (1) Lakṣmī's association with wealth and prosperity, (2) her association with fertility and abundant crops, and (3) her association with good fortune in the coming year. Perhaps the most obvious indication that Lakṣmī is identified with prosperity is her popularity among merchants. During this festival, it is customary for people, especially businessmen, to worship their account books.[61] It seems to be clearly understood by merchants that wealth will not arise without Lakṣmī's blessing or presence.

Agricultural motifs are also fairly clear in this festival as it is celebrated in some places. Cultivators are enjoined to worship their crops (which, at this time of year, have been harvested) and offer sacrifices of goats and sheep. "Moreover they visit the dunghill which is collected for manuring the field for future crops and fall prostrate and beg to fertilize their lands and to procure abundant crops. In the Decan and Orissa the heap of cowdung is also worshiped by every householder on this day."[62]

Lakṣmī is also associated with crops and food in Orissa on the occasion of the Kaumundī-pūrṇimā festival. On these days, women invoke Lakṣmī on a mound of new grain and recall a story in which Lakṣmī's disappearance results in the disappearance of crops and food and her return brings the return of abundance.[63] The worship of Lakṣmī during Durgā Pūjā is also significant in terms of her association with agriculture. Although Durgā Pūjā as it is celebrated today in India is not primarily a harvest festival, many indications exist that the renewed vigor of the crops is still an aspect of the festival.[64]

Lakṣmī's association with good fortune in the coming year during the Dīpavalī festival is also significant. During this festival, end-of-the-year motifs are clear. It is a time when ghosts of the dead are said to return,[65] when Bali, a demon, is said to emerge from the underworld to rule for three days, when goblins and malicious spirits are about,[66] and when gambling, profligate spending, and boisterous activity are commanded. Throughout the festival, Lakṣmī is invoked to ward off the dangerous effects of the returned dead and the emergent demon king and his hosts and to bless the gambler with success that will betoken his good luck during the entire coming year. The banishment of Alakṣmī, the female spirit associated with bad luck and misfortune, is also associated with this festival. Lighting lamps, which is one of the most beautiful and characteristic features of this festival, and making noise with pots and pans or instruments are believed in many places to drive Alakṣmī away for the coming year.[67] On another occasion in Bengal, an image of Alakṣmī is made and then ceremoniously disfigured by cutting off its nose and ears, after which an image of Lakṣmī is installed to signify the presence of good luck in the future.[68]

Another aspect of Lakṣmī is the focus of a summer festival in honor of her and Viṣṇu. This festival signals the point at which Viṣṇu is believed to fall asleep for several months. It is common to pray to Viṣṇu at this time to prevent losing one's wife or husband. In this festival, Lakṣmī and Viṣṇu are the embodiment of marital harmony and bliss. Lakṣmī is understood to be the faithful, loving, and obedient wife.[69] At another festival in honor of her and Viṣṇu, Lakṣmī plays the role of a jealous wife and protector of the home. Viṣṇu is said to go off with another consort during this festival, and Lakṣmī, in anger over his unfaithfulness, breaks his vehicle and temporarily locks him out of their home (the temple).[70]

Chapter **4**

Amaterasu, the Japanese Ancestral Goddess

Immaculate as the sacred tree,
        Her spirit pure and clear,
She lights the far corners
        Of Heaven and earth—
The Great Kami of the Sun

This Way is the way
        Of the Great Sun Kami,
Whose radiance from above
        Lightens the very bounds
Of Heaven and earth.[1]

Introduction

In traditional Japanese culture, the world was perceived to be pervaded by powerful forces, many of which were associated with natural powers or specific natural objects. These beings were called *kami*, which means "a highly placed being" who is worthy of veneration.[2] The *kami* are often described as having human characteristics and are almost always said to be extremely powerful, although not necessarily omniscient or omnipotent.

One of the most important, popular, and revered of the Japanese deities is the goddess Amaterasu, who is preeminently associated with the sun. Amaterasu plays a central role in ordering and civilizing the earth and is intimately associated in Japanese mythology and history with the Japanese royal family. She has strong associations with nature (the sun), culture (the institution of agriculture and the silk industry), and society (she is associated with the ruling elite). Although her importance has diminished somewhat in recent history, particularly as the Japanese royal family, with whom she was intimately related, has declined from political power, she remains a well-known and widely revered deity.

The Creation of the World and the Birth of Amaterasu

Prior to the creation of the world, there existed in heaven several deities whose forms were not visible. Eventually, the divine couple Izanagi, He Who Invites, and Izanami, She Who Invites, came into being. These two deities were commanded by the other deities to create or to solidify the earth and prepare it for human habitation.[3] Taking a jeweled spear, the couple stirred the watery chaos, and when they pulled the spear from the water the brine that dripped from the spear congealed into an island. The divine pair descended to this island and built a dwelling in which to live. Having discovered sex, they then created the eight principal islands of Japan.[4] They also created several deities associated with certain natural phenomena: the god of the sea, the god of the winds, the god of the trees, and others. According to the *Kojiki*, they also created the god of fire; however, he severely burned Izanami when she gave birth to him. Badly injured, she retreated to the underworld, the land of the dead. Izanagi wished to visit her and followed her into the underworld. Izanami could not return to the land of the living, however, and had already begun to decay. She was insulted when Izanagi saw her and chased him from the land of the dead. Having escaped the nether world, Izanagi then purified himself by bathing in a stream. In this process, he gave birth to several important deities: from his nose was born Susanoo, a god who would become associated with the sea and the underworld; the god of the moon, Tsukiyomi; and the goddess of the sun, Amaterasu. Izanagi commanded Amaterasu to rule the upper world of heaven, the moon deity to rule the night, and Susanoo to rule the ocean.[5]

The account of Amaterasu's birth is quite different in the *Nihongi*, the other basic text of traditional Japanese mythology.[6] According to this text, after Izanagi and Izanami had created the island of Japan and various deities to pervade the land, they consulted each other and said: "Why should we not produce someone who shall be lord of the universe?"[7] A most glorious female child was then born whose brilliance filled the world. She was given the name Amaterasu-no-oho-kami, Heavenly Shining Great Deity. The moon god and Susanoo were born subsequently. In the *Nihongi*'s account, Susanoo is described as a wicked, cruel deity who is banished to the underworld lest he bring misery upon the world and humankind.[8]

The death of Izanami and the birth of the three siblings, Amaterasu, Tsukiyomi, and Susanoo, mark the transition between two distinct phases in the Japanese creation saga. The stories of Izanagi and Izanami deal with a phase of creation that is concerned with the origin of the Japanese islands and the institution of certain natural laws that indelibly mark human existence. After creating the physical world, upon which human life will proceed, Izanagi and Izanami perform certain actions that are prototypical of all human existence. Most important, they discover and take part in sex, and Izanami dies; thus come into the world the two irreducible facts of human existence: sex and death. With Izanagi and Izanami, then, we have the creation of what we might call the natural parameters of human existence: a physical world, procreation, and death. The further refinement of the world, the advent of culture, is primarily the task of the next generation of gods, and in this task Amaterasu is the principal figure.

The Assault on Heaven and the Eclipse of Amaterasu

Before departing to the land of the dead, where Izanagi had decided to send him, Susanoo wished to ascend to heaven and bid goodbye to his sister, Amaterasu. On his way to heaven he caused a great commotion: the mountains and rivers trembled; the earth itself shook. Amaterasu heard the sounds and sensed trouble. She bound up her hair, rolled her skirts into trousers, put on protective armor, and armed herself with a bow and arrows. She assumed a fierce demeanor and greeted Susanoo with a threatening appearance: "Shaking the upper tip of her bow, stamping her legs up to her very thighs into the hard earth, and kicking (the earth) about as if it were light snow, she shouted with an awesome fury, she shouted stamping her feet. Thus waiting for him, she asked him: 'Why have you come?'"[9]

Susanoo claimed that he had no evil intention and suggested that they collaborate in producing children as a sign of peaceful cooperation. Amaterasu agreed and took her brother's sword, broke it into three pieces, chewed them, and spat forth a mist from which three goddesses were born. Susanoo then took Amaterasu's jewels, chewed them in his mouth, and spat forth a mist from which were created five male children. The first of these, Amaterasu's eldest male child, was the deity through whom her lineage was passed to the imperial family in a later chapter of the myth.[10] The other deities produced in this incident became the ancestors of other great noble families of Japan.

After the creation of these children, however, Susanoo lost his self-control and began to create havoc in heaven. He broke down the ridges separating the rice fields and covered up the ditches that surrounded the fields, thus returning the land to formless sterility. Then he threw excrement into the temple of heaven, in which the first-fruits ceremonies were conducted (or in which Ama-

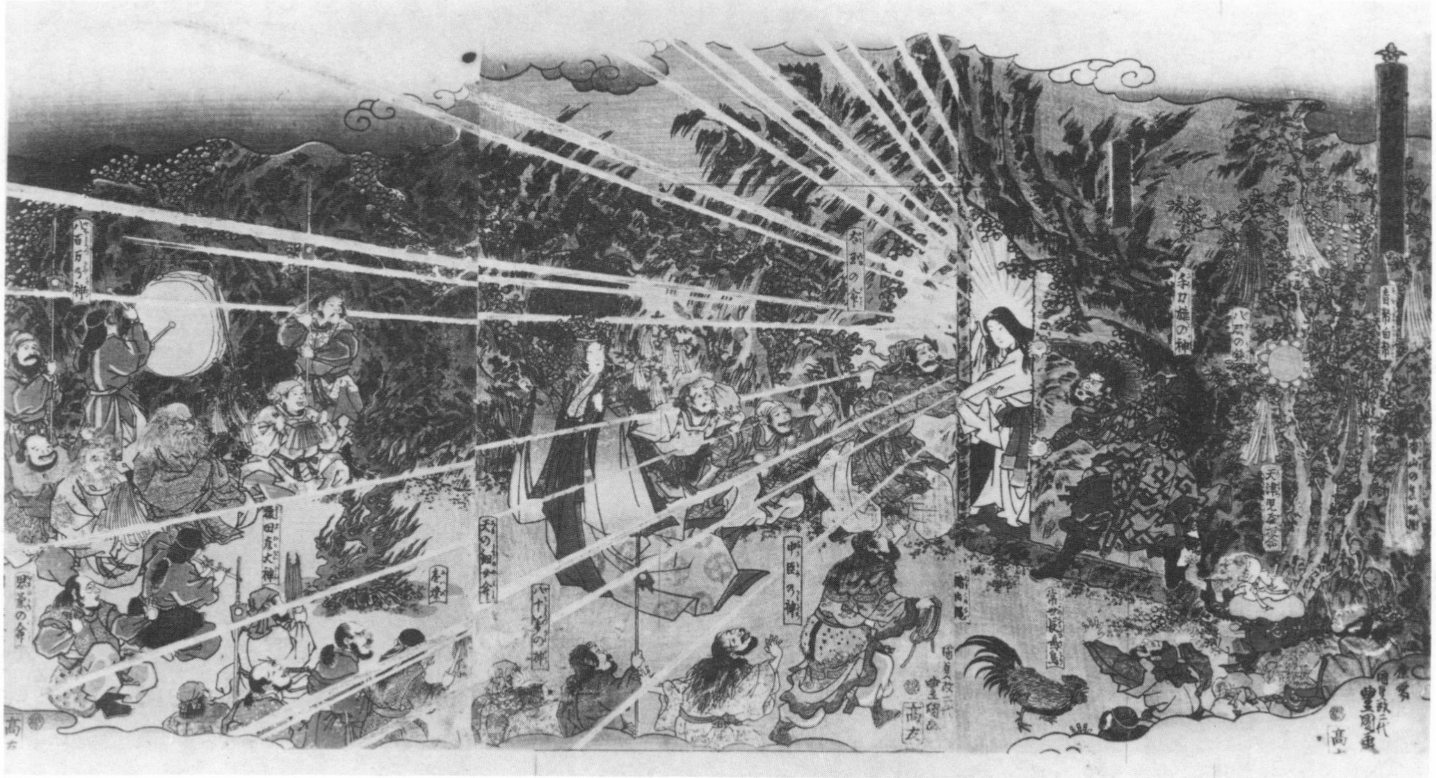

Amaterasu, painting by Utagawa Kunisada (1786–1864). Robert Graves, ed., *New Larousse Encyclopedia of Mythology* (London: Paul Hamlyn, 1968), p. 405.

terasu sampled the first fruits). Amaterasu at first tried to excuse her brother's destructive behavior. But then Susanoo broke open a house in which women were weaving garments and threw a flayed horse among them. One woman was so shocked at this that she struck herself in the genitals and killed herself.[11] Amaterasu was outraged at these actions of her brother and hid herself in a cave. She blocked the entrance with a great stone, and all light went out of the world.

In this episode, Amaterasu clearly represents civilization and order. Amaterasu's domain, the plain of heaven, is characterized by peace, harmony, and culture (represented by rice agriculture and weaving). Susanoo, associated with the underworld and the sea, is in many ways untamable. He storms heaven and violates Amaterasu and her orderly domain. His impetuous actions destroy cultured order and cause Amaterasu to withdraw from her kingdom. Susanoo, the wild spirit of the sea, the aggressive male deity, literally eclipses Amaterasu with his uncivilized actions and demeanor.

While it is not explicit in the myths, there is a suggestion, furthermore, of sexual violence in this episode. Amaterasu's breaking of Susanoo's sword and his crushing of her jewels result in the birth of children and hint at sexual union between the two. Sexual violence is clearer in the episode in which Susanoo destroys the house of the weavers and the women wound themselves by hitting their genitals with the shuttles. In the *Nihongi*, Amaterasu herself is said to do this.[12] Her outrage and disappearance from the world are due at least in part to having been sexually assaulted by her brother.

With Susanoo still unrestrained and Amaterasu hidden in a cave, the world of heaven had been reduced to dark chaos. The gods, in order to lure Amaterasu out of her cave and restore order, set to work devising ways to bring the goddess back into the world. They collected cocks and set them crowing. They made a large mirror and collected strings of jewels and hung these outside the cave in which Amaterasu was hidden. They decorated trees with cloth streamers and uttered ritual formulas (all of which are ordinarily done in the worship of Amaterasu). Finally, the goddess Ama no Uzume was invited to dance in the hope of attracting Amaterasu's attention. She stood on the top of an upturned tub and began to dance. She had adorned herself with different plants and held some bamboo shoots. Soon she became ecstatic and stripped off her clothes. She danced in a lewd fashion and caused the assembled gods to laugh loudly. Amaterasu heard the laughter and fuss and became curious to find out what was happening. She slid the boulder back a bit and peeked outside. She immediately was struck by her dazzling image reflected in the mirror and moved further out of the cave. One of the gods then forced her all the way out and closed off the entrance so that she could never return to it. Once more the world was lit by the rays of the sun. Susanoo was forced to pay a heavy fine and was banished from heaven.[13]

Amaterasu emerging from the cave. Richard Cavendish, ed., *Mythology, an Illustrated Encyclopedia* (New York: Rizzoli International Publications, 1980), pp. 78–79.

Amaterasu's retreat to a cave probably is concerned with solar eclipses—their causes and the ways in which their harmful effects might be offset. Violence such as Susanoo's, which threatens civilized order (wanton destruction of rice fields, sexual violence, perhaps even incest), can result in cosmic catastrophe because it threatens the established order of things. Culture and nature are understood to be intimately related. If the cultural order is upset, so is the natural order. The return of the sun, the offsetting of natural disaster, which is represented by solar eclipses, is brought about through actions and rituals that attract, amuse, or arouse the curiosity of the sun (Amaterasu).[14] The sound of cocks crowing (which always precedes dawn), mirrors and jewels that reflect light, and erotic dancing all help in this respect.

The timing of Amaterasu's retreat into a cave, which coincides with the end of the first-fruits ceremonies,[15] may also suggest that her retreat represents the sun's waning during the winter months. If this is so, the erotic dance of Ama no Uzume probably is associated with a spring festival concerned with the planting of crops and the waxing strength of the sun. In many cultures, human sexual vigor as expressed in obscene dances and practices and promiscuous sexual conduct is held to have a beneficial effect on the growth of crops.[16] That the waxing sun also has a dramatic effect on the growth of vegetation is obvious. It may well have been the case in traditional Japan that sexual license or obscene behavior was understood to promote not only vegetation but also the power of the sun, whose waxing strength coincided with the rebirth of vegetation.[17]

Amaterasu and the Origins of Culture

Amaterasu's association with culture is fairly clear in the previous episode. She is associated with agriculture and silk weaving, in particular, and with an orderly society, in general. A myth concerning the origin of food links Amaterasu specifically with the origins of agriculture, silk weaving, and possibly animal husbandry. In the myth, Amaterasu sent a messenger to earth to investigate the goddess Uke-mochi no Kami. When the messenger arrived in the presence of the goddess, she turned her head toward the land, and boiled rice came forth from her mouth; when she faced the sea, fish came from her mouth. The heavenly messenger was revolted by what he saw and killed the goddess. When he returned to heaven Amaterasu was furious and banished him. A second messenger was sent; when he arrived on earth he found that although the goddess was indeed dead various foods and animals had been produced from her corpse. "On the crown of her head there had been produced the ox and the horse; on the top of her forehead there had been produced millet; over her eyebrows there had been produced the silkworm; . . . in her belly there had been produced rice; in her genitals there had been produced wheat, large beans and small beans."[18] The messenger brought these things to Amaterasu in heaven. She used the millet, wheat, and beans for seeds when planting in dry fields and the rice for planting in wet fields. "She . . . forthwith sowed for the first time the rice seed in the narrow fields and in the long fields of Heaven. That autumn, drooping ears bent down, eight span long, and were exceedingly pleasant to look upon. Moreover she took the silkworms in her mouth, and succeeded in reeling thread from them. From this began the art of silkworm rearing."[19] Later in the myth, when Amaterasu sent her grandson to earth to rule over it, she sent along with him the seed rice that had been grown in her heavenly paddy fields.[20] As she sent him on his way, she said: "I . . . give over to my child the rice-ears of the sacred garden, of which I partake in the Plain of High Heaven."[21]

Amaterasu's role as a culture hero is stressed in early twentieth-century Japanese school books, which sought to inculcate nationalistic loyalty through reverence to the goddess. She is described as a great benefactress to the nation. "The Great Deity (Amaterasu-Ōmikami) . . . poured forth her benevolent will upon the people. She alloted the divisions of water and land, she taught the cultivation of the five cereals, such as rice, millet, and panic-grass, and also imparted the knowledge of sericulture and textile manufacturing. There is not one of our myriads of people who has not been bathed in her benevolence."[22]

The Institution of the Imperial Line

A central concern of the *Kojiki* and *Nihongi* is the legitimation of the Japanese imperial line. Indeed, both collections were compiled at the order of and in the context of the imperial court.[23] In both texts, the central myth of the imperial line concerns Amaterasu's institution of the royal house by sending her grandson, Ninigi, the August Grandchild, to earth to rule the Japanese islands. Ninigi marries a woman from the earth and subsequently has two sons, who, in turn, marry and have children. One of these children marries and gives birth to Jimmu, the first Japanese emperor.[24]

In her relationship to the imperial line, Amaterasu plays two interrelated roles. First, she is the founding heavenly ancestor of the royal house. She inaugurates imperial rule on earth by sending down from heaven her grandson, Ninigi. Her words of commission to him stress the importance of lineage vis-à-vis the imperial family's right to rule. "This Reed-plain-1500-autumns-fair-rice-ear Land is the region which my descendants shall be lords of. Do thou, my August Grandchild, proceed thither and govern it. Go! and may prosperity attend thy dynasty, and may it, like Heaven and Earth, endure forever!"[25] The importance of being able to trace the royal line directly back to Amaterasu is stressed in the *Jinnō Shōtōki* of Chikafusa (1293–1354). In the opening passage of this text we read: "Great Japan is the divine land. The heavenly progenitor founded it, and the sun goddess bequeathed it to her descendents to rule eternally. Only in our country is this true; there are no similar examples in other countries. This is why our country is called the divine land."[26] Elsewhere in the text, Chikafusa comments upon Amaterasu's commissioning words to her grandson and her bestowal of the three regalia: "We can clearly see in these decrees that the divine spirit of our country lies in the legitimate passage of the emperorship to the descendents of a single family. Transmission of the regalia through the generations is as fixed as the sun, moon, and stars in heaven."[27]

Amaterasu's role vis-à-vis the imperial line goes beyond that of ancestral progenitor, however. Amaterasu also is an ever-present model for the emperors, and in some cases it is even suggested that she dwells within the emperor. The emperor, then, is not merely Amaterasu's descendent. He is also her appointee, her representative, and in some cases even the goddess herself. When Amaterasu commands Ninigi to descend to rule the earth it is clear that she also intends him to rule as her regent and according to the ways in which she rules the heavenly world. As her regent Ninigi is given the three divine regalia by Amaterasu: the mirror, the jewels, and the sword. When she gives him the mirror she tells him that he should revere it as if it were she herself.[28] In possession of the sacred mirror, the emperor acts on behalf of the goddess. In this sense, Amaterasu is not a distant ancestor whose actions belong only to the past. She is an ever-present force, a living ancestor, as it were.

According to Chikafusa, the living presence of Amaterasu is especially evident in emperors when they perform particularly significant benevolent, educational, or cultural actions. Commenting on the emperors Ōjin and Shōtoku, for example, he states: "Both Ōjin and Shōtoku were avatars of the divine *kami* spirits and seem to have intended, in accordance with the wishes of Amaterasu, to spread and make people fully aware of the way of our country."[29] For Chikafusa, the emperor fulfills "Amaterasu's mandate"[30] not only in the very act of occupying the throne as her descendent but in the way he rules. Japanese society and culture are understood as having been modeled after divine paradigms. The emperor's role in maintaining that order is understood by Chikafusa as the carrying out of the goddess's mandate. "In our country . . . the mandate of Amaterasu is manifest and the positions of those high and low are fixed."[31]

The identity of the emperor and Amaterasu is put most explicitly by Hozumi Yatsuka (1860–1912) in his popular work *The People's Education: Patriotism.*

The ancestor of my ancestors is the Sun Goddess. The Sun Goddess is the founder of our race, and the throne is the sacred house of our race. If father and mother are to be revered, how much more so the ancestors of the house; and if the ancestors of the house are to be revered, how much more the founder of the country! The position of the head of the house is that of the authority of the ancestors; the throne is the place of the Sun Goddess. Father and mother are ancestors living in the present; *the emperor is the Sun Goddess living in the present.* For the same reason one is filial to his parents and loyal to the throne.[32]

The special relationship between the Japanese emperors and Amaterasu, according to which the two are often identified, is discussed by Motoori Norinaga (1730–1801) in terms of the emotional and intellectual harmony between the two.

To the end of time each Mikado is the goddess' son. His mind is in perfect harmony of thoughtful feeling with hers. He does not seek out new inventions, but rules in accordance with precedents which date from the age of the gods, and if he is ever in doubt, he has resort to divination, which reveals to him the mind of the great goddess. In this way the age of the gods and the present age are not two ages, but one, for not only the Mikado, but his Ministers and people also, act up to the tradition of the divine age.[33]

The Imperial Regalia

The role and meaning of the imperial regalia are important to the relationship between Amaterasu and the imperial line. The three regalia are the mirror, the jewels, and the sword. The mirror was fashioned by the gods to lure Amaterasu out of the cave in which she hid after Susanoo had created havoc in heaven. The jewels also were hung in a tree in front of the cave in the hope that they might attract the goddess.[34] The sword, on the other hand, was originally found by Susanoo when he slew a dragon and discovered the sword in the dragon's tail. Awed by the weapon, Susanoo gave it to his sister, Amaterasu.[35]

In the mythological texts, then, it is clear that the three regalia belong to Amaterasu or are closely associated with her. So, when she sends her grandson to rule the earth and gives him the three items, it is clear that she is bestowing upon him certain insignia that will associate him with her. Just how strong the association is between the regalia and Amaterasu herself is made clear in the *Nihongi*, where Amaterasu says as she gives Ninigi her mirror: "My child, when thou lookest upon this mirror, let it be as if thou wert looking on me. Let it be with thee on thy couch and in thy hall, and let it be to thee a holy mirror."[36] The emperor's possession of the regalia, especially the mirror, represents his legitimate right to rule and marks him as Amaterasu's representative.

The meaning of the regalia, together and separately, has been the subject of both traditional and scholarly speculation. Chikafusa, in addition to seeing the regalia as the material evidence of the emperor's divine descent, also understood the regalia symbolically, as suggestive of the type of rule Amaterasu intended when she commissioned Ninigi to govern the earth. Chikafusa has Amaterasu say as she gives her grandson the regalia: "As the mirror is bright, illuminate the world; as the jewels spread broadly, rule with their wonderful sway; and, with the sword, subdue all those who do not submit to your rule."[37] Chikafusa elaborates by saying that the mirror, which reflects everything faithfully, which "possesses nothing of its own, but with an unselfish spirit illuminates all things,"[38] is the embodiment of honesty. He says that the jewels are characterized by "gentleness and yielding and are the source of compassion."[39] The sword is characterized by strength and resolution and is the source of wisdom.[40] Furthermore, Chikafusa continues: "Unless a ruler possesses the virtues of all three of the regalia, he will find it difficult to govern the country. Amaterasu's mandate is clear: . . . the spirit of the mandate is embodied in the imperial regalia."[41]

While all three regalia are important both as insignia of imperial rule and as suggestive of what type of rule that should be, the mirror, according to Chikafusa, is the most important of the three items. The mirror is identified with Amaterasu herself, he says, and is the most sacred image of her at her central shrine at Ise. The mirror, which is enshrined there, is her *shōtai*, her god-body. More than either the jewels or the sword, the mirror suggests Amaterasu's nature, which is bright and clear. "Since the mirror is a true reflection of Amaterasu herself, she must have invested it with her most profound feelings. . . . Because Amaterasu is the divine spirit of the great sun, she governs the world with a brilliant virtue."[42] The qualities of the mirror—brightness, clarity, and honesty—furthermore, bring about or permit the qualities possessed by the other two regalia. "If one's nature is bright, then one will also possess compassion [the virtue of the jewels] and resolution [the virtue of the sword]."[43]

A different, but in some ways related, interpretation of the meaning of the royal regalia is inspired by the work of Georges Dumézil, who has characterized Indo-European culture as expressing itself in three interrelated functions: the priestly, the warrior, and the agricultural. According to this schema, the mirror represents the priestly dimension or function of the emperor's rule and Amaterasu's mandate. The emphasis here is upon the pure and sacred nature of Amaterasu (and the emperor) and on the emperor's role as high priest in the service of Amaterasu (the emperor actually does have priestly roles to play in the goddess's worship). The sword, quite obviously, symbolizes the second aspect or function and emphasizes the importance of the emperor's role as defender of the nation and Amaterasu's role as a national guardian. The jewels represent the third function, which is related to agriculture, prosperity, and abundance. While the fertility associations of the jewels might not be readily apparent, it is well to remember that the first generation of Amaterasu's children were born from her jewels when Susanoo chewed them and spit forth five male children, one of whom was the grandfather of Ninigi.[44] The fertility or agricultural aspects of Amaterasu (and, by implication, of the emperor) are clear in the annual cycle of festivals celebrated at Ise, during which the promotion of abundant crops is an important concern.

In short, both Chikafusa and modern scholars are inclined to see in the imperial regalia suggestions concerning the different facets of Amaterasu herself and of the type of rule she has mandated to her descendants, the emperors of Japan. Amaterasu is seen to be a goddess who is particularly pure and bright, that is, particularly sacred and holy; she is the deity who, on occasion, displays a fierce, protective role as guardian of heaven against Susanoo or against invaders of Japan; and a goddess whose presence brings about growth, fertility, and abundance. Similarly, the emperor is understood to combine in his reign the qualities of purity and honesty, bravery and resolution, and generosity and benevolence.

Amaterasu and the Japanese Nation: Nationalism and Universality

Amaterasu's relationship to the imperial line originally may have been similar to the role of other *kami* vis-à-vis other Japanese clans. That is, Amaterasu originally may have been primarily the tutelary deity (*uji-gami*) of the Yamato clan. Her rise to prominence may have followed the royal clan's rise to political power.[45] *Uji-gami* were understood primarily as clan ancestors and guardians of their descendants' territories. So, perhaps when the imperial house gained preeminence, the clan territory was extended to include the entire nation and Amaterasu became the national deity. Whether Amaterasu's origins lie in her role as an *uji-gami*, she did play for centuries (and still plays today, to some extent) the role of the national deity of Japan. She was seen as the ancestor not only of the imperial line but of all Japanese people. This is clearly stated in the teachers' manual that accompanied school history texts in Japan around 1920. "Amaterasu Ōmikami is not only the ancestor of the Imperial House, but also of all Japanese. If we . . . seek our ancestry and parentage the greater part of us will prove to be descendants of the Imperial House. [Those who are not are descendants of later immigrants, but since they intermarried] there is no reason now why our common ancestor should not be Amaterasu Ōmikami."[46]

Just as Amaterasu came to be regarded as the ancestor of all Japanese, so her inspiring influence was not restricted to the emperors and their families and governing retinues. During the Kamakura period (1192–1336) the idea that uprightness, proper behavior, and a pure life generally were in harmony with the mandate of Amaterasu was clearly articulated. The *kami* in general were said to be attracted by proper behavior and repelled by improper actions and thoughts. During this time, there emerged a series of revelations from important Shinto shrines concerning the importance of leading a pure life. The revelation that was said to have come from Amaterasu at Ise says: "Although intrigue produces immediate gain, it will certainly bring punishment of the Kami. Although correctness and uprightness do not bring temporary advantage, they will eventually have the sympathy of the sun and the moon."[47] Chikafusa also identified the sun goddess with uprightness generally. While he understood her mandate to express itself most intensely in the emperors, he did tend to speak of basic virtue in all Japanese as an expression of her presence.[48] The philosopher Ishida Baigan (1685–1744), who wrote extensively on Shinto, understood "the good person as united with the heart of Amaterasu."[49]

It is clear, then, that Amaterasu transcends the limitations of a clan deity. She may be associated with the imperial line and house, but she also came to be understood as a universal deity, the ancestor of all Japanese, and an inspiring presence in the lives of those who followed her mandate, which meant leading an upright life and having pure thoughts. Amaterasu's universal nature is strongly expressed in the writings of Motoori Norinaga (1730–1801), a leader of the eighteenth-century Shinto revival, and Kurozumi Munetada (1780–1850), the founder of a Shinto faith-healing movement (named Kurozumi Kyo after him).

In asserting Amaterasu's universality, Motoori disagreed with those who said that Amaterasu was merely a human being who lived in the distant past and was the ancient ancestor of the nation. He emphasized her identification with the sun, which shines on all countries throughout the world and nourishes and makes possible all life. Although it is only in Japan that the sun goddess's traditions and mandates have been fully revealed and preserved, she reigns everywhere.

The High Heavenly Plain is the high heavenly plain which covers all the countries of the world, and the Sun Goddess is the goddess who reigns in that heaven. Thus, she is without a peer in the whole universe, casting her light to the very ends of heaven and earth for all time. There is not a single country in the world which does not receive her beneficent illuminations, and no country can exist even for a day or an hour bereft of her grace. This goddess is the splendour of all splendours.[50]

When Kurozumi Munetada was thirty-four, on December 22, 1814, as he prayed to the rising sun, "he suddenly felt a oneness with Amaterasu,"[51] who commissioned him to share his faith and healing powers with others.[52] For Munetada, Amaterasu was the universal parent, "the source of all things, the sustaining providence which upholds and guides all phenomena, the impartial benevolence which fills heaven and earth."[53] "All events are the expression of her activity, all things of life are nourished in her light and health. Through the benevolence and power of this great deity the individual may participate in the vitality of the Absolute God and gain thereby security and the enjoyment of the blessings of truth, beauty and freedom from sickness. . . . The Great Parent is manifested in the external world as the activities and principles of nature and in human society as the moral law."[54]

Returning to Amaterasu's identification with the Japanese nation specifically, there is some indication that the very name of Japan in the past, Dai Nihon, which literally means "great sun source," may have derived from the belief that Amaterasu was the ancestral founder and protector of the nation.[55] Her identification with the nation is also made clear in the fact that the national flag displays her symbol, the sun circle, or the rising sun.[56] Specific locales and shrines are sometimes associated with Amaterasu's legendary activities. It is said, for example, that she took a midday meal at Sugizaka, and when she had finished she stuck her chopsticks in the ground. They then grew into large cryptomeria trees that may still be seen there today.[57] In this way, Amaterasu sacralizes the land in a very concrete and specific way. The nation is understood as the special place in which she has made herself known, in which she has acted. The national geography reveals her presence.

In a similar vein, we discover that during Japan's colonizing efforts in the late nineteenth and twentieth centuries, shrines to Amaterasu were erected in newly claimed territory. In 1925, an Amaterasu shrine was built in Korea, followed by other shrines in 1936 and 1937. An Amaterasu shrine was built in Port Arthur in 1938 and another in the imperial palace at Changchun in 1940.[58] Amaterasu's presence, indicated by her shrines, brought these territories within the hegemony of Japan. Her shrines indicated that her mandate had been extended to these territories, and her mandate was inextricably associated with Japanese culture and political policy.

Amaterasu also, quite naturally, came to be associated with the protection of Japan. She assumed the role of guardian and protector. Her role as a warrior can be traced back to her assuming a fierce attitude and arming herself in response to Susanoo's visit to heaven in the *Kojiki* and *Nihongi*. Chikafusa, commenting on the destruction of the invading Mongol fleet by the Japanese in 1281 (only twelve years before his birth), saw in this event the presence of Amaterasu:

> In 1281 the Mongol army assembled many ships and attacked our country. There was fierce fighting in Kyushu, but the gods, revealing their awesome authority and manifesting their form, drove the invaders away. Thus a great wind suddenly arose and the several hundreds of thousands of enemy ships were all blown over and demolished. Although people speak of this as a degenerate age, the righteous power displayed by the gods at this time was truly beyond human comprehension. We can see in these events how unalterable is Amaterasu's mandate that the imperial line shall rule our country eternally.[59]

Amaterasu and the Ise Shrine

The most famous Amaterasu shrine is the Grand Shrine at Ise, where the sacred mirror itself is housed. The Ise shrine is about thirteen hundred years old[60] and dates back to a time when the sacred mirror was moved from the imperial palace to Ise, where it has remained to the present.[61] According to Japanese legend, the shrine was established when Emperor Sunin's daughter, Yamato-hime, an imperial princess and priestess, made a pilgrimage and was instructed by the goddess to found a shrine for her at Ise.[62] It seems that women of the royal house who possessed shamanistic abilities were entrusted with the worship of and communication with Amaterasu during the early history of her cult and that a royal princess/priestess played an important ritual role at Ise before the establishment of large priestly families there whose male members eventually came to dominate shrine worship.[63]

The Ise shrine initially was primarily a royal chapel, but over the centuries it became the most sacred national center and today attracts more than five million visitors per year.[64] In the teachers' manual for school children that was in use during the 1930s, we read: "Inasmuch as Amaterasu-Ōmikami is the Ancestress of the Emperor, she is the most venerated deity in our land of Japan. And since the Grand Imperial Shrine is the sanctuary where this Great Deity is worshipped, those who are Japanese, in addition to being obedient to the Emperor, must always revere and honour this shrine. You children should also await a suitable opportunity for making pilgrimage to the Grand Imperial

Ise shrine, the main sanctuary from the northwest. Kenzo Tange, Noboru Kawazoe, and Yoshio Watanabe (photographs), *Ise, Prototype of Japanese Architecture* (Cambridge, Mass.: MIT Press, 1965), p. 119.

Shrine."[65] Pilgrims come to Ise to report to the goddess important events in their lives and the lives of their families, to ask favors, and to give thanks for blessings they have received.[66] "One . . . striking instance is that of Admiral Togo who, after his victory over the Russians, took his whole fleet to the Bay of Ise to pay homage."[67]

Traditionally, the emperor worships Amaterasu at the shrine, either through a representative or in person,[68] and performs certain rituals that express the close relationship between the emperor and the goddess. Twice a year, at the end of June and December, the emperor and his household come to Ise to perform the *ōbarae* ceremony, a ceremony of national purification. A priest recites a series of transgressions that are offensive to the goddess and then symbolically destroys the offenses by tearing up hempen strips. In this way, the faults of the entire nation are exposed to Amaterasu and then ritually destroyed.[69] The *ōbarae* ceremonies emphasize Amaterasu's association with purity and recall her role as protector of divine order and culture in heaven against the transgressions of Susanoo (several of the transgressions mentioned in the *ōbarae* ceremony were committed by Susanoo).

Another series of ceremonies concerns the agricultural cycle and is intended to ensure good crops. In the autumn, a first-fruits ceremony is held, and this is said to be patterned on the ceremony that Amaterasu herself performed in heaven.[70] In the ceremony food is offered to Amaterasu and other *kami*, and prayers are offered to give thanks for the harvest.[71] In these rituals Amaterasu's association with the inauguration of agriculture is emphasized. Her association with the fertility and growth of crops also may be implied. She is, after all, clearly associated with the sun, which has a dramatic effect on the growth of crops.

Another type of ceremony involves informing Amaterasu of important national events or important matters in the life of the royal family and clearly emphasizes her role as national ancestor and national guardian.

> Because of her importance and preferred position the Sun Goddess is formally consulted on all important occasions of imperial and national life. Visits to Ise are still regularly undertaken by members of the imperial family. . . . They coincide with important events in the life of the imperial family and have been part of its annual schedule since the beginning of the Meiji era in the nineteenth century. . . . In modern times, the prime minister and the cabinet usually visit Ise at New Year and after the inauguration of a new government or even after a reshuffling of the cabinet.[72]

Amaterasu, then, is viewed as a concerned ancestor or parent to whom one must report all important business pertaining to the family (which, in this case, is the entire nation) or from whom one must ask advice.

Popular Worship of Amaterasu

Amaterasu's close connection with the imperial family and the ruling elite until very recent times is clear. Amaterasu's worship, however, is not limited to these associations. She is also a very popular deity among the Japanese people and occupies "the place of honour on practically every family shrine."[73]

> The number of shrines, big and small, consecrated to her, is enormous. In a small region of the Shikoku, about fifteen miles by ten, south of Tsurugisan and west of the Monono-

be River alone, one finds about a hundred temples . . . , in all of which she is enshrined. In the single locality of Fukuno-machi, with about 15,000 inhabitants, in Toyama-ken, she is the Kami of thirteen [shrines] . . . , all erected before the eighteenth century.[74]

Worship of Amaterasu is not restricted to shrines. She is commonly revered by showing reverence to the sun itself.

Many Japanese are still sun-worshippers. Particularly old folks, both in cities and in rural areas, are seen worshipping the sun every morning. Rising early, they step outside, and facing the eastern sky, they clap their hands and bow towards the sun. To these people, the sun rules their lives. The sun gives them food, and so they must be thankful for it. When children waste food, mothers tell them that they will anger the sun and be punished.[75]

A young Japanese student gives this description of his grandmother's ritual actions at dawn:

The sun rises early, but cannot be seen for some time because of the walls of high buildings that surround the house. Yet an old woman rises with the sun. Climbing slowly out of her heavy bedding, she walks across the *tatami* floor to the window. Opening it, she faces the east and twice claps her hands loudly: "Please protect everyone today, too."

The small cup of water and offering of rice are replaced with new ones on the white wood *kamidana* [god shelf] in the shape of a shrine, in the heart of which is a small mirror.

Again she claps twice. Having thus satisfied her *kami*, she goes outside to sprinkle the front porch with water. . . .

This is a typical morning for my eighty-year-old grandmother.[76]

The custom of *hi-machi*, "waiting for the sun," is often celebrated by groups of people who gather on particular days and worship the sun together.[77] Members of the Shinto healing movement called Kurozumi Kyo emphasize a mystical union with Amaterasu, a union that was realized by their founder. "Its members inhale the divine vitality by facing the Sun in the morning and praying to Amaterasu-o-mikami."[78]

By far the most appropriate time to worship the sun is at sunrise, and particularly sunrise on New Year's Day.[79] Amaterasu is strongly associated with holiness, which to a great extent means purity in Shinto. The rising sun, and particularly the rising sun on New Year's Day, is held to be especially pure, fresh, and new, uncontaminated by the world and time. Amaterasu, then, is associated with the sun, but particularly with the rising, new sun, which, like her, is pure and holy.

When Amaterasu is worshiped at a public shrine, it is appropriate to make an offering to her. Money, sake (rice wine), and leaves from certain holy trees are the most appropriate offerings. These items are usually given to a

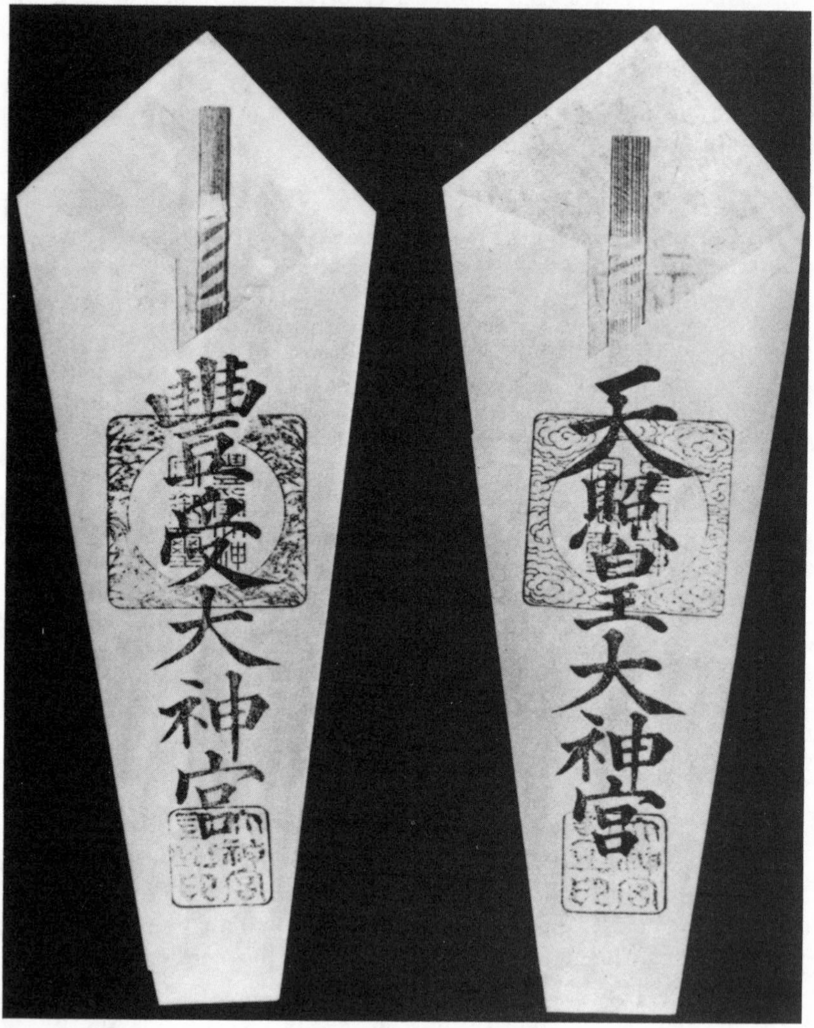

Ofuda representing Amaterasu. Robert Graves, ed., *New Larousse Encyclopedia of Mythology* (London: Paul Hamlyn, 1968), p. 406.

priest, who offers them on behalf of the devotee. In the case of sake, the priest may return the offering to the devotee, who may then consume the wine as a way of communing with the goddess.[80]

Amaterasu is not anthropomorphically represented in her shrines. The most common representations of her are a mirror and a sun symbol. Sometimes a phoenix (representing the rising sun) may represent her, or a sword or a necklace (representing the imperial regalia). Often, however, there is no object representing the goddess in her shrines. Sometimes, in fact, there are not even any confining walls, only a *torii*, a gateway, to frame a particular geographical scene. The idea in these cases, perhaps, is that Amaterasu is the land, the country, or the nation itself, insofar as she is identified with Japan itself as a cultural and geographical reality.

Chapter **5**

Sītā, the Ideal Wife

She came, and with her wise maidens escorting her, singing sweet-voiced songs. The mother of creation was she, of incomparable beauty; her delicate frame veiled in a fair white robe, and with a profusion of brilliant and tasteful ornaments, with which her maidens had bedecked her every limb. When she set her foot within the lists, all beholders, men and women alike, were fascinated by her charms; the gods in their delight sounded their kettledrums and rained down flowers midst the singing of the *apsarās* [heavenly nymphs].[1]

Introduction

One of the most popular heroines of Hindu mythology is Sītā. She is known primarily as the wife of Rāma, the hero of the epic *Rāmāyaṇa*. As one of the central protagonists of the *Rāmāyaṇa*, Sītā is revered as the model Hindu wife, who, although the victim of injustices, always remains loyal and steadfast to her husband. Although the divinity of Rāma and Sītā is not stressed in the early *Rāmāyaṇa* of Vālmīki (written sometime between 200 B.C.E. and 200 C.E., they increasingly become identified as manifestations of the god Viṣṇu and his consort Śrī-Lakṣmī in later vernacular renditions of the tale. As early as the fourteenth century, Rāma is praised as the supreme manifestation of the divine,[2] and in North India today he and Sītā are considered the supreme divine couple by millions of Hindus. Throughout this period of divinization, Sītā has achieved her status primarily in relation to Rāma. It is her wifely role, which has come to serve as a paradigm in Hindu mythology, legend, and folktale, that has defined Sītā and made her dear to so many Hindus. Unlike some other Hindu goddesses, who are either unmarried or unassociated with a male deity or who self-consciously seem to violate the norms of wifely duty, Sītā is the perfect model of wifely devotion.

Sītā, Madras bronze, seventeenth to eighteenth century C.E. Corvasji Jehangir Collection, Bombay. Ajit Mookerjee, *The Arts of India from Prehistoric to Modern Times* (Calcutta: Oxford and IBH Publishing House, 1966), fig. 112, p. 131.

Although Sītā is considered the wife of Rāma in the minds of all Hindus today, a female divinity named Sītā was known prior to Vālmīki's *Rāmāyaṇa*, and this deity was associated with agricultural fertility. Just why Vālmīki associated the name of this deity with his heroine is not entirely clear, but that he did so consciously seems beyond doubt, as we shall see below.

The Early History of Sītā

The word *sītā* means "furrow," "the line made by a plow," and is the name of a goddess associated with plowed fields in Vedic literature. In a hymn addressed to the lord of the fields, Kṣetrapati, Sītā is invoked as follows:

> Auspicious Sītā, come thou near:
> we venerate and worship thee
> That thou mayst bless and prosper us
> and bring us fruits abundantly.
>
> May Indra press the furrow down,
> may Pūshan guide its course aright
> May she, as rich in milk, be drained for us
> through each succeeding year.[3]

In the *Kauśika-sūtra,* Sītā is the wife of Parjanya, a god associated with rain. She is the "mother of gods, mortals and creatures" (verse 7c)[4] and is petitioned for growth and prosperity (verse 6).[5] In the *Parāskara-sūtra,* Sītā is the wife of Indra, a god often associated with rain and fertility, and is offered cooked rice and barley in the sacrificial fire (2.17.1–19).[6] In the *Vājasaneyi-saṁhitā,* Sītā is invoked when four furrows are drawn during a sacrifical ritual (12.69–72). This is reminiscent of plowing the ground upon which the fire altar is built during the Agnicayana ritual, an act apparently intended to ensure the abundance of fertility of the crops.[7] Sītā is also invoked as one of the names of the goddess Ārya in the *Harivaṁśa* (2.3.14).

> O goddess, you are the altar's center in the sacrifice,
> The priest's fee,
> Sītā to those who hold the plough,
> And Earth to all living beings.[8]

Sītā is not a very significant deity prior to the *Rāmāyaṇa* of Vālmīki. She is not mentioned very often and is overshadowed by much more popular goddesses associated with fertility, such as Śrī-Lakṣmī. Nevertheless, Sītā does seem to be part of a fundamental intuition concerning the fertility of the plowed earth and the necessity of a male power to awaken, arouse, and inseminate the earth. Underlying Sītā's connection with Indra, Parjanya, and other male deities associated with the inseminating effects of rain seems to be the basic perception that the ongoing fertility of the cosmos is the result of the interaction between the sky and the earth, between male and female, between the latent powers of the field and the inseminating effects of the plow, which opens the earth for the insertion of seeds into her fertile interior.

Kings and the Fertility of the Earth

The identification of Rāma's wife with a goddess of the plowed fields, with a goddess of fertility, seems to be related to the central role that kings in ancient India were assumed to play in promoting the fertility of the land.[9] The interrelation between fertility and the manly vigor and power of the ruler or king finds its prototype in the *Ṛg-veda*, where the mighty god Indra combats the demon Vṛtra, who withholds the creative, nourishing waters of creation. Having defeated the demon, the waters rush forth to fructify the earth and create a fertile, habitable cosmos fit for human civilization.[10]

The theme that the king brings forth the abundance and fertility of the earth is central in the myths concerning Pṛthu, the first human king. In these myths, the necessity of a king is related, in part, to the chaotic and barren nature of the earth in the mythic past. Prior to Pṛthu's reign the earth was inhospitable, her terrain impossible to cultivate, and her fertility untapped. In the *Mahābhārata*, Pṛthu is described as leveling the earth's mountains and hills to make her fit for agriculture and as milking the earth like a cow (7.69). As the legendary model for kings, one of Pṛthu's chief functions is to bring forth the fertility of the earth. According to the Pṛthu myths the earth, although fertile and potent, does not or cannot yield the abundance of her interior without being stimulated, activated, or, in the image of the *Mahābhārata*, "milked" by a heroic, royal figure. Conversely, it is understood that the king's reign will not be fruitful, that he will not be successful, unless he can draw forth the richness of the earth. Just as the king is needed to activate or provoke the earth into life and fertility, so the earth's fruitfulness is necessary to the king's success as a ruler.

Certain myths and certain Vedic rituals indicate the theme that the king wins the fruits of the earth. In various ways, the king relates to, interacts with, or captures things that are related to the earth, such as cows. These acts symbolize the king's ability to draw forth from the earth her treasures and abundance. They symbolize the king's ability to "milk" the earth of her richness for the benefit of all living creatures.[11]

The myth of the churning of the ocean also may be understood in this vein.[12] Viṣṇu, as the cosmic ruler, usually plays the central role and dominates the action in his various forms: as the tortoise that provides the foundation for the churning stick; as the cosmic serpent, Vāsuki, who provides the churning rope; as the seductress Mohinī, who prevents the demons from partaking of the nectar of immortality; and as the leader of the gods. The central action of the myth is the churning of the ocean of milk to make it yield the nectar of immortality. Viṣṇu represents the active ruler who brings his power and ingenuity to bear on the passive fertility of the cosmos. The result of Viṣṇu's actions is the drawing forth of representations of the abundance of the earth. Central among these are the nectar of immortality and the goddess Śrī-Lakṣmī. Śrī represents good luck, well-being, abundance, and fertility and also dwells wherever a righteous king reigns. She is sovereignty personified, and where she dwells, wealth and abundance of all good things always exist.

In the *Rāmāyaṇa*, care is taken to portray Rāma as the ideal king and his rule as a model of social perfection. It therefore is not surprising that we would encounter the theme of Rāma's relating to, interacting with, or winning the riches of the earth. In fact, his winning Sītā at her *svayamvara* (a suitors' contest for a bride), their subsequent marriage, and Rāma's regaining Sītā from the clutches of the demon Rāvaṇa probably should be understood as an expression of this basic and ancient pattern in Indian religion. It is clear in the *Rāmāyaṇa* that Sītā is no mere human being. Her birth is supernatural, while her abilities and appearance are exalted throughout the text. She is called *ayonijā*, "not born of a womb" (1.66; 2.30), for example, and in appearance she is often likened to Śrī-Lakṣmī (5.12).[13] The nature of her birth (as well as her name) makes it clear, too, that Sītā fits the theme of the mutual and necessary interaction between a king and the earth, which alone leads to fertility and abundance. According to the *Rāmāyaṇa*, Sītā is literally unearthed when her father, King Janaka, is plowing (1.66). Given Janaka's position as a great king, ruler of Videha, it seems extremely unlikely that he was simply in the fields farming when Sītā was discovered. What is more likely is that Janaka was involved in some royal ritual, part of which involved the king himself plowing the earth to bring about fertility.[14] It is also likely that the king's plowing of the field was likened to sexual intercourse, a symbolic coupling of the king (and the powers he represented or contained) with the latent powers of the earth.[15] The effectiveness of the ritual plowing, then, is manifest in the birth of Sītā, the earth's personified fertility, abundance, and well-being, which has been brought forth by Janaka.

The marriage of Rāma and Sītā represents a further interplay between a vigorous, virtuous, powerful king and a woman who represents the fecund forces of the earth, a woman who is literally the child of the earth. Their marriage institutes a relationship in which Sītā is, as it were, plowed by Rāma the

Rāma and Sītā, contemporary. Yves Vequaud, *Die Kunst von Mithila* (Brussels: Weber Genf, 1977), p. 86. Courtesy of Editions sous le vent, Paris.

king. The ultimate result of this auspicious relationship betweeen kingly virility and earthly fertility is the inauguration of Rāmrājya, "the rule of Rāma," an idealized reign in which harmony, longevity, order, fruitful crops, and all social, political, and economic virtues dominate society to the entire exclusion of all ills.

Interposed between the marriage of Rāma and Sītā and the inauguration of Rāmrājya is the central part of the epic narrative in which Rāma is banished from the capital city, Sītā is abducted by the villain Rāvaṇa, and Rāma and his allies defeat Rāvaṇa and recapture Sītā. During Rāma's exile, Ayodhya, the capital of Rāma's kingdom, is desolate. The citizens bemoan Rāma's absence, and in all respects the situation is contrasted with the times during which Rāma was present there.[16] Doubly traumatic is the situation when Sītā is kidnapped. At one point Rāma is reduced to a blubbering, half-maddened wreck and must be returned to sobriety by the appeals of his brother, Lakṣmaṇa, who tells him it is ummanly and improper to lament so.[17]

In summary, traditional Indian religion viewed the king as a figure who could stimulate, activate, or somehow draw forth from the earth her creative potential. Indeed, it was held that without the king's beneficial influence, without the manly vigor of the king, the earth's fecundity would remain untapped; the earth would remain unproductive. The king entered into a relationship with the earth in which he could stimulate her, a relationship that was understood as not unlike a marriage. "This marital relation of the ruler to the earth is directly expressed in the word *Bhupati* 'lord of the earth,' i.e. king."[18] In the *Rāmāyaṇa*, Rāma's wife is associated with the powers of the earth, or the earth itself, through her name and through her unusual birth. Underlying Sītā's epic character and personality is the ancient fertility goddess associated with the plowed field, who was worshiped for abundant crops and who was ritually activated by rulers in certain contexts. Sītā, the epic heroine, has ancient roots, and one important dimension of her character associates her with the primordial powers of the earth.

The Ideal Wife

In the *Rāmāyaṇa* and in the subsequent cult of Rāma, Sītā is defined almost entirely in relation to her husband. She is portrayed, from a clearly androcentric point of view, as the ideal Hindu wife, whose every thought revolves around her husband. For Sītā, Rāma is the center of her life. She is always steadfast in her loyalty to him. His welfare, reputation, and wishes are uppermost in her mind. In the *Manu-dharma-śāstra* the ideal wife is described as a woman who always remains faithful to her husband, no matter what his character might be: "Though destitute of virtue, or seeking pleasure elsewhere, or devoid of good qualities, a husband must be constantly worshiped as a god by a faithful wife" (5.154).[19] The same text, commenting on the necessity for protecting women throughout their lives, says: "Her father protects her in childhood, her husband protects her in old age; a woman is never fit for independence" (9.3).[20] Sītā is the ideal *pativratā*, the wife devoted entirely to her husband. In her selfless devotion and sexual fidelity, the *pativratā* nourishes an inner heat that both purifies her and provides her with a destructive weapon that can be used against those who might threaten her purity.[21] For a wife this inner heat generated as a result of marital fidelity seems to be similar to *tapas* in the context of asceticism. *Tapas* is both the act of doing asceticism, or something virtuous, and the result of doing that action, namely, an inner heat or fire.

Sītā's mythological role as the ideal wife and *pativratā* is illustrated in several incidents in the *Rāmāyaṇa*. When Rāma's father tells him that he will not inherit the kingdom and that he must go into exile in the forest for fourteen years, Rāma prepares to leave Sītā behind in the city of Ayodhya because he thinks that she could not bear the ordeals and discomforts of the forest. She is grief stricken at this plan and delivers a long discourse to him on her desire to go into exile with him. The point to which she returns often is that a husband is a god to his wife and that apart from him a wife might as well commit suicide, so meaningless would be her existence. She threatens to kill herself unless he relents and allows her to go with him to the forest. She begins her plea with these words:

> O Son of an illustrious monarch, a father, a mother, a brother, a son or a daughter-in-law enjoy the fruit of their merits and receive what is their due, a wife alone follows the destiny of her consort, O Bull among Men; therefore, from now on, my duty is clear, I shall dwell in the forest! For a woman, it is not her father, her son, nor her mother, friends nor her own self, but the husband, who in this world and the next is ever her sole means of salvation. If thou dost enter the impenetrable forest to-day, O Descendant of Raghu, I shall precede thee on foot, treading down the spiky Kusha Grass. . . . I shall willingly dwell in the forest as formerly I inhabited the palace of my father, having no anxiety in the Three Worlds and reflecting only on my duties towards my lord. Ever subject to thy will, docile, living like an ascetic, in those honey-scented woodlands I shall be happy in thy proximity, O Rama, O Illustrious Lord. (2.27)[22]

Rāma replies to her by describing all the dangers and discomforts of the forest and tells her that he cannot bear to inflict these things on her, that she must stay behind in the comfort of the city under the protection of her in-laws. She replies by saying:

> The hardships described by thee, that are endured by those who dwell in the forest, will be transmuted into joys through my devotion to thee. . . . Separated from thee I should immediately yield up my life. . . . Deprived of her consort a woman cannot live, thou canst not doubt this truth where I am concerned. . . . O Thou of pure soul, I shall remain sinless by following piously in the steps of my consort, for a husband is a God. (2.29)[23]

In her utter loyalty to Rāma she compares herself to Sāvitrī, who followed her husband to the realm of the dead, and says that she has never seen the face of another man, even in her thoughts (2.30). She says that the forest discomforts will be enjoyed by her as pleasures as long as she can be with him. She sums up her plea to Rāma by saying: "To be with thee is heaven, to be without thee is hell, this is the truth!" (2.30).[24]

When Rāvaṇa abducts Sītā and takes her to Laṅka, he keeps her prisoner in a garden surrounded by demonesses. Several long descriptions portray Sītā's pitiful condition in the absence of Rāma. Through a series of metaphors, Vālmīki tries to capture both Sītā's great beauty and her great grief. The latter has clearly eclipsed the former but cannot altogether hide it. In the words of the *Rāmāyaṇa*, she was

> resplendent with a radiance which now shone but dimly so that she seemed like a flame wreathed in smoke.

Sītā, Rāma, and Lakṣmaṇa in the forest, Kangra style, ca. 1780 C.E. Mrs. Douglas Barrett Collection, Drayton Parslow. Douglas Barrett and Basil Gray, *Painting of India* (Geneva: Editions d'Art Albert Skira, 1963), pl. 80, p. 184.

> . . . she resembled a lotus pool stripped of its flowers. Oppressed, racked with grief, and tormented, she was like unto Rohini pursued by Ketu [the moon in eclipse]. . . .
>
> Entangled in a mighty web of sorrow, her beauty was veiled like a flame enveloped in smoke or a traditional text obscured by dubious interpretation or wealth that is melting away or faith that is languishing or hope that is almost extinguished or perfection unattained on account of obstacles or an intellect which is darkened or fame tarnished by calumny. (5.15)[25]

Musing on her appearance, Hanuman, the loyal monkey ally of Rāma, says: "For a woman the greatest decoration is her lord and Sita, though incomparably beautiful, no longer shines in Rama's absence" (5.16).[26]

Although her beauty is dimmed, although she lacks the presence of Rāma, who alone gives her life meaning, she is described throughout this section of the narrative as constantly remembering Rāma. Keeping him always in her mind, she is sometimes described as shining beautifully as a result of this steadfastness. "Though that blessed one was shorn of her beauty, yet her soul did not lose its transcendency, upheld as it was by the thought of Rāma's glory and safeguarded by her own virtue" (5.17).[27]

Rāvaṇa comes to the garden and proposes that Sītā abandon Rāma and take him as her husband. She is shocked at this suggestion and refuses. Rāvaṇa threatens that he will give her two months to agree to his wishes. If, after that time, she refuses, he will cut her up and have her for breakfast (5.22). Sītā shows great pride and courage in the face of Rāvaṇa's threats. At one point she tells him that if she wished she could burn him to ashes with the fire that she has accumulated from her chastity (5.22). She refuses to do so, she says, simply because she has not been given Rāma's permission.

When Hanuman finds Sītā in her garden prison he proposes to return her to India by carrying her on his back. Given Sītā's predicament and her longing to see Rāma again, it would be natural for her to accept this offer of rescue joyfully. She does not agree to return with Hanuman, however, because to do so would mean touching another male besides her husband, which would violate her devotion to Rāma. She also refuses to accept Hanuman's offer because it would mean that Rāma would not obtain the glory involved in rescuing her. Sītā displays in this scene her habit of always thinking of Rāma first. His welfare and reputation are uppermost in her mind. To her it would be wrong to think of her own safety first if it would mean adversely influencing Rāma's reputation or opportunity for fame and glory (5.37).

In Rāvaṇa's attempt to persuade Sītā to accept him as her new husband, he has his court magician create a head that resembles Rāma's and a bow like Rāma's. Taking these to Sītā, Rāvaṇa claims that Rāma has been defeated in battle and slain. In her shock and lamentation Sītā's chief thought is that it must

Sītā in a garden, contemporary. Yves Vequaud, *Die Kunst von Mithila* (Brussels: Weber Genf, 1977), p. 92. Courtesy of Editions sous le vent, Paris.

have been some fault of hers that resulted in Rāma's untimely and undignified death. A virtuous woman sustains her husband and prevents his untimely death. Only some shortcoming or unvirtuous act, she thinks, can explain the tragedy. She begs Rāvaṇa to take her to the body of her husband and slay her there so that she can be united with him in death (6.31–32).

After Rāma defeats Rāvaṇa, Sītā's loyalty to her husband is severely tested. Sītā is brought before Rāma, and she beams with joy at seeing him. He, however, scowls at her and announces that he has only undertaken the defeat of Rāvaṇa in order to uphold his family's honor and not out of love for her. He says that it would be lustful and ignoble for him to take her back after she had spent time under the control of another man. He disclaims her and even invites her to associate with one of his brothers or one of the surviving demon heroes. He concludes this frosty interview with her by saying: "Assuredly Rāvaṇa, beholding thy ravishing and celestial beauty, will not have respected thy person during the time thou didst dwell in his abode" (6.17).[28]

Sītā is shocked at this accusation and protests her innocence, saying that although it is true that Rāvaṇa handled her, she could have done nothing to

Sītā proves her innocence by an ordeal of fire, contemporary lithograph.

prevent it, that he abducted her by means of superior strength, and that thoughout her ordeal and stay in Laṅka she remained completely faithful to her husband and thought of him constantly. Grieved by Rāma's false accusations, she asks Lakṣmaṇa to make a funeral pyre for her. Having displeased Rāma and having been renounced by him publicly, she wishes to die (6.118). When the fire has been kindled, Sītā prepares to enter it by circumambulating Rāma and then addressing Agni, the god of fire, with the words: "As my heart has never ceased to be true to Raghava, do thou, O Witness of all Beings, grant me thy protection! As I am pure in conduct, though Rāma looks on me as sullied, do thou, O Witness of the Worlds, grant me full protection!" (6.118).[29] Because of her innocence and purity, Agni refuses to harm her and returns her to Rāma so unscathed that even her flower garland remains unwithered by the heat of the flames. Rāma, convinced of her purity, accepts her back and says that he will protect her forever (6.120).

Back in Ayodhya, however, when everyone is living happily ever after and the glorious era of Rāmrājya is underway, Rāma hears that his citizens are unhappy that he accepted Sītā back after she was under Rāvaṇa's control. To stop this gossip and to set a stainless example for his subjects, Rāma decides to banish Sītā from his kingdom, even though he has just learned of her pregnancy. He commands his brother, Lakṣmaṇa, to take Sītā to a deserted place and abandon her (7.45). When Lakṣmaṇa tells Sītā of Rāma's decision, her predilection is again to blame some fault of her own, either in this life or a past life, for bringing about her ill luck. She does not blame Rāma, nor does it seem to occur to her that he might be in the wrong (7.48). She asks Lakṣmaṇa to send Rāma this message:

> O Raghava, thou knowest I am truly pure and that I have been bound to thee in supreme love, yet thou hast renounced me in fear of dishonour, because thy subjects have reproached and censured thee, O Hero. . . . As for me, I am not distressed on mine own account, O Prince of Raghu, it is for thee to keep thy fair name untarnished! The husband is as a God to the woman, he is her family, and her spiritual preceptor, therefore, even at the price of her life, she must seek to please her lord. (7.48)[30]

After Sītā has given birth to twin sons and has spent several years in exile in a forest hermitage, Rāma summons her back to Ayodhya to undergo an ordeal that will absolve him of all shame and demonstrate her innocence once and for all. Although he himself is convinced of her innocence, he demands a public ordeal to convince his subjects. Sītā agrees, but it seems that she no longer relishes life; she asks, on the basis of her purity and loyalty to Rāma, to be taken back into the bosom of her mother, the goddess Earth. She says: "If, in thought, I have ever dwelt on any but Rāma, may the Goddess Madhavi receive me!" (7.97).[31] As she finishes this act of truth, a throne rises from the ground sup-

Sītā in flames. Jagdish Mittal, *Andhra Paintings of the Rāmāyana* (Hyderabad: Lalit Kala Akademi, 1969), pl. 48, detail.

ported by serpents. Earth embraces Sītā, seats her on the throne, and then the throne and Sītā sink back into the ground (7.97). Although Rāma angrily demands Sītā's return, the earth remains silent and closed, and Rāma lives out his life in sorrow. He does not remarry and has a golden image of Sītā made, which he uses in her place at religious rituals requiring the presence of a wife.

Sītā's self-effacing nature, her steadfast loyalty to her husband, and her chastity make her both the ideal Hindu wife and the ideal *pativratā* from the androcentric point of view of most Hindu texts. In a sense, Sītā has no independent existence, no independent destiny. In all things she sees herself as inextricably bound up with Rāma. Apart from him her life is meaningless. Throughout the *Rāmāyaṇa*, she constantly thinks of Rāma and his welfare and always remains faithful to him despite provocations on his part. Although Rāma is considered the ideal king, he is not a very good husband to Sītā. He would have been perfectly willing to leave her behind for fourteen years during his exile, he entertains doubts about her chastity while she was under Rāvaṇa's control, he allows her to undergo an ordeal by fire, he exiles her from his kingdom to stop the gossip of the citizens and to protect his own reputation, and

Sītā prays to return to the lap of her mother, Earth. Contemporary Indian comic book, "The Sons of Rama," Amar Chitra Katha.

finally he demands that she undergo a public ordeal. Throughout all this, Sītā remains steadfast, usually blaming herself instead of Rāma for events that cause her suffering and separation from Rāma. In her loyalty and chastity, furthermore, it is understood that she supports and nourishes Rāma's strength and reputation. A common Hindu belief is that a man is strengthened, indeed, is made nearly invulnerable, by his wife's chastity, while he is weakened and endangered by her faithlessness. Thus, when Rāvaṇa shows Sītā Rāma's head and bow, she immediately blames herself. Although she cannot remember being faithless in act or thought, she assumes that she must have been at some time (perhaps in a past life) for Rāma to have met such an untimely end. It does not occur to her that some fault of Rāma's own might have led to his misfortune.

In Hinduism, it is generally true that the good woman and ideal wife should express submission and docility to her in-laws. Speaking of the training of girls in Mysore, M. N. Srinivas says:

> It is the mother's duty to train her daughter up to be an absolute docile daughter-in-law. The *summum bonum* of a girl's life is to please her parents-in-law and her husband. If she does not "get on" with her mother-in-law, she will be a disgrace to her family, and cast a blot on the fair name of her mother. The Kannada mother dins into her daughter's ears certain ideals which make for harmony (at the expense of her sacrificing her will) in her life.[32]

In the Hindu tradition, a woman is taught to understand herself primarily in relation to others. She is taught to emphasize in the development of her character what others expect of her. It is society that puts demands upon her, primarily through the agents of relatives and in-laws, and not she who places demands upon society that she be allowed to develop a unique, independent destiny. A central demand placed upon women, particularly vis-à-vis males, is that they subordinate their welfare to the welfare of others. Hindu women are taught to cultivate an attitude that identifies their own welfare with the welfare of others, especially that of their husbands and children. "In the *bratas*, the periodical days of fasting and prayer which unmarried girls keep all over India, the girl's wishes for herself are almost always in relation to others; she asks the boons of being a good daughter, good wife, good daughter-in-law, good mother, and so forth. Thus, in addition to the 'virtue' of self-effacement and self-sacrifice, the feminine role in India crystallizes a woman's connections to others, her embeddedness in a multitude of familial relationships."[33]

In inculcating the nature of the ideal woman in India, Sītā plays an important role, perhaps the dominant role of all Hindu mythological figures. The *Rāmāyaṇa*, either in its original Sanskrit version or in one of several vernacular renditions, is well known by almost every Hindu. Many of the leading characters have come to represent Hindu ideals. In the context of the Daśa Puttal

Vrata, for example, Bengali girls wish that, "I shall have a husband like Rāma, I shall be *sati* like Sītā, I shall have a Devara [younger brother-in-law] like Lakshman. I shall have a father-in-law like Dasaratha; I shall have a mother-in-law like Kousalya."[34]

Sītā represents all the qualities of a good woman and ideal wife. Although other goddesses, such as Pārvatī and Lakṣmī, and other heroines from Hindu mythology, such as Sāvitrī and Damayantī, express many of these qualities, Sītā is by far the most popular and beloved paradigm for wifely devotion, forbearance, and chastity.

> From earliest childhood, a Hindu has heard Sita's legend recounted on any number of sacral and secular occasions; seen the central episodes enacted in folk plays like the *Ram Lila*; heard her qualities extolled in devotional songs; and absorbed the ideal feminine identity she incorporates through the many everyday metaphors and similies that are associated with her name. Thus, "She is as pure as Sita" denotes chastity in a woman, and "She is a second Sita," the appreciation of a woman's uncomplaining self-sacrifice. If, as Jerome Bruner remarks, "In the mythologically instructed community there is a corpus of images and models that provide the pattern to which the individual may aspire, a range of metaphoric identity," then this range, in the case of a Hindu woman, is condensed in one model, and she is Sita.[35]

Ideal Devotee and Intermediary

After Vālmīki's *Rāmāyaṇa*, Rāma increasingly ascended to a position of supreme deity for many Hindus. Today in India he is one of the most popular deities of all and is the recipient of fervent devotion from millions of devotees. The shift in Rāma's status, from that of a human hero or incarnation of Viṣṇu in Vālmīki's *Rāmāyaṇa* to that of the lord of the worlds, is evident in the sixteenth-century Hindi work of Tulsī Dās, the *Rāmcarit-mānas*, an extremely popular devotional work in North India. Although the central narrative remains the same, even in most particulars, Tulsī Dās frequently alters the story in such a way that opportunities are afforded to express devotion to Rāma as the Lord. Throughout the text it is clear tht the central point of the narrative is Rāma's descent to earth so that his devotees may have a chance to worship him.[36]

In the process of Rāma's elevation to divine supremacy, Sītā also undergoes certain changes. Her status is similarly elevated when Rāma becomes identified with the highest god. In his poem *Kavitāvalī*, Tulsī Dās refers to Sītā as the world's mother and to Rāma as the world's father (1.15).[37] Elsewhere in the poem Rāma and Sītā are praised in fervent, devotional language by village women who see them walking along the road. The two are compared to various divine couples, and the very sight of them has redemptive effects (2.14–25; 7.36). In another of Tulsī Dās's works Rāma and Sītā are worshiped and ad-

Sītā, early Choḷa bronze, 1000 C.E. Government Museum, Madras. C. Sivaramamurti, *South Indian Bronzes* (New Delhi: Lalit Kala Akademi, 1963), fig. 40b.

dressed in devotional tones. "My mind now tells me that save for Rāma's and Sītā's feet I shall go nowhere else."[38] In his invocation to his *Rāmcarit-mānas*, Tulsī Dās invokes several deities and includes this verse to Sītā: "Hail to Rama's own beloved Sita, victor o'er all suff'ring, / Mistress of birth, life, death, and of all happiness the giver."[39] In the popular folk dramas of North India, the Rām Līlās, in which whole villages act out the story of Rāma over the course of several weeks, the actors playing the roles of Rāma and Sītā are worshiped by the spectators as deities.[40]

Consistent with her role in Vālmīki's *Rāmāyaṇa* as the ideal wife who subordinates herself to her husband, Sītā never achieves the position of a great, powerful, independent deity. Even compared to such goddesses as Lakṣmī and Pārvatī, who in most respects are portrayed as ideal wives in Hindu mythology, Sītā lacks an identity, power, and will of her own. She remains in Rāma's shadow to such an extent that she is often hardly visible at all. In such devotional works as Tulsī Dās's *Kavitāvalī* and *Vinaya-patrikā*, Sītā is rarely mentioned. Hanuman and Lakṣmaṇa, in fact, are mentioned more often than she is. And when Rāma's consort is referred to, Tulsī Dās often prefers to identify her as Lakṣmī, not as Sītā.[41] In fact, Tulsī Dās expresses devotion more often to Pārvatī and Gaṅgā as goddesses than he does to Sītā.[42]

If Sītā does not assume the role of a popular, powerful goddess more or less equal to her husband, Rāma, she does play two important roles in the context of devotion to Rāma: the role of intermediary and the role of ideal devotee. Addressing her as world mother, Tulsī Dās petitions Sītā to act as his advocate before Rāma.[43] She is not approached directly for divine blessing but as one who has access to Rāma, who alone dispenses divine grace. Again, consistent with her subordinate position vis-à-vis Rāma in the *Rāmāyaṇa*, consistent with her role as one who always subordinates her will to his, Sītā here acts primarily as a messenger between Rāma and his devotees. In her loyalty and devotion she has gained the Lord's ear, and because of this she is sometimes approached by his devotees for help in seeking Rāma's favor.

Sītā also assumes the role of devotee in the later Rāma cult and thus assumes a place as model to Rāma's devotees. Although Hanuman is the most popular model of Rāma devotion in the later Rāma cults, Sītā is often pictured as an ardent devotee. In the *Rāmcarit-mānas*, for example, she is typically pictured as intoxicated by the appearance of Rāma and steadfastly devoted to him. Indeed, in the *Rāmcarit-mānas*, Tulsī Dās has sometimes altered the narrative in such a way as to emphasize Sītā's devotion and love for Rāma. For example, in the Vālmīki *Rāmāyaṇa*, Sītā pleads to accompany Rāma to the forest by appealing to law and custom. She argues that a wife's duty is to be with her husband. In the *Rāmcarit-mānas*, however, Rāma and others argue that religious custom and law dictate that she should stay behind and take care of her in-laws. Backing up these arguments are other reasons why she should stay behind, including the argument that someone as delicate as Sītā could not endure the difficulties of forest life. Sītā's reply does not dwell on the fact that it is socially accepted that a wife always be with her husband, as in the Vālmīki *Rāmāyaṇa*, but on the fact that separation from her husband will be unbearable agony. It is not her sense of duty but her love for and devotion to Rāma that gives Sītā's plea its force and passion in the *Rāmcarit-mānas*.[44]

As in Sītā's role as intermediary, here, too, she plays a subsidiary role vis-à-vis Rāma. He is the supreme deity, the object of devotion; she is the ideal devotee, the model for the human devotee. Wifely devotion has here become a metaphor for ideal devotion to God.

Part II

Goddesses of the West

Queen Nefertari guided by Isis (on the right), from the tomb of Queen Nefertari at Thebes. K. Lange and M. Hirmer, *Egypt: Architecture, Sculpture, Painting in Three Thousand Years* (3d ed., rev.; London: Phaidon Press, 1961), pl. 247. Permission of Hirmer Verlag, Munich.

Chapter **6**

Inanna, Queen of Heaven and Earth

Mighty, majestic, and radiant,
You shine brilliantly in the evening,
You brighten the day at dawn,
You stand in the heavens like the sun and the moon,
Your wonders are known both above and below,
To the greatness of the holy priestess of heaven,
To you, Inanna, I sing![1]

The goddess Inanna was worshiped in Sumer from the beginning of the third millenium B.C.E. to the beginning of the first millenium B.C.E., and in the form of the Babylonian goddess Ishtar, until near the end of the first millenium B.C.E.. During this period, furthermore, Inanna (Ishtar) was an extremely popular deity and played a central role in Sumerian mythology, theology, and cult. She was strongly associated with the fertility of the crops and animals and with life in general; she played a central role in the royal marriage ceremony in which kings were ritually united with Inanna in order to engender the fertility of the kingdom; and she was described as reigning in heaven, where she controlled the cosmic rhythms and oversaw all happenings on the earth below. She was, in short, affirmed to be queen of heaven and earth.

Fertility, Growth, and Abundance

Early references to Inanna link her with a male deity names Dumuzi-Amaushumgalanna, whose name means "the one great source of the date clusters."[2] This god, it seems, represented the vitality of the date palm by which it produced a large cluster of fruit each year. Inanna, on the other hand, in early references, seems to have been associated with the storehouse in which the date harvest was kept. An early epithet of Inanna is Ninanna, which means "lady of the date clusters,"[3] and her early emblem is "a gatepost with rolled up mat to serve as a door, a distinguishing mark of the storehouse."[4] In an early hymn from the city of Uruk, these two deities are described as uniting in marriage. A long section of the hymn describes Inanna adorning herself with gems (which in some cases may also be dates) before receiving Dumuzi into her house.[5] While this hymn may have been part of the celebration of the sacred marriage rite in which the king united with Inanna to promote fertility in the world, it suggests, perhaps, a preanthropomorphic aspect of Inanna that identified her with the numen of the date storehouse.[6] If this is the case, it means that from earliest times Inanna's identity was associated with abundance and the vitality of the crops. Indeed, throughout her history this aspect of Inanna persists as central to her character.

In a hymn that may have been used in the sacred marriage rite, Inanna speaks of meeting Dumuzi and pouring forth food from herself:

He made me enter, he made me enter,
My brother made me enter his garden,
Dumuzi made me enter his garden,
He made me approach with him a high grove,
Made me stand with him by a high bed.

Steadily I kneel by an apple tree,
My brother comes chanting,
The lord Dumuzi comes up to me,
Comes up to me out of the reddish oak-leaves,
Comes up to me out of the midday heat—
I pour out before him legumes from my womb,
I bring into being legumes before him, I pour out legumes before him,
I bring into being grains before him, I pour out grains before him.[7]

In another hymn in which Inanna and Dumuzi address each other, Dumuzi compares Inanna's breasts to broad, fertile fields:

O Lady, your breast is your field.
Inanna, your breast is your field

Your broad field pours out plants.
Your broad field pours out grain.
Water flows from on high for your servant.
Bread flows from on high for your servant.
Pour it out for me, Inanna,
I will drink all you offer.[8]

In one hymn, Inanna praises her body and in doing so compares her vulva to a well-watered field that is ready to be plowed.[9] She longs to have herself plowed, and in the end Dumuzi fulfills her longing. His awakening is reflected in the general quickening of vegetation. The hymn ends like this:

At its mighty rising, at its mighty rising,
did the shoots and the buds rise up.
The king's loins! At its mighty rising
did the vines rise up, did the grains rise up,
did the desert fill (with verdure)
like a pleasure garden.[10]

Another song features Inanna comparing her hair to lettuce.[11] To further the analogy, Inanna would be compared to the earth itself, particularly the mysterious power within the earth that causes vegetation to bubble forth in such vigor and profusion.

Inanna's control over, if not identification with, the powers of growth and fertility is made explicit in a hymn that describes the destruction she causes to her enemies, to lands where she is not praised and honored. "In the mountain where homage is withheld from you vegetation is accursed."[12] In that land, sexual attraction is absent. "Its woman no longer speaks of love with her husband. At night they no longer have intercourse. She no longer reveals to him her inmost treasures."[13]

In the Babylonian account of Ishtar's descent to the underworld, which is modeled on the Sumerian account of Inanna's descent to the land of the dead, sexuality and fertility vanish from the world when the goddess leaves it.

After Lady Ishtar [had descended to the nether world],
The bull springs not upon the cow, [the ass impregnates not the jenny],
In the street [the man impregnates not] the maiden.
The man lies [in his (own) chamber, the maiden lies on her side].[14]

From earliest times, then, Inanna's presence was seen in full storehouses, in the mysterious powers of the earth to promote growth and produce crops, and in the vigor of life itself.

Sexuality

Related to Inanna's identification with growth, abundance, and fertility is her association with sex. Her presence, indicated in the last two examples above, is revealed in the attraction between the sexes. In her absence, sexual desire is nonexistent. Many songs and hymns describe Inanna herself as eager for sex and as sexually active. In a hymn entitled "The Sister's Message," Dumuzi's sister, Geshtinanna, tells of meeting Inanna and of how Inanna invited Geshtinanna to her house and in her bedroom confessed of her longing for Geshtinanna's brother. In describing the scene to her brother she says that Inanna

> wore herself out moaning to me,
> and I was fetching (things) for her the while,
>   as for someone (very) weak,
> and a disposition to tremble, from the ground up—
>   exceedingly much—befell her.
> O my brother, smiting her hips (in anguish)
> does my sweet darling pass the day.[15]

In the following hymn, in which Inanna praises her vulva, her longing is equally strong:

> My vulva, the horn,
> The Boat of Heaven,
> Is full of eagerness like the young moon.
> My untilled land lies fallow.
>
> As for me, Inanna,
> Who will plow my vulva?
> Who will plow my high field?
> Who will plow my wet ground?
>
> As for me, the young woman,

Who will plow my vulva?
Who will station the ox there?
Who will plow my vulva?

To which Dumuzi replies:

Great Lady, the king will plow your vulva.
I, Dumuzi the King, will plow your vulva.

And Inanna says:

Then plow my vulva, man of my heart!
Plow my vulva![16]

In another hymn Inanna describes her love play with Dumuzi:

I bathed for the wild bull,
I bathed for the shepherd Dumuzi,
I perfumed my sides with ointment,
I coated my mouth with sweet-smelling amber,
I painted my eyes with kohl.

He shaped my loins with his fair hands,
The shepherd Dumuzi filled my lap with cream and milk,
He stroked my pubic hair,
He watered my womb.
He laid his hands on my holy vulva,
He smoothed my black boat with cream,
He quickened my narrow boat with milk,
He caressed me on the bed.

Now I will caress my high priest on the bed,
I will caress the faithful shepherd Dumuzi,
I will caress his loins, the shepherdship of the land,
I will decree a sweet fate for him.[17]

In her later form as Ishtar, she is described as beautiful and alluring:

Ishtar, terracotta plaque, ninth to eighth centuries B.C.E. Fitzwilliam Museum, Cambridge. Pierre Grimal, ed., *Larousse World Mythology* (London: Paul Hamlyn, 1965), p. 65.

She is clothed with pleasure and love.
She is laden with vitality, charm, and voluptuousness.
Ishtar is clothed with pleasure and love.
She is laden with vitality, charm, and voluptuousness.

In lips she is sweet; life is in her mouth.
At her appearance rejoicing becomes full.
She is glorious; veils are thrown over her head.
Her figure is beautiful; her eyes are brilliant.[18]

There is a certain overpowering quality to Inanna's sexuality. One hymn, in which her lover pleads to be released, suggests that she is insatiable. Inanna speaks:

My beloved, the delight of my eyes, met me.
We rejoiced together.
He took his pleasure of me.
He brought me into his house.

He laid me down on the fragrant honey-bed.
My sweet love, lying by my heart,
Tongue-playing, one by one,
My fair Dumuzi did so fifty times.

Now, my sweet love is sated.
Now he says:
"Set me free, my sister, set me free."[19]

In the *Epic of Gilgamesh*, Ishtar's sexuality is presented as dangerous and disruptive and possibly excessive. Approaching Gilgamesh, she is struck by his beauty and says: "Come Gilgamesh, be my lover! / Give me the taste of your body." She promises him wealth and power. He will live in a sumptuous house with her and be served by kings and princes. His goats will bear triplets and his ewes have twins. Gilgamesh, however, refuses her and taunts her with a long list of lovers whom she has destroyed or discarded.[20]

Inanna is associated with prostitutes and with the rising evening star, which "raises its head" in the early evening and spreads its soft light to provide the proper setting for erotic evening activities.[21] She herself is described as a harlot who sets out in the early evening to solicit men.

O harlot, you set out for the alehouse,
O Inanna, you are bent on going into your (usual) window
(namely, to solicit) for a lover—
O Inanna, mistress of myriad offices,
no god rivals you!
Ninegalla, here is your dwelling place,
let me tell of your greatness!
As the herds make the dust (they kick up)
settle in layers,
as oxen and sheep return to pen and fold,
you, my lady, dress like one of no repute
in a single garment,
the beads (the sign) of a harlot
you put around your neck.
It is you that hail men from the alehouse!
It is you, tripping along into the embrace
of your bridegroom Dumuzi![22]

Although Inanna on occasion is described as sexually innocent—"That which pertains to women—copulation—I know not, / That which pertains to women—kissing—I know not, / I know not copulation, I know not kissing"[23]—she usually is described as unabashed about expressing and indulging her sexual desires. Indeed, she *is* sexual desire, without which creation could not proceed, without which the flocks would not multiply, and without which humankind would cease to reproduce itself. There is about her sexuality a certain unrestrained eagerness that might threaten social stability and marital harmony. Her reputation as a threat to men, for example, is well known by the hero Gilgamesh. For the most part, however, Inanna's sexuality (along with her identification with fertility and abundance) is understood to be a very positive reality. This is clear in the many hymns that celebrate her marriage with kings, who usually are associated with her lover Dumuzi. In these hymns, which probably were sung in the context of sacred marriage rituals, Inanna's sexual eagerness is joyously and warmly channeled in unison with the king (Dumuzi) for the welfare of all. The following hymn expresses this well.

The queen bathes her holy loins,
Inanna bathes for the holy loins of Dumuzi,

She washes herself with soap.
She sprinkles sweet-smelling cedar oil on the ground.

The king goes with lifted head to the holy loins,
Dumuzi goes with lifted head to the holy loins of Inanna.
He lies down beside her on the bed.
Tenderly he caresses her, murmuring words of love:
"O my holy jewel! O my wondrous Inanna!"

After he enters her holy vulva, causing the queen to rejoice,
After he enters her holy vulva, causing Inanna to rejoice,
Inanna holds him to her and murmurs:
"O Dumuzi, you are truly my love."[24]

The Sacred Marriage Rite

It seems clear that a central concern of Mesopotamian culture was the vigor and fertility of life, particularly the fertility of the soil and the flocks. The vegetative cycle reflected a pattern in which growth and fertility were not constant, a pattern is which they periodically waned and seemed to disappear. The situation was similar with the flocks. Sexual desire did not seem constant. There were long periods when it seemed absent or in abeyance.

The sacred marriage rite is perhaps partly understood against this background of uncertainty and anxiety concerning the waxing and waning of sexual vigor and fertility. It seems to have been an attempt to promote, arouse, and perpetuate vitality, fertility, and sexuality by uniting a king (or ruler) with Inanna, who personified or controlled these mysterious powers.[25]

The sacred marriage rite seems to have been a central part of Mesopotamian religion for around two thousand years. It was probably celebrated, at least once, by each ruler of each major city in Mesopotamia. The rite may have served to legitimate the ruler in question by ritually signifying that he had established a productive relationship with the powers of fertility and abundance and that under his rule the city and surrounding countryside would prosper. If this was the case, in some places the rite may have formed part of an inauguration or coronation scenario. The rite also may have been celebrated annually at some periods and some places. It is not clear whether the rite was usually practiced at a certain time of year, but some texts say that the rite took place at harvest time or just after the harvest.[26] In some cases, the sacred marriage rite seems to have been part of a New Year's scenario, the rite itself marking the end of one cycle and the beginning of another, potentially fruitful, cycle.

The two central protagonists in this ritual drama were Inanna and Dumuzi. The king or ruler played the role of Dumuzi, while a priestess probably played the role of Inanna. Even though the specific details of the rite are not well known, it does seem apparent that the climax of the ritual involved the sexual copulation of the two on a specially prepared bed, which in some cases may have been set up in Inanna's shrine.[27] The following hymn, almost certainly used in the context of the sacred marriage rite, mentions the preparation for the rite, the careful selection of the appropriate day, the fact that the rite took place as part of the New Year's celebrations, and the preparation of the marriage bed on which the two protagonists will make love:

> The people of Sumer assemble in the palace,
> The house which guides the land.
> The king builds a throne for the queen of the palace.
> He sits beside her on the throne.
>
> In order to care for the life of all the lands,
> The exact first day of the month is closely examined,
> And on the day of the disappearance of the moon,
> On the day of the sleeping of the moon,
> The *me* are perfectly carried out
> So that the New Year's Day, the day of rites,
> May be properly determined,
> And a sleeping place be set up for Inanna.
>
> The people cleanse the rushes with sweet-smelling cedar oil,
> They arrange the rushes for the bed.
> They spread a bridal sheet over the bed.
> A bridal sheet to rejoice the heart,
> A bridal sheet to sweeten the loins,
> A bridal sheet for Inanna and Dumuzi.[28]

In some hymns, the emphasis is on Inanna's awakening sexual vigor and fertility in Dumuzi, or the king who assumes the role of Dumuzi in the rites.[29] In other hymns, the emphasis seems to be on Dumuzi's, or the ruler's, arousing Inanna, or fulfilling her desire to be invigorated.[30] The overall intention of the rite is clear, however: to arouse and ensure the future fertility and productivity of the realm by uniting two figures that symbolize the powers of sexual vigor and fertility. It is implied in the sacred marriage rite hymns that, for fertility to persist, a fruitful union must occur between a male and a female. Dumuzi himself, or Inanna herself, alone cannot ensure or invigorate the powers that produce growth and abundance. The ruler alone cannot bring about a fruitful realm without establishing a relationship between the earth and his productive powers, while the earth by itself cannot yield crops and be fruitful without being infused by the potency of the ruler. The relationship was probably understood to be symbiotic.

Perhaps the goals of the sacred marriage rite are most clearly catalogued in a hymn in which Inanna's maidservant, having led Dumuzi to her mistress's bed, gives the following list of blessings that she prays her mistress will bestow on Dumuzi:

May the lord, the choice of your heart,
may the king, your beloved bridegroom,
    pass long days in your sweet thing, the pure loins!
Grant him a pleasant reign to come!

Grant him a royal throne, firm in its foundations;
grant him a scepter righting (wrongs) in the land,
    all shepherds' crooks;
grant him the good crown, the turban that
    makes a head distinguished.

From sunrise to sunset
from south to north
from the Upper Sea to the Lower Sea,
from (where grows) the *huluppu*-tree, from
    (where grows) the cedar-tree,
and in Sumer and Akkad,
    grant him all shepherds' crooks,
and may he perform the shepherdship
    over the dark-headed people.

May he like a farmer till the fields,
may he like a good shepherd make the folds teem,

may there be vines under him,
    may there be barley under him,
may there be carp-floods in the river under him,
may there be mottled barley in the fields under him,
may fishes and birds sound off in the marshes under him.
May old and new reeds grow in the canebrake
    under him,
may shrubs grow in the high desert under him,
may deer multiply in the forests under him,
may (well) watered gardens bear honey and wine
    under him,
may lettuce and cress grow in the vegetable plots
    under him,
may there be long life in the palace under him.

May the high flood rise (?)
    in the Tigris and Euphrates under him,
may grass grow on their banks,
    may vegetables fill the commons,
may the holy lady (of the grains), Nidaba,
    gather grainpiles there!
O milady, queen of heaven and earth,
    queen of all heaven and earth,
may he live long in your embrace![31]

Queen of Heaven and Earth

Another of Inanna's dominant characteristics is her royal status, which is captured in one of her most common epithets, "queen of heaven and earth." In many hymns and myths she is pictured as a strong, willful regent who dwells in heaven, from where she rules the gods and the peoples of the earth. She also is often pictured as dwelling as an earthly queen in her various city temples.

In one story, she is described as setting her mind on obtaining the powers of rulership from the god of wisdom, Enki, who, in some cases, is said to be Inanna's father. She is described in the initial scene as putting on her crown and leaning against a tree and taking pride in her beauty:

Inanna, second half of third millenium B.C.E. Musée du Louvre. André Parrot, *Sumer und Akkad* (Munich: Verlag C. H. Beck, 1983), pl. 205, p. 214.

When she leaned against the apple tree, her vulva was wondrous to
behold.
Rejoicing at her wondrous vulva, the young woman Inanna applauded
herself.

She said:
"I, the Queen of Heaven, shall visit the God of Wisdom.
I shall go to the Abzu, the sacred place of Eridu.
I shall honor Enki, the God of Wisdom, in Eridu.
I shall utter a prayer to Enki at the deep sweet waters."[32]

Arriving at Enki's realm, the goddess was treated hospitably. She was given water to wash herself. Enki gave her beer and cake and treated her respectfully. As they drank beer together, they "toasted each other; they challenged each other."[33] As Enki became increasingly drunk, he sought to impress Inanna by offering her the different powers, the divine *me*, with which he ruled the world.

Enki, swaying with drink, toasted Inanna:
"In the name of my power! In the name of my holy shrine!
To my daughter Inanna I shall give
The high priesthood! Godship!
The noble, enduring crown! The throne of kingship!"

Inanna replied:
"I take them!"[34]

It is not long before Enki has bequeathed to Inanna all of the *me*, "a set of universal and unchangeable rules and laws which had to be obeyed willy-nilly by everybody and everything."[35] Among the *me* mentioned in the story are: giving judgments, making decisions, lovemaking, and descent to the underworld (that is, death). After receiving the *me* from Enki, Inanna sings a song of triumph in which she lists the many areas of which she is now mistress. The list represents in neat, schematic form the many offices Inanna controls in her role as queen of heaven and earth. Prominent among the *me* are powers associated especially with the priesthood, kingship, weapons, eroticism, fertility, and the arts of culture such as carpentry, metalworking, making leather, and weaving with reeds.[36]

After Inanna has sailed off in her heavenly boat for her own realm with all the *me*, Enki sobers up and regrets having given her all his power. He sends his army after her to gain back the *me*, but Inanna steadfastly resists them and keeps the *me* for herself. In possession of the *me*, in possession of authority over nature and culture, over life and death, Inanna celebrates herself in the following exultant hymn:

My father gave me heaven, gave me earth,
I, the Queen of Heaven am I,
Is there a god who can vie with me?
Enlil gave me heaven, gave me earth,
I, the Queen of Heaven am I!
He has given me lordship,
He has given me queenship,
He has given me battle, he has given me combat,
He has given me the Flood, he has given me the Tempest,
He has placed heaven as a crown on my head,
He has tied earth as a sandal at my foot,
He has fastened the holy garment of the *me* about my body,
He has placed the holy scepter in my hand.[37]

Elsewhere she proudly sums up her control over the natural world this way:

I step onto the heavens, and the rain
rains down;
I step onto the earth, and grass and herbs
sprout up.[38]

Inanna's position as heavenly queen is sometimes associated with her identification with certain celestial bodies, especially the evening star, the sun, and the moon. Perhaps the regularity of the movements of the heavenly bodies was associated with Inanna's control of the rhythms of nature, which possession of the *me* empowered her to affect.

The great queen of heaven, Inanna,
I will hail!
The only one, come forth on high,

I will hail!
The great queen of heaven, Inanna,
I will hail!

The pure torch that flares in the sky,
the heavenly light, shining bright like the day,
the great queen of heaven, Inanna,
I will hail!
The holy one, the awesome queen of the Anunnaki,
the one revered in heaven and earth,
crowned with great horns,
the oldest child of Suen, Inanna,
I will hail!

Of her majesty, of her greatness,
of her exceeding dignity
of her brilliant coming forth
in the evening sky
of her flaring in the sky—a pure torch—
of her standing in the sky
like the sun and the moon,
known by all lands from south to north,
of the greatness of the holy one of heaven
to the lady I will sing.[39]

If Inanna's presence was revealed in the movements of the heavenly bodies, if she was associated with the predictable rhythms of the natural world, she was also associated with the regularity of the social order. Her presence was manifest in kingship and the arts of culture, and especially in the matter of rendering judgment on human actions.

When in the bed-chamber sweet sleep had come to an end,
When all the lands and the black-haired people had assembled—

. . . .

And uttering orisons approached her, brought their words to her,
Then did she study their words, knew the evildoer,

Against the evildoer she renders a cruel judgment, she destroys the wicked,
She looks with kindly eyes on the straightforward, gives him her blessing.[40]

In her Babylonian form as Ishtar, the goddess is often celebrated as supreme among the gods, as the one who is most respected and highly exalted by the other deities.

Praise the goddess, the most awesome of the goddesses.
Let one revere the mistress of the peoples, the greatest of the Igigi [a collective name for the gods].
Praise Ishtar, the most awesome of the goddesses.
Let one revere the queen of women, the greatest of the Igigi.
. . . .

The goddess—with her there is counsel.
The fate of everything she holds in her hand.
At her glance there is created joy,
Power, magnificence, the protecting deity and guardian spirit.
. . . .

Who—to her greatness who can be equal?
Strong, exalted, splendid are her decrees.
Ishtar—to her greatness who can be equal?
Strong, exalted, splendid are her decrees.

. . . .
Ishtar among the gods, extraordinary is her station.
Respected is her word; it is *supreme* over them.

She is their queen; they continually cause her commands to be executed.
All of them bow down before her.
They receive her light before her.
Women and men indeed revere her.[41]

Inanna's Violent Nature

While Inanna is usually described in terms that emphasize her positive roles—her association with fertility and abundance and her role as guardian of the natural and social orders—she is sometimes said to behave in violent, disruptive, and dangerous ways. This violent aspect is often mentioned in the context of natural calamity or battle. The following excerpts from the hymn of Enheduanna, a high priestess of Inanna, portray a wrathful, vengeful aspect of Inanna. She lays waste the land through flood and storm, people tremble before her in expectation of being punished, and even the gods fly from her glance in fear.

> Like a dragon you have deposited venom on the land.
> When you roar at the earth like Thunder, no vegetation can stand up to
> you.
> A flood descending from its mountain,
> Oh foremost one, you are the Inanna of heaven and earth!
> Raining the fanned fire down upon the nation,
> Endowed with me's by An, lady mounted on a beast,
> Who makes decisions at the holy command of An.
> (You) of all the great rites, who can fathom what is yours?
> Devastatrix of the lands, you are lent wings by the storm.
> Beloved of Enlil, you fly about in the nation.
> You are at the service of the decrees of An.
> Oh my lady, at the sound of you the lands bow down.
> When mankind comes before you
> In fear and trembling at (your) tempestuous radiance,
> They receive from you their just deserts.
> Proffering a song of lamentation, they weep before you,
> They walk toward you along the path of the house of all the great sighs.
> In the van of battle everything is struck down by you.
> Oh my lady, (propelled) on your own wings, you peck away (at the land).
> In the guise of a charging storm you charge.
> With a roaring storm you roar.
> With Thunder you continually thunder.
> With all the evil winds you snort.
> Your feet are filled with restlessness.
> To (the accompaniment of) the harp of sighs you give vent to a dirge.
> O my lady, the Anunna, the great gods,

Fluttering like bats fly off from before you to the clefts,
They who dare not walk (?) in your terrible glance,
Who dare not proceed before your terrible countenance.[42]

In Enheduanna's hymn, Inanna elicits awe. Her presence is overwhelming, her actions often furious. Near the end of her hymn, Inanna's priestess declares:

That you are lofty as Heaven (An)—be it known!
That you are broad as earth—be it known!
That you devastate the rebellious land—be it known!
That you roar at the land—be it known!
That you smite the heads—be it known!
That you devour cadavers like a dog—be it known!
That your glance is terrible—be it known!
That you lift your terrible glance—be it known!
That your glance is flashing—be it known!
. . . .
That you attain victory—be it known!
. . . .
O my lady, beloved of An, I have verily recounted your fury![43]

In another hymn, the poet speaks of Inanna's "troubled heart" and depicts the goddess as uncontrollably restless. She is associated with the extremes of the natural environment: storms and great heat. She is also associated with the eeriness of the night breezes and with the quaking of the earth. These are all the overflowings of her impetuous nature, her strong emotions.

Proud Queen of the Earth Gods, Supreme Among the Heaven Gods,
Loud Thundering Storm, you pour your rain over all the lands and all the
    people.
You make the heavens tremble and the earth quake.
Great Priestess, who can soothe your troubled heart?

You flash like lightning over the highlands; you throw your firebrand
    across the earth.
Your deafening command, whistling like the South Wind, splits apart
    great mountains.

Inanna, detail from cylinder-seal impression. Oriental Institute, University of Chicago.

> You trample the disobedient like a wild bull; heaven and earth tremble.
> Holy Priestess, who can soothe your troubled heart?
> Your frightful cry descending from the heavens devours its victims.
> Your quivering hand causes the midday heat to hover over the sea.
> Your nighttime stalking of the heavens chills the land with its dark
> breeze.
> Holy Inanna, the riverbanks overflow with the flood-waves of your
> heart.[44]

Inanna's violent nature is clearly seen in her love of battle. She does not seem attracted primarily by the skills, or even the cunning, of war and combat but by the emotion and blood lust of it.

> Lordly queen of the awesome *me*, garbed in fear, who rides the great *me*,
> Inanna, you who have perfected the *a-ankara* weapon, who are covered
> with its blood,

Who storm about in great battles, who step upon shields,
Who initiate the flood-storm,
Great queen Inanna who are knowledgeable in planning combat,

. . . .

Like a lion you roared in heaven and earth, you smote the flesh of the
people,
Like a big wild-ox you stood up eager to battle the inimical *kur*,
Like an awesome lion you annihilated with your venom the hostile and
the disobedient.[45]

For the Sumerians, battle was known as "the dance of Inanna."[46] In the tumult, fury, fear, and slaughter, Inanna's presence was made forcefully known. In the following hymn, she describes herself as the very heart of battle, as the one who goads the combatants on into the fray.

When I stand in the front (line) of battle
I am the leader of all the lands,
when I stand at the opening of the battle,
I am the quiver ready to hand,
When I stand in the midst of the battle,
I am the heart of the battle,
the arm of the warriors,
when I begin moving at the end of the battle,
I am an evilly rising flood,
when I follow in the wake of the battle,
I am the woman (exhorting the stragglers):
"Get going! Close (with the enemy!)"[47]

Descent to the Underworld

Perhaps Inanna's most famous myth, and the most perplexing as well, is the story of her descent to the underworld. At the beginning of the story,[48] we are told that Inanna turns her attention to the netherworld and decides to go there, a most unusual decision, because only the dead travel and dwell there. She dresses in her finest royal garments and adornments and with her faithful servant, the female Ninshubur, approaches the underworld. Before arriving, however, she instructs Ninshubur on what to do in the event that she does not return in three days. Leaving Ninshubur in the upper world, Inanna arrives at the gates of the netherworld and hammers on them for admittance. The gatekeeper is told by the queen of the underworld, Ereshkigal, who is angry at the news of Inanna's arrival, to admit the goddess of the upper world. As Inanna passes through the seven gates of Ereshkigal's domain, she is gradually stripped of all her robes and finery. When she comes before Ereshkigal's throne she is stripped bare and made to crouch down. For Inanna, this is a complete humiliation. However, the spirited goddess still has plenty of fight left in her. She rushes at Ereshkigal, pulls her off her throne, and sits upon it herself. Ereshkigal's powerful companions, the Anunnaki gods, however, coldly sentence Inanna to death; when Ereshkigal looks on her with the eye of death, Inanna dies. She is unceremoniously hung on a peg and turns into a rotting piece of putrid meat.

After three days Ninshubur, following her mistress's instruction, begins mourning ceremonies and seeks the help of the gods Enlil and Nanna, neither of whom is able to help her rescue Inanna. When Ninshubur asks the god Enki for his help, however, she is successful. Enki fashions two expert mourners and instructs them on the way to enter the netherworld undetected. He also tells them how to ingratiate themselves with Ereshkigal and gives them the waters of life with which they might revive the dead Inanna. When Ereshkigal, flattered by the mourners' attentions to her, offers them a blessing, they ask for Inanna's body. Although Ereshkigal offers them other boons instead, the mourners are persistent; having been given Inanna's body, they revive her with the waters of life. Before Inanna can gain permission to leave the underworld, however, she is told that she must provide a substitute for herself.

Inanna then leaves to return to the upper world accompanied by guardians from the netherworld, who are described as an unruly, wild group with no benevolent feelings. These are messengers of death who have been released into the world of the living along with the resurrected Inanna. Every person Inanna meets is suggested as a substitute for Inanna by the guardians, but she refuses each person when she learns that he or she has mourned and lamented her recent death. It is not until she discovers that her husband/lover Dumuzi has not mourned her absence that she consents to have him take her place in the land of the dead. Dumuzi's sister, Geshtinanna, out of compassion for her brother, agrees to spend half the year there in his place, and so Dumuzi is ordained to spend half the year in the world of the living and half in the land of the dead.

One likely meaning of this myth concerns cycles of vegetation and Inanna's early identification with the spirit of the storehouse in which food was kept for the long, relatively barren winter months. Inanna's disappearance from the world marks the withering of vegetation and probably corresponded to the searing summer heat of Mesopotamia, which dries up most plant life. Indeed, in the Babylonian version of this myth, in which the goddess Ishtar is the protagonist, it is said that when the goddess descended to the underworld sexual desire and fertility left the world.[49] The disrobing and stripping of Inanna, furthermore, might be an allusion to the gradual emptying of the storehouse during the months between harvests. The revival of Inanna with the waters and grasses of life is probably an allusion to the return of cool, wet weather and the revival of vegetation.[50]

Inanna's return to the land of the living and the necessity of finding a substitute for her to appease the powers of the underworld also suggest that Mesopotamian culture, like others,[51] perceived a clear connection between the powers of fertility that produced food and the reality of death and decay. For Inanna to return to the land of the living, for the power of fertility and abundance to reappear in the world, a sacrifice or substitution had to be made. The powers of fertility, growth, and abundance had to be fed, as it were, nourished by the death of a powerful being, in this case, Dumuzi. The myth of Inanna's descent also may suggest the connection, understood in many agricultural societies, between death, burial, and new life.[52] For crops to reappear one must first bury the seeds of the old, "murdered" crop in the ground. For Inanna to reinvigorate herself, she must descend to the underworld; she must die in order to be reborn fresh and strong.

Another quite different way of interpreting Inanna's descent to the underworld is as a journey of discovery or self-discovery on the part of the goddess. In this interpretation, Inanna's decision to leave her own domain and to explore unknown territory might be understood as a personal quest for self-knowledge, a descent into, or a journey to, the unconscious, which is equivalent to a kind of death and rebirth for the individual as he or she is initiated into the mysteries of the unconscious world.[53] In this approach to the myth, Ereshkigal is Inanna's subconscious self, who, once known, can be overcome and used to provide new power with which Inanna can assert a more complete and encompassing identify. Inanna's descent, during which she is stripped of all shreds of her former identity, represents the individual's searching beyond or going beyond inherited social identities that are not inherent to one's real identity, which is to be found only within one's own deepest recesses.[54]

Personal Savior

Inanna, the mighty queen of heaven and earth, the impetuous goddess of fertility and sex, the violent goddess of nature and battle, was also approached by her devotees for help in daily affairs. In this aspect she played the role of personal savior. In the following poem, Inanna's gracious response to the pleas of King Ishme-Dagan is specified in detail:

The Queen of the searching eye, the guide of the land, the all-

compassionate,
Removed from that man the bruising cane that had been laid upon him,
Attacking on his behalf the demons of disease and sickness, she extirpated them from that man,
The whip that had been laid cruelly upon him she made into a cloth bandage,
She made the silver-ore as bright as good silver, purified it,
She gazed upon him with joyous heart, gave him life,
She returned him to the gracious hand of his god,
Placed the ever-present good angels at his head,
Had Utu provide him with truth, dressed him with it like a lion,
Blessed his womb, gave him an heir,
Gave him a spouse who bore him a son, spread wide his stalls and sheepfolds.
Gave him a faithful household, decreed a sweet fate for him.[55]

There are several examples of Ishtar's protective, motherly roles vis-à-vis certain Babylonian rulers. She told the king Esarhaddon in an oracle: "I was the senior midwife (at) your (birth)" and "I am your kindly wetnurse."[56] When Ashurbanipal, frightened at the prospect of being attacked by the king of Elam, sought her help, she is said to have had compassion for him and to have appeared to him saying: "You (better) stay here where you are, eat food, drink dark beer, make merry and praise my godhead while I go and do that job and achieve your heart's desire—your face shall not blanch, your legs not tremble, you shall not (have to) wipe off your sweat in the midst of battle."[57] She is then said to treat him like a child, coddling him in the crook of her arm and protecting him.[58]

In another hymn, a priest intercedes on behalf of one of Ishtar's devotees and asks her to have pity and accept her devotee's admission of wrongdoing.

Ishtar, who but you can clear a path for him?
Hear his entreaties!
He has turned to you and seeks you.
Your servant who has sinned, have mercy on him!
He has bowed down and loudly implored you.
For the wrongs he committed he shouts a psalm of penance.[59]

In the following hymn, the goddess's devotee describes himself as physically sick, troubled at heart, and cursed with inauspicious portents. He pleads for her to take pity on him and end his sufferings.

> I have cried to thee, (I) thy suffering, wearied,
> distressed servant,
> See me, O my lady, accept my prayers!
> Faithfully look upon me and hear my supplication!
> Say "A pity!" about me, and let thy mood be eased.
> "A pity!" about my wretched body
> that is full of disorders and troubles,
> "A pity!" about my sore heart
> that is full of tears and sobbings,
> "A pity!" about my wretched, disordered,
> and troubled portents,
> "A pity!" about my house, kept sleepless,
> which mourns bitterly,
> "A pity!" about my moods,
> which are steadily of tears and sobbings.[60]

Despite her lofty title and queenly roles, then, the goddess Inanna/Ishtar is often petitioned by individual devotees to help them in their specific troubles. It is clear from the above hymns that she was seen by at least some people as a tenderhearted deity who could be moved to compassion by the pitiable plight of a particular human being.

Impetuous Energy and Power

It is not at all surprising that a goddess who was worshiped for approximately thirty-five hundred years had a variety of characteristics and roles. Indeed, one of Inanna's epithets is "lady of myriad offices."[61] Nevertheless, at the core of her character there seems to be an impetuousness that manifests itself in great, often unrefined, power, energy, and exuberance. Inanna is associated consistently and unambiguously with sex and vigor and often with war and natural violence. She usually plays roles that portray great emotion: lover, bride, widow. She is rarely described in the roles of helpmate, wife, or mother. She is not a patient, responsible type of being.[62] As queen of heaven and earth, a title suggesting a rather dignified, sober, and responsible position, she is often described as acting violently, aggressively, or impetuously. She is, in short, identified with life in all its rambunctious, teeming, vigorous manifestations and bubblings. As such, she is tireless, fresh, often tumultuous, and always restless.

Chapter **7**

Athena, Goddess of Culture and Civilization

I . . . sing of Pallas Athene, the glorious goddess, bright-eyed, inventive, unbending of heart, pure virgin, saviour of cities, courageous. . . . From his awful head wise Zeus himself bare her arrayed in warlike arms of flashing gold, and awe seized all the gods as they gazed. But Athene sprang quickly from the immortal head and stood before Zeus who holds the aegis, shaking a sharp spear: great Olympus began to reel horribly at the might of the bright-eyed goddess, and earth round about cried fearfully, and the sea was moved and tossed with dark waves, while foam burst forth suddenly; the bright Son of Hyperion stopped his swift-footed horses a long while, until the maiden Pallas Athene had stripped the heavenly armour from her immortal shoulders. And wise Zeus was glad.[1]

Introduction

The goddess Athena was one of the most popular deities of classical Greece. She was well known for hundreds of years and appears as a prominent goddess in the works of many classical writers. She was counted among the group of powerful and popular deities known as the twelve Olympians[2] and was particularly close to her father, Zeus, king of the gods. Athena was closely identified with the city of Athens, where her most famous temple, the Parthenon, was located. In her role as guardian of Athens, she was associated with the arts of war. As the embodiment of civilization, she was associated with domestic skills. Throughout her history she is described as a virgin. Although she inspired male heroes to deeds of valor and discovery, she never had sexual relations with them. She is described consistently as an independent deity who refuses to submerge her identity in that of a male through sexual liaison or marriage. Athena also is associated with wisdom, an attribute of Zeus. Her

Head of Athena Lemnia by Pheidias, Roman copy, ca. 440 B.C.E. Museo Civico, Bologna. Gisela M. A. Richter, *A Handbook of Greek Art* (London: Phaidon Press, 1959), pl. 154, p. 121.

"mother" was Metis (whose name means intelligence or wisdom),[3] and Athena sometimes is said to have inherited from her a practical sagacity and intelligence. Athena also has some connection with procreation and fertility. She is the protector of and promoter of marriage and is associated with the olive tree. In her mythology, however, she is rarely spoken of as a mother or as a deity associated with fertility. She is primarily described as a martial maiden, the inventor and protector of culture, she who inspires and accompanies heroes in their adventures, and a virgin who disdains the traditional female roles of mother and wife because they would restrict her active participation in politics, war, and public life generally.

Early Background

Several distinctive characteristics of the goddess Athena make it very likely that she has roots in Minoan and Mycenaean culture and religion.[4] These were quite sophisticated city cultures located in Crete and the Greek mainland and preceded the migration of the Greeks into this area sometime during the second half of the second millennium B.C.E. Prominent in Minoan-Mycenaean religion was a goddess who often was associated with, or took the form of, a snake and guarded palaces or large houses. In its association with the earth and the nether regions within the earth, the snake may have been identified with fertility (especially the fertility of the lineage) and with the ancestors of the palace.[5] The Minoan-Mycenaean palace goddess also was associated with birds.[6] Athena is strongly identified with both snakes and birds. In many images and descriptions of Athena, she is adorned with snakes, and there are indications that Athenians believed that Athena lived on the Acropolis in the form of a snake.[7] Athena also is associated with birds, particularly the owl, and is sometimes said to take the form of birds.[8]

Although the palace goddess in Minoan Crete did not have martial aspects, the more warlike Mycenaean kings who lived in fortified strongholds did depict their guardian goddess holding a shield. Athena is typically shown holding a shield, and several scholars have not hesitated to refer to the Mycenaean shield-bearing goddess as "a forerunner of Athena."[9] It also is tempting to find in the Minoan-Mycenaean palace goddess a forerunner of Athena in terms of what seems to have been one of her central functions, namely, guarding a specific locality. The Minoan-Mycenaean goddess, like Athena, seems to have been a tutelary goddess who embodied and was embedded in a particular place: a house, palace, or city. In short, Athena, that most Greek of Greek goddesses, probably embodies important aspects and characteristics of an ancient, pre-Greek divinity. In some respects, Athena suggests an archaic tradition that is strongly related to Greek geography (as distinct from Greek culture) and that ties her symbolism and cult to the earth and fertility, ties only weakly hinted at in her mythology.

Athena may have had roots in the ancient Greek tradition itself (the tradition of the Indo-Europeans who migrated into Greece in the latter half of the second millennium B.C.E.). Although exceedingly little is known about the religion and culture of these people prior to their establishment in Greece, it has been suggested that Athena may hark back to a warlike maiden goddess. In discussing the common epithet of Athena, Pallas, which he says is probably a Greek term meaning "girl," W. K. C. Guthrie says: "This makes it likely that the invading Greeks themselves had a maiden goddess, who considering their way of life may well have been a martial, Valkyrie-like figure, and that they identified her with the ancient powerful native goddess when hellenic and aboriginal civilizations came into contact."[10]

Athena and the City of Athens

A consistent theme in the mythology and cult of Athena is her identification with the city of Athens. Some scholars consider this association to have been geographical originally, Athena being the spirit who was associated with, or who lived upon, the mountainous rock, the Acropolis, which dominates the city of Athens. "The Akropolis at Athens was originally called *Athene*, a place-name comparable with the pre-Greek *Mykene*, *Pallene*, *Mitylene*, *Priene*, etc. . . . The goddess was named *Athene* like the rock, because at the outset she *was* the rock, the mountain-mother of the usual Anatolian sort."[11] As the spirit of the place upon which the city of Athens develops, Athena, then, is understood to have preceded the city. The city is an extension of her, as it were, something that spreads and grows from the sacred center, the Acropolis, which is not only the dwelling of the goddess but the goddess herself. She *is* the city in a physical sense.

Athena also is implicated in the birth and nurturing of an early Athenian king (the first king in some accounts),[12] Erichthonius (or sometimes Erechtheus, who in some accounts of the story is the grandson of Erichthonius). The god Hephaestus tries to seduce Athena, but she resists him. He spills his semen on her thigh, and she, in disgust, wipes it off with a rag and throws it on the ground. The earth then becomes pregnant. The infant Erichthonius is born, and Athena takes responsibility for raising and nurturing him in her temple. When he matures, Erichthonius is made king and introduces worship of the gods and inaugurates state government. In this myth, Athena is cast in the role of nurturer and tutor to the founder of Athens. An intimate relationship is described in which the goddess helps bring into being an able and qualified leader, who establishes civic law and governmental structures.[13]

Another myth that features Athena as the reigning deity of the city of Athens involves a contest between her and the god Poseidon to determine who will rule the city. The two deities meet on the Acropolis, and Poseidon creates a

Athena and Poseidon, ca. 540 B.C.E. Bibliothèque Nationale, Paris. John Boardman et al., *The Art and Architecture of Ancient Greece* (London: Thames & Hudson, 1967), pl. 115.

saltwater spring by striking the ground with his trident. Athena, in turn, creates the olive tree. Her creation is deemed more useful to the Athenians (the olive tree became the basis of their economy), and Athena is declared ruler of the city.[14] This myth of a divine contest may suggest a rivalry or tension between people engaged in a seafaring and fishing economy and people engaged in land-based economies, such as agriculture, horticulture, and animal husbandry. Athena then would be associated with the latter, at least in this particular myth.

Athena's creation of the olive tree suggests two important aspects of her nature. Athena's gift to Athens, the olive tree, is practical, forming the basis of its economy. In contrast to Poseidon, whose feat is impressive but of no practical value, Athena acts in a way that creates and supports culture, that makes civilized existence possible. Her creation of the olive tree also suggests her association with vegetation and fertility. An olive tree was known to grow on the Acropolis (and was believed to be the very tree Athena created) and was revered as a manifestation of Athena herself. Its miraculous vigor was suggested in its great age and its ability to recover quickly if damaged.

Although Athena is not usually or typically represented as a goddess associated with fertility in classical Greek mythology, an archaic strand in her makeup links her to an earth-mother type of deity, which is quite in harmony with her role as guardian of Athens. In one story, the women of Elis pray to Athena to make them fertile when their husbands return after a long absence. The women subsequently become fruitful.[15] There are examples of images of Athena holding a pomegranate in her right hand. The pomegranate is usually a symbol of fertility and probably suggests Athena's role in providing agricultural produce.[16] Another image of Athena shows her holding the cornucopia.[17] In speaking of the image of Athena that was worshiped in the northern sanctuary of the Acropolis, one scholar refers to her as a "farmer's goddess, the peaceful mother of the fruits and the offspring of the land,"[18] whose "chief original function was to watch over the increase of the land."[19]

Athena's association with Athens, however, is not based primarily on her powers of fertility and growth, which, in fact, are rarely emphasized in her myths and character. In Aristides' sketch of her character, it is said that "cities are the gifts of Athena."[20] Athena's intimate relationship with Athens (which may be taken as a symbol of cities per se in many cases), and her role as protector of other cities as well,[21] has to do far more with her identification with culture and civilization than with nature. As the centers of culture, as places where culture and civilization are distilled, refined, and concentrated, cities are Athena's natural dwelling places. Indeed, it is her presence that inspires and engenders Athens, and other cities, in the first place. In her role as a citifying presence, Athena often is associated with political structures, the administration of justice, and the arts of persuasion, such as rhetoric.[22] She represents practicality, normality, and rationality, qualities useful, even necessary, for the building and maintaining of cities.

She is associated with humane rule as well. In the trial of Orestes for the murder of his mother, Clytemnestra, Athena establishes a court of justice in which democratic voting by leading citizens decides the fate of the accused, thereby doing away with the archaic and disruptive law of blood revenge.[23]

It is probably in her role as the protector of cities and civilization that Athena's association with weddings, marriages, and children should be understood. She herself, of course, never marries and shows no sexual interest in males. Furthermore, she is only a reluctant foster mother in the case of Erichthonius. In her role as guardian of weddings, marriage, and children, Athena acts primarily in defense of culture and not as a source of fecund power.[24] "Athene . . . is not a goddess of procreation, but of creation."[25] Her association with children is not in terms of childbirth but of "caring for young children and their socialization."[26] Unlike Hera, Zeus's wife, who embodies married life and the marital role of women, Athena is not interested in the intrinsic value of marriage and the procreation of children. Rather, the institution of marriage provides the proper setting for the nurturing, education, and civilizing of children and is therefore necessary to the well-being and survival of the state and city. It also has been suggested that Athena's protection and promotion of the institution of marriage was in defense of a patriarchal society that demanded a carefully structured and restricted marriage institution in order to provide reliable male heirs.[27] Athena's interest in marriage and children is not as a wife or mother but as a defender of the social order.

Athena, then, personifies or embodies the spirit of Athens as the expression of ideal civilized human existence. She expresses what the Athenians thought about their city (and about culture) ideally. Speaking of her worship during the age of Pericles (495–429 B.C.E.), one author has said about Athena: "To the Pericleans . . . Athena *is* Athens; the best that Athens stands for. Athena's attributes, victorious prowess in war, intelligence, love of the arts, are precisely the attributes of the Athenian people as Pericles describes them. . . . In this sense, every thinking Athenian who had been fired by the Periclean ideal 'believed in' Athena."[28]

Athena's association with Athens in her role as inaugurator and protector of culture is also dramatically suggested in the four main scenes pictured on the outer walls of the Parthenon, her famous temple on the Acropolis. On the north side of the temple, the fall of Troy was depicted; on the west, the battle between the Greeks and Amazons; on the south, the battle of the Lapthis and the Centaurs; and on the east, the battle of the gods and the giants. The main theme here for the Athenians was "civilization overcomes barbarism."[29] Athena represented enlightened, sophisticated, refined, city life; she was the enemy of anything crude, uncivilized, or barbaric.

The Warrior Goddess

Of Pallas Athene, guardian of the city, I begin to sing. Dread is she, and with Ares she loves deeds of war, the sack of cities and the shouting and the battle. It is she who saves the people as they go out to war and come back.

Hail, goddess, and give us good fortune with happiness![30]

Head of Athena by Euboulides, marble, 150–100 B.C.E. National Archaeological Museum, Athens. J. J. Pollitt, *Art in the Hellenistic Age* (Cambridge: Cambridge University Press, 1986), pl. 169, p. 167. Reproduced by courtesy of the Trustees of the British Museum.

Athena, Aegina, temple of Aphaia, ca. 500–480 B.C.E. K. Papaioannou, *L'Art et la civilisation de la Grèce ancienne. L'Art grec* (Paris: Editions d'art Lucien Mazenrod, 1972), pl. 86, facing p. 261.

Athena is often associated with war and battle. She typically is shown wearing a helmet, holding a large shield in one hand and a poised spear in the other, and striding forward in an aggressive attitude. Her warlike nature is suggested in the story of her birth. Athena is born directly from the head of Zeus. In agony over a terrible headache, Zeus summons Hephaestus to relieve him. The smithy god splits Zeus's head open, and Athena springs forth, fully armed, brandishing a spear. In his *Theogony*, Hesiod calls her a "waker of battle noise, leader of armies / goddess queen who delights in war cries, / onslaughts and battles."[31] Pindar says that at her birth she gave forth "an earth-shattering battle-cry, so that the heavens shook and the mother earth."[32]

Athena's warlike aspect is related to her role as guardian of Athens and protector of civilization. The enemies of the Greeks, such as the Persians, were undoubtedly understood to be barbarians bent on the destruction of civilized life. In her protection of civilization, it is only natural that Athena would assume a warlike demeanor.

There may be a more archaic tradition in Athena's warrior role, however. This is suggested in her rather gruesome attire, the serpent-ringed aegis, which seems to have been the skin of a goat, and the head of the Gorgon Medusa, a mythical demon, which was fastened to the aegis. The practice of sacrificing animals (sometimes maidens) before battle to ensure victory was fairly common in Greece. At the end of the battle, if victory was attained, a restitution to the sacrificial victim was made by setting up a stake with a captured enemy helmet, shield, and spear. Sometimes the skin of the sacrificial victim was added to this war trophy. "By adding to the tropaion the skin of the goat, the *aigis*, which had been slaughtered before battle, the stake came to represent the goddess Athena with her helmet, shield, and aegis. The 'virgin' thus came into being through the battle, just as her symbolic substitute had been slaughtered in the preliminary sacrifice."[33]

This argument that relates Athena to sacrifice performed to ensure victory is lent credibility not only by images of Athena with a helmet, spear, shield, and aegis but by the story that during a tournament Athena once accidentally killed her companion, Pallas, daughter of her teacher, Triton. In memory of her beloved companion, Athena created a statue of herself in the likeness of Pallas. This style of image is called the Palladium and shows Athena in battle dress advancing with a raised spear.[34] It is also the case that one of Athena's popular forms is Athena Nike, Athena of Victory.

A certain, though not very strong, undercurrent of frenzy and passion in Athena's warlike aspect also suggests an archaic strand to her nature. Although she is almost always restrained in her actions, tempering practical cunning with passionate aggression, and is often said to be calm and controlled compared to the furious, raging Ares, god of war, there are hints that Athena has (or had) a wild aspect that was unleashed in battle. In the *Iliad*, for example, "Ares re-

Athena, the "Herculaneum Pallas," marble, probably a Roman copy of an original of the second century B.C.E. Archaeological Museum, Naples. J. J. Pollitt, *Art in the Hellenistic Age* (Cambridge: Cambridge University Press, 1986), pl. 193, p. 184. Reproduced by courtesy of the Trustees of the British Museum.

proaches Zeus for giving birth to such a daughter and describes at the same time her terrifying force in battle. In his rage he gives her the epithet *aphrōn* ('crazed,' 'frantic'), by which he calls into question any association she might have to prudence and wise counsel."[35] Athena's battle attire, especially the aegis ringed with serpents and the awful Gorgon's head that she wore on her breast, also suggests a frightening, gruesome aspect. "Her titles continually bear witness to her warlike character. In various places she is called Promachos (Champion), Sthenias (Mighty), Areia (Warlike, or Companion of Ares), and so forth."[36] And in one account of her birth she "leaps and dances a war-dance and shakes her shield, and brandishes her spear, and is filled with ecstasy."[37]

It is much more typical of Athena, however, to act with restraint, even in battle. Indeed, she is often shown as an enemy of Ares[38] and reveals a strong distaste for the gruesome, frenzied blood lust of battle. This is clear in the story of Tydeus, one of Athena's favorite heroes. So fond of him was she that when he lay dying on the battlefield she approached him with the potion of immortality, intending to make him divine. As she came near, however, Tydeus was tearing open the skull of a slain enemy to eat the victim's brain in a fit of cannibalistic frenzy. Athena was repulsed by the sight and abandoned Tydeus to death. In her eyes, his frenzy was a degradation and extremely offensive.[39]

Athena is much more likely to reveal herself in situations that demand clear thinking, the calming of emotions, and the restraint of violence. She is apt to appear when feelings of vengeance and blood lust are curbed and controlled. Very much in keeping with her role as an effective and prudent combatant is her appearance in the beginning of the *Iliad* when Agamemnon insults Achilles. Achilles feels rage rising within himself and reaches for his sword, intent upon slaying Agamemnon on the spot. At this point Athena appears to him, catching him by the hair from behind and making herself visible only to him. Achilles turns toward her and beholds her terribly shining eyes. She is not there to incite him, however. She has appeared to stay his hand. She counsels him to return Agamemnon's insult with words of his own but to resist his urge to violence.[40] In return for restraint, Athena promises him greater rewards in the future.

Athena's interest in war and battle, then, does not seem to be intrinsic. She does not fight and seek out battle for the thrill of it. She does not express herself most fully in the blood lust and tumult of battle and killing, as does Ares. For her, warfare is primarily political, tactical, and expedient—one way among others to obtain some goal or to protect some cherished value. She is more interested in the arts of war, the skillful use of weapons, and the strategy of war—the use of cunning and reason—than she is in the din and frenzy of violent struggle. Her presence in battle does not incite rage and fury; her presence incites courage and daring, tempered with control of the passions that can make a person reckless and vulnerable.

Heroic Inspiration

A striking characteristic of Athena is her affection for and close association with several important Greek heroes. She is not an aloof deity who dwells in a far-off heaven or in wild places far removed from the society of human beings. Athena is often found involved in the affairs of human society (in some ways she is a personification of society) and is frequently pictured as the helper and companion of heroic leaders and adventurers, who represent the human tendency to explore and civilize the world. She assists Perseus in his quest to obtain the head of the Gorgon Medusa, which he has promised as a wedding gift to his friend, Polydectes. Medusa's face is so fearful that anyone who glances upon it is turned to stone. Athena presents Perseus with a brightly polished shield and advises him to use it as a mirror in his fight with Medusa to avoid having to look directly upon her face. At the critical moment, Athena guides his hand when he cuts off Medusa's head.[41] Eventually, Perseus gives Athena the head of Medusa, which she fastens upon her aegis. Still capable of turning to stone anyone who looks upon it, the head functions as an awe-inspiring, powerful weapon for Athena.

Heracles, perhaps the most famous of all Greek heroes, is a special favorite of Athena's. Heracles is the son of Zeus by the human maiden Alcmene. Shortly after Heracles' birth, Alcmene abandons the child, fearing Hera's jealousy. In league with her father, Zeus, Athena takes Hera to the area where the child has been left and induces her to nurse the child, which will bestow immortality on him. Hera agrees, thereby symbolically adopting the child.[42] From the very beginning, then, Athena protects Heracles, and in many of his adventures she stands by him or comes to his aid. After Heracles slays envoys from King Erginus who have come to Thebes, Heracles' native city, to collect tribute, Erginus seeks to capture and slay Heracles. Heracles gathers his young companions to offer resistance, and they roam the city seeking weapons in temples where they have been stored as spoils from earlier battles. At this point, Athena appears and, "greatly admiring such resolution, girded these on him and on his friends."[43] After the battle, in gratitude for her help, Heracles dedicates two stone images to Athena the Girder-on-of-Arms.[44]

When the jealous Hera, who has learned that Zeus had fathered Heracles, drives Heracles mad, he begins to murder his own family thinking that they are his enemies. To stop him Athena knocks him out by hitting him on the head with a large rock.[45] Heracles is told by the Delphic oracle that he should submit himself to Eurystheus for twelve years, in reward for which he will be granted immortality. During his service to Eurystheus, Heracles performs his famous twelve labors. Most of these heroic exploits involve slaying a monster who has plagued the earth and its inhabitants in some fashion. When he seeks out the many-headed serpent monster, Hydra, Athena advises him to make Hydra emerge from her lair by shooting fire arrows at her, and then Athena tells him to hold his breath while fighting Hydra lest her evil odor overcome him.[46] When Heracles is commanded by Eurystheus to rid the world of the man-eating birds of the Stymphalian Marsh, he finds it impossible to approach close enough to make the birds take flight so that he can shoot them with his arrows. Athena appears and gives him brass castanets (or in some versions a rattle), which he bangs so loudly that the birds take to the air in terror and confusion and present easy targets for his arrows. It is Athena, too, who guides Heracles in his final heroic feat, the slaying of the dog Cerberus, who dwells in the underworld. She accompanies him down into the netherworld and helps him cross the river Styx.[47] In his battle against the city of Pylus, Athena and Heracles fight together against Hera, Poseidon, Hades, and Ares.[48] In another battle, Athena helps Heracles defeat Cycnus, who is supported by the war god, Ares. She advises Heracles before the battle not to slay Ares or deprive him of his horses or armor; that is, she counsels restraint on his part, sparing him the possible disaster of divine retribution.[49] At the end of his earthly adventures, Heracles is borne up to heaven by Zeus in a chariot, "where Athene took him by the hand and solemnly introduced him to her fellow deities."[50]

Although Heracles sometimes behaves in wild, furious ways and is stricken with periods of madness in which he commits terrible deeds, he plays primarily the role of slayer of monsters and protector against barbarism in those episodes in which Athena plays a role.[51] This is consistent with Athena's association and identification with culture and civilization. Heracles, in ridding the world of monsters who are wreaking havoc on the world, acts in defense of those things that Athena holds dear: rational social order, cultural refinement, and city life. Athena's association with and affection for Heracles (and other heroes) involves more than her interest in protecting civilization and culture, however. She is attracted by his extraordinary strength, daring, and adventuresome spirit. It is Heracles' spirit, which continually seems to break the bonds of ordinary human limitations and strives for divine greatness, that attracts the goddess and is also the mark of her presence.

> The grandeur which ennobles the deeds of Heracles and makes them the paradigm for the heroic course that conquers heaven is the expression of Athena's spirit. In poetry as in plastic art we see her ever at his side; she accompanies him upon his journeys, she helps him to encompass the superhuman, and finally she leads him into heaven. . . . Always she appears at the right moment as the true counsellor and helper of the almighty hero who proudly challenged monsters and paved his own path to the gods by glorious struggle.[52]

Athena's relationship with Odysseus emphasizes both her attraction for those of bold spirit and her role as wise counselor to those she befriends. When the Achaian army, which has been besieging Troy, loses heart and begins to talk of returning home, Odysseus, one of the Achaian leaders, despairs of being able to inspire his men to continue the fight. As with saddened heart Odysseus watches his men begin to prepare their ships for the return voyage, Athena appears beside him, having descended swiftly from heaven. Athena challenges Odysseus to speak individually to each of his men "and with thy gentle words refrain every man."[53] Odysseus recognizes Athena's voice and immediately does as she has advised. Going quickly among his men, speaking to them individually, calling upon their courage and steadfastness, he gradually begins to turn the tide of discontent and to instill resolve in them to see through the fight. Soon the men cease to prepare the ships for the return voyage and sit down, waiting to hear the issue debated. When his turn comes to address the army, Odysseus rises. "And by his side bright-eyed Athene in the likeness of a herald bade the multitude keep silence, that the sons of the Achaians, both the nearest and the farthest, might hear his words together and give heed to his counsel."[54] Inspired by Athena's counsel, Odysseus is able to persuade the army to remain.

A particularly intimate scene between Athena and Odysseus takes place when he finally returns home after his adventures. He is washed ashore and does not recognize his native land at first. When Athena appears to him in the guise of a shepherd boy, he refuses to identify himself, claiming that he is a Cretan sailor who has been cast ashore because of a crime he committed. Having listened to his artful lies, Athena reveals herself to him.

> The goddess, gray-eyed Athene, smiled on him,
> and stroked him with her hand, and took on the shape of a woman
> both beautiful and tall, and well versed in glorious handiworks,
> and spoke aloud to him and addressed him in winged words, saying:
> "It would be a sharp one, and a stealthy one, who would ever get past
> you in any contriving; even if it were a god against you.
> You wretch, so devious, never weary of tricks, then you would not
> even in your own country give over your ways of deceiving
> and your thievish tales. They are near to you in your very nature.
> But come, let us talk no more of this, for you and I both know
> sharp practice, since you are far the best of all mortal
> men for counsel and stories, and I among all the divinities
> am famous for wit and sharpness; and yet you never recognized
> Pallas Athene, daughter of Zeus, the one who is always

standing beside you and guarding you in every endeavor. . . . "

. . . .

"Always you are the same, and such is the mind within you,
and so I cannot abandon you when you are unhappy,
because you are fluent, and reason closely, and keep your head always. . . . "[55]

After convincing him that he is, indeed, back in his native land, Athena suggests that they discuss how he should return to his wife and home so as to defeat the many suitors who have come to lodge in his dwelling in the hope of seducing his wife, Penelope. "The two sat down against the trunk of the hallowed olive / and plotted out the destruction of the overmastering suitors."[56] Listening to her wise counsel, and grateful for her advice, Odysseus praises Athena with these words:

"Surely I was on the point of perishing by an evil
fate in my palace, like Atreus' son Agamemnon, unless
you had told me, goddess, the very truth of all that has happened.
Come then, weave the design, the way I shall take my vengeance
upon them; stand beside me, inspire me with strength and courage,
as when together we brought down Troy's shining coronal.
For if in your fury, O gray-eyed goddess, you stood beside me,
I would fight, lady and goddess, with your help against three hundred
men if you, freely and in full heart, would help me."[57]

When Odysseus returns home and eventually engages his wife's suitors, Athena aids him by making the suitors' spears miss their mark and by bewildering them when she waves her aegis.[58] Taking the form of a swallow, she "flew twittering around the hall until every one of the suitors and their supporters lay dead."[59]

What attracts Athena is exceptional courage combined with cunning and skill, in short, the hero who has the daring and ability to attempt what others dare not, and to succeed in his attempt despite all obstacles. Indeed, Athena *is* that quality of heroism; she instills heroism in her favorites and encourages, inspires, and sustains those whom she befriends. "What Athena shows man, what she desires of him, and what she inspires him to, is boldness, will to victory, courage. . . . She is the ever-near whose word and whose lightning glance encounter the hero at the right moment and summon him to his most intelligent and manly prowess."[60]

Athena Lemnia, marble replica of a bronze statue by Pheidias from before 450 B.C.E. Dresden Staatliche Kunstsammlungen. John Boardman et al., *The Art and Architecture of Ancient Greece* (London: Thames & Hudson, 1967), pl. 200.

The Counselor

One of Athena's most distinctive features is evident in her relations with heroes: her tendency to employ wisdom, knowledge, and cunning in bending events in directions that she favors. She is reluctant to use brute force and passion in battle, and just as reluctant to use her physical charms in dealing with males. Her way of achieving success is through reason, intelligence, and skill. Her natural rivals among the gods are Ares,[61] the passionate, impulsive god of war, and Aphrodite, the goddess of sexual passion and lust.

Athena's association with intelligence and reason is expressed in the story concerning her birth from the head of Zeus. Zeus chooses the goddess Metis, whose name means "thought," as his first wife. Hesiod describes her as "wisest among gods and mortal men."[62] After being warned that Metis will produce a child who will be greater than he, however, Zeus swallows Metis to prevent his own possible downfall. Metis, in the meantime, has conceived, and the embryo survives and grows to term in Zeus's head. Eventually Athena is born directly from his head when Hephaestus splits it open to relieve Zeus of his monumental headache. In this myth, Athena's association with intelligence and rationality is doubly emphasized. Although Metis's maternity is attenuated, Athena does have her mother's superior intelligence. Her birth from Zeus's head probably is also meant to stress her association with rationality rather than passion and emotion.[63] This is in direct contrast to Aphrodite, preeminently associated with emotion and sexual passion, who is born from the foam caused when Cronos castrates his father, Uranus, and throws his genitals into the sea.[64] Although Athena is not without emotion in some contexts, she is much more prone to rely on her sagacity and intelligence in dealing with a problem.

One of Athena's most common descriptions is "bright eyed" (*glaukopis*), and this probably relates to her intelligence. Her association with the owl, whose large, luminous eyes are so striking, also might be understood as suggesting her intelligent nature. Commenting upon Athena as bright eyed and sharp eyed, Walter Otto says: "When we imagine the presence of the goddess, this spirit of brightest vigilance which grasps with lightning speed what the instant requires, which always and with serenity never troubled devises counsel and encounters the most difficult tasks with poised and ready energy—we can think of no better mark and symbol for such a being than the bright and luminous glance of the eye."[65]

The attribute "of many counsels" that characterizes Athena does not describe a goddess of brooding introspection. The knowledge or wisdom of which she is mistress is not esoteric, magical, or transcendent. Her knowledge is practical, tending toward the clever and cunning. She knows how to accomplish things successfully. Her intelligence is useful and pragmatic, not mysterious and otherworldly. She is the companion and counselor of heroes, not mystics.

Her intelligence and knowledge are applied to the worldly concerns of defeating representatives of chaos, such as the various monsters that Heracles defeats, and establishing civilization and the arts of civilization.

> Athena exemplifies the value of *mētis*. . . . In Athena's case *mētis* implies arts and crafts (including women's domestic ones), masculine skills, such as shipbuilding and carpentry, and, more generally, all manner of skill, persuasiveness, and courteous or appropriate deceit in conversation or public debate or other types of verbal exchange. The idea of skill in word and deed was one of the most integral values in the civilization of the ancient Greeks, who contrasted themselves with both barbarian peoples and wild nature by virtue of possessing it.[66]

Athena and the Arts of Civilization

Athena's role as creator and protector of civilization and her character as the giver of practical knowledge and skill are evident in her association with domestic arts and the skills of civilization. As mentioned earlier when discussing Athena's role as guardian of Athens, she is associated with the olive tree and its cultivation, which formed a central place in Athenian economy. She also is associated with the discovery of agriculture in general. Aristides says that Athena taught human beings to use the plow.[67] In some places, Athena was worshiped as Athena Boarmia, the "yoker of oxen."[68]

Although Athena seems to have been depicted most commonly in warlike garb, with shield, helmet, and spear, many of her images showed her holding a spindle.[69] She was famous for (and jealous of) her artistry as a weaver, which is emphasized in the story of Arachne. Arachne also became famous for her ability to weave, but when her art rivaled Athena's in its beauty, Athena transformed her into a spider.[70] Athena is said to have given Odysseus's wife, Penelope, superior skill in weaving and to have woven the robe that Hera wears to seduce Zeus.[71] Athena is eminently dexterous and is said to teach young girls "skill in handiwork."[72]

Athena inspired and founded many other practical arts of civilization. The *Iliad* says that Athena instructs those who have mastered shipbuilding[73] and is fond of those who practice this art.[74] When the hero, Jason, is preparing to embark on his adventures, Athena appears and fits a special beam on the prow of his ship.[75] Her association with shipbuilding emphasizes her interest both in extending economic dominion over the seas and in furthering human exploration and discovery, both important aspects of the establishment and extension of civilization.

Athena taught humans the art of the wheelwright. "She first taught earthly craftsmen to make chariots of war and cars variously wrought with bronze."[76] Those who make vessels of silver and gold are said to be her disciples.[77] The strongest plow is one made when "one of Athena's handmen has fixed in the share-beam and fastened it to the pole with dowels."[78] Athena also was propitiated by potters. "Come, then, Athena, with hand upraised over the kiln. Let the pots and all the dishes turn out well and be well fired."[79] Athena also is implicated in taming horses. In the myth of Bellerophon's taming of Pegasus, the winged horse, Athena gives the hero a bridle with which to subdue the horse, while some versions of the myth say that she presented Pegasus to Bellerophon already bridled.[80]

On the Acropolis of Athens during the classical age, two temples housed images of Athena. The southern sanctuary, the Parthenon, contained the famous image of Pheidias, which was thirty feet tall and showed Athena fully armed and standing.[81] In the northern sanctuary, however, the image of Athena "was eminently a *peaceful* goddess. Her statue certainly showed her unarmed but for the aegis, and probably seated. Further, it was made of olive-wood, and draped with a robe of wool: and much else about her suggests that her chief original function was to watch over the increase of the land."[82] This peaceful, and older, image of Athena emphasized her concern with the order necessary for civilization, in which the arts that she so dearly loved herself and that she inspired could flourish. This peaceful goddess is more at home with the concentration of the artist and artisan at work than she is on the battlefield. In Greek mythology, Athena may make her most dramatic appearances on the battlefield or in scenes of high adventure, but her presence also was felt and acknowledged in the less dramatic settings where the arts and crafts of culture were taught and practiced.

Virginity

One of Athena's most famous epithets is Parthenos, "the virgin." She is not inclined to marriage or to sexual love. Although she prefers to associate with males, especially heroic men of courage, imagination, and intelligence, she is never depicted as having romantic or sexual feelings toward those whom she befriends. In the Homeric hymn to Aphrodite, Athena is said to be one of three goddesses (the other two are Artemis, virgin goddess of the hunt, and Hestia, goddess of the home and hearth) who are immune to the influence of Aphrodite, whose presence arouses sexual desire and love. In that hymn, the poet says that Athena "has no pleasure in the deeds of golden Aphrodite, but delights . . . in strifes and battles and in preparing famous crafts."[83]

Athena is often described as a fair, striking woman, and there are indications that she is proud of her beauty. When Paris is selected by Zeus to judge which of the three goddesses, Athena, Hera, or Aphrodite, is the fairest, Athena does not hesitate to compete in the impromptu beauty contest. Nor does she

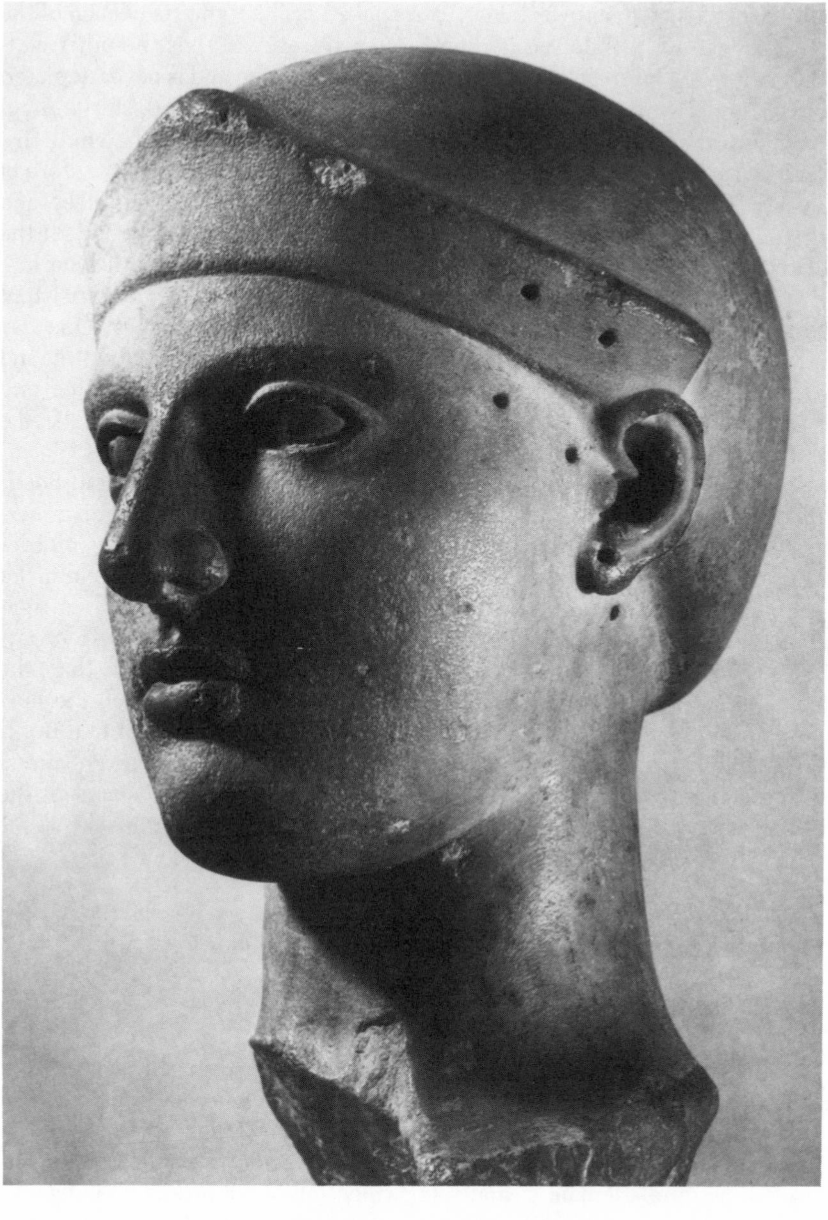

Athena, island of Aegina, middle fifth century B.C.E. Musée du Louvre, Paris. K. Papaioannou, *L'Art et la civilisation de la Grèce ancienne. L'Art grec* (Paris: Editions d'art Lucien Mazenrod, 1972), pl. 123, facing p. 296.

indicate reluctance to appear before Paris naked, as he requests of each of the three goddesses.[84] While she is proud of her beauty vis-à-vis the other goddesses, she is not interested in attracting sexual attention and is never depicted flaunting her charms or beauty in order to influence men. Indeed, she is antagonistic toward any man who shows sexual interest in her and can be vindictive to one who catches her in a compromising situation. This is clear in the story of Teiresias. One day she and the nymph Chariklo stripped themselves and bathed at midday in a forest pool. Chariklo's son, Teiresias, happened on the spot and saw Athena's naked body. She became angry and blinded the youth.[85]

Athena's reaction to Hephaestus's attempt to seduce her is consistent with her steadfast refusal to engage in sexual liaisons with males. One day Athena went to Hephaestus to obtain a new suit of armor. She stood by and watched him work the red-hot metal, when suddenly he turned on her and tried to embrace her. She held him off, and he ejaculated on her thigh. She wiped off the sperm with a cloth and threw it on the ground in disgust.[86]

Athena's distaste for sex does not have to do with a dislike of men. She is often depicted as being most at home with men. Sometimes she disguises herself as a man, as when she appears to Odysseus as his friend Mentor, in order to approach males more closely.[87] In the trial of Orestes for the revenge murder of his mother, Clytaemnestra (who had conspired to kill Orestes' father, Agamemnon), Athena presides over the proceedings. Apollo, in defense of Orestes, argues that biologically the father is much more important than the mother, that the mother is "no more than the inert furrow in which the husbandman cast his seed; and that Orestes had been abundantly justified in his act, the father being the one parent worthy of the name."[88] When the vote of the jury, composed of the leading citizens of Athens, is tied, Athena casts the deciding vote, which is to acquit Orestes. In casting her vote in his favor, she agrees with Apollo, asserting the dominance of the male and confessing:

> There is no mother bore me for her child,
> I praise the Man in all things (save for marriage),
> Whole-hearted am I, strongly for the Father.[89]

Athena's virginity, her refusal to become involved sexually or romantically with men, then, has to do more with a distaste for sex and romance than it does a distaste for men. Indeed, Athena prefers men. Athena's virginity symbolizes her independence. She refuses to be reduced to a sexual object. She refuses to assume a female sexual role, which might subordinate or demean her. As a female, she competes in, excels at, and dominates the male world of warfare, adventure, and politics. As a virgin, she refuses to be sexually manipulated and dependent upon a male; she is unapproachable sexually. However, this very unapproachability, this stubborn sexual independence, permits her to be spiritually, psychologically, even physically close to the male heroes she champions. "Athene is not a virgin in order to be alone but in order to be with others without entanglement."[90] Her alliances with males are based on mutual skill, superior cunning and rationality, great courage, and mutual respect for these qualities. Her alliances are not based upon or dependent upon sexual charm, expectations, or favors. Perhaps it is her very refusal to engage in sexual roles and games that enables Athena to get close to her favorites, who see in her neither a potential sexual conquest nor a potential sexual threat. Athena does not need a sexual relationship with a man to express her identity. Neither romantic love and sex nor motherhood is central to her character and nature. She is complete in herself, essentially independent and self-sufficient. This does not mean, however, that she does not appreciate and seek out friendships with those whom she admires for their superior abilities and courage. For the most part, however, it is not they who fulfill a need in her but she who inspires them to greater deeds and nobler efforts.

Contemporary Interpretations

Several contemporary authors have sought to interpret Athena in the context of modern concerns or to understand Athena in the light of recent ideologies. In his "translator's afterthoughts" to Kerényi's book on Athena, Murray Stein sees in Athena a being, attitude, or tendency that is epitomized in certain typically American attitudes. "Athene's spirit is the spirit of achievement, competence, action in the world: she gets us out there to win, and gives us the heart to do so, and the wit. It is hard to keep from seeing Athene in the American statue of liberty and in the American spirit of enterprise, in American expansionism, military heroes and Pentagon planning . . . , and in American football (especially in the position of the quarterback, the strategist)."[91] For Stein, Athena's influence prevents human beings from being distracted by mystical or emotional tendencies. She keeps people focused on the tasks at hand. "Athene keeps us in the 'real world'; she gives us the wherewithal to confront its problems, the joy of conquering ourselves, others, problems, and the sagacity and confidence to slay its dragons. She keeps us grounded in 'real projects,' out of vain and idle speculations."[92]

Relating Athena to the dynamics of the psyche, James Hillman interprets Athena as the psychological tendency toward normalization, the tendency of the mind to organize reality according to the practical norms of the dominant culture. "When psychology speaks in terms of norms, when it attempts to normalize, when it represents the point of view of the cultural canon and gives wise counsel from the practical understanding—protective, hygienic, politic, sensible—then psychology is enacting Athene."[93] Athena represents the psychological tendency to take care of the "maintenance of daily, practical life"[94] and not to get distracted by impractical dreamings, musings, and emotional fits. "The dynamic emotionalities, rages, possessions, moist hysterics, depressions, and wild nature outside the *polis* do not belong within the cosmos of Athene's normalization. They cannot be held in her wide, but shallow, bowl."[95] Psychologically, Athena represents the tendency of ego consciousness to keep the subconscious from overwhelming the psyche. "Athene's counsel presents the norms of this world, and its necessities, in close cooperation with the ego's interests."[96]

Jean Shinoda Bolen, a psychiatrist, understands Athena, and the Greek goddesses in general, to represent patterns of thought and behavior that characterize women. "The goddesses are patterns or representations of what women are like—with more power and diversity of behavior than women have historically been allowed to exercise. . . . They represent inherent patterns of archetypes that can shape the course of a woman's life."[97] Bolen's use of mythic images from Greek mythology, and specifically her construction of a map of the dynamics of the feminine psyche using Greek goddesses, is an attempt to correct certain difficulties in the Jungian portrait of the psyche, which seems more applicable to men than to women.[98]

> Athena is a feminine archetype: she shows that thinking well, keeping one's head in the heat of an emotional situation, and developing good tactics in the midst of conflict, are natural traits for some women. Such a woman is being like Athena, not acting "like a man." Her masculine aspect, or animus, is not doing the thinking *for* her—she is thinking clearly and well for herself. The concept of Athena as an archetype for logical thinking challenges the Jungian premise that thinking is done for a woman by her masculine animus, which is presumed to be distinct from her feminine ego.[99]

The woman dominated by the Athena archetype has a strong tendency to be practical and down-to-earth. Political and economic considerations are prominent in her calculations, while a tendency to resist emotions and sentimentality is strong. "The Athena archetype rules in women . . . whose intelligence is geared to the practical and pragmatic, whose actions are not determined by emotions or swayed by sentiment. With Athena in her psyche, a woman grasps what must be done and figures out how to achieve what she wants."[100] Bolen also characterizes the Athena-dominated women as loyal to the partriarchal norms of her culture and as politically conservative. "The father's daughter quality may make an Athena woman a defender of patriarchal right and values, which emphasize tradition and the legitimacy of male power. Athena women usually support the status quo and accept the established norms as guidelines of behavior. Such women are usually politically conservative; they resist change. Athena has little sympathy for the unsuccessful, downtrodden, or rebellious."[101]

Speaking autobiographically, Christine Downing describes her early admiration for Athena as a life's model. "She was all I wanted to be and I gave my soul to her—self-confident and courageous, clear-eyed and strong, intelligent and accomplished, judicious and fair. I delighted in her ability to make full use of the given possibilities in any situation, in her gift for deep friendship unentangled with the confusion of passion, in her pleasure in struggle and challenge. Her dedication to the world of art and culture, of clear thought and realized accomplishment, were important testimony to me of how a woman might order her life."[102]

Although at a certain point in her life Downing came to view Athena as "too cool and distant, too suspicious of the emotional and sensual, too extroverted and ambitious—too 'heady,'"[103] she continued to find in Athena positive inspiration, and inspiration that is not just rational but also spiritual and passionate. She speaks of Athena coming to her in "the guise of a man, recalling me to the deep excitement of shared intellectual concerns, the passion inherent in the kind of competitive rivalry where each partner urges the other to high achievement, to consummated accomplishment."[104] For Downing, Athena's presence gives courage and confirmation, the sudden bright idea or the seasoned reflection. She does not actively take command over the men whom she supports but brings them into touch with their own highest potentiality."[105] Athena is not just the cunning, pragmatic, rational, success-oriented tendency of people; she is that, but she is also an inspiring, creative, artistic presence who speaks to the soul or spirit of those whom she befriends. "Athena is thus soul-giver, soul-maker."[106]

If Athena is admired in the context of feminine thought as a presence that encourages women to escape from traditional feminine roles in which they are exploited and not valued, the admiration is often less than complete. Speaking in the early part of the century, Jane Harrison said of Athena: "We cannot love a goddess who on principle forgets the Earth from which she sprang."[107] Bolen sees in Athena the tendency to lose touch with one's emotions and physical self. "Living in her head, the Athena woman misses the experience of being fully in her body. She knows little about sensuality and about what it feels like to push her body to its limits. Athena keeps a woman 'above' the instinctual level, so she does not feel the full strength of maternal, sexual, or procreative instincts."[108]

Bolen also speaks of Athena's "Medusa effect," by which she means the tendency of Athena women to turn people into stone by focusing exclusively on facts and logic to the neglect of other aspects of human experience.

Through her focus on facts and details, her need for logical premises and rationality, she can turn a conversation into a dry recital of details. Or she can be devastatingly insensitive and can thus change the atmosphere dramatically from deeply personal to superficial and distant. With her critical attitude and dissecting questions, an Athena woman can unintentionally and unconsciously demean another person's subjective experience. She can be unempathetic about spiritual or moral issues that others consider of vital importance, intolerant of the problems people have with their relationships, and critical of any weaknesses. Such lack of empathy is killing.[109]

Bolen, Christine Downing, and the radical feminist Mary Daly all argue, in one way or another, that Athena, in order to represent a complete, wholesome model for women, must be viewed as having a dimension that is more affirming of the "powerful instinctual side" of reality. The Athena-dominated woman, Bolen says, must try to recapture a childhood self (Athena was born a full adult) and try to establish an appreciation for motherhood (Athena was born from her father).[110] Downing sees the missing aspect of the stereotypically cool, rational, and practical goddess in the Gorgon's head that Athena wears on her chest. This fearsome countenance represents, Downing says, Athena's "shadow side," which suggests "the dark sources of her power."[111] Mary Daly speaks of "hacking off with our Dreadful double-axes the Athena-shells designed to stifle our Selves"[112] and searching for the Great Hag that lies deep within. For Athena, and for women, Daly says, it is necessary to deny the overbearing influence of the father and patriarchal society and to recover and remember the mother, who for Athena is Metis, the goddess of wisdom.

Chapter **8**

Isis, Heavenly Queen

The gods above adore you, the gods below do homage to you, you set the orb of heaven spinning around the poles, you give light to the sun, you govern the universe, you trample down the powers of Hell. At your voice the stars move, the seasons recur, the spirits of earth rejoice, the elements obey. At your nod the winds blow, clouds drop wholesome rain upon the earth, seeds quicken, buds swell. Birds that fly through the air, beasts that prowl on the mountain, serpents that lurk in the dust, all these tremble in a single awe of you.[1]

Egyptian Origins

During the first few centuries of its history, one of the most powerful rivals to Christianity in the Greco-Roman world was the religion of the goddess Isis. During these centuries, she was widely worshiped throughout the Mediterranean world for a variety of blessings: health, fertility, family security, and immortality. She was popular among the nobility as well as among the lower classes and was especially dear to women. She was widely known for her warm approachability as well as her great cosmic power.

By the time Isis became popular in the Greco-Roman world she had been one of the most important deities in Egyptian religion for more than three thousand years. The central myth in the religion and mythology of Isis concerns the death and resuscitation of Osiris. The myth dates back all the way to the Pyramid Texts (late third millennium B.C.E.) and remained central to Egyptian religion up to the Greco-Roman period (fourth century B.C.E.). The myth suggests several central characteristics of Isis in Egyptian religion. In brief outline, the myth is as follows:

Isis and Osiris are twins and so love each other that they sexually embrace in their mother's womb. After their birth they become husband and wife. While bringing order and civilization to the world, however, Osiris is slain by his wicked brother, Seth, who lures Osiris to a beautiful wooden chest, traps him in it, and casts the chest into a river. Isis hears of the murder of Osiris and undertakes mourning. The earliest references to her portray her primarily as a mourner in the context of this myth. The chest or coffin eventually floats to Byblos, on the Lebanon coast, where it becomes hidden inside a tree, which subsequently is used as a pillar in the king's house. Isis wanders about in distress, asking everyone she meets if they have seen Osiris's coffin. She eventually traces it to Byblos. Gaining entry into the house of the king as a nurse, Isis transforms herself into a swallow every night and flies about the pillar containing the dead Osiris and laments loudly. Finally, she reveals to the king that she is the wife of Osiris and asks for the pillar. Having been given the chest, she takes it to a secluded place, opens it, and caresses the body of Osiris. By means of her great magical power and strong affection, Isis is able to revive Osiris's penis. She has intercourse with Osiris, and the child Horus is conceived. Horus is born prematurely and is weak in his lower limbs. Seth again appears and steals the body of Osiris, cutting it into pieces this time and scattering them everywhere. Isis sails through the marshes of the Nile Delta in search of the parts of her husband's body and eventually retrieves them all, except his genitals. Osiris, his body having been restored by Isis, goes on to the land of the dead. However, he returns from the dead long enough to instruct Horus in the martial arts so that he can defeat Seth. In the ensuing battle with Seth, Horus is successful. Throughout his infancy, when he was a weakling, Horus had been patiently nourished and protected by Isis until he was able to assume mature strength and defeat Seth.[2]

In the context of Egyptian religion, this myth seems to have two primary meanings—one associated with the Nile River and the other with the birth, death, and rebirth of the pharaohs. The rhythmic, seasonal rising and falling of the Nile River provides a long, narrow thread of habitable land in the immense wastes of the Northeast African deserts. With predictable regularity, and with little fluctuation from year to year, the Nile floods its banks in the spring, swollen with the snows of mountains far to the south. When the river subsides, vast stretches of land along its banks are left enriched by the silt left by the floods. For thousands of years, these fertile lands along the Nile River have been cultivated and have provided a dependable food supply for stable, civilized life. Without the Nile, and without its rhythms of regular flooding, life in the North African desert would be tenuous at best.

The myth of the birth, death, and resurrection of Osiris, in part at least, suggests the rhythm of agriculture and vegetative life. Like the crops, Osiris grows to maturity, is then slain (harvested), only to be reborn in the spring. In the context of Egyptian geography, the rebirth of vegetation (the rebirth of Osiris) is inextricably bound up with the flooding of the Nile before spring planting. Indeed, the land would not be renewed, the crops would not be reborn, if the Nile did not annually swell its banks and renourish the land. This periodic flooding is caused by the tears of Isis when she laments for her dead husband. In the myth, Isis brings back life through much effort, after a long and trying search, and after much mourning and shedding many tears.[3] Osiris (vegetation) is revived through both Isis's emotion (her tears) and her efforts. Isis's steadfast love and her heroic refusal to cease trying to recover and revive her husband bring back the power of vegetation every year. In the myth as it relates to Egyptian geography, then, Isis may be said to be the land itself, which is left barren without the annual rebirth of vegetation, while Osiris is the spirit of the crops, the fecund power that yields food from the land.[4] In this sense, one of the central tasks of ancient Egyptian religion was to help Isis in her mythic quest to find and revive Osiris so that the land, upon which all life and civilization depended, could be renourished.

The other fundamental meaning of the myth of Osiris and Isis in the context of ancient Egyptian religion concerns the periodic death and rebirth of the pharaohs. In Egyptian political mythology, when the pharaoh died he was identified with Osiris, while the new pharaoh, usually young and inexperienced, was identified with Horus. In Egyptian cosmology, the pharaoh was far more than a political leader who might be experienced in administration, warfare, and statecraft. The pharaoh was the living, concrete presence of divinity in the land of the living. From his sublime and powerful presence emanated civilization, well-being, and order. He was no mere representative of the divine, he was the divine, and as long as he prospered, as long as he waxed strong and vigorous, the kingdom that he ruled would prosper also. Like Osiris, however, the pharaoh eventually became exhausted in exerting himself in the civilizing process on behalf of his people. Like Osiris he died, worn out with the immense effort of his task. Through the effort, love, and magic of Isis, the powerful, divine genius of the pharaoh as a fructifying and civilizing force was transferred or recycled in refreshed form from the dead pharaoh to his successor. Isis shepherded the dead pharaoh to the land of the dead, guaranteeing him eternal existence there; Isis also successfully preserved the divine essence of the pharaoh so that it could be passed on in the land of the living to the next embodiment of divinity in the form of the new pharaoh. In the myth, Isis's function in preserving and passing on the pharaoh's divinity is expressed in her ability to impregnate herself with Osiris's corpse, her giving birth to Horus, and her nurturing him to full maturity. In terms of the destiny of the pharaoh, then, Isis acts as both the psychopomp who guides the dead pharaoh to the land of the dead, granting him immortality there, and the one who, through love, persistence, and patience, saves a germ of the pharaoh's divinity to renourish and mold into the next mature ruler. In her role in granting immortality to the dead pharaoh (which Isis does through the art of mummification), she is often pictured as a bird "hovering over the king's mummy," holding "in one hand the billowing sail 𓊡 , the hieroglyph for the wind or breath of life, and in the other the *ankh* ☥ ," the symbol of life itself.[5] According to Egyptian mythology, cult, and religion, "the resurrection of the dead Osiris was the result of Isis breathing into his nostrils the breath of life by flapping the air with her wings."[6] In the myth, Isis took the form of a swallow and flew about the pillar that entombed her dead husband and so began the resuscitation process; it was believed that during the mummification rituals of the dead pharaoh she was similarly present, imbuing the corpse with fresh life.

In her role as protector, nourisher, and mother of all pharaohs, Isis is represented by a hieroglyph that has as its basic element the throne of the pharaohs, 𓊨𓏏 . So basic was she to the well-being and power of the ruler that she was understood to be the seat of his power, quite literally. It was she who had given him birth, continued to nourish him in his vulnerable infancy and youth, and sustained and invigorated him in his maturity and old age. As the fertile land itself, Isis was the ground upon which the pharaoh sat, and he was the genius of fecundity, the presence of order and civilization that made her habitable, beautiful, and ever fruitful.

Mistress of Life and Health

In 332 B.C.E., Alexander the Great conquered Egypt, and the reign of the pharaohs, which had lasted more than three thousand years, came to an end. This was not the end of the religion of the goddess Isis, however; far from it. Alexander was extremely impressed with the antiquity and greatness of Egypt and decided to establish a new city there as the center for his far-flung empire. So it was that the city of Alexandria was founded near the mouth of the Nile and came to be a cosmopolitan center for the intermingling of different religions and cultures and the dissemination of Egyptian religion, duly modified in several ways, to the Greco-Roman world. Of all Egyptian exports to the wider world, Isis became the most adored and popular deity. In her spread throughout the Greco-Roman world, her character became elaborated, often modified, and in many cases she was identified with or associated with non-Egyptian (especially Greek) deities.[7] In this process, her character and cult were greatly enriched. The majority of the motifs that remained central in her religion outside Egypt, however, seem to have been rooted in her Egyptian past and indicated an impressive persistence of her central character and meaning.

One of the most striking features of the Osiris myth is Isis's ability to retrieve life from the dead Osiris. By undertaking a dangerous trip in search of her dead husband (suggestive of a trip to the land of the dead), exerting her magical powers, and venting her passionate love, she is able to recover from Osiris's corpse the seed of life from which Horus is conceived. She brings back

Fragment of Isis suckling Horus, blue faience, Ptolemaic, 305–330 B.C.E., Egypt, site unknown. Brooklyn Museum, Charles Edwin Wilbour Fund.

the body of her husband, performs the revivifying rites of mummification, and thus restores him to a condition in which he is able to make the journey to the land of immortality. Isis's ability to vivify, her ability to breathe life into the weak and ailing, is also a central point in her relationship with the young Horus, who is born weak and fragile. It is not surprising, then, that both in Egypt and in the Greco-Roman world, where she became popular later, Isis was preeminently associated with life and was typically shown bearing the *ankh*, the symbol of life. Isis suckling Horus became a particularly popular way of depicting the great goddess of life, and to her devotees she was understood as nourishing all creatures and all life with the life-giving nectar of her breasts.[8] "Everything that drew breath and whatever held sap could praise Isis,"[9] because they could not exist without her presence, which was coincidental with life itself.

Her presence brought vigor, her absence decay. Lucius, the hero of Apuleius's *Metamorphoses*, says of Isis's life-giving character: "She is the shining deity by whose divine influence not only all beasts, wild and tame, but all inanimate things as well, are invigorated; whose ebbs and flows control the rhythm of all bodies whatsoever, whether in the air, on earth, or below the sea."[10] Just as her tears annually returned fecundity to the Nile River Valley by making the river overflow, just as she restored Osiris to wholeness through her affectionate presence, and just as she nourished the weak child Horus to maturity with the milk from her breasts, so she restored life and nourished it everywhere in the world, revealing her presence wherever life arose and flourished.[11]

In the Greco-Roman world, Isis quite naturally became associated with both Demeter and Aphrodite. In Isis, the Greco-Roman world saw the fertile powers of the great grain goddess, Demeter, whose presence imbued the crops with the miraculous ability to renew themselves annually.[12] The Greco-Roman world also saw in Isis the irresistible power of sexual attraction associated with Aphrodite.[13] The attraction of the sexes resulting in the continual renewal of life was easily associated with Isis, whose presence anywhere aroused life even from the dead or failing.[14]

Isis's association or identification with the universal life force is connected to her ability to maintain and restore health. Isidorus, writing in the first century B.C.E., says in one of his hymns to Isis: "All who are bound in mortal illnesses in the grip of death, / if they (but) pray to you, quickly attain your (renewal of) Life."[15] Again, her magical ability to bring about health and wholeness is clearly reflected in the Osiris myth: she succeeds in restoring Osiris himself and in bringing wholeness and strength to Horus. In an Egyptian text dating back to the sixteenth century B.C.E., we find this prayer to Isis: "O Isis, thou great Mage, heal me, release me from all things that are bad and evil and that belong to Seth, from the demonic fatal sicknesses—as thou hast saved and freed thy son Horus."[16]

According to Egyptian tradition, Isis gained her miraculous power to heal by wresting from the great god, Re, his sacred and secret names and infusing herself with them.[17] The great potency of her spells resides in the use of these names, which are held to contain the essence of reality and divinity. Isis, however, is never stingy with her healing abilities, and, having taken Re's power from him, she uses it to bring about cures for anyone calling on her for help.

Isis's mastery of pharmacology was known throughout the Greco-Roman world, and tales about her nourishing Horus with special medicines were widely told. Indeed, Isis is said to have taught the branches of medical science—anatomy, pathology, surgery, and pharmacology—to her son, Horus.[18] Several of her temples were famous depositories of ancient medical lore (especially those at Koptos and Panopolis).[19] Isis also was reputed to have discovered, and to possess, the elixir of immortality, and reading her scriptures was said to yield eternal life. "Her name was given to a drug which won universal praise, according to the medical writer Galen, because it could staunch

The goddess Isis, temple of King Sethos I at Abydos, chapel of Osiris. K. Lange and M. Hirmer, *Egypt: Architecture, Sculpture, Painting in Three Thousand Years* (3d ed., rev.; London: Phaidon Press, 1961), pl. 24.

wounds, cure headaches, and was good for lesions, ulcers, fractures and bites of every kind."[20]

Having successfully treated the most dire sickness of all, namely, death, by restoring Osiris to wholeness, Isis naturally was affirmed to have in her possession great healing powers. For many of her devotees, Isis's presence, her glory, resided in her wondrous acts of healing.

> Her epiphany, the manifestation of her glory, is witnessed all over the world in the mighty acts and the cures she performs. Isis does not dwell in the clouds on top of Olympus far away from the everyday ills and sorrows of men and women. She unites with them when they are asleep. She can save them when their lives are despaired of by their own doctors. Those who obey her can be suddenly restored to health. At her hands the maimed are healed and the blind receive their sight. Her name has magical virtue and power, for she is sorceress, apothecary and physician.[21]

A common means of procuring Isis's curative powers was to dwell within her temple for a certain period of time. The practice was known as incubation, and by means of it devotees sought to place themselves in Isis's hands so that she would bless them through a dream or some other indication of her presence.[22] Like Osiris and Horus, devotees sought renewed life as a result of Isis's ministrations.

An important part of the curing process involving Isis was the faith of the devotee. "What is so striking in the therapy that Isis promises to perform is the need of faith and the sureness of hope on the side of those who patiently await the indubitable dream which will bring them health."[23] An example of a prayer to Isis from an Egyptian papyrus calls upon her to protect the petitioner from sickness: "May Isis heal me as she healed her son Horus of all the pains (which were) brought on him. . . . Thou great enchantress, heal me, save me from all evil things of darkness, from the epidemic and deadly diseases and infections of all sorts that spring upon me, as thou hast saved and freed Horus. . . . Free me from all possible evil, hurtful things of darkness, from epidemic and deadly fevers of every kind."[24] Another devotee thanked Isis for curing his afflicted eyes. "With these eyes. . . . I saw the sun and I see the world, which is yours: I am convinced that you will help me in every way. Indeed, you came when I invoked you for my health."[25]

In Isis temples many *ex-voto* offerings were left by those whom the great goddess had cured or rescued from calamity. In her temple at Pompeii, images of various human limbs dedicated to the goddess have been found and presumably were presented to Isis as a request or in gratitude for healing that particular limb or part of the body.[26] One need not have belonged to Isis's cult to approach her for health or to respect her healing power. She was popular, it seems, even among Jews. Her shrine at Philippi was dedicated by a doctor named Q. Mofius (Moses) Euhemerus, presumably a Jew who had either witnessed or directly experienced her curative powers.[27]

Wife, Mother, and Guardian of the Family

Another important motif in the religion of Isis is her role as guardian of family love and family relationships. She was associated with Aphrodite in the Greco-Roman world and was affirmed to be the mysterious, powerful force that attracted men and women to each other. Isis had willed in the beginning that "men and women should anchor together"[28] and was thus at the root of the attraction upon which marriage and family life were based. Although Isis in her association with Aphrodite sometimes was characterized as inspiring unrefined sexual lust, her sexual passion is almost always described as channeled in undestructive, traditional ways. That is, she is nearly always adored as the wife who would make any effort or sacrifice on behalf of her husband. "Although she was eventually identified with Hathor, goddess of sexual love in Egypt, and later with Aphrodite, in contrast to these goddesses, Isis represented sexuality only within the bounds of wifely fidelity which she perfectly embodied."[29]

Her love is constructive, even redemptive in the case of Osiris and Horus, and presents a model of affection that is supportive of society and the family. She herself is portrayed as deeply experiencing the emotions of a devoted wife. She therefore is understood as promoting such devotion and as attentive to those who petition to secure or preserve such love. The central elements of the Osiris myth are motivated by Isis's all-consuming love for her husband, which refuses to let her accept his final loss.

Isis's maternal love is similarly passionate and devoted and, like her love for Osiris, is constructive and redemptive in relation to society. Her doting loyalty to her weakling child, Horus, offers to her devotees a model of love that is patient, protective, and nourishing. Under her motherly presence the half-withered and helpless child gradually gains his strength and vigor and eventually assumes the position of mighty pharaoh, protector of civilization, victor over the destructive influences of Seth. Both in Egypt and later in the Greco-Roman world, one of the most popular ways of representing Isis was to show her suckling the infant Horus.[30] Although this symbolized more than just maternal nourishment, representing as it did the infusion of immortality to devotees of Isis,[31] it did confirm the centrality of motherly qualities in her makeup.

The motherly devotion of Isis for Horus is reciprocated by Horus's love for his mother. Horus is represented as a model of filial piety. His devotion to his parents is indicated in two of his Egyptian epithets, "pillar of his mother" and "savior of his father."[32] In his affection for his parents, Horus rounds out the picture of the divine family as marked by loyalty, love, and service. Presided over by Isis, this family represented an inspiration to cultivate and protect family bonds. Isis not only loves her child, she causes him to love her by her devotion to him, and in so doing she perpetuates by her presence one of the strongest human bonds, a bond necessary to the perpetuation of the human species.

Sister-in-law of Ramose, detail of festival relief, Hall of Pillars in the tomb of Ramose at Thebes. K. Lange and M. Hirmer, *Egypt: Architecture, Sculpture, Painting in Three Thousand Years* (3d ed., rev.; London: Phaidon Press, 1961), pl. 172. Permission of Hirmer Verlag, Munich.

In her roles as exemplar of wifely devotion and maternal love Isis presided over marriage, pregnancy, and birth. In hymns to her, she is said to have founded the institution of marriage, she is sometimes mentioned in marriage contracts, and she also appears at times as a witness to marriage ceremonies.[33] Betrothals of marriage were made at her temples, and she is depicted as witnessing lovers' vows to each other, thereby making them binding.[34] Isis also is said to have instituted parenthood by embodying in her own relationship with Horus all the ideal qualities of a parent. She also bestowed fertility. In one of his hymns, Isidorus says: "All indeed who wish to beget offspring, / if they (but) pray to you, attain fruitfulness."[35] She also was said to protect pregnant women and to be present at childbirth. In an Egyptian charm, a pregnant woman identifies herself with Isis and summons the gods to prepare her room for birth.[36] Isis also was associated or identified with the goddess Bubastis, whose primary function was to oversee women and protect them at childbirth and during maternity.[37] It was to Isis that the poet Philinus prayed when his wife was in the midst of a difficult pregnancy and to Isis also that Ovid looked when his wife lay on her deathbed after an attempted abortion.[38]

Completing her image as the protectress, promoter, and embodiment of orderly domestic life is the tradition that it was Isis who invented spinning and weaving.[39] Isis may have been viewed by many of her devotees as queen of the cosmos; creator of the sun, moon, and stars; and the dramatic savior who answered the pleas of her devotees when they were threatened by danger. But the oldest strand in her mythology and worship locates her in the home and pictures her at domestic tasks. In this setting, she invents the domestic arts (spinning, weaving, cooking, etc.) and thus is involved in cultural refinement and civilization at the most basic level of human society. These most fundamental arts are those upon which the more elaborate civilized arts depend.

Especially for women, then, Isis played a very important role as model and protector of domestic life.

> Isis in the Greco-Roman world was above all else the faithful wife and indeed the divine patroness of family life and instructress in such domestic arts as weaving and spinning. . . . She was esteemed as the model spouse. She was hymned as upholder of the marriage covenant. It was her ordinance that parents should be loved by their children and that in the wedding service of the Egyptians the husband should make a solemn contract to be obedient to his wife. The tale of Isis and Osiris, whatever the discrepancies of detail, contained just those elements which for later antiquity could serve as the pattern of family bonds of affection.[40]

Although she may have been exceptional in her wifely and maternal devotion, Isis was seen as motivated and overcome by the same human emotions that every woman experiences. Her concerns, her preoccupations, her passions were those of her devotees, especially her female devotees.[41]

Isis nursing Horus, bronze, Egyptian. Courtesy of Walters Art Gallery, Baltimore.

> In sum, she was a protectress during the most important occasions of the life-cycle—birth, marriage, and death. Every emotion experienced by the ordinary person at such events had already been experienced by Isis. At death she provided an emotional outlet through the enactment of her sufferings. . . . One's chastity was preserved by Isis before marriage, and troth was pledged with Isis as witness. Finally, she provided protection during childbirth and nurtured infants. All of these matters were of primary concern to women, and it was they who sought Isis out most eagerly to fill a need which the Greek and Roman religions failed to fill.[42]

Isis understood the pleadings of her devotees, was present and sympathetic when they experienced the passions and affections and traumas of domestic life, was nearby at birth and death and at weddings and during lovemaking, because she too had experienced these same things deeply in her relationships with Osiris and Horus.

Isis's establishment and protection of domestic life is expressed in cosmic fashion when she creates culture and an orderly universe. In addition to the domestic arts, she was said to have invented agriculture, the basis of Egyptian economy, and in this vein was identified with the ancient Egyptian goddess Renenutet,[43] associated with grain, and with the Greek deity Demeter, also associated with grain.[44] Isidorus says that she gave humankind various skills to make life comfortable,[45] such as the domestic arts of weaving, spinning, and cooking. The exemplification in her own life of family relations and her protection of marriage underline her support for the basic values that support society and ally her strongly with the forces of order and civilization.

On a cosmic scale, Isis is affirmed to have created the world in all its orderliness. Isidorus praises her for creating the world:

> Because of You heaven and the whole earth have their being;
> And the gusts of winds and the sun with its sweet light.
> By Your power the channels of Nile are filled, every one,
> At the harvest season and its most turbulent water is poured
> On the whole land that produce may be unfailing.[46]

In Apuleius's *Metamorphoses*, Isis appears enrobed in the stars and at several points is praised as the presence or reality who creates and governs nature and the cosmic rhythms.[47] She personifies the orderly cosmos itself. She has created it and has entered into it directly.

Savior and Cosmic Queen

Perhaps the most important role that Isis played was that of savior. Again, this role is implied in her mythology and in other characteristics already discussed. Her magical power to revive Osiris, her role as his guide to the land of immortality, and her power to instill vigor in the crippled Horus all point to her ability to bring about miraculous change. Similarly, her successful part in the eventual overthrow of Seth, who represents danger, chaos, and death, marks her as a guardian of safety, security, and order. Her association with health and healing also points to her involvement in bringing about dramatic cures, a task that savior deities are often called upon to undertake. In her role as a gracious savior, Isis also granted her devotees various worldly blessings, in addition to health. In his third hymn to her, Isidorus mentions the following blessings that Isis gives her devotees: wealth, happiness, good fortune, understanding, long life, and good harvests.[48]

Her most miraculous power, however, and the power that was perhaps most cherished by her devotees, was her ability to grant immortality, to thwart death, as she had done with Osiris.[49] Her ability to grant immortality is ancient; in the Egyptian context, she was believed to be present during the rituals of mummification, which guaranteed the dead person a safe passage to the land of immortality.[50] With her companion deity, Anubis, she played the role in traditional Egyptian religion of psychopomp, guiding the souls of the dead to their new homes in the other world.[51]

In the Greco-Roman world, at a time when the so-called mystery religions were offering different forms of personal immortality, Isis understandably was seen to be especially qualified and capable. Although the inner mysteries of her religion are not known, nor of other mystery religions, it does seem apparent that an important part of the candidate's initiation was a period of incubation in an Isis temple or shrine, during which period he or she was left alone with the image of the deity and underwent some kind of transformative experience. In Apuleius's account of Lucius's initiation into the religion of Isis, the candidate clearly underwent a symbolic death and rebirth at the hands of the goddess. In the inner sanctuary of Isis's temple, alone during the whole night, Lucius described his experience as follows: "I approached the very gates of death and set one foot on Proserpine's threshold, yet was permitted to return, rapt through all the elements. At midnight I saw the sun shining as if it were noon; I entered the presence of the gods of the underworld and the gods of the upper-world, stood near and worshipped them."[52] The morning after his initiation, he was presented to a crowd of admirers, "That day was the happiest of my initiation, and I celebrated it as my birthday with a cheerful banquet at which all my friends were present."[53]

Early in her history, Isis was associated with ships and with journeys over vast seas. She sailed all the way to Byblos in search of her husband and criss-crossed the Nile Delta in search of his dismembered corpse in her heroic efforts to rescue and revive him. In her role as savior, she was particularly associated with protecting sailors, travelers, and ships. In one of his hymns,

Isidorus praises Isis as a savior and specifically mentions her ability to rescue sailors at sea.

> As many as are bound fast in prison, in the power of death,
> As many as are in pain through long, anguished, sleepless nights,
> All who are wanderers in a foreign land,
> And as many as sail on the Great Sea in winter
> When men may be destroyed and their ships wrecked and sunk . . .
> All (these) are saved if they pray that You be present to help.[54]

In this aspect, she impressed herself upon her devotees as a deity who was not tied down to one place, as a deity who was on the move in the world and hence attentive to the pleas of her devotees wherever they might be. For those who viewed human life and destiny as a precarious journey across difficult seas, Isis was known to dwell with voyagers, to be at home on the oceans, and to provide, ultimately, safe haven and a safe passage to the land of immortality.[55] As in the case of Osiris and Horus, Isis was famous for exerting herself for those for whom she cared. She was not aloof, she was not afraid, she was aggressive, accomplished, and caring. She too was a voyager and was ready to stand by the side of other voyagers in trouble.

An important characteristic of Isis in her role as savior was her approachability and accessibility. In contrast to the Olympian deities, who often were aloof from the daily concerns of mortals, Isis often was referred to as "the one who listens."[56] Not only did she listen, not only was she attentive to the cries of her devotees, she acted on their behalf in the world. "Isis toiled without rest on behalf of her beloved human family, sheltering them on land and sea, banishing the storms that beset their lives, and stretching out to them a strong right hand of a Savior."[57] According to some scholars, the dominant image of Isis, particularly after the spread of her religion to the Greco-Roman world, was that of the "divine nurse-mother."[58] Appropriately, her temples and shrines were constructed, not in inaccessible places, but in places frequented by her devotees. She was willing to dwell among the lowly, among those who needed her most, and was not afraid to busy herself in the mundane affairs of her children.

> Vitruvius, an authority on Roman architecture, contracts the siting of temples to such Olympian deities as Jupiter, Juno and Minerva with those of Isis and Sarapis. The traditional champions of city-states have their dwelling high on an acropolis, whereas the Egyptian pair are worshipped in a market place. . . . Isis and her companion gods from Egypt gain a foothold in Italian cities by a readiness to take a comparatively low

rank. She enters as the friend of the masses. She makes her home hard by the business and trading centre where she can be near and dear to the common man.[59]

Perhaps the most dramatic and vivid account of Isis's role as a savior who is attentive to the pleas of her devotees is found in the closing scene of Apuleius's *Metamorphoses*. The hero of the novel, Lucius, a Roman nobleman, is cursed to take the form of an ass, a particularly lowly and brutish beast, because of his careless meddling in magical spells. Near the end of the novel, the bulk of which tells of Lucius's adventures in his animal form, the hero decides in desperation to petition Isis to transform him back into human form. He closes his initial petition to her with these words: "I beseech you, by whatever name, in whatever aspect, with whatever ceremonies you deign to be invoked, have mercy on me in my extreme distress, restore my shattered fortune, grant me repose and peace after this long sequence of miseries. End my sufferings and perils, rid me of this hateful four-footed disguise, return me to my family, make me Lucius once more."[60] Isis appears in response to this plea, shining, radiant, emerging from the sea. After introducing herself to her petitioner, she reassures him: "I have come in pity of your plight, I have come to favour and aid you. Weep no more, lament no longer; the hour of deliverance, shone over by my watchful light, is at hand."[61]

In return for her blessing Isis asks Lucius to serve her devotedly for the rest of his days. This service is described, not as a burden, but as a path that will bring him joy, long life, and divine protection. She says to him:

> Only remember, and keep these words of mine locked tight in your heart, that from now onwards until the very last day of your life you are dedicated to my service. It is only right that you should devote your whole life to the Goddess who makes you a man again. Under my protection you will be happy and famous, and when at the destined end of your life you descend to the land of ghosts, there too in the subterrene hemisphere you shall have frequent occasion to adore me. From the Elysian fields you will see me as queen of the profound Stygian realm, shining through the darkness of Acheron with a light as kindly and tender as I show you now. Further, if you are found to deserve my divine protection by careful obedience to the ordinances of my religion and by perfect chastity, you will become aware that I, and I alone, have power to prolong your life beyond the limits appointed by destiny.[62]

The next day, during a procession in honor of Isis, one of her priests presents Lucius the ass with a bunch of roses. While eating the roses offered by the priest, Lucius is suddenly changed back into his human form. He willingly and joyfully presents himself for initiation into the religion of the goddess and her sacred mysteries, at the end of which he speaks of being born he closing scene of the book, Lucius once again prays to Isis, capturher salvific presence:

Holiest of the Holy, perpetual comfort of mankind, you whose bountiful grace nourishes the whole world; whose heart turns towards all those in sorrow and tribulation as a mother's to her children; you who take no rest by night, no rest by day, but are always at hand to succour the distressed by land and sea, dispersing the gales that beat upon them. Your hand alone can disentangle the hopelessly knotted skeins of fate, terminate every spell of bad weather, and restrain the stars from harmful conjunction.[63]

Isis's power and majesty, finally, were most extravagantly exalted when she was praised as queen of heaven. Although Isis shared divine control of the universe throughout her history with other divinities, and in the Egyptian context was inextricably associated with Osiris and Horus, both of whom had central roles in the cosmic economy, her devotees often came to appreciate her and praise her as the ultimate power in the universe, the creator and sustainer of all things, the queen of heaven. In the context of her Roman cult she was popularly referred to as *regina* (queen), *domina* (mistress), and *augusta* (the glorious one).[64]

In her aspect as cosmic queen, ruler of the universe, Isis was strongly associated with law, order, and justice. In the Egyptian setting, she resided over *maat*, the idea of just, righteous, moral, and cosmic order, or was associated with or identified with the goddess Maat, the daughter of the sun god, Re; Maat personified this idea.[65] *Maat* was the idea of the intrinsic rightness of the cosmic order, the idea that the world as it had been created operated in a predictable, benign manner. *Maat* was evident in both the rule of the pharaohs and the regularity of the Nile's flooding. In all this, Isis was seen to be present.[66] In Greece, Isis was given the title *thesmophorus*, "the lawgiver." In this role, she was understood as punishing those who transgressed the moral order. In Isidorus's third hymn to Isis, he describes her as a heavenly judge who carefully watches the conduct of human beings: "You are directing the world of men, looking down on the manifold / deeds of the wicked and gazing down on those of the just."[67] As the all-seeing and all-knowing queen of the cosmos it was impossible for those who broke her laws to escape her anger and punishment.[68] "She has established laws that shall never be broken. She has caused what is right to prevail. She has destroyed the empires of despots, and has made righteousness stronger than gold and silver. She has established the overriding sanctity of the oath. When one person forms a plot unjustly against another, then Isis hands the perpetrator over to his intended victim. She assigns vengeance on those who deal unjustly."[69]

To her devotees, Isis was evident everywhere, particularly in other female beings.[70] To them, other goddesses were essentially particularized manifestations of Queen Isis's many-faceted personality. In Lucius's prayer to her, Isis is said to appear in the world in many forms and in many roles.

Blessed Queen of Heaven, whether you are pleased to be known as Ceres, the original harvest mother who in joy at the finding of your lost daughter Proserpine abol-

Isis, Eighteenth Dynasty, ca. 1450 B.C.E., from Karnak. Egyptian Museum, Cairo. Claude Vandersleyen, *Das alte Ägypten* (Berlin: Propyläen Verlag, 1975), pl. 178.

ished the rude acorn diet of our forefathers and gave them bread raised from the fertile soil of Eleusis; or whether as celestial Venus, now adored at sea-girt Paphos, who at the time of the first Creation coupled the sexes in mutual love and so contrived that man should continue to propagate his kind for ever; or whether as Artemis, the physician sister of Phoebus Apollo, reliever of the birth pangs of women, and now adored in the ancient shrine at Ephesus; or whether as dread Proserpine to whom the owl cries at night, whose triple face is potent against the malice of ghosts, keeping them imprisoned below earth; you who wander through many sacred groves and are propitiated with many different rites—you whose womanly light illuminates the walls of every city, whose misty radiance nurses the happy seeds under the soil, you who control the wandering course of the sun and the very power of his rays—I beseech you, . . . grant me repose and peace.[71]

When Isis comes to Lucius in answer to his prayer, her appearance is majestic. She wears a robe bedecked by stars, and in the center of her robe gleams the full moon. She bears fruits and grains symbolizing her great fertile powers and is adorned with emblems of victory. When she introduces herself, her self-portrait is similar to Lucius's praise of her. She describes herself as the underlying power, or the divine essence, of all the gods. Overwhelming the awestruck Lucius with her appearance and intoxicating fragrance, the mighty Queen of Heaven says to him:

You see me here, Lucius, in answer to your prayer. I am Nature, the universal Mother, mistress of all the elements, primordial child of time, sovereign of all things spiritual, queen of the dead, queen also of the immortals, the single manifestation of all gods and goddesses that are. My nod governs the shining heights of Heaven, the wholesome sea-breezes, the lamentable silences of the world below. Though I am worshipped in many aspects, known by countless names, and propitiated with all manner of different rites, yet the whole round earth venerates me. . . . Some know me as Juno, some as Bellona . . . others as Hecate, others again as Rhamnubia, but . . . the Egyptians who excel in ancient learning and worship me with ceremonies proper to my godhead, call me by my true name, namely, Queen Isis.[72]

Chapter **9**

Golden Aphrodite

I will sing of stately Aphrodite, gold-crowned and beautiful, whose dominion is the walled cities of all sea-set Cyprus. There the moist breath of the western wind wafted her over the waves of the loud-moaning sea in soft foam, and there the gold-filleted Hours welcomed her joyously. They clothed her with heavenly garments: on her head they put a fine, well-wrought crown of gold, and in her pierced ears they hung ornaments of orichalc and precious gold, and adorned her with golden necklaces over her soft neck and snow-white breasts, jewels which the gold-filleted Hours wear themselves whenever they go to their father's house to join the lovely dances of the gods. And when they had fully decked her, they brought her to the gods, who welcomed her when they saw her, giving her their hands. Each one of them prayed that he might lead her home to be his wedded wife, so greatly were they amazed at the beauty of violet-crowned Cytherea.

Hail, sweet-winning, coy-eyed goddess![1]

Introduction

Aphrodite was one of the most widely worshiped goddesses of ancient Greece.[2] Although historically her roots are outside Greece, in the ancient Near East and in Indo-European traditions, she became very much a central Greek deity. Her sanctuaries are found all over Greece, and she is an important, powerful deity in most of Greek literature. "As the goddess of physical coupling . . . she expressed feelings which . . . were . . . common to every man or woman. . . . She was necessary, or so the Greeks felt; therefore her temples, large and small, stood everywhere, in the sunlight of the Aegean, the Mediterranean, the Adriatic and the Black Sea; her name was spoken by everyone, as a common fact of life for more than fifteen hundred years."[3]

She is often stereotyped as having only one dimension or function—to stir sexual desire—but in her cult and mythology it is clear that she had many

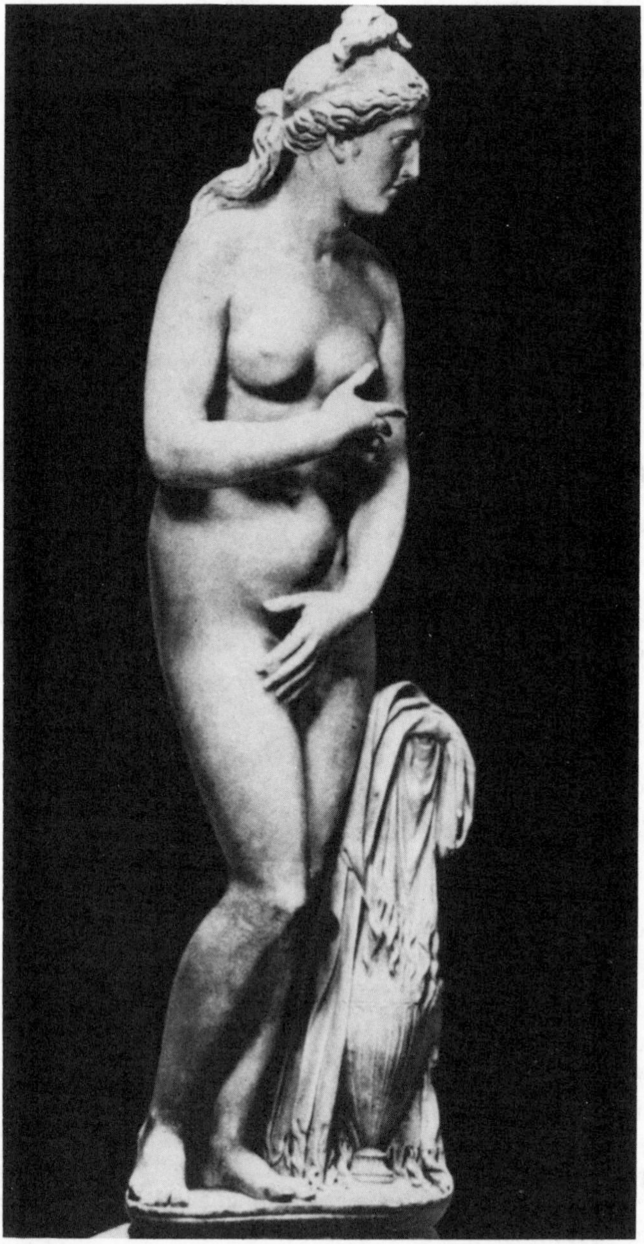

Venus of Capitole, a variation of Aphrodite of Cnide, second century B.C.E. K. Papaioannou, *L'Art et la civilisation de la Grèce ancienne. L'Art grec* (Paris: Editions d'art Lucien Mazenrod, 1972), fig. 814, p. 460. Permission of Giraudon/Art Resource, New York.

facets. She was strongly associated with desire and longing, to be sure, and many myths that feature her stress her power to arouse sexual feelings. Her presence often drives gods and mortals into a frenzy of passion. Aphrodite, however, also was associated with growth and fertility in general, and in much of her cult she was approached no so much to arouse sexual passion as to grant vigor and well-being. She was also associated with marriage and prosperity, and in some cases she was considered a city guardian.

In some mythological scenes and in the writings of some scholars, Aphrodite is dismissed as an ineffective deity who suffers abuse and mockery by other deities and by mortals.[4] However, it is clear in most texts, and from the wide extent of her worship, that Aphrodite was revered as an extremely powerful presence who was mocked or ignored at great risk. Greek mythology has many tales that feature the dire consequences of ignoring or challenging Aphrodite's power.

Early Background

There is general agreement among scholars of Greek religion and mythology that Aphrodite was not an indigenous Greek goddess. Most scholars and writers, furthermore, tend to trace Aphrodite's origin to the East.[5] Aphrodite's Eastern origin is suggested by the fact that she is strongly associated with Cyprus, where one of her most famous shrines was located at Paphos. Among her most common epithets are the Cyprian and the Paphian. Cyprus was an important center of contact between Semitic, Near Eastern culture and Minoan-Mycenaean and Greek culture. It has been suggested, and is likely, that Aphrodite, or a goddess much like her, was worshiped by the Phoenicians, who had strong contacts with both the Near East and Cyprus.[6]

Aphrodite's strong identification with islands (particularly Cyprus and Cythera) and with the sea also suggests that she came to Greece from outside, most likely from the East. In one version of her birth, she is born from the sea and is blown ashore at either Cythera or Cyprus after a long sea voyage.[7] From the Greek point of view, that is, tradition stated that Aphrodite had undertaken a sea voyage in order to come to the Greek homeland.

It also has been argued in support of Aphrodite's Eastern origin that she has strong similarities with goddesses who were popular in the Near East. Such goddesses as the Canaanite Anat and Astarte and the Assyrian Ishtar (the earlier Sumerian Inanna) had strong associations with fertility and sexuality. Herodotus (fifth century B.C.E.) saw clear similarities between worship of these Near Eastern deities and Aphrodite. Speaking of the association of temple prostitution with the worship of Ishtar, he actually calls Ishtar, and other goddesses associated with this custom, "Aphrodite." That is, he saw in these goddesses the equivalents of the Greek Aphrodite. He also mentioned that similar practices were found in Cyprus, where Aphrodite was widely worshiped.[8] It should be pointed out, however, that Anat and Ishtar in particular had strong associations with war. Aphrodite, on the other hand, although she does appear on the battlefield occasionally[9] and does associate with the god of war, Ares, who is often said to be her lover, is not a warrior goddess and is generally not at home on the battlefield. It is clear, that is, that Aphrodite is no mere import from the Near East.

Another possible historical tradition that may have contributed to the making of Aphrodite is the Indo-European (or proto-Indo-European) tradition. In particular, the goddess Dawn (Eos in Greek and Ushas in Sanskrit) has certain attributes that are shared by Aphrodite. It may be that Aphrodite absorbed certain aspects and attributes of this goddess as she achieved her fully developed character. Eos and Ushas, like Aphrodite, are often said to be very beautiful. The goddess Dawn, naturally, is associated with the sky, and is often said to be sky-born. Aphrodite, although she nearly always is referred to as water-born or ocean-born, is associated with the sky. Both goddesses are attracted to mortal lovers, although Aphrodite's sexual vigor seems far greater than that of Eos or Ushas. Both Eos and Aphrodite are associated strongly with the sun and light. Quite unlike many other goddesses associated with fertility, Aphrodite's chthonian qualities are almost entirely lacking. Her great power, which affects growth and fertility as well as sexuality, seems to come more from the vigor of such sky-associated phenomena as the sun and rain than it does from the mysterious powers residing in the earth.[10] Indeed, one of her widely used epithets was Aphrodite Ourania, Aphrodite of the Sky (or Heavens).[11]

There is no strong evidence that a goddess like Aphrodite was known in the Minoan-Mycenaean culture. Seashells littered the floor of places where Minoan goddesses were worshiped, suggesting an association with the sea, and Aphrodite has strong associations with the sea and with certain shellfish.[12] Furthermore, some Minoan female figurines are shown with birds, which some scholars have identified as doves, a bird strongly associated with Aphrodite. One particular figure is shown nude, which is quite exceptional, and has birds attached to her head and elbows.[13] This reminds us of Aphrodite's connection with birds (although she is not the only goddess connected with birds) and of the later preference for depicting Aphrodite naked.

What seems clear is that the Greek goddess Aphrodite had historical roots in at least two traditions, ancient Near Eastern and proto-Indo-European, and may have had roots elsewhere as well,[14] but that at one point she assumed a specifically Greek identity. Aphrodite, as we know her from Greek myth and cult, certainly has similarities with goddesses in other traditions. Her distinctive character, however, cannot be reduced to either the proto-Indo-European goddess Dawn or any of the ancient Near Eastern goddesses of love and war. By the time of Sappho and Homer, and probably much earlier, Aphrodite had succeeded in becoming an established part of the Olympian pantheon and was acknowledged to be (mythologically) one of the oldest and most powerful of the Greek deities.

Vigor and Growth

Aphrodite's presence is apparent throughout the living world, for it is she who quickens all life. She is the power that stirs seeds to grow, mature, flower, and reproduce themselves. She is the underlying, pervasive power that renews plant life in its season and imbues animals with the urge to mate and multiply themselves.[15] In Hesiod's account of her birth from the sea, she is said to have come ashore at Cytherea and then Cyprus, and "grass grew up about her beneath her shapely feet."[16] In the *Iliad*, Hera borrows Aphrodite's girdle, which makes its wearer irresistible, and with Aphrodite's help arouses sexual desire in her husband, Zeus. Zeus speaks sweetly to her, and when they lie down to make love he surrounds them with a thick cloud so they will go unseen. In their great desire, infused with the presence of Aphrodite, vegetation becomes lush and bursts into bloom beneath and around them: "So speaking, the son of Kronos caught his wife in his arms. There underneath them the divine earth broke into young, fresh grass, into dewy clover, crocus and hyacinth so thick and soft it held the hard ground deep away from them. There they lay down together and drew about them a golden wonderful cloud, and from it the glimmering dew descended."[17] At one of her temples, located on Mount Eryx in Sicily, it was said that each night all sign of ashes from sacrifices on the altar disappeared and "each morning dewy green grew in their stead."[18]

Aphrodite's identification with fertility and growth is stressed in her association with fruits and flowers. Fruits suggest fertility and progeny, and Aphrodite is often shown holding fruits, particularly the apple, which is probably associated with sexual desire as well as fertility, and the pomegranate, which suggests fecundity because of its many seeds.[19] She is even more strongly associated with flowers. She is "celebrated as the lady of spring blossoms, especially of roses in bloom;"[20] she wears garments that have been dyed in spring flowers by the Graces;[21] she wears roses in her hair;[22] the rose is called "the image of Venus" (the Roman name for Aphrodite) by the poet Tiberianus;[23] and she is often associated with gardens in bloom.[24] In images of her, Aphrodite is "almost stereotypically represented holding the lily."[25] While flowers represent growth and fresh life, they also suggest the generative organs.[26] Flowers are both beautiful and sensual when linked with Aphrodite.

In later phases of her worship and cult, Aphrodite becomes increasingly associated with fragrances (often floral) that arouse sexual yearning.[27] "Scent is important in the roses of Aphrodite, scent and its emotional effect. The three vegetal attributes that have most to do with Aphrodite are all sweet-scented, her roses, her myrtle, her quinces. Certainly the Summer Damasks emit that spicy, slightly sharpened sweetness which can be named aphrodisiac."[28] In addition to the aroma of flowers, she becomes identified with the scents of myrrh, cinnamon, fennel, and other aromatic spices that were believed to enhance sexual arousal.[29]

It is not surprising, given Aphrodite's strong identification with growth and fertility, that at times she should be identified or associated with Kore (Persephone), who also was held to personify the power of vegetation.[30] It also seems clear that some of Aphrodite's sexual adventures had an underlying fertility motif.

> Adonis' annual comings and goings obviously symbolize the seasonal vegetative cycle, and in many parts of the eastern Mediterranean his death was mourned annually in city-wide rites. . . . Most scholars and, again, many ancient authors accept the (fairly unquestionable) parallelism between Adonis and Aphrodite, Osiris and Isis of Egypt, Astarte and Tammuz of the Semites, and, finally, the Sumerian Inanna and Dumuzi. Not only do we have a regional structure of great geographical extent and time depth, but the Greek variant specifically resembles that of the Sumerians, as in the detail that Adonis died in a field of lettuce.[31]

Aphrodite's attempts to give her lovers Anchises and Adonis immortality, and their subsequent deaths, are reminiscent of the myths featuring the goddesses Isis and Inanna/Ishtar, who also unsuccessfully strove to grant their lovers/husbands immortality. The periodic death of vegetation probably is suggested in these relationships. "An important element of the Marriage of the Fertility Goddess is the attempt of the goddess to give immortality to her mortal lover, an attempt that is somehow frustrated. Fertility and increase are given instead."[32] Anchises is granted progeny as a result of his encounter with Aphrodite, and certain flowers appear in the world from the blood of the dying Adonis. It has been suggested that the scene in the myth of Aphrodite and Anchises, in which Aphrodite strips off all her adornments and clothing before making love to Anchises, is reminiscent of the scene in Sumerian mythology when Inanna is stripped of all her clothing and regal insignia when she appears in the underworld. Inanna subsequently dies and must be reinvigorated before returning to the realm of the living. This is usually taken to represent the death and rebirth of the crops.[33]

Aphrodite's presence also was seen in the animal world. The mutual attraction of the sexes represents Aphrodite's influence. On her way to meet her human lover Anchises, Aphrodite passes through a wooded area, and the animals there are attracted to her. "After her come grey wolves, fawning on her, and grim-eyed lions, and bears, and fleet leopards, ravenous for deer: and she was glad in heart to see them, and put desire in their breasts, so that they all mated, two together, about the shadowy coombes."[34]

Aphrodite, bronze statuette, second century C.E., Verulamium. Courtesy of the Verulamium Museum, St. Albans, England.

Aphrodite has a strong indentification with birds, especially those suggestive of fertility and eroticism. Doves, in particular, are associated with her. In this case, it seems clear that "certain obvious features of a goddess of love are paired with the equally obvious billing and cooing of the dove in an excellent case of natural symbolism."[35] "The dove remained Aphrodite's bird, . . . the essence of that affinity having been that doves coo and are gentle and are publicly amorous. . . . Doves croon, and are comfortable: their crooning to each other is a music of the preliminaries, their comfortable quality is the langour of afterwards."[36] The poet Sappho says that Aphrodite's chariot was drawn by sparrows. Sparrows were "notorious for their wantonness and fecundity" and "their flesh and eggs were eaten for aphrodisiac effects."[37] Pindar says that Aphrodite sent forth the wryneck, which was believed to be a passionate bird, to undertake her wishes. In the Adonis myth and cult, the wryneck featured prominently. Commenting on its role, Detienne says: "The wryneck has only one function: to unite the lover with his mistress or the mistress with her lover."[38]

Aphrodite's presence also was revealed, in a somewhat more abstract way, in such natural phenomena as the rain, the cycles of the seasons, and other natural rhythms that accompany fertility, growth, and fruitfulness. Aeschylus, in the *Danaids*, has Aphrodite speak of the primordial longing that earth and heaven have for each other, a longing that produces the rain that satisfies and fertilizes earth and makes her fruitful. "The holy heaven is full of desire to mate with the earth, and desire seizes the earth to find a mate; rain falls from the amorous heaven and impregnates the earth; and the earth brings forth for men the fodder of flocks and herds and the gifts of Demeter; and from the same moistening marriage-rite the fruit of trees is ripened. Of these things I am the cause."[39]

Empedocles spoke of the primordial force of love pervading the creation, stirring all species of life to harmonious and productive interaction.

> At one time in life's season of flower does
> Love bring together the limbs that belong
> To the body. At another, cruel strife
> Divides them and they wander alone by
> The breaking waves of life's sea. It is so
> With the plants and the fishes that have
> Their homes in the sea. It is so with the beasts
> couch on the hills, and so with
> tumbling birds who wander around on the wing.[40]

Several centuries later the Roman Lucretius wrote about Aphrodite's (Venus's) omnipotence over all nature this way:

> Mother of Aeneas, darling of gods and men,
> Venus our nurse, below the wheeling
> Stars of heaven you fill ship-bearing
> Sea and fruitful lands with life. Through you
> All manner of things alive first are
> Conceived and then emerge and see the light
> Of day. Goddess, ahead of you storms clear,
> When you arrive clouds empty from the sky.
> And sweet Daedalian earth brings out its
> Flowers for you. The flats of ocean smile
> For you, and through the calm of heaven light
> Spreads and shines. The day Spring shows herself
> The west wind's generative breath regains
> Its life, the birds of the air make you
> And your arrival known, their hearts pierced
> By your power. Then rich provender
> Makes wild beasts leap and swim quick streams.
> Captives of your charm follow, wherever
> You may lead. And so through seas and heights
> And grasping streams, through leafy homes of birds,
> And the green fields, into the hearts of all you
> Strike persuasive love, by which eagerly,
> Race by race they multiply their kind.[41]

Recently, attention has been drawn to certain images of Aphrodite that show her spinning, and these have been interpreted as illustrating her association or identification with natural rhythms that transform certain inorganic substances into organic life. Commenting on a vase painting showing Aphrodite riding a flying goose and holding a distaff, Elmer Suhr says: "The swan or goose plays the role of the clouds from which the divinity plucks the fibers for spinning the golden thread of life which, in turn, produces the plant life of the fertilized soil. She is an outstanding example of the Heavenly Aphrodite actually engaged in spinning. . . . The power of pneuma flows through her body,

Aphrodite riding a goose, Attic cup, ca. 470 B.C.E. British Museum. Geoffrey Grigson, *The Goddess of Love* (London: Constable, 1976), fig. 56, p. 206.

she combines it with other elements in the cosmos—the water and air of the cloud—before pneuma can realize itself in the generation of life."[42]

As the cosmic spinner, Aphrodite not only quickens, renews, and excites life and growth, she creates life. She is the mysterious quality or rhythm that is able to produce life in its great variety from the lifeless elements of the universe. She is able, by means of her spinning, to instill the rhythms of the inorganic world with living rhythms that fill the world with plants, animals, and human beings, all possessed of her own creative power, which tends to attraction, pairing, and progeny. Sweeping through the heavens astride her great bird, Aphrodite gathers the potent energy of the sun and the life-giving moisture of the clouds and spins them into semen, the distilled essence of life, and with the semen/rain she fertilizes the earth, which brings forth life abundantly, rhythmically, and beautifully.

A fairly minor, but interesting, aspect of Aphrodite, which should probably be understood in the context of her identification with vegetation and animal life, concerns her association with death. "At Delphi . . . there was worship . . . in the first and second centuries A.D., of an Aphrodite Epitymbia, an Aphrodite on the Grave. By her statue the dead were called up, eager for the libation poured into the ground."[43] Plutarch mentions funeral ceremonies that were held in honor of Aphrodite in Aegina to commemorate those who died at Troy.[44] At Thebes, Aphrodite was associated with Persephone, the queen of the underworld.[45] On Crete and Cyprus, a goddess named Aphrodite Gorgo, who represented a "goddess conceived as dead and represented in frozen slumber," was worshiped.[46] Although Aphrodite's association with death may have to do with her role in punishing people who ignore her power, and with her driving them to ruin and sometimes death by suicide,[47] her association with death probably should be interpreted as part of the cycles of vegetation and life generally. In many cultures, renewal of vegetation, especially invigoration of the spirit of the crops, was accomplished by offering a blood sacrifice. It was assumed that the energy of the earth that yielded life had to be renourished. This was done by offering life to the source of life in the form of sacrifice.[48] Although blood sacrifice does not seem to have been at all central in the worship of Aphrodite, there are references to sheep, goats, and other animals being offered to her.[49] That the periodic renewal of life necessitated the regular return of energy to the goddess through death may have been a part of the logic or symbolic significance of these sacrifices.

Civic Associations

Yet there are three hearts that she cannot bend nor yet ensnare. First is the daughter of Zeus who holds the aegis, bright-eyed Athene; for she has no pleasure in the deeds of golden Aphrodite. . . . Nor does laughter-loving Aphrodite ever tame in love

Aphrodite, copy of an original by Scopas of Lysippe, fourth century B.C.E. K. Papaioannou, *L'Art et la civilisation de la Grèce ancienne. L'Art grec* (Paris: Editions d'art Lucien Mazenrod, 1972), fig. 809, p. 459. Permission of Giraudon/Art Resource, New York.

Artemis, the huntress with shafts of gold. . . . Nor yet does the pure maiden Hestia love Aphrodite's works. She was . . . a queenly maid whom both Poseidon and Apollo sought to wed. But she was wholly unwilling, nay, stubbornly refused; and touching the head of father Zeus . . . she that fair goddess, sware a great oath which has in truth been fulfilled, that she would be a maiden all her days.[50]

There is much to be learned, no doubt, from reflecting on why it is that these three goddesses—Athena, Artemis, and Hestia—are immune to Aphrodite's power. It is pointed out, for example, that sexual desire, excitement, and lust do not belong in the realms of civic order (Athena), the hunt (Artemis), and the structure of the home and family (Hestia). Conversely, it is also often pointed out that Aphrodite herself cares little or nothing for civil order and propriety, hunting, or the domestic routines of the hearth and home. However, instances of Aphrodite's association with civic affairs exist, and although these are not central and do tend to be overshadowed by her preference for sexual independence, sexual adventure, and strong physical passion, it is clear that in her cult Aphrodite was understood to play the role, in some places and at some times, of guardian of social and civic order.

Although in Greek mythology Aphrodite herself seems restless within the confines of marriage, considerable evidence suggests that at several places she was associated with, and was the patroness of, marriage. This probably suggests a concern on her part for social and civic harmony. Sometimes before a marriage she was propitiated with a sacrifice.[51] At Sparta she assumes the name of Hera, the wife of Zeus, who is strongly associated with marriage.[52] She is known by names that emphasize her role in bringing couples together in marriage and in presiding over their union in the bridal chamber.[53] In some places, widows and unmarried girls made offerings to Aphrodite to help them in obtaining husbands,[54] while Aphrodite herself is mentioned trying to arrange the marriage of daughters of Pandareos in the *Odyssey*.[55] Aphrodite's association with marriage had to do, in part at least, with the central role that sexual attraction plays in marriage. Without her presence a marriage might fade and die. Her association with the clan,[56] the city, and children,[57] however, makes it clear that her role in marriage was not strictly sexual in every case.

Aphrodite's nonsexual, civic aspect is even clearer in those cases where she is depicted fully clothed and armed[58] or in which she is shown with "the turreted crown, the badge of the state."[59] In these cases, Aphrodite's role seems to be primarily that of a tutelary deity who is associated with a specific geographical area or a specific local, city tradition or who is the defender of the city. In Greek mythology, Aphrodite is rarely depicted in either role, and in the few instances in which she is depicted on the battlefield she is said to be ineffective. It seems clear, though, that in some places she did play the role of a deity whose concern was the preservation of social order. It is possible that these aspects of her cult—warrior and city guardian—were inherited from such goddesses as Ishtar in the ancient Near East. Ishtar and others combined love and war and sometimes were strongly identified with particular cities that they defended fiercely.

Aphrodite's later association in Greek mythology with the war god, Ares, does not seem to represent a continuation of her role as a civic guardian. Their relationship is primarily sexual and suggests, perhaps, the mutual attraction of two strong passions—violence/war and sex/love.

Golden Aphrodite

One of Aphrodite's most distinctive qualities, a quality central to her character in most descriptions, has to do with what is suggested in her epithet the Golden One. Beauty, light, sunshine, warmth, and what has been called a smiling "sunlit sexuality" are all part of this quality of goldeness that Aphrodite possesses to a much greater extent than any other Greek goddess.

Aphrodite's physical appearance is supremely beautiful and is often said to have a stunning impact upon those who behold her. Other Greek goddesses such as Athena, Hera, and Artemis are also said to be beautiful, but Aphrodite is the most beautiful, and her beauty seems an intrinsic part of her character. Her physical beauty is not at all incidental to her character (as might be said of Athena's or Artemis's) but is an essential part of who she is and of the roles she plays in the world. Her physical features are often mentioned and the impact of their beauty described. "We are told of her flashing eyes, her soft skin, her smile and golden ornaments."[60] Aphrodite becomes the standard for female beauty. To compare a woman to her is "the most eloquent way to extol a woman's beauty."[61] Even when Aphrodite disguises herself as an old woman, as she does when she appears to Helen in a scene from the *Iliad*, she is recognized because of her beauty. Helen at once is struck by the "sweet throat of the goddess / and her desirable breasts and her eyes that were full of shining."[62]

Aphrodite is often described bathing, dressing, or adorning herself, which calls attention to her physical attractiveness. Before going to seduce Anchises, she visits her temple at Paphos on Cyprus. "There she went in and put to the glittering doors, and there the Graces bathed her with heavenly oil such as blooms upon the bodies of the eternal gods—oil divinely sweet, which she had by her, filled with fragrance. And laughter-loving Aphrodite put on all her rich clothes, and when she had decked herself with gold, she left sweet-smelling Cyprus and went in haste towards Troy, swiftly travelling high up among the clouds."[63] After having been caught in the act of adultery by her husband, Hephaestus, and mocked by the gods, Aphrodite is released. She seems quite unruffled by the incident and returns to her sanctuary at Paphos,

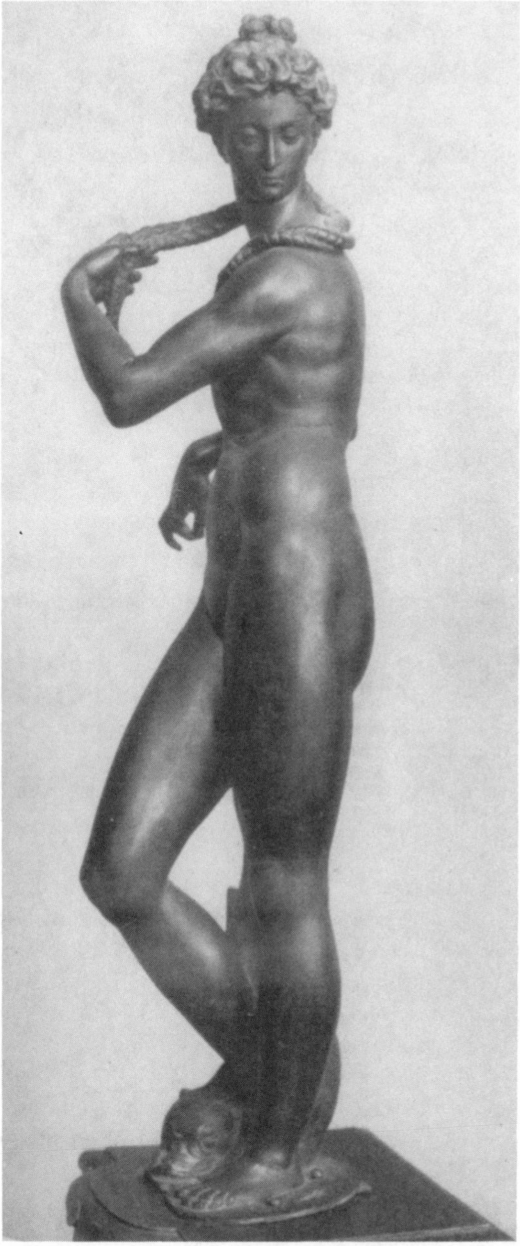

Venus by Ammanati, sixteenth century C.E., Italian. Bargello Museum, Florence. Kenneth Clark, *The Nude* (Princeton, N.J.: Princeton University Press, 1956), p. 137.

. . . where lies her smoky alter
and there the Graces bathed her and anointed her with ambrosial
oil, such as abounds for the gods who are everlasting,
and put delightful clothing about her, a wonder to look on.[64]

And while the male gods may have mocked her, caught as she was in flagrant adultery lying naked in the arms of Ares (the goddesses were too embarrassed to join the gods in gazing on the erotically entwined couple), at least two of the gods, Hermes and Poseidon, are enamored of her beauty and charmed by her presence. At one point Apollo asks Hermes how he would like to be in Ares' place, caught under a tight net in bed with Aphrodite under the gaze of the assembled gods. Hermes replies:

" . . . I wish it could only
be, and there could be thrice this number of fastenings,
and all you gods would be looking on and all the goddesses,
and still I would sleep by the side of Aphrodite the golden."[65]

Images of Aphrodite frequently depict her in poses that call attention to her body and her physical beauty. As Aphrodite Kallipygos, Aphrodite of the Lovely Backside, she is sometimes shown lifting her gown and turning her head to admire her sleek rump.[66] She is often shown bathing, about to bathe, or wringing her hair after bathing (or after having arisen from the sea). She is sometimes shown adjusting a sandal or putting on a necklace.[67]

Aphrodite's clothing and adornments are also consistently described as splendid, dazzling, and radiant. They emphasize and enhance her beauty and contribute to the overpowering effect of her appearance. When she appears to Anchises his initial reaction is to "wonder at her."[68] Soon "love seizes him"[69] as he gazes at her stunning physical appearance. "His feelings are described mainly in terms of his reactions to her outward appearance, including both her body and her clothes: her robe 'more shining than fire' . . . ; her shining ear rings, bracelets, and necklaces of gold . . . ; and, above all, the light glowing around her soft breasts 'like the moon.' "[70] Aphrodite's clothes and adornments are meant not to cover, mask, or deemphasize her physical appearance but to accentuate and heighten her beauty.

Her gold ornaments are mentioned frequently. Gold in association with Aphrodite seems to have at least two meanings. First, gold is bright and shiny. Its glitter is attractive in itself and calls attention to the person who wears it. In the case of Aphrodite and the world of classical Greece, gold was held to be synonymous with beauty itself.[71] Second, gold does not tarnish. It stays forever bright and in this respect seems immune from aging and decay. Aphrodite's ever-young, ever-beautiful, ever-fresh appearance is reflected in the ever-bright nature of gold and reminds us of Aphrodite's epithet "the putter-off of old age."[72] A third possible meaning of Aphrodite's association with gold may have to do with the symbolic associations between gold, honey, mellifluous speech, and semen. "At a deeper level there is an association between gold, honey, speech, and sexual fluids. . . . Gold and its semantic cognates in speech, honey, and semen . . . symbolize the yet deeper Aphrodite values of procreation, verbal creation, and so forth."[73]

Although images of Greek goddesses unclothed are rare before the fifth century B.C.E., Aphrodite's nudity after that period became an important part of her character. Images of her partially clothed, undressing, or totally naked became so common that exposure of her body became expressive of her nature. Initially, images of Aphrodite naked were seen as exceptional, perhaps even shocking. One of the most famous images of naked Aphrodite, a statue carved by Praxiteles around 330 B.C.E., was rejected by the citizens of Cos in favor of a draped image of the goddess. Presumably, the naked image was too shocking. The image was subsequently purchased by the people of Cnidus and became famous throughout the Greek world. People came from all over to gaze upon the beauty of the image. So famous did she become that a king offered to pay off all the municipal debts of Cnidus in exchange for the statue. The Cnidians refused this request.[74] It seems that the image, which must have been remarkable, had a certain "sensual tremor which, for five hundred years, led poets, emperors, and boatloads of tourists to linger in the sanctuary of Knidos."[75]

Increasingly, portraying Aphrodite naked became acceptable, and this is appropriate in that she more and more was associated with physical beauty. She came to be associated with the power inherent in the beauty of the body to rivet the attention, stir admiration, and arouse sensual feelings. Her nudity expresses the truth that the beauty of the human body is complete unto itself. It needs no additional adornment, no ornamentation. It is, as it were, divinely attractive, compelling, and arresting in itself. Speaking of the Cnidian Aphrodite of Praxiteles, Kenneth Clark says: "Perhaps no religion ever again incorporated physical passion so calmly, so sweetly, and so naturally that all who saw her felt that the instincts they shared with beasts they also shared with the gods."[76] The shimmering beauty of the naked female body can only be attenuated by clothing. In her goldenness, then, Aphrodite is appropriately shown unclothed so that her physical beauty can be appreciated in its fullness and completeness.

The radiant, sparkling quality of Aphrodite that is suggested in her name the Golden One is emphasized in one of her most famous epithets, "smile loving" or "laughter loving" (*philommeides*). Rarely is Aphrodite depicted as brooding, angry, or resentful. Although she does punish those who deny her power, the darker aspects of passion and lust rarely express themselves in Aphrodite herself. She does mourn for her lover Adonis, and she occasionally is associated with the underworld, but a strong preference is shown in literary and plastic depictions of Aphrodite to emphasize her delight in sensual pleasure. Her smile conveys a playful, affectionate nature. Her smile, her graceful nudity, her ornaments of gold and flowers, her association with birds, the sky, and the sun all convey a divine presence that is almost totally removed from chthonian regions and powers. Her impressive power in affecting fertility, growth, and sexuality seems derived primarily from the warmth, light, and brightness of the sun, rather than from the mysterious powers of the earth.

Aphrodite's association with the sea also might be seen as related to her goldenness, particularly goldenness as suggesting positive, pleasant, fortunate, auspicious qualities. The sea, of course, can suggest chaos and is often used as a symbol of unrefined, primordial power that can seem threatening and overwhelming. Poseidon, the Greek god who is most consistently associated with the sea, is sometimes characterized as turbulent and wrathful. He often expresses himself in wild ocean storms. Aphrodite's association with the sea, however, is consistently peaceful and calm. It is the smooth, glittering sea that Aphrodite is associated with, not the dark, turbulent ocean. She is known as the "goddess of the serene sea,"[77] "goddess of the haven," and "goddess of the prosperous voyage."[78] Her relationship to the shining, calm sea is made clear in the story of Herostratus of Naucratis, who took a sea journey and found himself in the midst of a storm that threatened to destroy his ship. He prayed to a small image of Aphrodite that he had purchased at Paphos, and "when prayer was offered to the image, pure myrtle sprouted all round it, a sweet aroma filled the ship, and the passengers who had already given up hope reached land in safety."[79]

Aphrodite's association with smooth seas and successful voyages is also related to good luck in love. Indeed, it seems that in some cases references to Aphrodite's influence in creating smooth seas and prosperous journeys over them are used as metaphors for happy and successful love relationships.[80]

Watcher over the Surf, I send you these cakes
    And gifts of simple offering, for tomorrow
I traverse the wide Ionian Sea, hurrying to our
    Eidothea's arms. Shine with fair
Favour on my sailing and my love, Cyprian,
    Queen of the bedroom and the shore.[81]

The same connection is made in this poem in which Aphrodite herself speaks:

Because I delight in the wide
Frightening sea
And in seafarers who look
For assistance from me.

Give me my due, and fair wind will
Flow out from me
Behind you in love, or
Across the grey sea.[82]

Aphrodite is often shown with a dolphin, which relates both to her association with the sea and with what we have referred to as her goldenness. Among the Greeks, the dolphin was associated with fair weather and smooth seas. Stories were told of the friendliness and helpfulness of dolphins to voyagers in distress. In its playfulness and friendliness, perhaps also in its sociability, its disinclination to travel alone, the dolphin reflected Aphrodite's own nature.[83]

Aphrodite is often accompanied by the Graces, three maidens whose names are "Algaïa, the Bright One, Euphrosyne, the Glad One, and Thaleia, the One of Abundance."[84] They help her bathe, they dress and adorn her, and in every way they reflect Aphrodite's golden nature. They are often shown dancing together, fair haired, arms linked around each other.[85] They are said to give delight; "they give life its vigour, and make it bud."[86] They surround Aphrodite with an air of harmonious growth, charm, winsomeness, youthful vigor, and maidenly grace. They are extensions of herself.

Love, Longing, and Sex

Aphrodite's dominant characteristic is her powerful sexuality. It is this aspect of her nature that so clearly distinguishes her from the other major Greek goddesses (with the possible exception of Hera, whose sexuality, though powerful, is much more restricted, expressing itself almost exclusively in her relationship with Zeus). Unlike Athena and Artemis, who are ever virgin, Aphrodite is never virgin. No story tells of the loss of her virginity, nor do any tell of her being raped or overpowered sexually by a male. Her own great sexual strength would make this unlikely.[87] Not only is Aphrodite sexually powerful, she is "sexually generous."[88] In some myths she is said to be married to Hephaestus, but this relationship in no way limits or fulfills her sexual expression. Indeed, marriage does not seem to befit Aphrodite. Among the gods, she is intimate with Ares, Hermes, Poseidon, and Hephaestus, while she has sexual encounters with Anchises, Adonis, and Theseus among mortals.[89] In these relationships, furthermore, Aphrodite is not the passive recipient of male attention. She is usually active in seeking out love and is sometimes depicted seducing her lover, as in the case of Anchises.

It is clearly Aphrodite's close identification with sexual desire itself that lends her a power and an overwhelming presence that prompted one scholar to say: "Of all the Twelve Olympians she is the most alarming and the most alluring."[90] Indeed, the Greek term *aphrodite* meant sexual desire or sexual intercourse.[91] To experience sexual desire or sexual pleasure, to be in a state of *aphrodite*, was to be infused by the goddess Aphrodite. In this sense, Aphrodite is ever present and close to hand in the living world, where all life is perpetuated by sexual attraction. Her primordial power, manifest in sexual desire and attraction, is a main theme in descriptions of her. In the opening lines of one of the *Homeric Hymns* in praise of her, we read: "Muse, tell me the deeds of golden Aphrodite the Cyprian, who stirs up sweet passion in the gods and subdues the tribes of mortal men and birds that fly in air and all the many creatures that the dry land rears, and all that the sea: all these love the deeds of rich-crowned Cytherea."[92] Empedocles speaks of Aphrodite as "planted deep in our fabric" and says that it is "she by whom men are impelled to / Have thoughts of love."[93] In Euripides' *Hippolytus* one of the characters says of Aphrodite: "Her path is in the sky, and mid the ocean's surge she rides; from her all nature springs; she sows the seeds of love, inspires the warm desire to which we sons of earth all owe our being."[94]

Aphrodite's identification with sexual desire and sexual pleasure is often explicit. The account of her birth in Hesiod's *Theogony* makes a clear identification between the goddess and sexual desire by describing her creation from the severed genitals of Uranus.[95] Just as Athena's nonsexual, rational nature is suggested by her birth from Zeus's head, so Aphrodite's sexual, sensuous, and emotional nature is suggested in her birth from the genitals of her father. Aphrodite's association with several male deities also makes her identification with sexual desire and pleasure clear. She is often said to be accompanied by Eros, a masculine counterpart to herself, a deity clearly identified with sexual desire. In his *Theogony*, Hesiod makes Eros one of the oldest of the gods, born in the very first stages of creation, suggesting his primordial importance. Hesiod describes him at his birth as "fairest among the deathless gods, who unnerves the limbs and overcomes the mind and wise counsels of all gods and all men within them."[96] In Euripides' *Hippolytus*, the chorus praises Aphrodite and Eros together and describes the effects they bring about on all beings.

> Ah! Cypris, thine the hand that guides the stubborn hearts of gods and men: thine, and that attendant boy's, who, with painted plummage gay, flutters round his victims on lightning wing. O'er the land and booming deep on golden pinion borne flits

the god of Love, maddening the heart and beguiling the senses of all whom he attacks, savage whelps on mountains bred, ocean's monsters, creatures of this sun-warmed earth, and man; thine, O Cypris, thine alone the sovereign power to rule them all.[97]

In the striking image of Sappho:

> Eros shivers my heart,
> Like a wind down the mountain
> Which falls on the oaks.[98]

Aphrodite also is said to be accompanied by the spirits Himeros, Pothos, and Peitho, the "geniuses of longing and persuasion."[99] She is also paired quite often with Hermes and Priapus, both of whom have fairly obvious phallic identities. Indeed, Priapus is primarily a personification of the erect phallus. He represents sexual arousal, sexual longing, and as such is appropriately associated with Aphrodite.[100] The god Hermes was often represented by stone pillars topped with a bearded head of the god. On many of these pillars there was also shown an erect phallus.[101] In some places, appropriately, Hermes and Aphrodite were worshiped together.[102] A second-century B.C.E. terracotta image in the British Museum shows a pillar of Hermes with bearded head and erect phallus being crowned and embraced by Aphrodite.[103]

These associations with Priapus and Hermes suggest an alternative, or additional, translation or meaning to Aphrodite's common epithet *philommeides*. While this is almost always translated as "smile loving," some scholars have said that it also might have been understood to mean "penis loving," "loving a (man's) penis (or genitalia),"[104] or "Lover of Genitals."[105] This is suggested on the basis of the very similar epithet *philommedes*, which does mean "penis loving" or "genital loving" and is used by Hesiod in the *Theogony* when he describes Aphrodite's birth from the genitals of Uranus.[106] Grigson and Friedrich suggest that *philommeides* may have had a double entendre, then, suggesting the more sexually explicit name that is so close in sound.

Another association that to us moderns may not appear explicit, but that well may have had explicit sexual meaning to the ancient Greeks, is Aphrodite's identification with seashells. Around the fourth century B.C.E., images of Aphrodite emerging from a scallop shell became known and by the second century B.C.E. were quite common. She is usually shown naked. It is as if she were being born from the shell. The association of the scallop shell with the female genitals is not unlikely if these images can be taken to depict Aphrodite's actual birth. The matter is made quite certain when we learn that the Greek word for scallop, *kteis*, "also meant the private parts of a woman."[107] In some renditions of this theme, Aphrodite holds a phallus.[108] It seems fairly clear that, whatever

Head of Aphrodite, bronze, Hellenistic, second century B.C.E., from Satula, Armenia Minor (northeast Turkey). British Museum. Geoffrey Grigson, *The Goddess of Love* (London: Constable, 1976), fig. 19, p. 87.

else the scallop might suggest, these images suggest Aphrodite's identification with genitals, especially female genitals.

Aphrodite's identification with sex also is explicit in her association with prostitutes. Such epithets as Aphrodite the Whore (Aphrodite Hetaira or Aphrodite Porne), Aphrodite of Copulation, Aphrodite Who Rides Astride, and Aphrodite Who Opens Herself Up all make explicit Aphrodite's identification with prostitutes and with sexual intercourse and sexual pleasure. That she was served and worshiped by courtesans, or *hetairai* (literally, companions), and that she was in some sense identified with them, is not surprising. Although prostitutes were not associated with most Aphrodite temples,[109] sacred prostitution was practiced at some famous temples. The most famous of these was at Corinth. Although the precise details of the relationship between the *hetairai* and Aphrodite are not known, it is clear that the women were all vowed to the goddess and lived in or near the temple on the Corinthian acropolis. It is also known that these Corinthian *hetairai*, in addition to being beautiful and accomplished in the erotic arts, were often well-trained in such fine arts as music, dancing, and conversation.[110] Many of these women were purchased by the wealthy as offerings to Aphrodite.[111] A famous example of this concerns the athlete Xenophon, who vowed one year to supply the Corinthian temple with one hundred girls if he won the crown at the Olympic games, which he did. Pindar then wrote a poem describing the dancing of the girls at the temple when they were dedicated there.[112] Pindar is supposed to have read this poem before the image of Aphrodite in the temple. It reads in part:

> Young girls, hospitable to many guests, servants of
> Persuasion in wealthy Corinth, you who burn the golden
> tears of fresh frankincense, many times soaring upward
> in your thoughts of Aphrodite, heavenly mother of loves:
>
> To you, girls, she has granted blamelessly on lovely beds
> to harvest the fruits of delicate spring, for under love's
> necessity all things are fair.[113]

Aphrodite's votaries, the *hetairai*, like Aphrodite herself, were no mere sexual athletes interested only in the pleasure of the physical act of making love. They, and she, were accomplished in the arts and pleasures of seduction. In Hesiod's *Theogony*, when Aphrodite is taken to the assembly of the gods, "the portion allotted to her amongst men and undying gods" is said to be "the whisperings of maidens and smiles and deceits with sweet delight and love and graciousness."[114] Aphrodite's seductive nature is embodied in her girdle, which lends to the wearer an irresistible ability to seduce anyone whom he or she chooses. In Hera's seduction of Zeus, which she accomplishes with the help of Aphrodite's girdle, there is the suggestion that "all seductions are ultimately performed by Aphrodite herself."[115] The girdle itself is described this way when Aphrodite takes it off to lend it to Hera: "She spoke, and from her breasts unbound the elaborate, pattern-pierced zone, and on it are figured all beguilements, and loveliness is figured upon it, and passion of sex is there, and the whispered endearment that steals the heart away even from the thoughtful."[116]

The story concerning the judgment of Paris reveals Aphrodite's seductive nature. Zeus asks Paris to determine which of the three goddesses—Hera, Athena, or Aphrodite—is the fairest. Although Paris is impressed by Hera's beauty and her promise to make him powerful and rich, and by Athena's stately grace and her intention of making him handsome, rich, and victorious in battle, he is unable to resist Aphrodite.

> Aphrodite sidled up to him, and Paris blushed because she came so close that they were almost touching.
>
> "Look carefully, please, pass nothing over. . . . By the way, as soon as I saw you, I said to myself: 'Upon my word, there goes the handsomest young man in Phrygia! Why does he waste himself here in the wilderness herding stupid cattle?' Well, why do you, Paris? Why not move into a city and lead a civilized life? What have you to lose by marrying someone like Helen of Sparta, who is as beautiful as I am, and no less passionate? I am convinced that, once you two have met, she will abandon her home, her family, everything, to become your mistress. Surely you have heard of Helen?"

Paris admits that he has not heard of Helen, so Aphrodite describes her charms with some care, and then says that, if he wished, he could have Helen. Paris says:

> "How is that possible, if she is already married?"
>
> "Heavens! How innocent you are! Have you never heard that it is my divine duty to arrange affairs of this sort? I suggest now that you tour Greece with my son Eros as your guide. Once you reach Sparta, he and I will see that Helen falls head over heels in love with you."[117]

Paris, overcome by her beauty, flattery, charm, and promises of having Helen, awards her the apple, signifying he has chosen her over Hera and Athena.

In her seduction of Anchises, Aphrodite breaks down his defenses against her godlike appearance. He is fearful of consorting with a goddess even though he is struck by her beauty. So Aphrodite invents a story, asserting that she is a mortal woman and wishes to marry him and bear him fine children. She even describes herself as "stainless and unproved in love."[118] Eventually

Anchises is overcome with desire for Aphrodite and, believing her to be a mortal woman, makes love with her.[119]

Such epithets as the following make clear Aphrodite's association with the arts and wiles of seduction: Aphrodite the Persuasive, Aphrodite Who Contrives Ways and Means for Lovers, Aphrodite Who Turns the Hearts of Men to Love, Aphrodite Who Gives Success in Love,[120] Aphrodite Who Whispers, Aphrodite of the Mandrake (which was believed to be a love drink), Aphrodite Who Gives Joy, and Aphrodite the Side-Glancer.[121] She is also called Aphrodite the Slayer of Men[122] and is sometimes shown holding a poppy. Her epithet She Who Lulls the Senses and Gives Sweet Sleep may be related to the effects of the poppy.[123]

Her stunning beauty, her golden nature, her amiable and smiling character, her delectable fragrance, her uninhibited display of her gorgeous features, her charm and grace, her warmth and generosity, and her seductive skills usually overcome gods and mortals with a divine madness, the madness of the lover, which Socrates in Plato's *Phaedrus* declares the highest form of madness.[124] This lover's madness is an "all-powerful yearning which can forget the whole world for the sake of the one beloved, that can shatter honorable bonds and break sacred faith only to melt into oneness with him."[125] "Her powerful enchantment causes oblivion of all duty and leads to resolves that later seem incomprehensible to the enchanted person himself."[126] Anchises, finally overwhelmed by Aphrodite, who has charmed him, declares: "Willingly would I go down into the house of Hades, O lady, beautiful as the goddesses, once I had gone up to your bed."[127] Aphrodite herself is also overcome by the madness of love, as when she first sees Anchises: "When laughter-loving Aphrodite saw him, she loved him and terribly desire seized her in her heart."[128]

While divine madness sometimes can lead to living life "happily ever after," it usually leads to tragedy in Greek mythology. Quite often, the relationship is set in motion by Aphrodite herself to punish someone who has slighted her or denied her power. Hippolytus dedicated himself to the chaste goddess Artemis and a life of celibacy, refusing to honor Aphrodite. Aphrodite then caused Phaedra, his stepmother, to fall madly in love with him. When Hippolytus discovered Phaedra's love for him, he was furious and berated her in horrified tones. She was humiliated and hanged herself. Before killing herself she accused Hippolytus of raping her. Her husband, Theseus, furious at his son, called upon Poseidon to slay his son, and Hippolytus was duly dragged to his death by his own horses when they became frightened while pulling his chariot along the sea coast.[129] Pasiphae, the mother of Phaedra, became inflamed with passion for a bull, and in Euripides' *Cretan Women*, she blames Aphrodite for her consuming and ruinous passion.[130] Aphrodite caused Myrrha, the daughter of one of her own priests, to fall in love with her father. She did this either because Myrrha's mother had boasted that Myrrha was more hrodite herself or because Myrrha had neglected to worship disguise, and at night, Myrrha went to her father and made love him. When he discovered who she was, he was horrified and tried to kill her. She ran away and was "saved" when she prayed to the gods for help and was turned into a myrrh tree.[131]

There is a deep, terrifyingly powerful passion exhibited by many of those whom Aphrodite "blesses." This passion often has about it a dark, violent aspect. This dimension of Aphrodite's power is nicely expressed by the Sicilian Greek poet, Ibykos, who lived in the sixth century B.C.E.

> But for me love is alert
> In all seasons.
> Love is a north wind
> On fire with flashes of lightning,
> Sent by the Cyprian.
> It brings a withering madness,
> It is black, it is shameless,
> Our hearts through and through
> Are wrung by its violence.[132]

In a similar vein, the second-century B.C.E. poet Meleager wrote:

> Love is a terror, a terror,
>   But how does it help if
> I sigh and repeat over and over again,
>   Love is a terror?
> . . . .
> O how did you manage,
>   Cyprian, born of the blue
> Green sea, all the same to bring
>   Out of the water flame?[133]

When she infuses a devotee/victim with her power or presence, his or her world becomes greatly intensified. Obsessive preoccupation with a lover is common, a preoccupation that is often incapacitating, ruinous, disruptive, and tragic. But under her influence—absorbed, overpowered, drugged, maddened by her—nothing else matters.

Perhaps the most eloquent testimony from Greek culture concerning the overpowering influence of Aphrodite comes from one of her own devotees, in the poetry of the great sixth-century B.C.E. poet Sappho, who lived in the city of Mytilene, the principal city of the island of Lesbos. We find in Sappho's poetry a glimpse of the interior turmoil created by love. Her poetry is personal, subjective, filled with sentiment that hints at the way Aphrodite overwhelms the entire person. Physical desire, no doubt, is one indication that Aphrodite has infused the lover, but emotional yearning, mental turmoil, agonized separation, maddening jealousy, and tearful reproaches are dominant also. It is the mind that is enraptured in Sappho's poetry. Her mind and emotions are completely dominated by a vision of the beloved (in the case of Sappho, her lovers were usually women). Yearning to mingle in love with her beloved, Sappho summons Aphrodite to help her. In a most interesting way, Sappho's poetry suggests two quite distinct ways of thinking of Aphrodite. When she summons Aphrodite to help her,[134] we imagine a deity or a presence that is outside Sappho, who may be addressed as an objective reality quite apart from the poet. Elsewhere in her poems, we are quite sure that Aphrodite infuses the poet herself, that Sappho is in a condition of Aphrodite, as it were; that her longing, passion, sensitivity, yearning, anguish, and sensuous needs are tangible manifestations of the powerful love goddess herself; that the fundamental reality of Aphrodite is found precisely in Sappho, or in any lover, overcome by the longing for the beloved. A few examples of Sappho's poetry will convey the deep, powerful nature of Aphrodite aroused in the heart and mind of one of her devotees.

> O Brocheo, I see you
> and speech fails me,
> the tongue shatters,
> my skin runs with delicate
> flame—my eyes dim;
> I'm hearing things!
> and sweat cascades,
> a trembling clutches
> my whole body,
> paler than grass
> lacking little to death.[135]

In the above poem she is physically impaired by the divine madness that has overcome her to the extent that she thinks she may die. She is lovesick, as it were—her body and mind no longer under her control. In the following poem, too, she uses images of being struck dumb, of being staggered by her strong passion.

> Let the depths of my soul be dumb
> for I cannot think up
> a clarion song about Adonis
> for Aphrodite who staggers me
> with shameful lust
> has reduced me to dull silence,
>
> and Persuasion (who maddens one)
> from her gold vial
> spills tangy nectar on my mind.[136]

Modern Reflections on Aphrodite

Although Aphrodite to a great extent was a deity who "made sense" within her own culture, which was able to "read" her symbols and myths in all their complexity, it is obvious that Aphrodite is associated with an aspect of reality so basic to human experience that it could be said that she has never died. Writing at the turn of the century, Jane Ellen Harrison said: "She is the only goddess who in passing to the upper air yet kept life and reality. Artemis becomes unreal from sheer inhumanity; Athene, as we have seen, becomes a cold abstraction; Demeter, in Olympus, is but a lovely metaphor. As man advanced in knowledge and in control over nature, the mystery and the godhead of things natural faded into science. Only the mystery of life, and love that begets life, remained intimately realized and utterly unexplained; hence Aphrodite keeps her godhead to the end."[137] Of all the goddesses of the ancient world, it does seem that Aphrodite is the one whose existence is most difficult to deny. She is the one goddess who seems familiar to us, we moderns who also know well the power, mystery, and beauty of relationships on which she has spilled her "tangy nectar." We, no less than the ancient Greeks, have been staggered by her, driven mad by her. Especially in North American culture, in which such a premium has been placed on romantic relationships as a source of ultimate meaning, Aphrodite is known very well. Indeed, she is sought after, invoked, and propitiated to an extravagant degree in our culture.

In speaking of Aphrodite as an archetype that characterizes many women, Jean Bolen says: "Aphrodite is the archetype most involved in sensual or sensory experience. Therefore, cultivating a keenness of perception and a here-and-now focus invites Aphrodite."[138] A woman who is dominated by the Aphrodite archetype "engages in intense relationships, moving from one to another. . . . Such a woman follows whatever and whoever fascinates her, and may lead an unconventional life."[139]

The Aphrodite archetype, Bolen says, is usually at odds with other tendencies, which she identifies with other Greek goddesses. The Athena (and to some extent the Artemis)[140] archetype is goal directed and interested in social and cultural stability in one's life. The Hera[141] archetype tends to value long-lasting, secure relations with a spouse, and the Demeter[142] tendency extolls the centrality of the mother's role. The Hestia[143] archetype focuses a woman's attention primarily on the hearth and home, discouraging the kind of romantic adventuring that expresses a woman's predilection for cultivating Aphrodite. To varying degrees, the intense relationships that the Aphrodite tendency urges women to immerse themselves in are threatening to all of the above archetypes. For many women, Bolen says, the psyche, expressing itself in the forms of the above-mentioned archetypes, is very judgmental of the Aphrodite tendency. A woman's desire to cultivate Aphrodite is often pronounced to be frivolous, destructive, self-indulgent, shallow, and immature—incompatible with the demands of the other more culturally and less sensuously inclined tendencies expressed in the images of the other goddesses. These other archetypes (especially the Athena and Hestia archetypes) may be so inhibiting that Aphrodite will be totally excluded from a woman's life, reminding us of the Homeric hymn to Aphrodite in which it is said that Aphrodite has power over all beings except Athena, Artemis, and Hestia.[144]

A woman who is open to her Aphrodite instincts or tendencies will prefer to seek out relationships that are sensuous, passionate, and intense. A woman whose Aphrodite archetype is dominant, Bolen says, has "magnetic warmth" and an "unselfconscious sensuality."[145] For such a woman, what is most important in life is not stability, success, or power (either domestic or professional). What is important is experiencing deep, fiery, passionate relationships that can transform perception, permitting a new depth of vision into the mysteries of life and love. Sexual, erotic intimacy is usually an important, perhaps necessary, part of such relationships for the Aphrodite-dominated woman, Bolen says.[146]

Christine Downing's treatment, or appreciation, of Aphrodite emphasizes some similar themes. Aphrodite represents for Downing the "life-infusing warmth," the "grace and desirability" that enlivens any relationship and lends to it a dimension that shatters routine ways of relating that prevent individuals from knowing each other deeply.[147] Sometimes, of course, this aspect of a relationship will include "passionate intimacy" of a sexual kind.[148] But sexual intimacy is not always present when Aphrodite makes her presence known and does not exhaust the meaning of her influence in human affairs.

For Downing, Aphrodite is that tendency in human beings to trust their feelings and values and to think and act according to these emotions and convictions.[149] While sexual attraction and enchantment and the lure of the sensuous and beautiful may be part of heeding Aphrodite's call, her reality is much more pervasive and fundamental than this, according to Downing. Aphrodite is she whose presence encourages people to undertake spontaneous self-giving,[150] to be receptive to others who react openly to them, and she who in the end brings about transformative consummations of relationships that shake the participants to the roots and change their outlooks, dreams, and basic perceptions about themselves. Such relationships are not undertaken in order to accomplish anything else. "It is the quality and intensity of the relationship that marks it as Aphroditic—its existence for its own sake, for the pleasure and fulfillment of both partners, rather than for power or offspring. In [Aphrodite's] sphere, reaching toward the other is an essential activity of the self."[151]

Chapter **10**

Mary: Virgin, Mother, and Queen

Hail, holy Queen, Mother of mercy; hail, our life, our sweetness and our hope. To you do we cry, poor banished children of Eve. To you do we send up our sighs, mourning and weeping in this valley of tears. Turn, then, most gracious Advocate, your eyes of mercy toward us. And after this our exile show unto us the blessed fruit of your womb, Jesus. O clement, O loving, O sweet Virgin Mary.[1]

Introduction

According to Christian teaching and tradition, the Virgin Mary is not divine; she is not a goddess. In the Christian monotheistic vision of reality, there is simply no place for a goddess. According to Christian orthodoxy (whether Roman Catholic, Eastern Orthodox, or Protestant) Mary is no more (and no less) than an exceptional human being who enjoys (according to the Roman Catholic and Eastern Orthodox communities) special privileges and a unique status among her fellow beings. Officially, Mary has been accorded extraordinary powers and unique characteristics that set her apart from all other human beings (except Jesus), but she is not acknowledged as divine. She is denied the status of a goddess.

In comparison with the goddesses we have considered earlier, and in comparison with many other goddesses we have not mentioned, however, Mary appears very much a goddess, and a very popular and powerful one at that. As will be seen, Mary has the characteristics of many goddesses (such as omniscience, omnipotence, immortality) and plays many of the roles associated with goddesses (such as savior, protector, promoter of fertility). She is no less powerful and awesome than the other goddesses we have discussed, nor are her special roles all that different from those of other goddesses. Indeed, for her millions of devotees Mary functions in exactly the same ways that other goddesses function for their devotees.

Mary with child, detail of an image, about 1500 C.E., Güttingen, TG. Courtesy of Schweizerisches Landesmuseum, Zurich.

The question of Mary's divinity, her status as a goddess, is actually primarily a question of relative views of divinity. In some cultures, divinity is understood as an ever-present, implicit aspect of the creation; in such contexts and cultures divinity veritably bubbles forth in a great variety and richness. It is apparent in a wide range of phenomena: unusual or awesome natural objects such as rivers, mountains, and celestial bodies; impressive, particularly pious, or unusual human beings; and unusual, eerie, or unpredictable events. In the context of Hinduism, for example, one expects to encounter the divine, the sacred, or the power of *brahman* everywhere. In other cultures, however, the divine is thought of as radically separate from the world or the creation, as beyond or outside the normal world of human beings and events. For the divine to appear in the world of human beings and creation is startling. In such traditions the divine is not expected to erupt into everyday life in any kind of routine or predictable way. In the Judaic-Christian-Muslim tradition, furthermore, the divine is thought of as indivisible, a supreme unity that is compromised, even threatened, by any notion of divine multiplicity.

Mary, of course, belongs to the latter type of tradition; to suggest that she is divine or a goddess is both threatening and insulting to many Christians. Nevertheless, in cross-cultural perspective, Mary is no less powerful, awesome, effective, responsive, active, sublime, wise, merciful, and omnipresent than any of the goddesses considered thus far. In cross-cultural perspective, there is no question that Mary is supremely divine—equal or superior to a host of other powerful and revered female beings commonly called goddesses.

In discussing Mary as a goddess, another difficulty arises. This concerns the varied views of Mary that we find in the different Christian traditions, and the varied views of Mary found even within one Christian tradition. It is apparent, for example, that most Protestant traditions do not glorify Mary. Like the rest of humankind, she is fallen and in need of divine grace. The Roman Catholic and Eastern Orthodox traditions, however, exalt Mary much more. These traditions affirm that Mary has transcended most human shortcomings and limitations.

In my discussion of Mary as an important figure of adoration and theological and philosophical musings, I will concentrate on the Roman and Eastern Orthodox traditions. Even within these traditions, however, one is faced with a further complication. Particularly in the Roman tradition, one finds diverse opinions, beliefs, and practices in relation to Mary. In general, one finds that the popular tradition, in which Mary's position tends to be greatly exalted, especially in worship and devotion, is in tension with the official tradition, which tries to temper and control the popular tradition by insisting that Mary's nature, role, and status are to be understood only in relation to, and in subordination to, her son, Jesus. In the Roman or Latin tradition of Marian thought, it is rarely the church hierarchy that leads the way in proclaiming Mary's exalted

Nativity, detail of a tapestry, 1600 C.E., Kloster Rathausen, LU. Courtesy of Schweizerisches Landesmuseum, Zurich.

nature and status. The church hierarchy is almost always slow, conservative, skeptical, and grudging in following the yearnings, practices, and beliefs of the popular tradition vis-à-vis Mary.

In my discussion of Mary, I do not limit myself to the official teachings of the Roman and Orthodox traditions. Mary is, among other things, an extremely popular being who very much belongs to the piety of unlettered, unsophisticated, and earnest believers throughout the Christian world. Their testimony about Mary, past and present, should be taken seriously, even when it has been declared heterodox by church officials. Where possible, I indicate what the official Roman and Orthodox positions are on Mary but also include in my account of Mary popular beliefs and practices that have not (or have not yet) gained official recognition or that have even been declared heterodox.

The Life of Mary in Early Literature

Information about Mary is scant in the canonical writings of Christianity. In these writings Mary is not a central figure. She is alluded to only once in the writings of Paul when in Galations he says that Jesus was "born of woman" (4:4). In the Gospel of Mark, Mary is mentioned as Jesus' mother twice (6:3 and

3:31), the latter reference being somewhat uncomplimentary, as Jesus contrasts his biological mother and brothers with those who follow him, whom he says are his true mother and brothers. In the Gospel of John, Mary appears in two places: at the wedding feast in Cana (2:1–11) and at the crucifixion (19:25–27). In the Acts of the Apostles Mary is mentioned only once, when shortly after the resurrection of Jesus she joins the disciples in a room in Jerusalem for prayer. It is primarily in the birth accounts of Jesus in the Gospels of Matthew and Luke that Mary plays an important role in the New Testament.

The account of Jesus' birth in Matthew is preoccupied with setting the event within the context of biblical prophecy. The story clearly is modeled on biblical imagery and events in such a way that there can be no doubt in the account that Jesus is the fulfillment of a divine plan referred to in the Hebrew scriptures. The narrative opens with a geneology that demonstrates that Joseph, Mary's husband, is a direct descendent of both Abraham and David. This is meant to establish that Jesus is the savior who was promised in the Davidic line and that he is also in the line of Abraham, the father of Israel's faith. The fact that Matthew's narrative later says that Joseph had no part in the conception of the savior (1:18) rather weakens the significance of this geneology, however. The exceptional nature of Jesus' conception is put this way in Matthew: "When his mother Mary had been betrothed to Joseph, before they came together she was found to be with child of the Holy Spirit" (1:18).[2] Joseph is reassured in a dream that Mary's pregnancy is part of a divine plan. After Jesus is born in Bethlehem, he is visited by wise men from the East, who find the place of his birth with the help of a special star. King Herod's jealousy is aroused at the possibility of a rival, and he undertakes to find and kill the child. An angel appears to Joseph and warns him to flee to Egypt to escape Herod's massacre of children, which indeed follows. At this point Matthew notes, in typical fashion in order to underline the predestined nature of Jesus' coming: "And he rose and took the child and his mother by night, and departed to Egypt and remained there until the death of Herod. This was to fulfill what the Lord had spoken by the prophet, 'Out of Egypt have I called my son'" (2:15). Eventually, after another angelic visitation to Joseph, the holy family returns and settles in Galilee in the town of Nazareth.

The story of Jesus' birth in Luke differs from Matthew's account in several ways. Although Joseph is said to be of the "house of David" (1:27), the long lineage of Matthew is omitted. The account of Jesus' conception and birth are closely intertwined with the conception and birth of John the Baptist. The story of the wise men and the flight to Egypt are not mentioned in Luke. In Luke, the angel Gabriel visits Mary in Nazareth and greets her with the famous words: "Hail, O favored one, the Lord is with you!" Mary is troubled, and the angel seeks to comfort her by saying: "Do not be afraid, Mary, for you have found favor with God. And behold, you will conceive in your womb and bear a son, and you shall call his name Jesus. He will be great, and will be called the Son of the Most High; and the Lord God will give him the throne of his father David, and he will reign over the house of Jacob for ever; and of his kingdom there will be no end" (1:31–34). Mary is still troubled, as she is not yet married to Joseph, only betrothed to him, and asks: "How can this be, since I have no husband?" The angel replies: "The Holy Spirit will come upon you, and the power of the Most High will overshadow you; therefore the child to be born will be called holy, the Son of God." Mary acquiesces: "Behold, I am the handmaid of the Lord; let it be to me according to your word" (1:34–38). As in Matthew, then, the conception of Jesus is said to be miraculous, the result of special divine intervention. In Matthew, however, the announcement of this miracle is made to Joseph, while in Luke the visit of the angel of God is to Mary and elicits her surprise, confusion, and eventual cooperation. It is Mary's confession of cooperation in Luke that later becomes the foundation of her role as co-redeemer in some Christian theology.

After Gabriel's appearance, Mary visits her relative Elizabeth, who is pregnant with John the Baptist. When Mary approaches Elizabeth, the infant John leaps in her womb at the presence of the embryonic Jesus, and Elizabeth greets Mary with the words that later became famous as part of the Marian prayer Ave Maria: "Blessed are you among women, and blessed is the fruit of your womb!" (1:42). Mary replies in words that later became famous as the Magnificat: "My soul magnifies the Lord, and my spirit rejoices in God my Savior, for he has regarded the low estate of his handmaiden. For behold, henceforth all generations will call me blessed; for he who is mighty has done great things for me, and holy is his name" (1:47–49).

The birth of Jesus in Luke's account takes place when Joseph and Mary travel to Bethlehem. A whole host of traditions and imagery surrounding Jesus' birth is based on this passage from Luke: "And she gave birth to her first-born son and wrapped him in swaddling clothes, and laid him in a manger, because there was no place for them in the inn" (2:7). Shepherds are visited by an angel and told to go visit the newborn child, which they do, and there they praise him. The child is duly circumcised and later is taken to Jerusalem by his parents, where they make a sacrifice at the temple, as was the custom at that time. In Jerusalem, Jesus is recognized and adored by certain people. After this the holy family returns to Nazareth in Galilee.

Mention also should be made of a passage from Revelation that refers to the appearance of a pregnant woman. Although there is no indication in the text that the woman is meant to be Mary, the association was made in later Christianity, and the passage subsequently became important in Marian iconography and theology. The passage reads: "And a great portent appeared in heaven, a woman clothed with the sun, with the moon under her feet, and on

Nativity, altar panel, 1493 C.E., Ober-Aegeri. Courtesy of Schweizerisches Landes-museum, Zurich.

her head a crown of twelve stars; she was with child and she cried out in pangs of birth, in anguish for delivery" (12:1–2).

Additional details of Mary's life are known only from noncanonical, apocryphal sources. The most important of these is the *Protevangelium*, or *Book of James*, written sometime between 100 and 150 C.E. The work undertakes to tell the life story of Mary, supplying many details of her life that were missing in other sources up to that time. According to this text, Mary's parents are Joachim, a wealthy, generous, and pious man, and Anna. The couple are childless, and the high priest of the temple one day refuses Joachim's offerings because of this. Joachim is dejected and retreats to the desert for forty days. While he is gone, Anna weeps because of her barrenness. At this point, an angel appears and tells her that she will have a child. Simultaneously an angel appears to Joachim with the same message. He rushes home, and the two embrace at the city gates of Jerusalem. Anna becomes pregnant and promises to dedicate the child to God. Mary is duly born. When the child is six months old, Anna puts her on the ground, and Mary takes seven steps. After this, Anna vows that nothing impure will come in contact with the child and that the child will not even be allowed to step on the earth until she sets foot in the temple at age three. Anna makes Mary's bedroom a sanctuary, and only pure young women are allowed entrance. Everywhere Mary goes she is carried by her parents and servants.[3]

Mary's parents take her to the temple when she is three, and she dances near the altar to the delight of all present. Angels give her food there, and she begins to frequent the temple regularly and to receive instruction from the priests. When she reaches puberty, the priests do not wish her to remain in the temple lest she pollute it (with her menstrual blood, presumably) and arrange for her to be married. They assemble all the widowers in the area in the temple. The elderly Joseph is chosen as Mary's husband when a dove emerges from his staff and perches on his head. Joseph is reluctant to become betrothed to Mary because of his age, but is urged to do so by the priests. Joseph takes Mary to his house, but their marriage is not consummated. At this point the story begins to follow the birth narratives in Matthew and Luke. An angel appears to Mary and announces that she will conceive a child as a result of being overshadowed by the Lord. Mary then visits Elizabeth, whose infant leaps in her womb at the presence of the embryonic Jesus. Joseph is absent during all of this period, and when he returns he is troubled to find Mary pregnant. An angel reassures him of Mary's purity, however. The priests at the temple are similarly persuaded of Mary's purity and the miraculous nature of her conception.[4]

Late in her pregnancy, Joseph takes Mary to Bethlehem. Outside the town Mary suddenly begins to give birth, and Joseph finds a cave for her. He goes in search of a midwife, but by the time they return the child has been born, and an intense light emanates from the cave. The midwife is astonished at the miraculous birth and tells a friend of hers about the strange birth. The woman, Salome, wants to see for herself whether Mary has remained a virgin and tries to lift her dress. Her hand withers for her impertinence and lack of faith but is restored to wholeness when she takes the child in her arms and adores it.[5] The wise men now appear to adore the child, the wandering star having led them to the cave in Bethlehem. Herod is worried about the tale that a new king has been born and attempts to kill his potential rival by slaying many young children. Joseph is warned of Herod's intention by an angel and returns to his native town by a secret way to evade the King's wrath.[6]

Another body of apocryphal texts, some dating back to around the third century C.E., describe the circumstances of Mary's death and her assumption into heaven. Mary's earthly career comes to an end sometime between a few days and ten years after the resurrection of Jesus. She is assumed into heaven either directly or after she has died and been buried in a cave. In some versions only her soul is assumed into heaven, not her body, which is buried and awaits resurrection on the Last Day. In most versions, Jesus appears and announces to Mary and the disciples, who have been specially gathered for the event from the four quarters of the world, that he wishes to take Mary into heaven to dwell with him. In some accounts the disciples ask Jesus to let her linger on earth a while longer. In one version, that of *Pseudo-Melito*, it is only at the suggestion of the disciple Peter that Jesus raises Mary's body to heaven.[7]

Often in a glowing cloud, sometimes in a chariot, Mary is raised bodily into heaven, usually accompanied by Jesus. In one account, as she is rising from the earth, she lets her girdle fall to earth, where it is taken by the disciple Thomas.[8] In some accounts Mary requests Jesus the favor of allowing those who call on her name to be glorified. In the *Discourse of St. John the Divine concerning the Falling Asleep of the Holy Mother of God* (written sometime before the seventh century C.E.), Mary makes this request before her death and assumption:

> O Lord Jesu Christ, that hast all power in heaven and on earth, I entreat thine holy name with this supplication: At every time and in every place where there is a memorial of my name, sanctify thou that place, and glorify them that glorify thee through my name, accepting every offering of such, and every supplication and every prayer.[9]

Jesus replies to her:

> Let thine heart be glad and rejoice; for every grace and every gift hath been given thee of my Father which is in heaven and of me and of the Holy Ghost. Every soul that calleth upon thy name shall not be put to shame, but shall find mercy and consolation and succour and confidence, both in this world and in that which is to come.[10]

We have in these passages a clear indication that some people were supplicating Mary directly for help and blessing, that she was beginning to play the role of intercessor for her devotees, a role that becomes central throughout most of her subsequent history.

Mary's Virginity

Perhaps Mary's most outstanding characteristic is her virginity. It has served several purposes in the history of Christian doctrine and practice and is important in understanding Mary's nature as a powerful Christian presence. In the Gospel birth stories, Mary's virginity seems primarily a device to underline the exceptional nature of Jesus' conception and birth. It is never suggested that God chose Mary, or found favor with her, because she was a virgin. Her virginity is meant primarily as a statement about the nature of Jesus, not a statement about Mary's own nature. Mary's virginity after the birth of Jesus, furthermore, does not seem to interest the Gospel writers, who sometimes mention Jesus' brothers. In the Gospels, Mary's virginity underlines Jesus' divine filiation. His conception is extraordinary, involving the intervention of the divine in a special way.

The importance of virginity to the character of Mary herself increased as she became an object of reverence, devotion, and imitation and as Christian asceticism became prominent. As a central characteristic of Mary, virginity is less a device to emphasize the special circumstances of Jesus' conception and birth than it is a proof of her superior nature. The shift in focus from Mary's virginity as significant primarily in relation to Jesus' nature, to a concern for Mary's nature is evident in the debates that took place among early church leaders concerning whether Mary was a virgin after the birth of Jesus and whether she remained a virgin until her death. Against the background of considerable debate among Christian leaders, Mary's perpetual virginity was declared at the Second Council of Constantinople in 381. She was given the title "ever virgin" (*aeiparthenos*) at the Council of Chalcedon in 451, and belief in her perpetual virginity was made dogma at the Lateran Council of 649.[11]

This period in Christianity (the fourth through seventh centuries) was a time during which many church leaders adopted celibacy as a way of life and during which tens of thousands of Christians abandoned the world to undertake ascetic and monastic lives in the deserts of Egypt and Syria. In this context, sex came to be viewed as dangerous or evil or both. To master the sexual urge by abstaining from it entirely was considered heroically Christian and came to be praised as a spiritually superior way of life. Virginity, especially among women, was regarded as a sure means of overcoming one's natural inclinations to evil and sin. Saint John Chrysostom, speaking of Adam and Eve, saw a direct relationship between sex, death, and disobedience to God: "Scarcely had they . . . turned from obedience to God than they became earth and ashes, and all at once, they lost the happy life, beauty and honour of virginity . . . they were made serfs, stripped of the royal robe . . . made subject to death and every other form of curse and imperfection; then did marriage make its appearance . . . Do you see where marriage took its origin? . . . For where there is death, there too is sexual coupling; and where there is no death, there is no sexual coupling either."[12]

Augustine is quite clear that Mary's virginity was attractive to God and was important in his choosing her to bear Jesus. "Let us love chastity above all things, . . . for it was to show that this was pleasing to Him that Christ chose the modesty of a virgin womb."[13] Mary's perpetual virginity is also equated with moral and physical purity in this statement of Ambrose (339–97): "Would the Lord Jesus have chosen for his mother a woman who would defile the heavenly chamber with the seed of a man, that is to say, one incapable of preserving her virginal chastity intact?"[14]

In exalting Mary's chastity and virginity, early church writers elevated her above what they considered to be the degrading aspects of life in the flesh, especially life in female flesh. The virgin woman escaped what were considered the impurities of sex and childbirth and thus enhanced her spiritual status. According to Jerome, the female virgin transcends her sex to such an extent that she comes to approximate the male! "As long as a woman is for birth and children, she is different from man as body is from soul. But when she wishes to serve Christ more than the world, then she will cease to be a woman, and will be called man."[15]

To many early Christian writers (all males), the female virgin represented wholeness, integrity, and purity. Sexual intercourse ruptured, soiled, and compromised the wholeness of the female body. Saint Methodius of Olympus in his *Symposium of Ten Virgins* has his leading character say: "It is imperative that anyone who intends to avoid sin in the practice of chastity must keep all his members and senses pure and sealed—just as pilots caulk a ship's timbers—to prevent sin from getting an opening and pouring in."[16] Such biblical images as: "a closed gate" (Ezek. 44:2), "a spring shut up," and "a fountain sealed" (Song of Sol. 4:12) were applied to Mary as a virgin in an exclusively positive way. As ever virgin she came to represent the spiritually supreme manifestation of her sex. To a great extent, Mary's high status was understood as inextricably associated with her vow to abstain totally from sex.[17] She had refused to fall into sexual indulgence and hence had refused to fall into the fallen human condition. She had remained pristine and whole physically and hence had achieved a superior (indeed, supreme) moral and spiritual state. For the celibate leaders and members of the church she became a model to revere and imitate. Throughout the history of Christianity (especially for Roman Catholics) Mary has played a central role as an ideal to be imitated by all celibate members of the church, especially nuns.

Mother of God, Mother of Sorrows, Mother of Mercy, the Great Mother

Complementing and enriching Mary's virginal, ascetic character is her role as a mother. Initially, and to a great extent throughout her history, Mary's status was dependent upon her son, Jesus. She was of interest to early Christians primarily as the mother of the savior. As the nature of Jesus came to be affirmed as divine, as his status as God became clearer in Christianity, Mary's status, correspondingly, became more elevated in the minds of some Christians. In some places, Mary began to be referred to as Mother of God (*theotokos*). A debate developed among Christians concerning whether Mary was only the mother of the man Jesus or whether she was also the mother of God, the mother of the divine Jesus. The debate was primarily between the Christians of Antioch, who opposed the use of the term *theotokos*, and those of Alexandria, who favored it. Appropriately, the debate was settled at a council held at Ephesus in 431. Ephesus had been the center of a famous temple of the goddess Artemis, and in Acts, the apostle Paul is described as arousing the animosity of Artemis's devotees, who formed large crowds and praised the goddess as a way of denouncing Paul's new religion (Acts 19:23–41). During the Council of Ephesus in 431, Cyril, bishop of Alexandria and principal advocate of the title *theotokos* as an epithet of Mary, organized large processions of sympathizers to march through the streets chanting slogans in support of his position. After the Council of Ephesus, Mary rapidly became the center of a popular cult. She was celebrated in a series of feast days, during which churches and shrines were dedicated to her, and she increasingly took on majestic, divine aspects. It is hard not to suspect that Mary's title of *theotokos* meant a good deal more to many of her devotees than merely that she had given birth to the man Jesus.

In her role as the mother of Jesus, Mary comes to be thought of in two very important and distinctly different ways. First, she is thought of and often depicted as nourishing and protecting the infant Jesus; second, she is thought of as the Mater Dolorosa, the Mother of Sorrows, who suffers on account of her son's tribulations. Images of Mary and the infant Jesus are popular throughout the Christian world. In these images, Mary tends to dominate the child. She is his protector. He is dependent upon her. Images that show Mary suckling the child convey this relationship unmistakably. The infant savior is nourished at the breast of his human mother. Mary becomes the archetypal mother who nourishes the God-man who has created the heavens and the earth. Mary's milk takes on cosmic implications. Her milk becomes the symbol of ultimate nourishment. She nourishes him who nourishes the whole race. She becomes in this role the mother of salvation, and her milk becomes the milk of salvation.

In many contexts the salvific power of Mary's nourishing powers is effective quite apart from the role of Jesus. That is, Mary herself is understood to

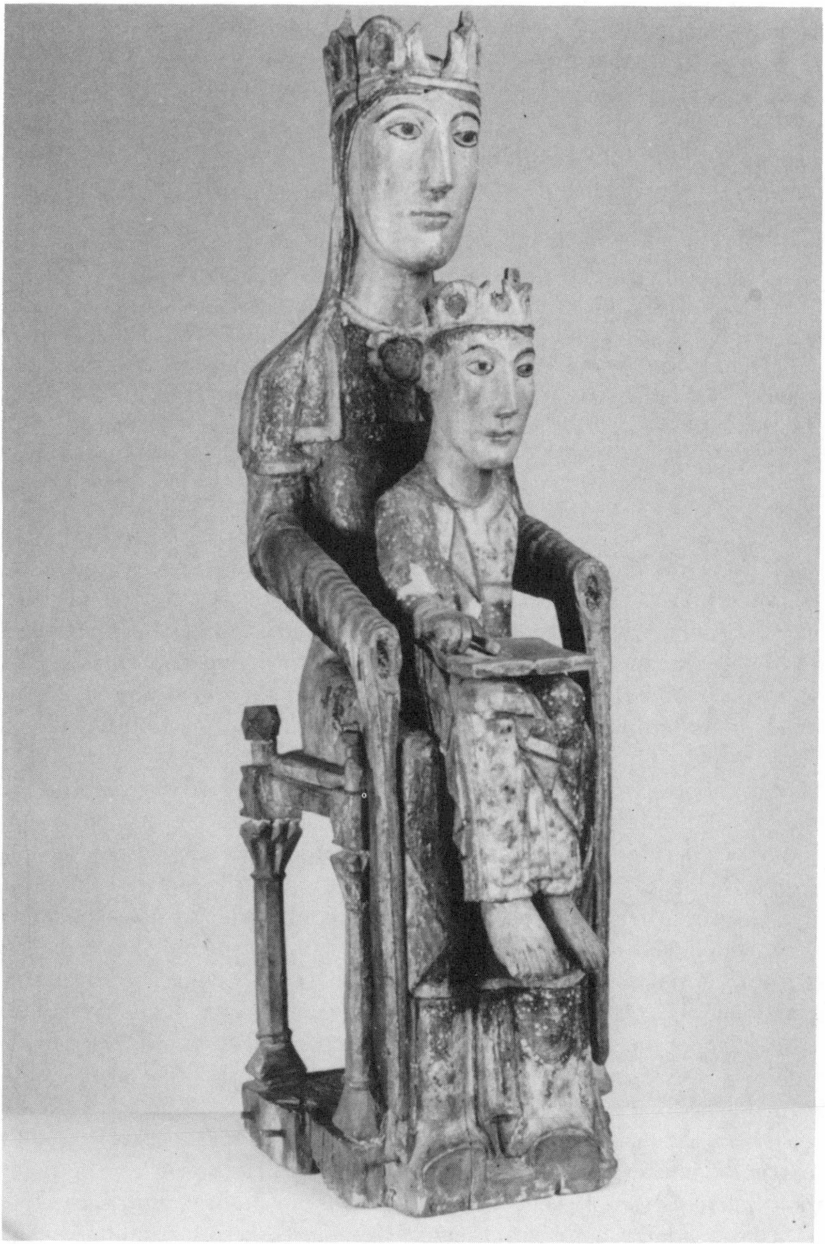

Mary with child, about 1150 C.E., Raron, VS. Courtesy of Schweizerisches Landesmuseum, Zurich.

be a nourishing presence to her devotees, and her milk is understood to have sacred power on its own. Her motherhood expresses itself directly to her devotees. She may be the mother of Jesus, the mother of God—and it is clearly established in Christian doctrine that this is the source of her superior status—but she is also the mother of those who petition her directly. Many miraculous stories have been collected describing the healing and salvific effects of Mary's milk.

A monk is dying of a putrid disease of the mouth, and his nose and lips have been eaten away by ulcers. His fellow monks have given him up for dead. He reproaches the Madonna, reminding her with bitterness that he has faithfully invoked her daily in the words of the woman of the Gospels: "Blessed is the womb that bare thee and the paps which thou hast sucked" (Luke 11:27). The Virgin, suitably chastened . . . , appears at his bedside and, . . . "With much sweetness and much delight, from her sweet bosom she drew forth her breast, that is so sweet, so soft, so beautiful, and placed it in his mouth, [and] gently touched him all about and sprinkled him with her sweet milk."

Needless to say, the monk was miraculously rendered whole again.[18]

Perhaps the most famous example of Mary's dispensing her milk in answer to the prayers of her devotees is that of Bernard of Clairvaux, an ardent admirer of Mary. "Bernard was reciting the *Ave Maris Stella* before a statue of the Virgin in the church of St. Vorles at Châtillon-sur-Seine, and when he came to the words *Monstra esse matrem* (Show thyself a mother), the Virgin appeared before him and, pressing her breast, let three drops of milk fall onto his lips."[19]

An important facet of Mary's role as mother involves the suffering she undergoes as a result of the pain, sorrow, and death of her son. Although Mary does not play a significant role in the passion of Jesus in the Gospel accounts (only the Gospel of John, 19:2, places her at the foot of the cross), a cult of the Mater Dolorosa, beginning in Western Christianity around the eleventh century, provided a whole series of incidents surrounding the crucifixion of Jesus that featured Mary as a suffering witness. These events, which constitute the passion of Jesus, are related through Mary's eyes and emotions. As Jesus is tried, accused, sentenced to death, mocked, and finally executed, Mary suffers with him in sympathetic agony. After his death on the cross, she takes his broken and bloody body into her arms and prepares his body for burial.

One of the most dramatic and compelling literary products of this cult is Jacopone da Todi's (1230–1306) hymn *Donna del Paradiso*. At several points during the sequence of events, Mary and Jesus speak directly to each other. Their conversation is familiar, intimate. When Jesus sees Mary at the crucifixion he says to her:

Mama, why have you come?

You cause me a mortal wound,
for your weeping pierces me
and seems to me the sharpest sword.

And she replies:

Son, white and ruddy,
Son, without compare,
Son, on whom shall I rely?
Son, have you also forsaken me?
Son, white and fair,
Son, of the laughing face,
Son, why has the world so despised thee?[20]

Eventually the cult of the Mater Dolorosa developed a mythology and piety that was in many respects a moving parallel to the suffering and agony of Jesus himself, and for many devotees a mythology and piety that were as important and efficacious as Jesus' own suffering. Confraternities developed that concentrated on Mary's sufferings and that spread this aspect of Mariology throughout Western Christianity. The number of Mary's sorrows ranged from five to fifteen, but in the seventeenth century were officially fixed at seven by the church. These were: Simeon's prophecy that Mary would be pierced by a sword of sorrow, the flight to Egypt, the disappearance of Jesus in the temple, meeting Jesus on the road to Calvary, the crucifixion, the deposition, and the burial.[21] Iconographically, Mary as the Mother of Sorrows is often shown being pierced by seven swords.[22] For many devotees, the suffering Mary became the primary figure with whom they identified and from whom they sought succor. Mary's suffering was understood to be no less than her son's, and was even understood to have been requested by her and bestowed upon her by God. Indeed, Mary becomes a cosufferer with her son and thus shares intimately in the divine drama of redemption. The parallel between Jesus' and Mary's sufferings is stressed by the Spanish nun Maria de Agreda de Jesus (d. 1665) in her book *City of God*: "She prayed that she might be permitted to feel and participate in her virginal body all the pains of the wounds and tortures about to be undergone by Jesus. This petition was granted by the blessed Trinity, and the mother in consequence suffered all the torments of her most holy son in exact duplication."[23]

The cult of the Mater Dolorosa parallels the cult of the Man of Sorrows. In both cases devotees are provided with a model of human suffering and sorrow with which they may identify. In the case of Jesus, his suffering is some-

Mary, "Mother of Sorrows," Kloster Mariastein, Switzerland. Pater Lukas Schenker, *Mariastein, Führer durch Wallfahrt und Kloster* (Kloster Mariastein, 1982), p. 9.

what abstract—he suffers on behalf of the whole race. In the case of Mary, her suffering is specific and concrete, focused as it is on one person, her own son. In Mary's sorrow, devotees can identify with her motherly agony and so participate in the central salvation drama of Christianity.

Both the intensity of Mary's suffering, caused by the anguish of her son, and the tendency of devotees to identify with her agony, are dramatically expressed in the *Stabat Mater*, a Latin hymn probably written in the thirteenth century. The opening lines depict Mary at the foot of the cross.

> At the cross her vigil keeping
> Mary stood in sorrow, weeping,
> When her Son was crucified.
>
> While she waited in her anguish,
> Seeing Christ in torment languish,
> Bitter sorrow pierced her heart.
>
> With what pain and desolation,
> With that noble resignation,
> Mary watched her dying Son.

A few verses later, the perspective changes and the devotee reciting the hymn repeats the following lines:

> At the cross, your sorrow sharing,
> All your grief and torment bearing,
> Let me stand and mourn with you.
>
> Fairest maid of all creation,
> Queen of hope and consolation,
> Let me feel your grief sublime.[24]

In her role as mother, Mary is often characterized as a protector of her devotees. Often, as we see below, she protects her devotees from the wrath of God or from the anger of Jesus in his role as judge. As a protective mother, Mary is sometimes shown protecting her children under her cloak, which provides them shelter from the vicissitudes of life. From the late thirteenth century to the Council of Trent in the sixteenth century (when worship of Mary in

Schuetzmantel-Maria (Mary with protective cloak) by Michael Erhart, ca. 1480 C.E., Ravensburg. Staatliche Museen Preussischer Kultur Besitz, Berlin. John A. Phillips, *Eve: The History of an Idea* (San Francisco: Harper & Row, 1984), p. 138.

this form was declared heterodox), the image of Mary as Our Lady of Mercy (Madonna della Misericordia) became very popular. In this form, Mary is shown with a cloak, sometimes decorated with stars, which she spreads over the pious who cluster around her, sometimes kneeling at her feet. As Our Lady of Mercy, Mary is usually shown without Jesus (except in some cases when she is protecting her devotees from his wrath), and achieves the status of an independent being, a kind of Christian version of the Magna Mater, who is appealed to directly for protection, nourishment, and spiritual fulfillment. A particularly stunning rendition of Our Lady of Mercy is the painting by Piero della Francesca (dated 1445–48). Mary is a monumental, powerful figure towering over the much smaller figures of her kneeling devotees, who gaze up at her with rapt adoration. With her long arms she spreads out her capacious cloak to shelter them and gazes on them with a look both serene and firm.[25]

As a mother, Mary is also associated with fertility and growth. Many churches and shrines dedicated to her are believed by pilgrims and devotees to be centers at which Mary bestows fertility. In some cases, such places enshrine a relic associated with Mary that is believed to have fecund power. Mary's sash, girdle, or cloak, which she let fall into the hands of the apostle Thomas as she ascended into heaven, is the central relic at several Marian shrines and is at times explicitly associated with fertility. This sash is believed to be the very one that Mary wore at the annunciation, when Gabriel told her that she was about to conceive a child by the spirit of God.[26] There are instances of powerful rulers supplicating Mary for progeny. Henri III and Louise of Lorraine made a fifty-mile pilgrimage barefoot to the cathedral at Chartres every winter for many years to petition Mary (unsuccessfully) for a child. Anne of Austria had Mary's girdle, which was enshrined at Le Puy, moved to her bedroom, and she subsequently conceived.[27]

In many Mary shrines noted for bestowing fertility, large collections of votive offerings have been left in thanks for blessings bestowed or in the hope of a child in the future. At Sant' Agostino cathedral in Rome, an image of Mary is surrounded by silver plaques that express thanks for the conception or birth of a child. Pilgrims to the shrine, mostly women, kiss the foot of the statue in gestures of hope or gratitude to the great being they know as the Madonna of Childbirth.[28] At other Italian shrines to Mary, women present their wedding gowns in the hope of having a fruitful marriage. Dolls, toy cribs, and children's clothes are also left at some Mary shrines as tokens of gratitude by devotees, usually women, who believe they have been blessed with fertility by Mary.[29] In Spain, a tradition many centuries old encourages young married couples to make a pilgrimage to the shrine of the black Virgin Mary of Montserrat so that they will be blessed with children. Stories tell of Mary's extraordinary powers of fertility at this site, and even the site itself (a rather barren, rocky, mountain-

Virgin Mary of Montserrat, Spain. Courtesy of FISA, Grupo Editorial Escudo de Oro, Barcelona.

ous area) is said to owe its amazing fertility to Mary (it is said to be especially abundant in flowers).[30]

Mary's fecund powers are sometimes extended to the natural world generally. Mary appeared to a medieval merchant of Milan as a grain goddess. Her robe was covered with ears of wheat in this vision. The merchant had a painting of this form of Mary made, and the popularity of her cult spread to Germany in the fifteenth century. Devotees would place garlands around the painting and ask Mary for fertility and plenty.[31] In the eighteenth century, Mary became associated with the month of May and the new growth that bursts forth at that time of year in Europe. Gradually she came to be identified with the Queen of the May, a figure representing fertility and sexuality who was traditionally worshiped with much gaiety, carousing, and sometimes sexual abandon. Although Mary's association with these May festivals rid them of much of their sexual features, the old rituals and meanings persist. "In Catholic countries, statues of the Virgin are bedecked in flowers and crowned on May 1, and carried in gay processions through flower-strewn streets and squares carpeted with blossoms. In Ireland, the may or thorn tree, which has a peculiar erotic aroma, is considered powerful magic, and is sacred to the Virgin in many of her sanctuaries."[32]

An image of Mary, Santa Maria, the patron of Lucera, "is showered with wheat, corn, and other sacrificial offerings on feast days, particularly on those which coincide with the planting and harvesting seasons. The Virgin is accorded powers relating to fertility: human, animal, and vegetal."[33] One tradition says that the church of Santa Maria of Lucera was originally built by the first Christian bishop, Saint Basso, on the exact location of a Roman temple dedicated to the goddess Ceres (the goddess associated with grain and fertility).[34]

Santa Maria of Lucera is one of several black Virgin Marys in Christian Europe. Most of these images are in locations that were once occupied by Roman armies, and it has been shown that many of the churches that enshrine these black Virgins are located in places that were once occupied by pre-Christian, often Roman, goddesses. It has been suggested that the blackness of the images relates to the blackness of the fertile earth and that the black Virgins represent a survival of pre-Christian goddesses. "The black madonnas are Christian borrowings from earlier pagan art forms that depicted Ceres, Demeter, Melaina, Diana, Isis, Cybele, Artemis, or Rhea as black, the color characteristic of goddesses of the earth's fertility."[35]

Savior and Redeemer

Throughout Mary's history there has been a tension between Mariology and Mariolatry. In general, popular reverence for and worship of Mary have sometimes emphasized her powers in ways that the official church has seen as exaggerated or heterodox. Official church teaching about Mary has always lagged behind popular devotion and traditionally has acted as a restraint in areas deemed excessive by the church hierarchy. This tension is probably nowhere more apparent than in the area of Mary's role as intercessor. For many devotees, Mary takes the place of Jesus himself as savior and redeemer. In their enthusiasm and devotion to Mary, many Christians in effect have elevated Mary to a position equal to, or superior to, that of Jesus.

The church's position on Mary's role as intercessor is clear. She, like the saints, can intercede on behalf of devotees. She can forward their prayers and petitions to God or to Jesus and even recommend the appropriate response. But she cannot act on her own. She is not divine, is not empowered by God to judge and forgive, even though she has a special and peculiar status. Mary's early role as the recipient of prayers and petitions no doubt was grounded in her special relationship to Jesus. Devotees probably felt that Jesus simply could not refuse the requests of his mother. Either through obedience to her, respect for her, love for her, or sympathy with her, Jesus, it was thought, did what his mother advised him to do. Therefore, to enlist Mary on one's side in any issue was tantamount to having the question decided favorably. Just as Jesus was understood to be an advocate of human beings before God the Father, Mary was understood to be an advocate for her individual petitioners before Jesus. This role of advocate became especially pronounced and popular in Christianity when and where Jesus was cast in the role of heavenly judge. In his role as the one who judges human beings at death or at the end of the world, Jesus is often portrayed as a determined, grim, angry, even hostile figure glowering down upon human beings, who have caused him so much undeserved pain and anguish on their behalf.[36] In this role, Jesus' aspect as advocate for humankind and as the good shepherd who protects and loves his human flock is often subsumed or forgotten. In this context, Mary enters to play the role that Jesus himself seems to have abandoned: friend and protector of the sinful devotee.

One of the earliest stories that features Mary in the role of redeemer is the legend of Theophilus. The story apparently arose in Eastern Christianity and seems to be the origin of the legend of Faust. Theophilus lived in the sixth century and is said to have been the treasurer and archdeacon of the bishop of Ardana in Cilicia in Asia Minor. When the bishop died, Theophilus was mistreated by the bishop's successor and dismissed from his post. Envious and frustrated, Theophilus made a pact with the devil. He sold his soul to Satan in return for wealth, fame, and power. However, Theophilus was struck with remorse at the bargain and asked the devil for a reprieve. The devil was not sympathetic, whereupon Theophilus called upon Mary for help. In a dream, Mary appeared to Theophilus and gave him back the contract he had signed with the devil. Mary had wrested it from the devil and returned it to her devotee. The legend was translated into Latin by Paul the Deacon (d. 799), a monk at Monte Cassino, and very rapidly became popular in Western Christianity. In the Latin version, Mary is called for the first time *mediatrix* and is portrayed as an independent power in answering prayers and rescuing her devotees. At one point she is addressed as follows: "Holy Mother of God, hope and support of Christians, redemption of the erring . . . who intercede for sinners, refreshment of the poor, mediatress between God and men."[37] The legend was often depicted in Christian art. In Notre-Dame de Paris, the legend is shown in a sequence of frames. In one of the frames, Mary is holding the devil down, threatening him with her sword, and taking the contract from him;[38] that is, she is shown acting independently on behalf of one of her devotees, defeating the devil by herself.

The tendency to see Mary as co-redeemer with Jesus, or as a saving power in her own right, is clear in the writings of the fourteenth-century mystic Saint Bridget of Sweden, who was a member of the Third Order of Saint Francis. Bridget emphasized Mary's sufferings, which paralleled the suffering of Jesus, and spoke of Mary and Jesus as cooperating in the salvation of humankind. She has Mary say this in one of her writings: "As Adam and Eve sold the world for one apple, so my Son and I have redeemed the world as it were with one heart."[39] At one point, Bridget even refers to Mary as *salvatrix*, savior.[40]

In the official theology of the church, Mary has never been deemed an independent savior. Her special role as an intercessor, however, has been underlined and emphasized by many Christian theologians. Saint Bernard of Clairvaux spoke of Mary as a unique channel through whom flowed the grace of God to human beings, as an aqueduct through whom divine mercy reaches the earth. In praying to God, Bernard advised, one is wise to offer one's petition through Mary.[41] Other theologians, in attempting to picture Mary's unique role as an intercessor or mediator between human beings and God, spoke of her as the neck that connects the head (God) with the body (the church, or human beings).[42]

One of the most common contexts in which Mary is featured in her role as intermediary or redeemer is in relation to the wrath, anger, and judgment of God or Jesus. Although the church has officially discouraged thinking of Mary (and Jesus) in this way, her role as one who tempers and restrains divine anger has been extremely popular and has cast her in the role of a very sympathetic figure, to whom one goes first for protection, understanding, and help. Jean-Jacques Olier (d. 1657) asserted that God has placed omnipotence in the hands of Mary and explained how she uses that power: "On the one hand she uses this power to do good; on the other she binds the power of Jesus Christ to prevent the evil he would do to the guilty."[43] Elsewhere he states: "It is she who stops the arm of God's justice, power and revenge by the force of her mercy and love."[44] Alphonsus Liguori (eighteenth century), in his popular work the *Glo-*

ries of Mary, stated the same idea: "If God is angry with a sinner, and Mary takes him under her protection, she withholds the avenging arm of her Son, and saves him."[45] Throughout this work, he tended to cast Jesus in the role of judge and avenger and Mary in the role of protector and advocate. At one point, he quoted with approval the position of an earlier church authority, to the effect "that the Eternal Father gave the office of judge and avenger to the Son, and that of showing mercy and relieving the necessitous to the Mother."[46] In one of the many miracle stories featuring Mary, she is said to break out in sweat when she attempts to stop Jesus from hitting a sinner with his mighty and vengeful arm.[47] A particularly explicit rendering of this theme, namely, the contrast between Mary's mercy and Jesus' wrath, is found in a dream of Brother Leo, a Franciscan monk.

> Leo saw two ladders leading up to heaven, one as red as blood, the other as white as lilies. At the top of the red ladder there appeared Christ, his face full of wrath. St. Francis beckoned to his brothers not to fear and to climb the ladder. They try, but fall. Francis prays, but Christ displays his wounds and thunders, "Your brothers have done this to me." So St. Francis runs down and leads his brethren to the white ladder, which they scale effortlessly and without mishap, to find Mary at the top, all smiles, to welcome them.[48]

In her role as redeemer and savior, Mary is consistently described as tenderhearted, compassionate, and always merciful. She seems incapable of refusing any request of a devotee, no matter how unworthy the petitioner and no matter how seemingly unworthy the request. Commenting on stories of Mary's miracles, Marina Warner says:

> The more raffish the Virgin's suppliant, the better she likes him. The miracles' heroes are liars, thieves, adulterers, and fornicators, footloose students, pregnant nuns, unruly and lazy clerics, and eloping monks. On the single condition that they sing her praises, usually by reciting the *Ave Maria*, and show due respect for the miracle of the Incarnation wrought in her, they can do no wrong. Her justice is loyalty to her own: whatever his conduct, anyone pledged to her protection is her liegeman and she his responsible suzerain. Through her the whole gay crew of wanton, loving, weak humanity finds its way to paradise.[49]

Mary's mercy and compassion for sinners is emphasized in legends contained in apocryphal works that tell of her descent to hell shortly before or after her death. When she sees the terrible suffering of the people in hell, she cries out to Jesus to show them mercy.[50] Mary is not concerned with the sins that have put individuals in hell. She is only concerned about the agony they suffer there and is moved to help them.

The theme of Mary's descending to hell and expressing compassion for those who dwell there is reiterated in the cult of the Carmelite Scapular, which was inaugurated in 1250 by Saint Simon Stock. Members of this movement wore a scapular, the original of which was believed to have been given to Saint Simon by Mary herself when she appeared to him in a vision. Mary promised Saint Simon that if anyone died while wearing this scapular she would release him or her from purgatory on the first Saturday after death. The scapular, then, was understood to be a kind of physical emblem of Mary's compassion toward those who suffer in purgatory or hell. The privilege bestowed by Mary to those of this confraternity was expressed in a papal bull of John XXII as follows: "I, the Mother of grace, will descend to purgatory on the Saturday after their death and will liberate all those whom I find there and lead them to the holy mount of eternal life."[51]

The importance of Mary as a savior in popular piety is vividly depicted in Roman Catholic areas where *ex-voto* pictures adorn church walls. These pictures depict situations in which, according to the devotee, Mary has intervened to save someone from catastrophe. In the Ticinese area of Switzerland, for example, *ex-voto* paintings depict accidents typical of that mountainous area, such as people falling off cliffs, road accidents, and avalanches. Many pictures portray people who are bedridden, sick, or injured. Others show children in danger of being burned, drowned, or crushed by rocks or vehicles. Some pictures show soldiers in combat or people being attacked by robbers. One picture shows a man being struck by lightning, while others show ships being tossed in stormy seas. Some *ex-voto* scenes include photographs of wrecked cars or motorcycles. In all of these pictures Mary is shown serenely floating in the sky above the scene of earthly danger, calamity, or distress. Many of the pictures have "G.R." written on them, which stands for *grazia ricevuta*, "for grace received." The message of these popular scenes seems clear. Mary is being thanked by her devotees for acts of grace whereby they or their relatives were spared death or misfortune.[52]

When the idea of purgatory became a significant part of Christian salvific geography, the Virgin Mary came to play an important role in aiding those who dwelt there. She was often petitioned to relieve the burdens of those in purgatory and was frequently credited with releasing souls from this realm in response to the pleas of her devotees. It was not uncommon in medieval Christianity for souls of the dead dwelling in purgatory to appear to the living and bear witness to the nature of purgatory and to the compassionate role of Mary in gaining their release or the moderation of their suffering. A work by Peter Damian of Ravenna written between 1063 and 1072 refers to a woman whose deceased grandmother appeared to her while she was praying in the basilica of Santa Maria in Compitello in Rome on the Feast of the Assumption of Mary. The daughter asked her mother how she could possibly appear among the liv-

An *ex-voto* painting showing Mary saving a woman caught in a rock slide, 1870 C.E., Swiss. Piero Bianconi, *Ex voto del Ticino* (Locarno: Amando Dado, 1977), fig. 11, p. 87.

An *ex-voto* painting showing Mary saving a woman who has fallen from a cliff, late nineteenth century C.E., Swiss. Piero Bianconi, *Ex voto del Ticino* (Locarno: Armando Dado, 1977), fig. 2, p. 69.

ing, whereupon her deceased mother replied: "Until today I was in the grip of no slight punishment, for when I was still of tender age I gave in to indecent lust and committed shameful acts with girls of my age, and alas! having forgotten them, even though I confessed to a priest, I did not submit to the judgment [of penance]. But today the queen of the world has poured forth prayers for us and liberated me from the places of punishment [*de locis poenalibus*] and by her intervention a multitude greater than the population of Rome has been plucked from torment. We are therefore visiting the holy places dedicated to our glorious lady to thank her for so great a boon."[53]

An image applied to Mary very early in her history, and often used in relation to her role as redeemer and savior, is that of Mary as the second Eve. Paul refers to Jesus as the second Adam (1 Cor. 15:22; 2 Cor. 5:17; Rom. 5:14), and by the second century, in the writings of Justin Martyr (d. 165), we find Mary referred to as the second Eve. In his *Dialogue with the Jew Trypho*, Justin makes the parallel this way: "Christ . . . became man by the Virgin so that the disobedience which proceeded from the serpent might be destroyed in the same way as it originated. For Eve, being a virgin and undefiled, having conceived the word from the serpent, brought forth disobedience and death. The Virgin Mary, however, having received faith and joy, when the angel Gabriel announced to her the good tidings . . . answered: 'Be it done to me according to thy word.'"[54]

Irenaeus (130–202), an early theologian, repeats the parallel between Eve and Mary in similar terms: "Mary the Virgin is found obedient, saying: Behold the handmaid of the Lord . . . Eve, however, disobedient: for she did not obey, even though she was still a virgin. Inasmuch as she, having indeed Adam for a husband, yet being still a virgin, became disobedient and was made both for herself and the whole human race the cause of death, so also Mary, having a husband destined for her yet being a virgin, by obeying, became the cause of salvation both for herself and the whole human race."[55]

Through Eve's disobedience, the human race was bequeathed a "garment of corruptibility," in the image of many early Christian writers. Through her actions, disobedience to God and mortality became inseparable from the human condition. Through Mary, however, the human race was bequeathed an incorruptible garment, the possibility of immortality through her divine son.[56]

In stressing Mary's role in reversing the actions of Eve, many Christian writers have emphasized Mary's purity in contrast to Eve's impurity after the Fall. Mary is pictured as living a sinless life, as totally removed from all human weaknesses. For many Christians, Mary's purity and sinlessness are intimately associated with her celibacy and vow of perpetual virginity. For many Christians, Eve's disobedience is understood to have led directly to the sexual seduction of Adam. Hence, sex has become for many Christians the peculiar mark or evidence of humankind's fallen condition. Mary, on the other hand, undoes or overcomes Eve's part in the Fall not only by being obedient but also by abstaining totally from sex. Some Christians have also drawn the conclusion, particularly during the centuries when the church extolled asceticism and monasticism, that obedience to God is more complete if one remains a virgin in imitation of both Mary and Jesus.[57]

As the second Eve, then, a relationship is established between Mary and Jesus, who is called the second Adam. Just as Eve and Adam broke communication between God and his creatures, so Mary and Jesus reestablished that communication. In drawing out this parallel, it becomes obvious that in some writings Mary is being given a role comparable to Jesus' role, that she also acts as redeemer. The symmetry of the parallel encourages this. What Adam *and* Eve bring about, namely, the Fall, Jesus *and* Mary reverse with the bringing of redemption. Mary is often seen as Jesus' partner, equal to him in nature and sanctity, in the great cosmic drama of the salvation of humankind. Although this theme never became official church teaching, it was, nevertheless, a strong tendency in some Christian writings. Lawrence of Brindisi, for example, is explicit in equating Jesus' and Mary's roles in salvation. He often compares Mary and Christ to Adam and Eve and at one point says: "Christ the Man (who, after all, cannot be separated from his Divinity) and the Virgin Mother of God are alike in nature, grace, virtue, dignity and glory."[58] He also claims that Mary "has reached the sanctity of Christ" because of her role in undoing what was done by Adam and Eve.[59]

As the second Eve, in her role as co-redeemer with Jesus, Mary is often described and depicted as victorious over the serpent who tempted Eve and who represents disobedience, sinfulness, and mortality. The dogma of the Immaculate Conception, proclaimed in 1854 by Pope Pius IX, declares that Mary was conceived and born without the stain of original sin (unlike all other human beings except Jesus) and says about Mary's participation in the drama of salvation: "Wherefore, as Christ, the mediator between God and man has . . . blotted out the handwriting of the decree of condemnation against us . . . so, in like manner, the most holy Virgin linked to him in the closest and most indissoluble bonds, in union with him and through him, waging eternal hostilities against the poisonous serpent, and obtaining a decisive triumph over him, completely crushed his head under her immaculate heel."[60]

Beginning with the image of Mary as the second Eve who parallels Jesus as the second Adam, and expanding and elaborating the comparison between the two, Christianity (at least in its Latin and Eastern aspects) provided itself a feminine counterpart to the male redeemer and savior, Jesus. Like Jesus' birth, Mary's is also special, if not miraculous. Like Jesus she is born free from sin and lives a sinless life. Like him she remains a virgin. Like Jesus she suffers innocently. She too descends to hell, or is given a glimpse of the beings in hell, immediately after her death or just before her assumption into heaven. Like

Jesus she is assumed bodily into heaven and resides there as a powerful monarch. In heaven, she hears the petitions of the faithful and acts as their advocate before the throne of divine judgment, as Jesus does, or is supposed to do. Although officially Mary's role and position in the economy of salvation are always subordinate to those of Jesus, it is clear that in many ways and for many Christians she has played the role of a female redeemer patterned on Jesus himself.

Queen of Heaven, Bride of Christ

In numerous hymns, prayers, and works of art Mary is described and depicted as a heavenly queen. For many Christians one of the most popular images of Mary is that of a regal monarch sumptuously dressed, wearing a crown, seated on a throne, and holding a staff of authority. Marina Warner describes an eighth-century image of Maria Regina, Mary the Queen, in the basilica of Santa Maria in Trastevere in Rome. The figure is in excess of eight feet tall and holds a cross-surmounted staff, a symbol of spiritual authority. The reigning pope, Pope John VII, kneels before her. "Angels stand at her side, carrying spears like the *protospathari*, the imperial guard. Mary is seated on an imperial purple cushion, stiff with jewels, with her feet resting above the ground, on a *subpedaneum*; a great arcaded diadem crowns her head and a huge nimbus irradiates about her."[61]

The legendary and mythological background to Mary's position as Queen of Heaven is the tradition concerning her ascension and bodily assumption into heaven. In Christian tradition, Jesus is believed to have ascended bodily into heaven, where he sits at the right hand of God the Father and judges humankind. In this role, Jesus takes on regal, magisterial attributes. Similarly with Mary, when she is assumed bodily into heaven she is pictured seated on a throne, often next to Jesus, who sometimes is shown setting a crown on her head. Mary's crowning by Jesus in heaven probably was understood by many Christians as an apt image of Mary's victory over corruption, a fitting finale to her pure, immaculate life and nature, which made her immune to death and decay.

Although the church through the centuries has steadfastly refused to declare Mary's divinity, her divine nature seems to declare itself particularly strongly in the images and hymns to her as Queen of Heaven. This is evident in cases where Mary is described or portrayed as Jesus' bride, or the bride of God. Doctrinally and theologically Mary becomes associated with Jesus as his bride because she represents, symbolizes, or embodies the church. As the church, she is wedded to Christ, who nourishes, sustains, and protects her. In many images and descriptions of Mary and Jesus as a bridal pair, inspiration was drawn from the biblical Song of Solomon, which describes the relationship between two lovers. In the Christian interpretation of this book, the love relationship is taken to be a description of God's love for his church and vice versa. Theologically, then, the relationship between Mary and Jesus is unequal; that is, Mary as the church is entirely dependent upon Christ or God for her existence.

Iconographically, and in the context of the cult of Marian piety, however, the two are often depicted, described, or understood to be equals in their marriage. The relationship, furthermore, strains the limitations of theological metaphor when enthusiastic devotees of Mary describe her marriage to Jesus in warm, erotic language. Bernard of Clairvaux, for example, writes this about Mary's ascension to heaven and her reception there by Jesus:

> With what a tranquil face, with what an unclouded expression, with what joyous embraces was she taken up by her son! . . . Happy indeed were the kisses he pressed on her lips when she was nursing and as a mother delighted in the child in her virgin's lap. But surely will we not deem much happier those kisses which in blessed greeting she receives today from the mouth of him who sits on the right hand of the Father, when she ascends to the throne of glory, singing a nuptial hymn and saying: "Let him kiss me with the kisses of his mouth."?[62]

In many paintings and images Mary and Jesus are seen seated or standing beside each other in heaven. In many cases, they are clothed very similarly, both robed and crowned, for example. In others, they are shown holding hands, a "formal and legal gesture of nuptial union."[63] In some cases the celestial couple is embracing, Jesus with his right arm around his mother/bride's shoulders.[64] All of this suggests an equality of status between the two.

Mary's regal nature and elevated status are even more pronounced in images and descriptions of her being crowned by or wedded to other persons of the Trinity. In the iconographic motif known as the Coronation of the Virgin, all three members of the Godhead are shown placing a crown upon Mary's head. God the Father is usually on the right and is an elderly, bearded man. Jesus is on the left, while the Holy Spirit usually is directly above Mary in the form of a bird, usually a dove. Mary is the central figure in this scene and dominates the viewers' attention. This scene is typically depicted on the ceiling of the dome of the apse in churches.[65]

The writings of Lawrence of Brindisi (d. 1619) refer explicitly to Mary as God's spouse. He says that Mary is "the woman . . . who is united (*copulata*) to God" in "divine marriage."[66] He describes the angel Gabriel's appearance to Mary as the point at which God proposes marriage to Mary and states that "the Virgin was conjoined and copulated with God in a legitimate and true marriage."[67] He also describes how God becomes enchanted with Mary and how she is able to influence him in all matters. Indeed, it is under Mary's influence, it is due to her enchantment of him, that God agrees to embody himself in

Diego Velásquez, *Coronation of the Virgin*. Museo del Prado, Marnel Collection.

human form and bring about the redemption of humankind. "She could turn God from a lion into the gentlest lamb and make God most loving to man, indeed, make him Man . . . as Queen Esther made King Ahasuerus most favourable to the Jews . . . O wonderful power!"[68] Jean-Jacques Olier (d. 1657), in similar fashion, describes the relationship between Mary and God as a marriage in which God acts in all things "according to the intentions, the desires and the prayers of Mary."[69] "As spouse of the eternal Father, she has also all power with him through her prayers; he wills what she wills; he does good to everyone to whom she wants it done. She has only to will and everything is done. . . . The power of the most holy Virgin as spouse is measured by the omnipotence of God, who gives her the use of all his goods; thus she is all-powerful to give everything . . . she is like a queen reigning on the throne of God."[70]

In her aspect as Queen of Heaven, Mary is often shown by herself or with the infant Jesus. A quite popular inconographic rendering of Mary in this vein is inspired by the reference in Revelation to "a woman clothed with the sun, with the moon under her feet, and on her head a crown of twelve stars" (12:1). Although it is unlikely that the author of this book was referring to Mary, the image eventually was affirmed to describe Mary, and images of her with a nimbus of flames behind her became common.[71] Images of her standing on the moon and bedecked with a crown of stars are also common.[72] These images, which associate Mary with natural and cosmic phenomena, assert her transcendent, heavenly nature and remove her from the realm of ordinary mortals. Her association with the heavenly bodies in iconography suggests (although it is never official church teaching) that Mary, like many other goddesses, controls or influences the cosmic rhythms.

Mary's queenly aspect is rendered magnificently in the many great cathedrals built in her honor, especially in France in the twelfth through sixteenth centuries. Befitting the names by which she was often called during those times—*coeli regina* (queen of heaven), *aula regalis* (court royal), *imperatrix supernorum* (empress of the highest), and *templum trinitatis* (temple of the Trinity)[73]—Mary was enshrined in these great structures as the most highly exalted heavenly queen. Commenting upon the extent to which Mary dominated Christian piety during the twelfth and thirteenth centuries, especially in France, Henry Adams writes:

> Nearly every great church of the twelfth and thirteenth centuries belonged to Mary, until in France one asks for the church of Notre Dame as though it meant cathedral; but, not satisfied with this, she contracted the habit of requiring in all churches a chapel of her own, called in English the "Lady Chapel," which was apt to be as large as the church but was always meant to be handsomer; and there, behind the high altar, in her own private apartment, Mary sat, receiving her innumerable suppliants, and ready at any moment to step up upon the high altar itself to support the tottering authority of the local saint.[74]

Diego Velásquez, *The Immaculate Conception*. National Gallery, London.

Seen against the background of very powerful queens such as Eleanor of Guienne (1122–1202) and Blanche of Castile (1187–1252), Mary, enshrined in her many sumptuous and grand cathedrals, is depicted and understood as the most powerful queen of all. Vis-à-vis the divine family and the divine economy she likewise plays the role of a powerful queen. Indeed, she dominates the palatial environs of her dwelling places to the almost total exclusion of God the Father and God the Holy Spirit. Jesus is present, and by implication the other persons of the Trinity, but he is often shown as an infant in Mary's arms; against the background of earthly politics, Mary probably was understood to dominate him. In her cathedrals, Mary is usually enthroned, crowned, and wielding symbols of power. Jesus is often shown as a child in her lap. At Chartres, "wherever we find her . . . , and of whatever period, she is always Queen. Her expression and attitude are always calm and commanding."[75]

"Our Lady": Mary as Patroness, Guardian, and Healer

Closely related to Mary's role as a queen is her role as a national, regional, and local guardian and patron. Throughout the Christian world, innumerable shrines, churches, and cathedrals are dedicated to, and enshrine, a wide range of images of Mary. Although doctrinally and officially there is only one Mary, there is a strong tendency in many places to regard local, regional, or national images of Mary as particular and peculiar to given places. It is as if for those devotees she has many manifestations, which differ from each other in significant ways. As mentioned above, in medieval France nearly every town and village had a church or cathedral dedicated to Mary, who was referred to in the affectionate and localizing way as Notre-Dame, Our Lady of such and such a place. In this fashion, Mary came to play the role of a tutelary deity in many parts of Europe. It was not uncommon for Mary's name to be used thus in battle in medieval France.

> . . . the greatest French warriors insisted on her leading them into battle, and in the actual mêlée when men were killing each other, on every battlefield in Europe, for at least five hundred years, Mary was present, leading both sides. The battle-cry of the famous Constable du Guesclin was "Notre-Dame-Guesclin"; "Notre-Dame-Coucy" was the cry of the great Sires de Coucy; "Notre-Dame-Auxerre"; "Notre-Dame-Sancerre"; "Notre-Dame-Hainault"; "Notre-Dame-Gueldres"; "Notre-Dame-Bourbon"; "Notre-Dame-Bearn";—all well-known battle-cries. The King's own battle at one time cried, "Notre-Dame-Saint-Denis-Montjoie"; the Dukes of Burgundy cried, "Notre-Dame-Bourgogne"; and even the soldiers of the Pope were said to cry, "Notre-Dame-Saint-Pierre."[76]

In Eastern Christianity from a very early time, Mary played the role of guardian and protector of the Christian Byzantine Empire.

Mary with child, fifteenth century C.E., Swiss. Courtesy of Schweizerisches Landesmuseum, Zurich.

> . . . in Byzantium, the emperors Maurice and Phocas and Heraclius and Constant II in the sixth and seventh centuries had struck the image of Nike, Goddess of Victory, from the imperial seals and replaced her with the Virgin and child. At the turn of the seventh century, the Emperor Heraclius had called his enemy Phocas "that Gorgon's head," and had turned against him another different magic face—"the awe-inspiring image of the pure Virgin," flying her image from the mastheads of his ships as he sailed into battle. During the siege of Constantinople by the Avars in 626, the patriarch had the Virgin and child painted on the west gates to commend the city into her hands, for the emperor and his army were far away; in 717, when the Arabs were attacking Constantinople, a picture of the Virgin and child and a relic of the True Cross were carried around the city walls as a charm against the besiegers.[77]

One of the oldest churches in Québec City is called Notre-Dame des Victoires because of Mary's assumed role in defeating a British attack on the city. In Latin America, similarly, many countries and cities came to identify Mary as their special guardian. "Each country placed itself under the protection of the national image of the Virgin: Guadalupe in Mexico; the Virgin of Lujan in Argentina; Our lady of Gualpulo in Ecuador; Our Lady of Copacabana in old Peru . . . ; Nuestra Senora de las Mercedes in modern Peru; Nuestra Senora de Caacupe in Paraguay. In fact, numerous cities of Latin America bear one of the names of the Virgin and are placed under her protection, for example, Our Lady of La Paz, capital of Bolivia."[78]

In some cases, Mary's role as a national, regional, or local guardian figure has involved her in pre-Christian or non-Christian traditions that have lent her an identity that is peculiarly national, regional, or local and that sometimes seems quite different from her doctrinal and theological identity in the established church. A good example of this is the Virgin of Guadalupe, the patron and protector of Mexico. In the gradual Christianization of Mexico, the Virgin of Guadalupe became a central symbol of mestizo and Indian spirituality, and eventually a national symbol of Mexico. Her cult contains clear examples of pre-Christian, specifically Indian, elements. In the story concerning the origin of her cult, she appears to Juan Diego, a poor Indian who had recently become a Christian.[79] She commands him to tell the local bishop to build her a church on the spot where she appeared. In order to convince the doubting bishop, Mary provides Juan Diego with a miraculous painting of herself on native fabric and executed in native style.[80] Images of the Virgin of Guadalupe, which are all patterned on this primordial revelation, depict her standing on the moon, wearing a star-spangled gown and a crown, with the rays of the sun emanating from behind her. Her complexion is dark. Jesus is not depicted.

The place where Mary appeared is also most significant, Tepeyac Hill, which was the exact location of an earlier shrine to the indigenous goddess Tonantsi. Tonantsi was a very popular Indian goddess, known for her benevolence, and in the early days of the Christian invasion of Mexico she protected her devotees from the anger of the new god. She was approached as a mother, and her devotees adopted the attitude of her children. She was said to attend to the prayers of the poorest people, to care especially for young children, to watch over midwives and women giving birth, and to preserve health, happiness, and life.[81] The tradition of Mary as the Virgin of Guadalupe protecting her devotees from an angry God, who was probably also associated with European Christians early in the history of the Guadalupe cult, was quite strong and probably represents a continuation of Tonantsi's role as a protective mother.[82] "Mother of gods and men, of stars and ants, of maize and agave, Tonantzin-Guadalupe was the imaginary compensation of the Indians for the state of orphanage to which the Conquest had reduced them. The Indians, who had seen the massacre of their priests and the destruction of their idols, whose ties with their past and their supernatural world had been severed, took refuge in the lap of Tonantzin-Guadalupe . . . a natural and supernatural mother, composed of American earth and European theology."[83]

Although she is clearly identified with Christianity as the Virgin Mary, it is also clear that there are motifs in Guadalupe's cult that stress her special role as guardian and patron of the Mexican people *against* foreign Christians. Guadalupe's special association with Mexican identity is also clear in the role she plays in the Mexican independence movement.

> During the eleven years of the Mexican Revolutionary Wars (1810–21) Guadalupe's image was carried on the banners of the insurgents, who began to refer to her as "La Conquistadora." General Manuel Felix Fernandez, who was active in the revolutionary wars against Spain, changed his name to Guadalupe Victoria. He was later one of the nation's presidents. Guadalupe's aid was also invoked in the war with the United States. . . . The Virgin also participated in the Civil War of 1911, which effectively curtailed the influence of the hereditary elite and made full citizens of the peasants and the urban poor. Victory for the nationalist forces increased Guadalupe's influence and popularity.[84]

In 1813, during the War of Independence, the revolutionary leader Morelos issued a proclamation in which he stated that all Mexican patriots should wear the emblem of Guadalupe and perform regular devotions to her.[85]

An intriguing corollary to Guadalupe's rise to national preeminence in Mexico was the corresponding decline in the popularity of the Virgin de los Remedios, a very popular image of Mary enshrined in Mexico City and a favorite of the Spanish rulers. During the Revolution, the Loyalists carried banners of the Virgin de los Remedios, while the Insurgents carried banners of Guadalupe. In this struggle "sentiments had become so polarized that soldiers led by Guadalupe or by Remedios shot at the banner bearing the image of the 'enemy' Virgin."[86]

The Virgin of Guadalupe has indeed become a "national symbol."[87] Her image appears everywhere in Mexico: "in churches, chapels, schools, and houses; on bridges; and even on liquor bottles."[88] Her image is also seen in almost every taxi in Mexico City, accompanied by the motto: "Holy Virgin, protect me!"[89] And in many Mexican churches it is Guadalupe's image and worship that completely dominate the spiritual atmosphere.

In modern times, especially in Europe, Mary has occasionally been depicted leading Christian armies against Communism. In this role, Mary reflects the quite conservative and anti-Communist attitude of the Roman Catholic church in Europe. Referring to the Civil War in Spain, one Catholic author has written: "The modern Red menace got its first hold west of Russia in Spain. But under the banner of Our Lady of Mount Carmel and the Sacred Heart, Catholicity had defeated it there. Yes, despite the cooperation of the great bear, despite the advantage of holding the reins of government, Communism has gone down into the dust before the meagre armies struggling for religious independence. . . . Against Satan in his red threats, we have Mary."[90]

In a different role, but one related to that of tutelary deity, protector, and guardian, Mary is a personal, individual protector for many pious Christians. Her devotees approach her with great tenderness and intimacy, often as a dear mother. The Virgin of Copacabana in Peru is called by her Indian devotees Pachamama, "mother of the peoples," or "mother goddess."[91] In medieval Europe, Mary was approached in the tradition and style of the troubadours. That is, she was understood in terms of courtly love as the beloved of her devotees, the perfect woman, and as such she was courted by and sometimes married to them. "The sensuous myth of Mary as the perfect ideal of womanhood merged into the chivalric pattern of thought which dominated Europe in the thirteenth and fourteenth centuries. Madonna (My Lady) now became for the first time the name by which the Virgin was most frequently honoured. Knights fought battles in her name. . . . She was also the confidante of all lovers and was the inspiration of all poets, minstrels and jongleurs."[92]

In many poems and descriptions, Mary is declared the only woman worthy of the devotee's love, and just as nuns were symbolically married to Jesus, so sometimes the male celibate clergy imagined themselves married to Mary.[93] There are even stories of devotees courting Mary in which, due to their disloyalty to her, her anger is aroused and she punishes them for their unfaithfulness to her.[94]

Mary's role as a personal protector is also clear in her aspect as a healer. At Lourdes in southern France, perhaps Mary's most famous shrine, millions of pilgrims approach her for mercy in the form of healing. There and at her many other healing shrines, Mary has made her presence known to her devotees as a loving, caring being who, in response to their prayers, touches them with her healing power. Mary is understood as a being of great compassion and concern for her devotees, who is available for protection, succor, comfort, and healing.[95]

Related to Mary's role as a protector and healer is her reputation as a comforter to the dying. She both protects them from the fires of hell in her role as merciful intercessor and advocate and brings peace to troubled souls. For many Christians it is Mary (not Jesus or God the Father) who is approached for refuge and comfort in the hour of death.

> . . . it is the jurisdiction over death accorded her in popular belief that gives her such widespread supremacy. When Catholics contemplate the darkness of death stretching before them, they cling to a light on the horizon that seems to them no will-o'-the-wisp but as constant as the moon. . . . At the moment the finite plane of a mortal life reaches its term it intersects with the timeless, undifferentiated, immortal beauty and bliss epitomized by the Virgin and makes death meaningless. At the moment the believer fears that step across the gulf, as every man who knows himself a sinner must fear, the promise of the Virgin's ungrudging, ever-flowing clemency sustains him. That is why the best-loved prayer of the Catholic world—the Hail Mary—ends with the plea that the Virgin should "pray for us sinners, now and at the hour of our death."[96]

The great appeal of Mary over the centuries undoubtedly is related to the fact that she is eminently approachable. She is not aloof and distant but near and available. She appears over and over again to the poor and dispossessed and repeatedly betrays a concern for personal, practical, worldly matters. She is approached by people about their ordinary, day-to-day troubles and joys. Although the official church generally tries to discourage and discipline those who claim to have seen an apparition of the Virgin, she continues to make dramatic appearances to ordinary people who are concerned about everyday problems.

> Mrs. Van Hoof of Necedah, Wisconsin, sends out regular mailings to a wide following who believe that Mary has warned her of the sure destruction that will be visited upon America unless short skirts and rock music are suppressed; and visions of Mary in Bayshore, Long Island, have inspired an active congregation of devotees whose concerns include the defeat of Communism and the restoration of the old Latin Mass. In June of 1981, the Boston *Globe* carried a front-page story about two women who claimed that a statue of Mary helped them to win two separate prizes in the Massachusetts state lottery. The cult of the Virgin Mary, replete with miracles and apparitions, is alive and well. Mary in the twentieth century is concerned with appropriately modern issues, including Communism, teenage morality, and the struggles of the poor.[97]

Mary in Contemporary Thought

The veneration of Mary persists very strongly to the present day. However, some of the roles and characteristics that were central to her character in the past have lost some of their relevance in the modern world. Mary as heavenly queen, for example, had more force and meaning in societies in which powerful monarchs dominated peoples' lives. Similarly, Mary's perpetual virginity had more significance in a society in which vast numbers of men and women were renouncing the world to become religious hermits and monks or nuns and in which a powerful church hierarchy staffed by celibates controlled society. Not surprisingly, in a time when women thinkers are seeking to raise people's consciousness about the pervasive sexism of many religious traditions, Mary has come under close scrutiny as a symbol that has been used by men against women.[98] So, for example, the emphasis in traditional Christian teaching and mythology on Mary's subservience, obedience, meekness, sexual abstinence, and subordination to the male aspects of the Godhead have been criticized as reinforcing male stereotypes about women and their place in the church and the world.

A good deal of thinking about Mary in contemporary writing, however, has sought to reinterpret or reevaluate Mary in positive ways. While being critical of the ways in which Mary has been stereotyped by the male-dominated Christian tradition, several writers have sought to find in Mary positive, spiritually relevant, and inspiring roles and characteristics. There are three general themes in modern attempts to reevaluate Mary that I shall briefly summarize: (1) Mary as a symbol by which the Christian image of the divine could be feminized; (2) Mary, freed from her theological and ritualistic trappings, as an exemplary model for women and the faithful generally; and (3) Mary as a revolutionary figure who sides with or supports the poor, the outcasts, the persecuted, and the lowly.

Although orthodox theology never gives Mary divine status, it is obvious that in many cases pre-Christian, pagan goddesses have survived, at least in part, through the veneration of Mary. It is also obvious that for many devotees Mary's status has transcended her official status in church doctrine. For them Mary is a great supernatural presence, closer and dearer to them than God or Jesus. Although the church has consistently sought to curb what it refers to as Marian excesses, some contemporary writers think that Mary's continued importance in modern Christianity is necessary because she introduces a feminine aspect into the Christian concept of the divine. In his book *The Mary Myth: On the Femininity of God*, Andrew Greeley says: "I . . . contend that Mary is a symbol of the feminine component of the deity. She represents the human insight that the Ultimate is passionately tender, seductively attractive, irresistibly inspiring, and graciously healing. . . . Mary is . . . part of a great tradition of female deities, all of whom reflect the human conviction that God has feminine as well as masculine characteristics."[99]

In his discussion of Mary, Greeley unhinges Mary from much traditional Christian theology and mythology and tries to understand her in the context of a universal goddess mythology/theology. Using Jungian archetypes as a framework,[100] Greeley reviews some of Mary's principal mythic roles—mother, virgin, bride, and sufferer—and tries to relate the meanings to the Christian view of the divine. In this way, Mary becomes for Greeley a window, as it were, on the nature of God through which certain qualities, which are otherwise hidden, become visible. Greeley is not alone in thinking that Mary provides the means through which a one-sided, overly masculine, and authoritative view of God in the Christian tradition can be made more complete. Teilhard de Chardin wrote of the "biopsychological necessity of the 'Marian' to counterbalance the masculinity of Yahweh" and said that in Catholicism the veneration of Mary corrects a "dreadfully masculinized conception of the godhead."[101] In a similar vein, a Protestant writer has said this about Mary's importance to the Christian tradition: "Ignoring the place of the Blessed Virgin in the Incarnation and the whole process of salvation has given Protestantism a harsh thoroughly masculine emphasis. . . . The development of a mature Mariology in Protestant thinking could do much to temper the harsh portrayal of the God of judgment and provide it with a healthy . . . concept of a God of mercy."[102]

The attempt to find in Mary a relevant model for women (and for humankind generally) is illustrated, in quite different ways, by Mary Daly and Rosemary Ruether. In the process of criticizing the male-dominated church for the thoroughgoing way in which it has used Mary to promote sexist views and practices, Mary Daly notes that several of the characteristics and roles of Mary—if taken from the context of Christian theology—have strong positive meanings for women. Daly argues, for example, that if Mary's virginity is taken from its Christian context, in which it is primarily a device to enhance the special nature of Jesus and to denigrate sexuality, it proclaims the independence of women.

> The image of Mary as Virgin . . . has an (unintended) aspect of pointing toward independence for women. . . . The woman who is defined as virgin is not defined exclusively by her relationships with men. . . . The message of *independence* in the Virgin symbol can itself be understood apart from the matter of sexual relationships with men. When this aspect of the symbol is sifted out from the patriarchal setting, then "Virgin Mother" can be heard to say something about female autonomy within the context of sexual and parental relationships. This is a message which, I believe, many women throughout the centuries of Christian culture have managed to take from the overtly sexist Marian doctrines.[103]

Similarly, if the doctrine of the Immaculate Conception is taken from its christological context, in which the intention is to affirm the special nature of Jesus, one finds an affirmative statement concerning women. "*As doctrine* it reinforces sexual caste. . . . *As free-wheeling symbol*, however, it can be read in another light. It can be seen as reflecting the power and influence of the Mother Goddess symbol which Christianity was never able to wipe out entirely. Sprung free from its Christolatrous context it says that, conceived free of 'original sin,' the female does not need to be 'saved' by the male. The symbol then can be recognized as having been an infiltrator into sexist territory, an unrecognized harbinger of New Being."[104]

The doctrine of the assumption—that Mary was assumed body and soul into heaven at the end of her earthly life—also has a positive message for women, according to Daly, if taken out of its christological context. In that male context, women's identification with earth, matter, and the physical world is often meant to be negative and derogatory; the assumption of Mary, physically, into heaven affirms women's physical nature. "In itself, the image of Mary 'rising' says something."[105]

Rosemary Ruether, like Daly, is critical of the ways in which Mary has been used by the church to perpetuate sexist views of women, but she sees in Mary meanings that are important for women and men alike. Ruether is reluctant to follow Greeley's interpretation of Mary as a symbol that is necessary in softening the Christian view of God. She thinks that the tendency to view Mary as important primarily because of her traditional "feminine" qualities (such as passivity, receptivity, self-abnegation, humility) simply leads to a continuation of sexist thinking.[106] Mary is an important symbol, Ruether says, because she represents something new. She represents a radical break from an old way of thinking and acting, a break from hierarchical power relationships in which men tend to dominate each other and, particularly, women. Ruether refers to the old order as masculine, insofar as it was (is) dominated by men. The new order, founded by Christianity, she refers to as feminine, an order in which power and dominance are absent, an order that allows the development of whole people.

> Mariology becomes a liberating symbol for women only when it is seen as a radical symbol of a new humanity freed from hierarchical power relations, including that of God and humanity. It is here that the revolutionary side of the image of Mary appears, as the representative of the original and eschatological humanity that is repressed from existence within patriarchy, the culture of domination and subjugation. Woman becomes the symbol of the unknown possibility of a humanity beyond and outside the entire system of such a world. . . . Mary stands for the eschatological humanity of the new covenant: that "new thing" which God has created on earth, "the female overcomes the warrior" (Jer. 31:22).[107]

Mary is also seen as a sympathetic figure in much contemporary Christian thought that emphasizes the solidarity of the Christian message with the lowly, the outcaste, the oppressed, the poor, and the powerless. Mary's own words from the famous hymn in the Gospel of Luke, known as the Magnificat, are often taken as central in this appreciation of Mary:

> My soul magnifies the Lord,
> and my spirit rejoices in God my Savior,

for he has regarded the low estate of his handmaiden.

. . . .

He has shown strength with his arm,
he has scattered the proud in the imagination of their hearts,
he has put down the mighty from their thrones,
and exalted those of low degree;
he has filled the hungry with good things,
and the rich he has sent empty away.

(Luke 1:47–48, 51–53)

Just as Mary, presumably a relatively powerless peasant of "low estate," was singled out and blessed by God, so Mary has singled out and supported the poor, the powerless, and the marginalized. Speaking of Mary's appearance on Tepeyac Hill in Mexico to the poor Indian peasant Juan Diego, one writer says: "The apparition is . . . a liberation from the socio-psychological oppression because she will *listen to the silenced poor*, she will call them by name, and place all her confidence in them. In the person of Juan Diego their crushed dignity is restored and from their imposed worthlessness, they are called upon to be the chosen servants and messengers."[108]

Mary as a symbol of liberation from tyranny, religious bigotry, financial exploitation, and sexism—liberation from the status quo wherever it impoverishes, humiliates, and crushes people—is the theme of a striking poem by the Swiss Protestant pastor Kurt Marti entitled "Und Maria." The poem, patterned on and inspired by the Magnificat, emphasizes Mary's opposition to and exclusion from established religion and society and her solidarity with those persecuted—indeed hounded, hunted, and murdered—by the church itself:

1. And Mary sang
to her unborn Son:
my soul magnifies the Lord
I rejoice in God my saviour
I: an unimportant woman. . . .

2. And Mary could hardly read
and Mary could hardly write
and Mary was not allowed to sing
or speak in the Jewish House of Prayer
where men serve the man-god

that is why she sang
to her oldest son
that is why she sang
to daughters to other sons
of the great grace and her
holy overthrowing . . .

5. later much later
Mary looked
in bewilderment at the altars
on which she
had been set
and she believed
there had been a change
as she
—the manifold mother—
was highly praised
as a maiden

but most of all
she was troubled
by the blasphemous kneeling
of potentates and officers
against whom she had once sung
full of hope

6. And Mary walked
out of the pictures
and climbed
down from the altars . . .
and she was
  burnt as a witch
  a million times over
  in a false god's honour

. . . .

and she was
  the lion Madonna naked
  on the lion's back
  riding for her Indians
and she was and she is
  many-bodied many-voiced
  the subversive hope
  of her song.[109]

CONCLUSION

Perhaps the most obvious conclusion one can draw after having meditated upon these ten goddesses[1] is that they are each impressive and distinctive presences or "personalities." There are similarities between them, to be sure, but what is more striking, I think, is their individuality, the extent to which each is a formidable reality in her own right. Even those goddesses who are strongly related to a male deity as wife or mother (for example, Sītā, Lakṣmī, Isis, and Mary) impress themselves upon us as strong, independent beings. Sītā might protest and insist that she is nothing without her husband, Rāma, and the church may insist that Mary is powerless except insofar as she is given power through her son, but devotees of both these female powers know better. Sītā provides, and has provided, an extraordinarily powerful reality for millions of Hindu women who have been caught in difficult social situations. It may well be argued (indeed, I think it should be argued) that Sītā has been used to legitimate a status quo that is oppressive of women, but this cannot detract from the powerful influence that she has had in helping Hindu women find meaning, value, and direction in the midst of difficult circumstances. Mary, similarly, transcends the limitations imposed by Christian doctrine. For millions of her devotees her power, influence, and grace have overflowed the categories that would restrict her to a subordinate, peripheral role in the economy of salvation.

The individuality of these goddesses, their distinctiveness, and the impressive ways in which they strike us seem to me to underline an important point, namely, that their sexual identity is not an overriding determinant of their character. All of these goddesses are certainly females, many of them emphatically so insofar as they epitomize what their respective cultures define as female characteristics or roles (for example, Sītā and Aphrodite). But it is unmistakably clear that it would be a violation of their individuality, their particular and peculiar natures or personalities, to see in these ten deities an irreducible essence that we might designate "feminine" or "female." I suppose this is not a very surprising conclusion to draw, for it certainly would never occur to us to take widely differing male deities and seek to attribute to them an underlying commonality by looking to their male natures. But this is exactly the kind of thing that we are often tempted to do with females, be they human or divine. The reason for this, I suspect, is a deep-seated sexism that persists in seeing females (women or goddesses) as in some sense peripheral to, secondary to, or dependent upon males or a male-centered vision of reality. If sexual reductionism is not appropriate in the case of male deities, why should it be appropriate in the case of female deities?

The second conclusion one is tempted to draw after reviewing these ten visions of the divine is that the East has far richer living goddess traditions than does the West. To a very great extent this may be explained historically. Christianity, and to some extent Judaism, has dominated Western religious thinking almost exclusively for two thousand years. In the Judeo-Christian vision of the divine there has not been much room for feminine expressions. To put the matter simply and bluntly, the Judeo-Christian tradition has found it nearly impossible to image the divine in female ways.[2] This tradition has been strongly dominated by a male vision of the divine. No matter how emphatically one may insist that in this tradition God is not really a person to whom sexual identity may be ascribed, the Judeo-Christian conception of the divine is very strongly compromised in the direction of male imagery and roles. Like it or not, the Judeo-Christian deity for centuries has been imagined as a male person, been assigned male roles, and been steadfastly referred to as "he," "father," and "king."

Mary, of course, is the exception, but then Mary is not actually a goddess; she is excluded from sharing in divinity according to Christian teaching. Her great popularity, power, and appeal, one suspects, derive primarily, not from the higher echelons of the church, but from the rank and file of the faithful, who found in Mary a sympathetic figure, and attributed to her powers that had been possessed by earlier goddesses in locales where Christianity usurped or replaced earlier religions in which female deities had been prominent. That is, Mary as a divine figure does not seem to be a logical development of Christian ideology and doctrine so much as she seems to reflect themes that were strong in pre-Christian, pagan religions in which goddesses were worshiped. It was left for the higher echelons of the church (dominated by male celibates) to try to conform Mary to orthodox Christian doctrine. The church hierarchy, that is, was in the position more of reacting to developments in the reverence and worship of Mary than fostering or promoting such piety. In general, I think, the role of the church hierarchy has been to keep Marian piety within bounds.

In the East, the situation is very different indeed. There we have lively goddess traditions in almost every region except those areas exclusively dominated by Islam (which, of course, is a continuation, or variant, of the Judeo-Christian tradition and is equally uncomfortable with female divine imagery). Large regions of Southeast Asia and the Orient veritably bubble with goddesses who are the centers of popular cults and elaborate festivals and who are the objects of prayer, pilgrimage, and petition by devotees, who seek from them every imaginable favor and blessing. In these areas one expects the divine to express itself in female form. In Hindu, Buddhist, Confucian, Taoist, and Shinto thought, to greater or lesser extents, the female aspect of reality is affirmed as fundamental and essential at all levels of reality in differing ways. Goddesses (or female superbeings), then, are not considered exceptional, extraordinary, deviant, or inappropriate expressions of the divine or the superhuman. The goddesses of the East, furthermore, as we have seen, are not stereotypical. There is a rich diversity among them. They do not seem to be mere male stereotypes about women projected to a spiritual realm. They often play male roles and violate codes of behavior dictated for women. Many of these Eastern goddesses seem to underline the point that theology (mythology, spirituality) is much more than a reflection of the social sphere.

A third conclusion that seems apparent after reflecting on these ten goddesses is that there was a time when the West also had lively goddess traditions and that these traditions were similar in many ways to the goddess traditions of the East. In the pre-Christian period, in the Ancient Near East, Egypt, Greece, and elsewhere, goddesses were popular and often central. We know also that goddesses were popular throughout pre-Christian Europe, the Americas, and indeed most lands where Christianity eventually spread and eventually came to dominate. The lack of goddesses in the West since the advent of Christianity, that is, seems to be the exception, not the rule, in the history of culture. The presence of many goddesses in the East should not strike us as anything remarkable. What is far more remarkable is the absence of goddesses in the Christian-dominated West. The pre-Christian West was just as rich in goddess traditions as the East is today. I do not wish to argue for a theory of prepatriarchal cultures in which goddesses were widely worshiped and equality between the sexes prevailed or in which women possibly dominated culture. I do think it is important, however, especially for those of us in the West who are heirs of the Judeo-Christian tradition, to reflect upon our notable lack of female divine imagery. It is this absence that is the remarkable phenomenon in the history of religions, I think, not the presence of goddesses elsewhere. The Christian-dominated West is the aberration in the goddesses' mirror for giving only a very limited reflection of the feminine divine.

Another conclusion is apparent on the basis of these ten examples of the divine feminine: although there are striking similarities among many of them, these similarities do not represent their essences. For example, it is clear that several of the goddesses we have portrayed are concerned with fertility, indeed, at times are identified with fertility (for example, Lakṣmī, Inanna, and Isis), while others are concerned with, or strongly related to, motherhood (Isis and Mary, for example). However to designate Lakṣmī or Inanna or Isis as a "fertility goddess" is not very helpful in describing who these goddesses are. Each of the goddesses who is strongly related to fertility is a complex "personality," with many other aspects that are unrelated to fertility. Similarly with the goddesses strongly associated with a maternal role: they are only very poorly and weakly defined as "mother goddesses." All too often, I think, we are tempted to simplify and breezily dismiss goddesses as expressions of a few themes we traditionally associate with women. It is natural, indeed it would be greatly surprising if it were not the case, that some goddesses are associated with fertility and motherhood. But then male deities also are sometimes associated with fertility and paternity; in these cases we are far less prone to reduce these deities to "fertility gods" or "father gods," although the practice is not entirely unknown. My point here is that I think the goddesses we find in the world's religions are often less stereotypical than we are prone to make them in our scholarly appraisals of them. I will be less suspicious of this tendency when I begin to hear of conferences devoted to "The Father God" instead of (or in addition to) conferences on "The Mother Goddess."

Finally, I would like to repeat what I said in the Introduction. There are innumerable goddesses in the history of religions. I am unfamiliar with most of them. The ten goddesses portrayed in this book were chosen, to some extent, arbitrarily—they attracted my fancy in one way or another. Also, as I said in the Introduction, the book is heavily weighted in terms of India and Greece. Because these things are so, any general conclusions we might be tempted to draw about all goddesses on the basis of these ten must be tentative indeed. It is my hope that this "sampler" of goddesses is sufficient for the reader to reach the conclusion that the divine as expressed in feminine form, image, and role is difficult to delimit, reduce, or otherwise circumscribe in a few themes, characteristics, or types. If there is a Goddess, one great female being who expresses herself wherever any particular goddess appears, as some theologians today are suggesting, then surely She is a being of great diversity who transcends and breaks the bounds of stereotypical thinking about the feminine.

NOTES

Introduction

1. Rosemary Radford Ruether, "The Future of Feminist Theology in the Academy," *Journal of the American Academy of Religion*, vol. 53, no. 4 (December 1985), p. 706.
2. See, for example, Virginia Ramey Mollenkott, *The Divine Feminine: The Biblical Imagery of God as Female* (New York: Crossroad, 1983).
3. See chap. 10 herein.
4. There are problems in referring to either Kuan-yin or the Virgin Mary as a goddess. These problems are discussed in the two chapters on Kuan-yin and Mary. At this point, suffice it to say, both Kuan-yin and Mary have, in comparative perspective, all the divine qualities possessed by goddesses in other traditions. That is, they look very much like goddesses, even if there are problems in using this term in their respective traditions.
5. David Kinsley, *Hindu Goddesses: Visions of the Divine Feminine in the Hindu Religious Tradition* (Berkeley: University of California Press, 1986).
6. M. and M. Vaerting. *The Dominant Sex* (London: Allen & Unwin, 1923), cited in Merlin Stone, *When God Was a Woman* (New York: Harcourt Brace Jovanovich, 1976), p. 31.
7. Adrienne Rich, "Prepatriarchal Female/Goddess Images," in Charlene Spretnak, ed., *The Politics of Women's Spirituality: Essays on the Rise of Spiritual Power within the Feminist Movement* (New York: Doubleday & Co., 1982), p. 33.
8. The two most important earlier books arguing in favor of prehistoric matriarchies are J. J. Bachofen, *Myth, Religion, and Mother Right*, trans. Ralph Manheim (Prince-

ton, N.J.: Princeton University Press, 1967), and Robert Briffault, *The Mothers* (abridged ed.; London: George Allen & Unwin, 1959; originally published in 1927).

9. Marija Gimbutas, *The Goddesses and Gods of Old Europe: Myths and Cult Images* (Berkeley: University of California Press, 1982).

10. Stone, *When God Was a Woman,* p. xii. For a review of the prepatriarchal theory, see Gerda Lerner, *The Creation of Patriarchy* (New York: Oxford University Press, 1986), pp. 15–35.

11. See, for example, Ean Begg, *The Cult of the Black Virgin* (London: Routledge & Kegan Paul, 1986); Pamela Berger, *The Goddess Obscured: Transformation of the Grain Protectress from Goddess to Saint* (Boston: Beacon Press, 1985); Leonard Moss and Stephen C. Cappannari, "In Quest of the Black Virgin: She Is Black because She is Black," in James J. Preston, ed., *Mother Worship: Theme and Variations* (Chapel Hill: University of North Carolina Press, 1982), pp. 53–74; Ethelbert Stauffer, "Antike Madonnenreligion," in Hildegard Temporini and Wolfgang Haase, eds., *Aufstieg und Niedergang der Römischen Welt,* vol. 17, pt. 3 (Berlin: Walter De Gruyter, 1984), pp. 1425–99; R. E. Witt, *Isis in the Graeco-Roman World* (London: Thames & Hudson, 1971).

12. Marija Gimbutas, "Women and Culture in Goddess-Oriented Old Europe," in Spretnak, ed., *The Politics of Women's Spirituality,* pp. 24–31.

13. See, for example, Elise Boulding. *The Underside of History: A View of Women through Time* (Boulder, Colo.: Westview Press, 1976), pp. 191–92; Ruby Rohrlich-Leavitt, "Women in Transition: Crete and Sumer," in Renate Bridenthal and Claudia Koonz, eds., *Becoming Visible: Women in European History* (Boston: Houghton Mifflin Co., 1977), pp. 38–57; Mary Wakeman, "Ancient Sumer and the Women's Movement: The Process of Reaching Behind, Encompassing and Going Beyond," *Journal of Feminist Studies in Religion,* vol. 1, no. 2 (Fall 1985), pp. 7–26; Lerner, *The Creation of Patriarchy,* p. 145.

14. See: Marylin Arthur, " 'Liberated' Women: The Classical Era," in Bridenthal and Koonz, eds., *Becoming Visible,* p. 61; Rosemary Radford Ruether, *New Woman, New Earth: Sexist Ideologies and Human Liberation* (New York: Seabury Press, 1975), pp. 9–10; William Irwin Thompson, *The Time Falling Bodies Take to Light: Mythology, Sexuality, and the Origins of Culture* (New York: St. Martin's Press, 1981), pp. 159–72; and Wakeman, "Ancient Sumer and the Women's Movement," p. 24.

15. Ruether, *New Woman, New Earth,* pp. 13–14; Wakeman, "Ancient Sumer and the Women's Movement," p. 19.

16. See, for example, Gimbutas, *The Goddesses and Gods of Old Europe,* pp. 9, 236–38, and passim; and Stone, *When God Was a Woman,* pp. 9ff. and passim. An exception to this tendency is Judith Ochshorn, *The Female Experience and the Nature of the Divine* (Bloomington: Indiana University Press, 1981), pp. xiv–xvii, in which the historic priority of polytheism is asserted.

17. Stone, *When God Was a Woman,* p. 18.

18. Gimbutas, *The Goddesses and Gods of Old Europe,* p. 9.

19. Gimbutas, "Women and Culture in Goddess-Oriented Old Europe," p. 29.

20. Ibid., p. 28.

21. Ibid.

22. Ibid., p. 24.

23. Anne L. Barstow, "The Prehistoric Goddess," in Carl Olson, ed., *The Book of the Goddess Past and Present: An Introduction to Her Religion* (New York: Crossroad, 1983), pp. 12–14.,

24. Gimbutas, "Women and Culture in Goddess-Oriented Old Europe," p. 23.
25. Stone, *When God Was a Woman*, pp. 10–13.
26. Elizabeth Schüssler-Fiorenza, *In Memory of Her: A Feminist Theological Reconstruction of Christian Origins* (New York: Crossroad Publishing Co., 1986), p. xxiii and passim.
27. See Arthur, " 'Liberated' Women: The Classical Era," pp. 60–89; and Christine Downing, "The Mother Goddess among the Greeks," in Olson, ed., *The Book of the Goddess Past and Present*, pp. 54–55.
28. See, for example, Gimbutas, *The Goddesses and Gods of Old Europe*, pp. 147–48.
29. Downing, "The Mother Goddess among the Greeks," pp. 49–59.
30. Barstow, "The Prehistoric Goddess," p. 12.
31. Ibid., p. 10.
32. David Kinsley, "The Image of the Divine and the Status of Women in the *Devī-bhāgavata-purāṇa*," *Anima*, vol. 9, no. 1 (Fall 1982), pp. 50–56.
33. Sarah B. Pomeroy, "A Classical Scholar's Perspective on Matriarchy," in Berenice A. Carroll, ed., *Liberating Women's History: Theoretical and Critical Essays* (Urbana: University of Illinois Press, 1976), p. 217.
34. Ibid., p. 218.
35. Ibid., pp. 222–23. Some examples of other scholars who are uneasy with, or disagree with, the theory of a prepatriarchal culture or matriarchal culture are Joan Bamberger, "The Myth of Matriarchy: Why Men Rule in Primitive Society," in Michelle Zimbalist Rosaldo and Louise Lamphere, eds., *Women, Culture, and Society* (Stanford, Calif.: Stanford University Press, 1974), pp. 263–80; Sally Binford, "Myths and Matriarchies," *Anthropology*, vols. 81/82, no. 1 (1981), pp. 150–53; Carolyn Fluehr-Lobban, "A Marxist Reappraisal of the Matriarchate," *Current Anthropology*, vol. 20 (June 1979), pp. 341–60; Dorothy Hammond and Alta Jablow, *Women in Cultures of the World* (Menlo Park, Calif.: Cummings Publishing Co., 1976), pp. 1–14; Ruether, *New Woman, New Earth*, pp. 6–11.
36. Martin King Whyte, *The Status of Women in Preindustrial Societies* (Princeton, N.J.: Princeton University Press, 1978), pp. 132–33, 171.
37. Ibid., p. 169; Evelyn Kessler, *Women, An Anthropological View* (New York: Holt, Rinehart & Winston, 1976), pp. 44, 51; Michelle Zimbalist Rosaldo and Louise Lamphere, "Introduction," in Rosaldo and Lamphere, eds., *Women, Culture, and Society*, pp. 3–4. For a rebuttal of the view that males tend to be everywhere dominant in traditional societies, see Eleanor Leacock, "Women in Egalitarian Societies," in Bridenthal and Koonz, eds., *Becoming Visible*, pp. 11–35.
38. A recent article that seeks to apply the theory of a shift from prepatriarchal to patriarchal culture to early Japanese religion is Robert S. Ellwood's "Patriarchal Revolution in Ancient Japan: Episodes from the *Nihonshoki* Sūjin Chronicle," *Journal of Feminist Studies in Religion*, vol. 2, no. 2 (Fall 1986), pp. 23–38. For some preliminary general remarks on India in this vein see Boulding, *The Underside of History*, pp. 187–91, and Stone, *When God Was a Woman*, pp. 69–73.

Chapter 1

1. Summary of *Devī-māhātmya* 2.55–67 following *The Glorification of the Great Goddess*, ed. and trans. Vasudeva S. Agrawala (Varanasi: All-India Kashiraj Trust, 1963), pp. 55–57.

2. *Taittirīya-aranyaka* 10.1.7.

3. M. C. P. Srivastava, *Mother Goddess in Indian Art, Archaeology & Literature* (Delhi: Agam Kala Prakashan, 1979), pp. 111–13; Jitendra Nath Banerjea, *The Development of Hindu Iconography* (2d ed.; Calcutta: University of Calcutta, 1956), pp. 495–500.

4. The most celebrated text describing Durgā's mythological exploits is the *Devī-māhātmya*, which constitutes chapters 81–93 of the *Mārkandeya-pūraṇa*. The myth about Durgā's defeat of Mahiṣa is also found in the *Vāmana-purāṇa* 19.1–21.52, *Varāha-purāṇa* 62.1–95.65, *Śiva-purāṇa* 5.46.1–63, *Devī-bhāgavata-purāṇa* 5.2–10, *Skanda-purāṇa*,and several *Upa-purāṇas*. The myth concerning Durgā's slaying of Śumbha and Nisumbha is also found in the *Vāmana-purāṇa* 29.1–30.73, *Śiva-purāṇa* 5.47.1–48.50, *Skanda-purāṇa* 7.3.24.1–22, and several *Upa-purāṇas*. The worship of Durgā is enjoined and described in the *Kālikā-purāṇa* 61, *Mahābhāgavata-purāṇa* 45–48, and *Devī-purāṇa* 21–23.

5. See, for example, the hymn to Āyrā in *Harivaṁsa* 3.3; *Viṣṇu-purāṇa* 5.1.95; and *Mahābhārata*, Virāṭa-parva 6.

6. M. Srivastava, *Mother Goddess*, p. 110.

7. *Devī-māhātmya* 5.38; *Vāmana-purāṇa* 28.6–25.

8. Heinrich Zimmer, *Myths and Symbols of Indian Art and Civilization*, ed. Joseph Campbell (New York: Harper & Row, 1962), pl. 56.

9. See David R. Kinsley, *Hindu Goddesses: Visions of the Divine Feminine in the Hindu Religious Tradition* (Berkeley: University of California Press, 1986), chaps. 8 and 10.

10. *Devī-māhātmya* 8.62.

11. The term *liminal* has been used by Victor Turner to designate boundary situations, charactertistics, and so on. He notes that many rituals purposely seek to involve participants in such situations to allow them to step outside their normal social roles and restraints. See his *Dramas, Fields, and Metaphors: Symbolic Action in Human Society* (Ithaca, N.Y.: Cornell University Press, 1974), pp. 231–70.

12. David Dean Shulman, *Tamil Temple Myths: Sacrifice and Divine Marriage in the South Indian Saiva Tradition* (Princeton, N.J.: Princeton University Press, 1980), pp. 186–87.

13. *Devī-māhātmya*, 5.56–65; *Devī-bhāgavata-purāṇa* 5.2–20.

14. *Devī-bhāgavata-purāṇa* 5.11.17–30.

15. See, for example, *Manu-dharma-śāstra* 5.147–49, 9.14–17.

16. See Victor Turner, *The Ritual Process: Structure and Anti-structure* (Ithaca, N.Y.: Cornell University Press, 1977).

17. Pearl Ostroff, "The Demon-slaying Devī: A Study of Her Purāṇic Myths" (master's thesis, McMaster University, Hamilton, Ont., 1978), pp. 56–57.

18. David Kinsley, "The Portrait of the Goddess in the *Devī-māhātmya*," *Journal of the American Academy of Religion*, vol. 46, no. 4 (December 1978), pp. 497–98.

19. *Devī-māhātmya* 2.9–10.

20. David Kinsley, *The Divine Player—a Study of Kṛṣṇa Līlā* (Delhi: Motilal Banarsidass, 1979), pp. 1–55.

21. Balram Srivastava, *Iconography of Śakti: A Study Based on Śrītattvanidhi* (Delhi: Chaukhambha Orientalia, 1978), plate facing p. 67.

22. Pandurang V. Kane, *History of Dharmaśāstra* (Poona: Bhandarkar Oriental Institute, 1930–62), vol. 5, p. 171; Pratāpachandra Ghosha, *Durga Puja: With Notes and Illustrations* (Calcutta: Hindoo Patriot Press, 1871), p. 39.

23. Abbé J. A. Dubois, *Hindu Manners, Customs and Ceremonies*, trans. Henry K. Beauchamp (3d ed.; Oxford: Clarendon Press, 1906), pp. 569–70; see also Paul Thomas, *Hindu Religion, Customs and Manners* (Bombay: Taraporevala, n.d.), p. 147. I am indebted to Pearl Ostroff for showing me the connection between Durgā and military themes in Hinduism.

24. Alexander Kinloch Forbes, *Rās-Mālā: Hindu Annals of Western India* (New Delhi: Heritage Publishers, 1973), p. 614.

25. Kane, *History of Dharmaśāstra*, vol. 5, p. 190.

26. Ibid., p. 193.

27. Krishna Kanta Handiqui, *Yaśastilaka and Indian Culture* (Sholapur: Jaina Saṁskṛiti Saṁrakshaka Sangha, 1949), p. 398.

28. *Garuḍa-purāṇa* 135.5; *Viṣṇudharmottara-purāṇa* 2.158; *Devī-purāṇa* 21.22.

29. *Vākpatirāja's Gauḍavaho*, trans. N. G. Suru (Ahmedabad: Prakrit Text Society, 1975), vv. 285–337.

30. *Worship of the Goddess according to the Kālikāpurāṇa*, trans. K. R. Van Kooij (Leiden: E. J. Brill, 1972), 62.24–27, 30–32, 41–43, 49; see also *Mahābhāgavata-purāṇa* 36–48 and *Bṛhaddharma-purāṇa* 1.18–22.

31. Narendra Nath Bhattacharyya, *History of Śākta Religion* (New Delhi: Munshiram Manoharlal Publishers, 1974), pp. 133, 149.

32. Ákos Öster, *The Play of the Gods* (Chicago: University of Chicago Press, 1980), p. 18.

33. P. K. Gode, "Hari Kavi's Contribution to the Problem of the Bhavāni Sword of Shivaji the Great," *New Indian Antiquary*, vol. 3 (1940–41), pp. 82–83.

34. Ibid., pp. 84–85, 92.

35. Ibid., p. 98.

36. James Tod, *Annals and Antiquities of Rajast'han* (New Delhi: M. N. Publishers, 1978), vol. 1, p. 465.

37. Ibid., p. 184.

38. Kane, *History of Dharmaśāstra*, vol. 5, p. 163; Gosha, *Durga Puja*, pp. 41–51.

39. Gosha, *Durga Puja*, p. 41.

40. Ibid., p. 47.

41. Ibid., p. 49.

42. Ibid., p. 50.

43. Ibid., p. 22.

44. Ibid., pp. 14, 23.

45. Ibid., p. 23.

46. Kane, *History of Dharmaśāstra*, vol. 5, p. 156.

47. Gosha, *Durga Puja*, p. 46.

48. Ibid., p. 14.

49. Ibid., pp. 76, lxvii.

50. Especially the Rudhirādhyāya (chapter on blood) of the *Kālikā-purāṇa* 71.

51. *Devī-māhātmya* 13.8.

52. *Harivaṁśa* 3.3.

53. Joseph Campbell, *The Masks of God: Primitive Mythology* (New York: Viking Press, 1959), pp. 216–24; Mircea Eliade, *Patterns in Comparative Religion,* trans. Rosemary Sheed (Cleveland, Ohio: World Publishing Co., 1958), pp. 341–47.

54. Kane, *History of Dharmaśāstra,* vol. 5, p. 177; *Bṛhaddharma-purāṇa* 1.21–22; *Kālikā-purāṇa* 61.

55. Gosha, *Durga Puja,* p. 82; Abhay Charan Mukerji, *Hindu Feasts and Fasts* (Allahabad: Indian Press, 1916), pp. 156, 162; *Kālikā-purāṇa* 61–63.

56. Eliade, *Patterns in Comparative Religion,* pp. 314–16, 332–34.

57. Edward J. Thompson and Arthur Marshman Spencer, trans., *Bengali Religious Lyrics, Śākta* (Calcutta: Association Press, 1923), p. 98.

58. Lawrence A. Babb, *The Divine Hierarchy: Popular Hinduism in Central India* (New York: Columbia University Press, 1975), pp. 216–24, argues that a typical theme in Hindu mythology is the danger presented by unmarried goddesses and females and argues that unmarried goddesses are generally aggressive and dangerous in their actions. This danger presumably might be said to arise from such goddesses' pent-up sexual energy.

59. This may reflect the male fear that in sexual intercourse the loss of semen is something spiritually harmful. An important notion in Indian asceticism is that by retaining his semen a male may build up great spiritual vigor.

60. Shulman, *Tamil Temple Myths,* pp. 176–91, 211–23.

Chapter 2

1. *The Journey to the West,* trans. and ed. Athony C. Yu (4 vols.; Chicago: University of Chicago Press, 1977–83), vol. 1, p. 185.

2. The term *goddess* is not, strictly speaking, appropriate to Kuan-yin, especially according to Buddhists. Technically, Kuan-yin is a bodhisattva. Bodhisattvas are human beings who have reached a certain degree of perfection. As one scholar bluntly puts it: "Never is it possible for a Bodhisattva to be a 'god' or a 'goddess' " (Dietrich Seckel, *The Art of Buddhism* [New York: Crown Publishers, 1964], p. 228). Indeed, to refer to Kuan-yin as a goddess is to greatly lower her status in the context of Chinese Buddhism. According to Chinese Buddhism, at least in the T'ien-t'ai school, there are ten realms of sentient beings. These are, in descending order: Buddhas, bodhisattvas, *pratyekabuddhas, Śrāvakas,* beings in heaven (gods and goddesses), human beings, demons, animals, hungry spirits, and beings in hell. In this scheme, only the first four realms are considered realms of enlightenment. The lower realms (which include heaven) are realms of transmigration; that is, the beings in these realms are subject to decay, death, and transmigration. Nevertheless, Kuan-yin is described in terms very similar to or identical with our Western idea of a goddess. That is, she is omniscient, omnipotent, and immortal. She also is approached by her devotees in exactly the same ways in which goddesses are approached: with reverence, worship, and pleas for help and understanding. Functionally, that is, Kuan-yin is a powerful, supernatural being—in short, a goddess.

3. Henry Dore, *Researches into Chinese Superstitions*. trans. M. Kennelly, vol. 6 (Taipei: Ch'eng-wen Publishing Co., 1920), p. 232.

4. John Blofeld, *Bodhisattva of Compassion: The Mystical Tradition of Kuan Yin* (Boulder, Colo.: Shambhala, 1978), p. 18.

5. A bodhisattva, technically, is a being who is destined for enlightenment. In Mahāyāna Buddhism, however, there is a group of what might be called super-bodhisattvas who have achieved great fame and popularity. Among these is Avalokiteśvara. These super-bodhisattvas are typified by wholly compassionate natures. They, in fact, have renounced the ultimate Buddhist goal of *nirvāna* in order to remain in the world to help suffering human beings.

6. Some scholars are relucant to admit that Kuan-yin ever came to be considered primarily female. "The idea that Kuanyin is feminine contradicts the notion that any Bodhisattva has overcome the difference between the sexes. . . . Moreover, it also contradicts the visual evidence in most of the sculpted and painted figures, including those from more recent epochs after the Sung period" (Seckel, *The Art of Buddhism*, p. 228). The evidence is overwhelming, however, that after the eleventh century Kuan-yin is usually understood to be female. See Diana Paul, *Women in Buddhism: Images of the Feminine in Mahāyāna Tradition* (Berkeley: University of California Press, 1985), chap. 8, for a discussion of the possibility of female Buddhas and bodhisattvas.

7. C. N. Tay, "Kuan-yin: The Cult of Half Asia," *History of Religions*, vol. 16, no. 2 (November 1976), p. 153.

8. Paul, *Women in Buddhism*, pp. 264–66; Diana Paul, "Kuan-yin: Savior and Savioress in Chinese Pure Land Buddhism," in Carl Olson, ed., *The Book of the Goddess Past and Present: An Introduction to Her Religion* (New York: Crossroad, 1983), pp. 165–66, 172.

9. Tay, "Kuan-yin," p. 151.

10. Ibid.

11. Ibid., p. 152.

12. Ibid.

13. Blofeld, *Bodhisattva of Compassion*, pp. 40–42.

14. Henri Maspero, "The Mythology of Modern China," in J. Hackin et al., eds., *Asiatic Mythology* (New York: Thomas Y. Crowell Co., n.d.), pp. 353–54.

15. Ibid., p. 354.

16. Ibid., p. 350.

17. Although it is possible to find Buddhist precedents for Kuan-yin's role as granting children in the figures of Avalokiteśvara and Hāritī, the continuities between Kuan-yin in this role and the indigenous Chinese goddess Sheng mu seem much greater than in the Buddhist figures. Hāritī was a demoness who attacked children. She was converted to a pious life by the Buddha and subsequently assumed the role of protector of children. See John H. Chamberlayne, "The Development of Kuan Yin: Chinese Goddess of Mercy," *Numen*, vol. 9 (January 1962), p. 51; Dore, *Researches into Chinese Superstitions*, p. 207; and Alice Getty, *The Gods of Northern Buddhism*, trans. J. Deniker (Rutland, Vt.: Charles E. Tuttle Co., 1962), p. 80.

18. Maspero, "The Mythology of Modern China," p. 355.

19. Laurence G. Thompson, *The Chinese Way in Religion* (Belmont, Calif.: Dickenson Publishing Co., 1973), p. 196; Dore, *Researches into Chinese Superstitions*, p. 216.

20. Thompson, *The Chinese Way in Religion*, p. 197.

21. Ibid., p. 201.

22. Ibid., p. 197.

23. Chamberlayne, "The Development of Kuan Yin," p. 51.

24. Dore, *Researches into Chinese Superstitions*, p. 223.

25. See Holmes Welch, *The Practice of Chinese Buddhism, 1900–1950* (Cambridge, Mass.: Harvard University Press, 1967), pp. 189, 297.

26. Dore, *Researches into Chinese Superstitions*, fig. 37 (facing p. 224).

27. Ibid., p. 205; see also Chamberlayne, "The Development of Kuan Yin," p. 50.

28. Glen Dudbridge, *The Legend of Miao-shan* (London: Ithaca Press, 1978), pp. 10–19.

29. My summary of the story follows ibid., pp. 22–34, 40–42; Blofeld, *Bodhisattva of Compassion*, pp. 66–71; and Dore, *Researches into Chinese Superstitions*, pp. 134–96.

30. Dudbridge, *The Legend of Miao-shan*, p. 27.

31. Ibid., p. 29.

32. Ibid., p. 94; Dore, *Researches into Chinese Superstitions*, pp. 161–62.

33. Dore, *Researches into Chinese Superstitions*, p. 164.

34. Dudbridge, *The Legend of Miao-shan*, pp. 33–34.

35. Ibid., p. 42.

36. Blofeld, *Bodhisattva of Compassion*, p. 108.

37. Paul, *Women in Buddhism*, p. 249; Kenneth Ch'en, *Buddhism in China: A Historical Survey* (Princeton, N.J.: Princeton University Press, 1964), p. 340.

38. Maspero, "The Mythology of Modern China," pp. 352–53; Dore, *Researches into Chinese Superstitions*, p. 226.

39. Paul, *Women in Buddhism*, p. 254.

40. Ibid., pp. 261–62.

41. Ibid., p. 258.

42. *The Journey to the West*, vol. 1, p. 439; vol. 2, pp. 279–80.

43. Dore, *Researches into Chinese Superstitions*, pp. 168–69.

44. Li sheng-hua, "Kuan-shih-yin p'u-sa chih yen-chiu" ("A Study of the Bodhisattva Kuan-shih-yin"), *Chung-shan-ta-hsüeh min-su chou-k'an* (September 1929), p. 8. I would like to thank Professor Bart Tsui and Mr. Yu-Kwan Ng for translating this article for me.

45. Welch, *The Practice of Chinese Buddhism, 1900–1950*, p. 517.

46. These examples are all described on a contemporary devotional lithograph that contains the mantra of Kuan-yin and a picture of her holding a child and flanked by her two attendants. Devotees are instructed to recite the mantra repeatedly and to keep count of their recitations by burning a hole in the sheet every time they recite the mantra fifty times. There are 240 circles to be burned out on the sheet. After completing the sheet (that is reciting the mantra twelve thousand times) the devotee is assured of getting his or her wish. The examples of Kuan-yin's miraculous interventions described on the sheet provide testimony to the efficacy of calling on the goddess in this fashion. I purchased this devotional "tally sheet" in a temple in Taipei in 1969. I am indebted to Mr. Yu-kwan Ng for translating it for me.

47. Blofeld, *Bodhisattva of Compassion*, p. 34.

48. Ibid., pp. 79–80.

49. Paul, "Kuan-yin: Savior and Savioress," p. 170.

50. *The Journey to the West,* vol. 1, pp. 186ff., 365; vol. 2, pp. 279–80.

51. Ibid., vol. 1, pp. 313–14, 322, 365.

52. Li sheng-hua, "Kuan-shih-yin," p. 14.

53. Blofeld, *Bodhisattva of Compassion,* pp. 114–15.

54. Dore, *Researches into Chinese Superstitions,* p. 161.

55. John P. Ferguson, "The Great Goddess Today in Burma and Thailand: An Exploration of Her Symbolic Relevance to Monastic and Female Roles," in James J. Preston, ed., *Mother Worship: Theme and Variations* (Chapel Hill: University of North Carolina Press, 1982), p. 286.

56. Dudbridge, *The Legend of Miao-shan,* p. 93.

57. Ibid, pp. 95–96.

58. Dore, *Researches into Chinese Superstitions,* p. 140.

59. Ibid., p. 142.

60. Ibid., pp. 145–46.

61. Ibid., p. 147.

62. Ibid., p. 150.

63. Dudbridge, *The Legend of Miao-shan,* p. 41.

64. Dore, *Researches into Chinese Superstitions,* p. 182.

65. Ibid., p. 193.

66. Chamberlayne, "The Development of Kuan Yin," p. 46. For a description of women worshiping Kuan-yin, see Blofeld, *Bodhisattva of Compassion,* pp. 18–19.

67. Maspero, "The Mythology of Modern China," fig. 76, p. 359.

68. The *Lotus-sūtra,* however, says that Avalokiteśvara grants children. *The Saddharma-puṇḍarīka or the Lotus of the True Law,* trans. H. Kern (New Delhi: Motilal Banarsidass, 1965), p. 409.

69. Maspero, "The Mythology of Modern China," p. 358.

70. Ibid., p. 358; Li sheng-hua, "Kuan-shih-yin," p. 21.

71. Daniel L. Overmyer, "Attitudes toward the Ruler and State in Chinese Popular Religious Literature: Sixteenth and Seventeenth Century *Pao-chüan,*" *Harvard Journal of Asiatic Studies,* vol. 44, no. 2 (December 1984), pp. 348–49.

72. Dudbridge, *The Legend of Miao-shan,* p. 86.

73. Ibid., p. 88.

74. Dore, *Researches into Chinese Superstitions,* pp. 166–68.

75. Getty, *The Gods of Northern Buddhism,* p. 84; Dore, *Researches into Chinese Superstitions,* pp. 168–69.

76. Getty, *The Gods of Northern Buddhism,* p. 83.

77. Dore, *Researches into Chinese Superstitions,* p. 229.

78. Li sheng-hua, "Kuan-shih-yin," p. 22.

79. *The Journey to the West,* vol. 2, p. 13.

80. Ibid., pp. 14–15.

81. Ibid., pp. 278–79.

82. *Saddharma-puṇḍarīka,* p. 412.

83. Blofeld, *Bodhisattva of Compassion,* p. 96.

Chapter 3

1. *Lakṣmī Tantra: A Pāñcaratra Text,* trans. Sanjukta Gupta (Leiden: E. J. Brill, 1972), 45.17–20, p. 303.

2. Throughout this chapter, I assume that Śrī and Lakṣmī are identical. It seems clear that in almost every case the names refer to the same goddess. For a discussion of the evidence suggesting their independent identity, see Bandana Sarawati, "The History of the Worship of Srī in North India to cir. A.D. 550" (Ph.D diss., University of London, 1971), pp. 291–96.

3. Jan Gonda, *Aspects of Early Viṣṇuism* (Delhi: Motilal Banarsidass, 1966), p. 188. Compare the role of Isis vis-à-vis the pharaoh, chap. 9 herein.

4. Although a process of personification seems evident in the origin of the goddess Śrī in Vedic literature, it may be that her origins lie in pre-Vedic, Indo-European traditions in which goddesses of royal power are common. It has long been known that the authors of the *Vedas* were Indo-Aryans and therefore related to other Indo-European peoples. As regards the goddess Śrī, it is significant to note that goddesses like her, goddesses associated with royal power and authority, are found in several Indo-European traditions. The Irish goddess Flaith or Flaith Erenn is a good example. See Alf Hiltebeitel, *The Ritual of Battle* (Ithaca, N.Y.: Cornell University Press, 1976), p. 176.

5. *Śatapatha-brāhmaṇa* 11.4.3.1ff.

6. For the text and translation of this hymn, see Saraswati, "History of the Worship of Srī," pp. 22–31.

7. Upendra Nath Dhal, *Goddess Laksmi: Origin and Development* (New Delhi: Oriental Publishers, 1978), p. 178; see also the Worship of Śrī later in this chapter.

8. F. D. K. Bosch, *The Golden Germ* ('s-Gravenhage: Mouton & Co., 1960), pp. 81–82.

9. Curt Maury, *Folk Origins of Indian Art* (New York: Columbia University Press, 1969), p. 114. Maury interprets the lotus as a symbol of the female sexual organ, which also emphasizes the meaning of the lotus as the source of all life or a symbol of all life (pp. 110–11).

10. Niranjan Ghosh, *Concept and Iconography of the Goddess of Abundance and Fortune in Three Religions of India* (Burdwan: University of Burdwan, 1979), p. 54: Bosch, *The Golden Germ,* p. 80; Ananda Coomaraswamy, *Yaksas* (Delhi: Munshiram Manoharlal, 1971), pt. 2, pp. 56–60.

11. For a discussion of these images, see Ghosh, *Concept and Iconography of the Goddess,* pp. 75–87; Saraswati, "History of the Worship of Srī," pp. 159–61; Kiran Thaplyal, "Gajalakṣmī on Seals," in D. C. Sircar, ed., *Foreigners in Ancient India and Lakṣmī and Sarasvatī in Art and Literature* (Calcutta: University of Calucutta, 1970), pp. 112–25.

12. Heinrich Zimmer, *The Art of Indian Asia* (New York: Pantheon Books, 1955), vol. 1, pp. 160–61.

13. Jan Gonda, *Ancient Indian Kingship from the Religious Point of View* (Leiden: E. J. Brill, 1969), pp. 7–8.

14. J. C. Heesterman, *The Ancient Indian Royal Consecration* (The Hague: Mouton, 1957), pp. 114–22.

15. Gonda, *Ancient Indian Kingship,* p. 37, notes that Lakṣmī is equated with *abhiṣekha* in some texts and is said to dwell in the royal umbrella.

16. Saraswati, "History of the Worship of Srī," p. 187.
17. Ibid., pp. 157–59.
18. Dhal, *Goddess Laksmi,* pp. 65–66; Saraswati, "History of the Worship of Srī," pp. 150–53.
19. Dhal, *Goddess Laksmi,* pp. 68–69.
20. Saraswati, "History of the Worship of Srī," pp. 138–47.
21. *Mahābhārata* 12.124.45–47.
22. *Vāmana-purāṇa* 49.14–50; *Māhābhārata* 12.216.16; *Devī-bhāgavata-purāṇa* 8.19.15. See Dhal, *Goddess Laksmi,* pp. 94–95.
23. *Mahābhārata* 12.221.14ff; Dhal, *Goddess Laksmi,* pp. 88–89.
24. For Indra's association with the plough, see *Ṛg-veda* 2.21.1 and 6.20.1. For Indra as a phallic god of fertility, see Wendy O'Flaherty, *Asceticism and Eroticism in the Mythology of Śiva* (London: Oxford University Press, 1973), pp. 85–86.
25. Maury, *Folk Origins of Indian Art,* p. 105, thinks that Śrī-Lakṣmī's association with wealth is subsidiary to her association with vegetation and calls her association with wealth the result of a crass preoccupation with "mundane vanities." Śrī-Lakṣmī's association with wealth, however, seems both ancient and consistent with her other qualities.
26. Dhal, *Goddess Laksmi,* pp. 91–93.
27. Saraswati, "History of the Worship of Srī," pp. 173–77.
28. See Coomaraswamy, *Yaksas,* pt. 1, pp. 32ff., for the woman-and-tree motif.
29. See ibid., pt. 2, pls. 34 and 35.
30. See, for example, *Mahābhārata* 12.220.44–46.
31. Banabhaṭṭa, *Kādambarī* (Bombay: Mathurānāth Śastrī, 1940), pp. 210 ff.; cited in Saraswati, "History of the Worship of Srī," pp. 287–88.
32. For the early history of Śrī's association with Viṣnu, see Saraswati, "History of the Worship of Srī," pp. 113–21.
33. Dhal, *Goddess Laksmi,* pp. 78–80.
34. The story of the churning of the ocean is found in the following texts: *Mahābhārata* 5.102.12ff; *Rāmāyaṇa* 4.58.13; *Viṣṇu-purāṇa* 1.9.105; *Padma-purāṇa* 5.4.1ff; *Bhāgavata-purāṇa* 8.8.7–28; Saraswati, "History of the Worship of Srī," pp. 299ff.
35. For a discussion of the water cosmology, see Coomaraswamy, *Yaksas,* pt. 2, pp. 19–26.
36. Zimmer, *Art of Indian Asia,* vol. 1, pp. 165–66.
37. *Viṣṇu-purāṇa* 1.9ff.; *Padma-purāṇa* 1.5.4ff.; Dhal, *Goddess Laksmi,* pp. 84–85.
38. Gonda, *Aspects of Early Viṣṇuism,* pp. 164–67.
39. See Zimmer, *Art of Indian Asia,* vol. 2, pl. 111; Saraswati, "History of the Worship of Srī," pp. 234–38.
40. For Śrī-Lakṣmī's accompanying Viṣṇu in his different *avatāras,* see Saraswati, "History of the Worship of Srī," pp. 133, 267–73; *Lakṣmī-tantra* 8.31–50; K. S. Behera, "Lakṣmī in Orissan Literature and Art," in Sircar, ed., *Foreigners in Ancient India,* pp. 96–97.
41. Behera, "Lakṣmī in Orissan Literature and Art," p. 101.
42. Saraswati, "History of the Worship of Srī," p. 242.
43. *Brahma-vaivarta-purāṇa* 3.23.19ff.; Dhal, *Goddess Laksmi,* p. 117.

44. *Garuda-purāṇa* 5.37; Dhal, *Goddess Laksmi*, p. 118.

45. Dhal, *Goddess Laksmi*, p. 118.

46. Saraswati, "History of the Worship of Srī," p. 239.

47. Ibid., p. 244.

48. D. C. Sircar, "Ardhanārī-Nārayaṇa," in Sircar, ed., *Foreigners in Ancient India*, pp. 132–41; Ghosh, *Concept and Iconography of the Goddess*, pp. 92–96.

49. Saraswati, "History of the Worship of Srī," pp. 133–35.

50. F. Otto Schrader, *Introduction to the Pāncarātra and the Ahirbudhnya Saṃhitā* (Madras: Adyar Library, 1916), pp. 34–35.

51. Translations are from Gupta's translation of the *Lakṣmī Tantra*.

52. See, for example, *Lakṣmī-tantra* 45.16–21.

53. Ghosh, *Concept and Iconography of the Goddess*, p. 28.

54. It is interesting to note that Śrī does *not* play a significant role in this respect in the thought of Rāmānuja, the most famous philosopher of the Śrī Vaiṣṇava movement; John Carman, *The Theology of Rāmānuja* (New Haven, Conn.: Yale University Press, 1974), pp. 238–44.

55. Vasuda Narayanan, "The Goddess Śrī: The Blossoming Lotus and Breast Jewel of Viṣṇu," in John Stratton Hawley and Donna Marie Wulff, eds., *The Divine Consort: Rādhā and the Goddesses of India* (Berkeley: Berkeley Religious Studies Series, 1982), p. 225.

56. Ibid., p. 226.

57. Vasudhā Nārāyaṇaṉ, "*Karma* and *Kṛpā*. Human Bondage and Divine Grace: The Teṅkalai Śrī Vaiṣṇava Position" (unpublished paper, DePaul University, Chicago, n.d.), p. 4.

58. Ibid., p. 5.

59. Maury, *Folk Origins of Indian Art*, pp. 101–2.

60. Dhal, *Goddess Laksmi*, pp. 164–84.

61. M. Srivastava, *Mother Goddess*, p. 189.

62. Dhal, *Goddess Laksmi*, p. 176.

63. Behera, "Lakṣmī in Orissan Literature and Art," pp. 104–5.

64. See chap. 1 herein.

65. Dhal, *Goddess Laksmi*, p. 179.

66. Ibid., p. 178.

67. Ibid., pp. 150–56, 177–78.

68. M. Srivastava, *Mother Goddess*, p. 190.

69. Dahl, *Goddess Laksmi*, pp. 166–67.

70. Behera, "Lakṣmī in Orissan Literature and Art," pp. 100–102, speaking of the festival tradition at the Jagannātha temple in Puri.

Chapter 4

1. Muraoka Tsunetsugu, *Studies in Shinto Thought*, trans. Delmer M. Brown and James T. Araki (Ministry of Education, Japan, 1964), p. 143.

2. Odette Bruhl, "Japanese Mythology," in Robert Graves, ed., *Larousse Encyclopedia of Mythology* (New York: Prometheus Press, 1960), p. 414.

3. *Kojiki*, trans. Donald L. Philippi (Princeton, N.J.: Princeton University Press, 1969), chap. 3.

4. Ibid., chap. 6.

5. Ibid., chaps. 10–12.

6. The *Kojiki* was compiled at the order of Empress Gemmyo (707–15) to preserve ancient legends. It was completed in 712. Empress Gemmyo also commissioned a national history, which was completed in the reign of her successor, Emperor Gensho (715–26). This was the *Nihongi*, completed in 720.

7. *Nihongi*, trans. W. G. Aston (London: George Allen & Unwin, 1956).

8. Ibid., pp. 19–20.

9. *Kojiki*, chap. 14, pp. 74–75.

10. Ibid., p. 77.

11. Ibid., chap. 16; in the *Nihongi* Amaterasu is described as injuring herself in this incident, p. 41.

12. *Nihongi*, p. 41.

13. *Kojiki*, chap. 17; *Nihongi*, pp. 42–45.

14. D. C. Holtom, *The National Faith of Japan: A Study in Modern Shinto* (New York: Paragon Book Reprint Corp., 1965), p. 147.

15. *Nihongi*, p. 47.

16. Mircea Eliade, *Patterns in Comparative Religion*, trans. Rosemary Sheed (Cleveland, Ohio: World Publishing Co., 1958), pp. 333, 354–61.

17. Bruhl, "Japanese Mythology," p. 418.

18. *Nihongi*, p. 33.

19. Ibid.

20. Ibid., p. 83; Jean Herbert, *Shinto: At the Fountain-head of Japan* (New York: Stein & Day Publishers, 1967), pp. 360–61.

21. *Nihongi*, p. 83.

22. Holtom, *The National Faith of Japan*, p. 129, quoting from the Teacher's Manual for the *National History for Ordinary Primary Schools*, vol. 1.

23. *Nihongi*, pp. xi–xv.

24. *Kojiki*, chap. 46; Holtom, *The National Faith of Japan*, p. 128.

25. *Nihongi*, p. 77.

26. Kitabatake Chikafusa, *A Chronicle of Gods and Sovereigns: Jinnō Shōtōki*, trans. H. Paul Varley (New York: Columbia University Press, 1980), p. 49.

27. Ibid., p. 76; see also Holtom, *The National Faith of Japan*, p. 130.

28. *Nihongi*, p. 83.

29. Chikafusa, *Jinnō Shōtōki*, p. 78.

30. Ibid., p. 78.

31. Ibid., p. 25.

32. Quoted in Robert J. Smith, *Ancestor Worship in Contemporary Japan* (Stanford, Calif.: Stanford University Press, 1974), pp. 32–33, italics mine.

33. Robert N. Bellah, *Tokugawa Religion* (Boston: Beacon Press, 1957), p. 101.

34. *Kojiki*, chap. 17, pp. 81–82; chap. 39, p. 139.

35. Ibid., chap. 19, p. 90.

36. *Nihongi*, p. 83.

37. Chikafusa, *Jinnō Shōtōki*, p. 76. Amaterasu does not say these words in the various mythical accounts of her commissioning of Ninigi. Very similar words, spoken by a chieftan to Emperor Chūai, are found in the *Nihongi*, however. Chikafusa, *Jinnō Shōtōki*, p. 76 n.

38. Ibid., p. 77.

39. Ibid.

40. Ibid.

41. Ibid.

42. Ibid.

43. Ibid.

44. See Atsuhiko Yoshida, *Nihon-shinwa no Gemryu* (Tokyo: Kodansha, 1976), translated for me by Hisayoshi Miyamoto; and I. A. Yoshida, "Japanese Mythology and the Indo-European Trifunctional System," *Diogenes*, vol. 98 (1977), pp. 93–116.

45. Smith, *Ancestor Worship in Contemporary Japan*, pp. 8–9.

46. Ibid., p. 32, quoting John Caiger, "The Aims and Content of School Courses in Japanese History, 1972–1945," in Edmund Skrzypczak, ed., *Japan's Modern Century* (Tokyo: Sophia University, 1968), pp. 67–68.

47. Tsunetsugu, *Studies in Shinto Thought*, p. 35.

48. Ibid., pp. 37–39.

49. Bellah, *Tokugawa Religion*, p. 155.

50. Ryusaku Tsunoda et al., *Sources of Japanese Tradition*, vol. 2 (New York: Columbia University Press, 1968), p. 17.

51. Smith, *Ancestor Worship in Contemporary Japan*, p. 62.

52. Holtom, *The National Faith of Japan*, p. 249.

53. Ibid., pp. 249–50.

54. Ibid., p. 251.

55. Chikafusa, *Jinnō Shōtōki*, p. 50.

56. Stuart D. B. Picken, *Shinto: Japan's Spiritual Roots* (Tokyo: Kodansha, 1980), p. 36.

57. Herbert, *Shinto*, p. 372.

58. Tsunetsugu, *Studies in Shinto Thought*, pp. 238–39.

59. Chikafusa, *Jinnō Shōtōki*, pp. 233–34.

60. Picken, *Shinto*, p. 36.

61. Herbert, *Shinto*, p. 412.

62. Kyoko Motomochi Nakamura, "The Significance of Amaterasu in Japanese Religious History," in Carl Olson, ed., *The Book of the Goddess Past and Present: An Introduction to Her Religion* (New York: Crossroad, 1983), p. 181.

63. Ibid., pp. 182–83; see also Robert S. Ellwood, "The Saigū: Princess and Priestess," *History of Religions*, vol. 7, no. 1 (August 1967), pp. 35–60.

64. Herbert, *Shinto*, p. 372.

65. Holtom, *The National Faith of Japan*, p. 136.

66. Herbert, *Shinto*, p. 373.
67. Ibid.
68. Wilhelmus H. M. Creemers, *Shrine Shinto after World War II* (Leiden: E. J. Brill, 1968), p. 32.
69. Picken, *Shinto*, pp. 39–40.
70. Floyd Hiatt Ross, *Shinto: The Way of Japan* (Boston: Beacon Press, 1965), p. 79.
71. Ibid., pp. 51–54.
72. Picken, *Shinto*, p. 37.
73. Herbert, *Shinto*, p. 371.
74. Ibid., p. 372.
75. Ibid., p. 466, quoting Mock Joya, *Things Japanese* (Tokyo: Tokyo News Service, 1960).
76. Picken, *Shinto*, p. 28.
77. Herbert, *Shinto*, p. 466.
78. Ibid., p. 521.
79. Picken, *Shinto*, p. 33.
80. Interview with Hisayoshi Miyamoto.

Chapter 5

1. *The Rāmāyaṇa of Tulasīdāsa*, trans. F. S. Growse (Delhi: Motilal Banarsidass, 1978), p. 153.
2. Edmour Babineau, "The Interaction of Love of God and Social Duty in the Rāmcaritmānas" (Ph.D. diss., McMaster University, Hamilton, Ont., 1975), pp. 46–48; R. G. Bhandarkar, *Vaiṣṇavism, Śaivism and Minor Religious Systems* (Strassburg: K. J. Trübner, 1913), pp. 75–76.
3. *Ṛg-veda* 4.47.6-7; *The Hymns of the Ṛgveda*, trans. Ralph T. H. Griffith (2 vols.; 4th ed.; Banaras: Chowkhamba Sanskrit Series Office, 1963), vol. 1, p. 461.
4. Cornelia Dimmitt, "Sītā: Mother Goddess and *Śakti*," in John Stratton Hawley and Donna Marie Wulff, eds., *The Divine Consort: Rādhā and the Goddesses of India* (Berkeley: Berkeley Religious Studies Series, 1982), p. 211.
5. Ibid., p. 212.
6. Ibid.
7. *Śatapatha-brāhmaṇa* 7.2.2.2–21.
8. Dimmitt, "Sītā," p. 212.
9. Jan Gonda, *Ancient Indian Kingship from the Religious Point of View* (Leiden: E. J. Brill, 1969), pp. 6–8, 129.
10. See, for example, *Ṛg-veda* 1.22.
11. Gonda, *Ancient Indian Kingship*, p. 130; Phyllis Kaplan Herman, "Ideal Kingship and the Feminine Power: A Study of the Depiction of 'Rāmrājya' in the Vālmīki Rāmāyaṇa" (Ph.D. diss., University of California, Los Angeles, 1979), pp. 65–75.
12. *Mahābhārata* 5.102ff.; *Rāmāyaṇa* 4.58; *Viṣṇu-purāṇa* 1.9.105; *Padma-purāṇa* 5.4.1ff.; *Bhāgavata-purāṇa* 8.8.7–28.

13. Herman, "Ideal Kingship and the Feminine Power," p. 56.

14. *Viṣṇu-purāṇa* 4.5.28; Herman, "Ideal Kingship and the Feminine Power," p. 114.

15. Mircea Eliade, *Patterns in Comparative Religion,* trans. Rosemary Sheed (Cleveland, Ohio: World Publishing Co., 1958), pp. 259–60.

16. *Rāmāyaṇa* 2.114.

17. Ibid. 3.63.

18. Ananda Coomaraswamy, "On the Loathly Bride," *Speculum: A Journal of Medieval Studies,* vol. 20, no. 4 (1945), p. 396.

19. *The Laws of Manu,* trans. G. Bühler (Delhi: Motilal Banarsidass, 1975), p. 196.

20. Ibid., p. 328.

21. *Rāmāyaṇa* 5.22.

22. *The Ramayaṇa of Valmiki,* trans. Hari Prasad Shastri (3 vols.; London: Shantisadan, 1957–62), vol. 1, p. 233.

23. Ibid., pp. 236–37.

24. Ibid., p. 238.

25. Ibid., vol 2, pp. 373–74.

26. Ibid., p. 377.

27. Ibid., p. 379.

28. Ibid., vol. 3, p. 336.

29. Ibid., p. 338.

30. Ibid., p. 529.

31. Ibid., p. 617.

32. M. N. Srinivas, *Marriage and Family in Mysore* (Bombay: New Book Co., 1942), p. 195.

33. Sudhir Kakar, *The Inner World: A Psycho-analytic Study of Childhood and Society in India* (Oxford: Oxford University Press, 1978), p. 62.

34. Akshaykumar Kayal, "Women in Folk-Sayings of West Bengal," in Sankar Sen Gupta, ed., *A Study of Women in Bengal* (Calcutta: Indian Publications, 1970), p. xxiii.

35. Kakar, *The Inner World,* p. 64.

36. Babineau, "Love of God and Social Duty," pp. 161–238.

37. Tulsī Dās, *Kavitāvalī,* trans. F. R. Allchin (London: George Allen & Unwin, 1964), p. 76.

38. *Vinaya-patrikā* 104.1; Tulsī Dās, *The Petition to Rām,* trans. Raymond Allchin (London: George Allen & Unwin, 1966), p. 155.

39. Tulsī Dās, *The Ramayana of Tulsidas,* trans. A. C. Atkins (New Delhi: Hindustan Times, n.d.), vol. 1, p. 1.

40. Norvin Hein, "The Rām Līlā," in Milton Singer, ed., *Traditional India: Structure and Change* (Philadelphia: American Folklore Society, 1959), p. 87.

41. See, for example, *Vinaya-patrikā* 53.4, 55.2, 58.1, 63.8, 77.1.

42. Introductory hymn to *Rāmcarit-mānas;* hymns introducing *Vinaya-patrikā* 15 and 16 to Pārvatī, Durgā, and Kālikā; 17-20 to Gaṅgā; and 21 to Yamunā.

43. *Vinaya-patrikā* 41–42.

44. Babineau, "Love of God and Social Duty," p. 287.

Chapter 6

1. Diana Wolkstein and Samuel Noah Kramer, *Inanna: Queen of Heaven and Earth* (New York: Harper & Row, 1983), p. 93.

2. Thorkild Jacobsen, *The Treasures of Darkness: A History of Mesopotamian Religion* (New Haven, Conn.: Yale University Press, 1976), p. 36.

3. Ibid.

4. Ibid.

5. Ibid., pp. 34–35.

6. Ibid., p. 36.

7. Samuel Noah Kramer, *From the Poetry of Sumer: Creation, Glorification, Adoration* (Berkeley: University of California Press, 1979), pp. 93–94.

8. Wolkstein and Kramer, *Inanna*, p. 39.

9. Jacobsen, *The Treasures of Darkness*, p. 45.

10. Ibid., p. 46.

11. James B. Pritchard, ed., *Ancient Near Eastern Texts Relating to the Old Testament* (3d ed.; Princeton, N.J.: Princeton University Press, 1969), p. 644.

12. William W. Hallo and J. J. A. Van Dijk, *The Exaltation of Inanna* (New Haven, Conn.: Yale University Press, 1968), p. 21.

13. Ibid.

14. Pritchard, ed., *Ancient Near Eastern Texts*, p. 108.

15. Jacobsen, *The Treasures of Darkness*, p. 28.

16. Wolkstein and Kramer, *Inanna*, p. 37.

17. Ibid., p. 44.

18. Pritchard, ed., *Ancient Near Eastern Texts*, p. 383.

19. Wolkstein and Kramer, *Inanna*, p. 48. See also Pritchard, ed., *Ancient Near Eastern Texts*, p. 645, for a translation of the same hymn.

20. *Gilgamesh*, trans. John Gardner and John Maier (New York: Alfred A. Knopf, 1984), pp. 148–49.

21. Jacobsen, *The Treasures of Darkness*, pp. 139–40.

22. Ibid., p. 140.

23. Kramer, *From the Poetry of Sumer*, p. 95.

24. Wolkstein and Kramer, *Inanna*, p. 108.

25. Samuel Noah Kramer, *The Sacred Marriage Rite: Aspects of Faith, Myth and Ritual in Ancient Sumer* (Bloomington: Indiana University Press, 1969), pp. 49, 57.

26. Jacobsen, *The Treasures of Darkness*, p. 39.

27. Kramer, *The Sacred Marriage Rite*, p. 80.

28. Wolkstein and Kramer, *Inanna*, pp. 107–8.

29. See, for example, Jacobsen, *The Treasures of Darkness*, p. 46.

30. See, for example, Wolkstein and Kramer, *Inanna*, p. 44.

31. Jacobsen, *The Treasures of Darkness*, pp. 41–42. See also Pritchard, ed., *Ancient Near Eastern Texts*, p. 641, and Wolkstein and Kramer, *Inanna*, pp. 46–47, for the same hymn.

32. Wolkstein and Kramer, *Inanna*, p. 12.

33. Ibid., p. 14.
34. Ibid.
35. Kramer, *The Sacred Marriage Rite,* p. 17.
36. Wolkstein and Kramer, *Inanna,* pp. 16–18.
37. Kramer, *From the Poetry of Sumer,* p. 96. See also Jacobsen, *The Treasures of Darkness,* p. 138, for the same hymn.
38. Jacobsen, *The Treasures of Darkness,* p. 136.
39. Ibid., pp. 138–39.
40. Kramer, *From the Poetry of Sumer,* p. 86. See Wolkstein and Kramer, *Inanna,* p. 103, for the same hymn.
41. Pritchard, ed., *Ancient Near Eastern Texts,* p. 383.
42. Hallo and Van Dijk, *The Exaltation of Inanna,* pp. 15–19.
43. Ibid., pp. 31–33. See Pritchard, ed., *Ancient Near Eastern Texts,* p. 581, for the same hymn.
44. Wolkstein and Kramer, *Inanna,* p. 95.
45. Kramer, *From the Poetry of Sumer,* p. 76.
46. Jacobsen, *The Treasures of Darkness,* p. 137.
47. Ibid.
48. My account of the myth follows ibid., pp. 56–63, and Pritchard, ed., *Ancient Near Eastern Texts,* pp. 52–57.
49. Pritchard, ed., *Ancient Near Eastern Texts,* p. 108.
50. Jacobsen, *The Treasures of Darkness,* pp. 62–63.
51. Mircea Eliade, *Patterns in Comparative Religion,* trans. Rosemary Sheed (Cleveland, Ohio: World Publishing Co., 1958), pp. 331–66.
52. Ibid., pp. 349–54.
53. See Sylvia Brinton Perera, *Descent of the Goddess: A Way of Initiation for Women* (Toronto: Inner City Books, 1981), for a psychoanalytical interpretation and appropriation of the myth of Inanna's descent to the underworld.
54. See also Wolkstein and Kramer, *Inanna,* pp. 158–59.
55. Kramer, *From the Poetry of Sumer,* pp. 90–91.
56. Jacobsen, *The Treasures of Darkness,* p. 237.
57. Ibid.
58. Ibid.
59. Ibid., p. 154.
60. Ibid., pp. 148–49.
61. Ibid., p. 141.
62. Ibid.

Chapter 7

1. *Homeric Hymns* 28: "To Athena"; Hugh G. Evelyn-White, trans., *Hesiod, the Homeric Hymns, and Homerica* (New York: G. P. Putnam's Sons, 1920), pp. 453–55.

2. W. K. C. Guthrie, *The Greeks and Their Gods* (Boston: Beacon Press, 1950), pp. 110–12.

3. See below for the attentuated sense in which Metis is Athena's mother.

4. The pre-Greek, indigenous culture of Greece is referred to as Minoan in Crete and as Mycenaean on the Greek mainland. Very little difference exists between them, and the culture is often referred to as Minoan-Mycenaean.

5. Martin P. Nilsson, *The Minoan-Mycenaean Religion and Its Survival in Greek Religion* (Lund: C. W. K. Gleerup, 1968), pp. 321–29, 496–97.

6. Ibid., p. 496.

7. Jane Ellen Harrison, *Prolegomena to the Study of Greek Religion* (Cambridge: Cambridge University Press, 1908), pp. 305–6.

8. Ibid., fig. 83, pp. 303–6.

9. Nilsson, *The Minoan-Mycenaean Religion*, p. 499.

10. Guthrie, *The Greeks and Their Gods*, p. 108.

11. Arthur Bernard Cook, *Zeus* (Cambridge: Cambridge University Press, 1940), vol. 3, p. 224; cited in Guthrie, *The Greeks and Their Gods*, p. 107.

12. O. Seemann, *The Mythology of Greece and Rome* (New York: American Book Co., 1875), pp. 251–52.

13. Robert Graves, *Greek Myths* (4th ed.; London: Cassell, 1965), pp. 96–98. See Benjamin Powell, *Athenian Mythology: Erichthonius and the Three Daughters of Cecrops* (Chicago: Ares Publishers, 1976), for a description and analysis of the many different forms of this myth.

14. Michael Senior, *Greece and Its Myths* (London; Victor Gollancz, 1978), pp. 38–39.

15. Lewis Richard Farnell, *The Cults of the Greek States* (3 vols.; Oxford: Clarendon Press, 1896), vol. 1, p. 302; Karl Kerényi, *Athene: Virgin and Mother: A Study of Pallas Athene*, trans. Murray Stein (Zürich: Spring Publications, 1978), p. 14.

16. Farnell, *The Cults of the Greek States*, vol. 1, p. 339.

17. Ibid., p. 342.

18. C. J. Herington, *Athena Parthenos and Athena Polias: A Study of the Religion of Periclean Athens* (Manchester: Manchester University Press, 1955), p. 46.

19. Ibid., p. 44.

20. Farnell, *The Cults of the Greek States*, vol. 1, p. 301.

21. Cities having an acropolis sacred to Athena included Argos, Sparta, Troy, Smyrna, Epidauros, Troezen, and Pheneus; Graves, *Greek Myths*, p. 47.

22. James Hillman, "On the Necessity of Abnormal Psychology: Ananke and Athene," in James Hillman, ed., *Facing the Gods* (Irving, Tex.: Spring Publications, 1980), p. 19.

23. Farnell, *The Cults of the Greek States*, vol. 1, p. 304.

24. Ibid., pp. 302–3.

25. Christine Downing, *The Goddess: Mythological Images of the Feminine* (New York: Crossroad, 1981), p. 118.

26. Ibid., p. 119.

27. Kerényi, *Athene*, pp. 14–16.

28. Herington, *Athena Parthenos and Athena Polias*, p. 56.

29. Ibid., p. 61.

30. *Homeric Hymns* 11: "To Athena"; Evelyn-White, trans., *Hesiod, the Homeric Hymns, and Homerica*, p. 437.

31. Hesiod *Theogony* 924–25; cited in Kerényi, *Athene*, p. 22.

32. Pindar *Olympia* 7.36; cited in Kerényi, *Athene*, p. 22.

33. Walter Burkert, *Homo Necans: The Anthropology of Ancient Greek Sacrificial Ritual and Myth*, trans. Peter Bing (Berkeley: University of California Press, 1983), pp. 66–67.

34. Kerényi, *Athene*, p. 26.

35. Ibid., p. 21.

36. H. J. Rose, *A Handbook of Greek Mythology* (London: Methuen & Co., 1958), p. 109.

37. Farnell, *The Cults of the Greek States*, vol. 1, p. 281.

38. Walter F. Otto, *The Homeric Gods: The Spiritual Significance of Greek Religion*, trans. Moses Hadas (New York: Pantheon Books, 1954), p. 46.

39. Ibid., p. 48.

40. Iliad 1.195–220.

41. Graves, *Greek Myths*, p. 239.

42. Ibid., p. 452.

43. Ibid., p. 460.

44. Ibid., p. 461.

45. Ibid., p. 522.

46. Ibid., p. 470.

47. Ibid, pp. 481, 515–16.

48. Ibid., p. 544.

49. Hesiod *Shield of Heracles;* Evelyn-White, trans., *Hesiod, the Homeric Hymns, and Homerica*, p. 243.

50. Graves, *Greek Myths*, p. 565.

51. G. S. Kirk, *The Nature of Greek Myths* (New York: Penguin Books, 1974), p. 204.

52. Otto, *The Homeric Gods*, p. 47.

53. Homer *Iliad* 2.180; *The Iliad of Homer,* trans. Andrew Lang, Walter Leaf, and Ernest Myers (New York: Random House, n.d.), p. 24.

54. Homer *Iliad* 2.280–82; trans. Lang *et al*., p. 27.

55. Homer *Odyssey* 13.287–300, 330–31; *The Odyssey of Homer,* trans. Richard Lattimore (New York: Harper & Row, 1965), pp. 205–6.

56. Homer *Odyssey* 13.372; trans. Lattimore, pp. 207–8.

57. Homer *Odyssey* 13.382–91; trans. Lattimore, p. 208.

58. Homer *Odyssey* 12.298–99; trans. Lattimore, p. 329.

59. Graves, *Greek Myths*, p. 734.

60. Otto, *The Homeric Gods*, p. 53.

61. Ibid., pp. 46–48.

62. Hesiod *Theogony;* Evelyn-White, trans., *Hesiod, the Homeric Hymns, and Homerica*, p. 143.

63. In some areas of Malaysia the belief exists that a child is conceived first in the mind of its father, where the embryo acquires its rational nature. The embryo, having gained

its intellectual aspect, is then transferred to the mother, where it grows to term in her womb. See Carol Laderman, "Giving Birth in a Malay Village," in Margarita A. Kay, ed., *Anthropology of Human Birth* (Philadelphia: F. A. Davis Co., 1982), pp. 81–100.

64. Graves, *Greek Myths*, p. 49.

65. Otto, *The Homeric Gods*, p. 59.

66. Paul Friedrich, *The Meaning of Aphrodite* (Chicago: University of Chicago Press, 1978), pp. 90–91.

67. Farnell, *The Cults of the Greek States*, vol. 1, p. 291.

68. Ibid.

69. Ibid., p. 338.

70. Graves, *Greek Myths*, p. 98.

71. Otto, *The Homeric Gods*, p. 56.

72. Ibid., p. 56.

73. *Iliad* 15.412.

74. *Iliad* 5.61.

75. Graves, *Greek Myths*, p. 579.

76. *Homeric Hymns* 5: "To Aphrodite"; Evelyn-White, trans., *Hesiod, the Homeric Hymns, and Homerica*, p. 407.

77. *Odyssey* 6.223.

78. Hesiod *Works and Days;* Evelyn-White, trans., *Hesiod, the Homeric Hymns, and Homerica*, p. 35.

79. *Homer's Epigrams* 14; Evelyn-White, trans., *Hesiod, the Homeric Hymns, and Homerica*, p. 473.

80. Graves, *Greek Myths*, p. 253.

81. Herington, *Athena Parthenos and Athena Polias*, p. 44.

82. Ibid.

83. *Homeric Hymns* 5: "To Aphrodite"; Evelyn-White, trans., *Hesiod, the Homeric Hymns, and Homerica*, p. 407.

84. Graves, *Greek Myths*, p. 633.

85. Charles Seltman, *The Twelve Olympians and Their Guests* (London: Max Parrish, 1952), p. 58.

86. Graves, *Greek Myths*, pp. 96–97.

87. Sarah B. Pomeroy, *Goddesses, Whores, Wives, and Slaves: Women in Classical Antiquity* (New York: Schocken Books, 1975), p. 4.

88. Graves, *Greek Myths*, p. 430.

89. Harrison, *Prolegomena to the Study of Greek Religion*, p. 303.

90. Downing, *The Goddess*, p. 119.

91. Kerényi, *Athene*, p. 75.

92. Ibid.

93. Hillman, "Ananke and Athene," p. 27.

94. Ibid., p. 28.

95. Ibid., p. 29.

96. Ibid., p. 31.

97. Jean Shinoda Bolen, *Goddesses in Everywoman: A New Psychology of Women* (San Francisco: Harper & Row, 1984), p. 23.

98. Ibid., pp. 9–10.

99. Ibid., p. 78.

100. Ibid., p. 80.

101. Ibid., p. 82.

102. Downing, *The Goddess*, p. 100.

103. Ibid.

104. Ibid., p. 102.

105. Ibid., p. 105.

106. Ibid.

107. Harrison, *Prolegomena to the Study of Greek Religion*, p. 303.

108. Bolen, *Goddesses in Everywoman*, p. 100.

109. Ibid., p. 101.

110. Ibid., pp. 105–6.

111. Downing, *The Goddess*, p. 124.

112. Mary Daly, *Gyn/Ecology: The Metaethics of Radical Feminism* (Boston: Beacon Press, 1978), p. 72.

Chapter 8

1. *The Golden Ass of Apuleius*, trans. Robert Graves (New York: Pocket Library, 1954), pp. 254–55.

2. The myth is told in its most complete form in *Plutarch's De Iside et Osiride*, ed. and trans. J. Gwyn Griffiths (N.p.: University of Wales Press, 1970), chaps. 13–20, pp. 137–47. For abbreviated versions of the myth see Sharon Kelly Heyob, *The Cult of Isis among Women in the Graeco-Roman World* (Leiden: E. J. Brill, 1975), pp. 40–42, and Barbara Watterson, *The Gods of Ancient Egypt* (London: B. T. Batsford Ltd., 1984), pp. 90–96.

3. Vera Frederika Vanderlip, *The Four Greek Hymns of Isidorus and the Cult of Isis* (Toronto: A. M. Hakkert Ltd., 1972), hymn 1, v. 11, p. 18; hymn 2, v. 16, p. 36.

4. *Plutarch's De Iside et Osiride*, chap. 32, p. 167.

5. R. E. Witt, *Isis in the Graeco-Roman World* (London: Thames & Hudson, 1971), p. 39.

6. Ibid.

7. For the spread of Isis and her religion to the Greco-Roman world, see Françoise Dunand, *Le Culte d'Isis dans le bassin oriental de la Mediterranée* (3 vols., Leiden: E. J. Brill, 1973).

8. Witt, *Isis in the Graeco-Roman World*, p. 30.

9. Heyob, *The Cult of Isis*, p. 50.

10. *The Golden Ass of Apuleius*, p. 236.

11. Witt, *Isis in the Graeco-Roman World*, p. 33.

12. Friedrich Solmsen, *Isis among the Greeks and Romans* (Cambridge, Mass.: Harvard University Press, 1979), pp. 23–24.

13. Dunand, *Le Culte d'Isis*, vol. 1, pp. 80–84.

14. Heyob, *The Cult of Isis*, pp. 48–49; Vanderlip, *The Four Greek Hymns of Isidorus*, pp. 35–36; and Witt, *Isis in the Graeco-Roman World*, pp. 126–27.

15. Vanderlip, *The Four Greek Hymns of Isidorus*, pp. 35–36.

16. Witt, *Isis in the Graeco-Roman World*, p. 187.

17. France Le Corsu, *Isis, mythe et mystères* (Paris: Société d'Edition "Les Belles Lettres," 1977), p. 20.

18. Witt, *Isis in the Graeco-Roman World*, p. 93.

19. Walter Jayne, *The Healing Gods of Ancient Civilization* (New Haven, Conn.: Yale University Press, 1925), p. 67.

20. Witt, *Isis in the Graeco-Roman World*, p. 195.

21. Ibid., p. 189.

22. Tran tam Tinh, "Sarapis and Isis," in Ben F. Meyer and E. P. Sanders, eds., *Jewish and Christian Self-Definition*, Vol. 3: *Self-Definition in the Greco-Roman World* (Philadelphia: Fortress Press, 1982) p. 111.

23. Witt, *Isis in the Graeco-Roman World*, pp. 195–96.

24. Jayne, *The Healing Gods*, pp. 66–67.

25. Cited in Tran tam Tinh, "Sarapis and Isis," p. 111.

26. Witt, *Isis in the Graeco-Roman World*, p. 196.

27. Dunand, *Le Culte d'Isis*, vol. 2, p. 198.

28. Heyob, *The Cult of Isis*, p. 48.

29. Ibid., p. 43. See also Le Corsu, *Isis*, pp. 15–16.

30. For examples of such images see: Witt, *Isis in the Graeco-Roman World*, pl. 8 (opposite p. 72); François Dunand, *Religion populaire en Egypte romaine* (Leiden: E. J. Brill, 1979), pls. 1–4 and 8–12; and Le Corsu, *Isis*, pl. 1, p. 16.

31. Heyob, *The Cult of Isis*, pp. 74–75.

32. Ibid., p. 51–52.

33. Ibid., p. 50.

34. Ibid., p. 69; Dunand, *Religion populaire*, pp. 68–69.

35. Vanderlip, *The Four Greek Hymns of Isidorus*, p. 36.

36. Heyob, *The Cult of Isis*, p. 51.

37. Ibid., pp. 52, 70–71.

38. Ibid., p. 71.

39. Ibid., p. 44.

40. Witt, *Isis in the Graeco-Roman World*, p. 41.

41. Tran tam Tinh, "Sarapis and Isis," p. 107.

42. Heyob, *The Cult of Isis*, p. 80.

43. Vanderlip, *The Four Greek Hymns of Isidorus*, p. 6.

44. Solmsen, *Isis among the Greeks and Romans*, p. 24.

45. Vanderlip, *The Four Greek Hymns of Isidorus*, hymn 1, vv. 5–6, p. 18.

46. Ibid., hymn 1, vv. 9–13, p. 18.

47. *The Golden Ass of Apuleius*, pp. 254–55, 238–39.

48. Vanderlip, *The Four Greek Hymns of Isidorus*, p. 50.

49. In some accounts of Isis's sojourn in Byblos, where she had gone to retrieve Osiris's corpse, she cared for the child of the king of Byblos. At night Isis would put the child into a fire to burn away its mortal parts. It was her intention to grant immortality to humankind in this way. However, she was interrupted by the distrustful queen one night and had to cease the fiery initiation of the child that would have won deathlessness for human beings (Watterson, *The Gods of Ancient Egypt*, p. 91). In the context of her cult, then, immortality was not a natural blessing of Isis to all people but a special, unusual blessing for her own devotees, which they achieved, presumably, through their initiation.

50. See, for example, Le Corsu, *Isis*, figs. 3–6, pp. 9–10.

51. Witt, *Isis in the Graeco-Roman World*, pp. 198ff.

52. *The Golden Ass of Apuleius*, p. 252.

53. Ibid., p. 253.

54. Vanderlip, *The Four Greek Hymns of Isidorus*, hymn 1, vv. 29–34, pp. 18–19.

55. Witt, *Isis in the Graeco-Roman World*, p. 183.

56. Ibid., p. 136.

57. Ibid., pp. 134–35.

58. Vanderlip, *The Four Greek Hymns of Isidorus*, p. 4; Solmsen, *Isis among the Greeks and Romans*, p. 95.

59. Witt, *Isis in the Graeco-Roman World*, pp. 136–37.

60. *The Golden Ass of Apuleius*, p. 237; see also Vanderlip, *The Four Greek Hymns of Isidorus*, hymn 1, vv. 15–22, p. 18.

61. *The Golden Ass of Apuleius*, p. 239.

62. Ibid., p. 240.

63. Ibid., p. 254.

64. Heyob, *The Cult of Isis*, p. 79; Dunand, *Le Culte d'Isis*, vol. 3, pp. 337–40.

65. Watterson, *The Gods of Ancient Egypt*, p. 36.

66. Dunand, *Le Culte d'Isis*, vol. 3, p. 274.

67. Vanderlip, *The Four Greek Hymns of Isidorus*, hymn 3, vv. 26–27, p. 51.

68. Witt, *Isis in the Graeco-Roman World*, p. 128.

69. Ibid., p. 106.

70. For a discussion of theories concerning how Isis came to be considered supreme among the deities of the Greco-Roman world, and in the process came to be identified with other goddesses, see Dunand, *Le Culte d'Isis*, vol. 1, pp. 27–108, and Tran tam Tinh, "Sarapis and Isis," pp. 103–5.

71. *The Golden Ass of Apuleius*, pp. 236–37.

72. Ibid., pp. 238–39.

Chapter 9

1. *Homeric Hymns* 6: "To Aphrodite"; Hugh G. Evelyn-White, trans., *Hesiod, the Homeric Hymns, and Homerica* (New York: G. P. Putnam's Sons, 1920), pp. 427–29.

2. Lewis Richard Farnell, *The Cults of the Greek States* (3 vols.; Oxford: Clarendon Press, 1896), vol. 2, p. 618.

3. Geoffrey Grigson, *The Goddess of Love: The Birth, Triumph, Death and Return of Aphrodite* (London: Constable & Co., 1976), p. 97.

4. Paul Friedrich, *The Meaning of Aphrodite* (Chicago: University of Chicago Press, 1978), pp. 62–64.

5. See, for example, Lewis Campbell, *Religion in Greek Literature* (Freeport, N.Y.: Books for Libraries Press, 1971), p. 234; Farnell, *The Cults of the Greek States,* vol. 2, pp. 636–43; G. S. Kirk, *The Nature of Greek Myths* (New York: Penguin Books, 1974), p. 258; Walter F. Otto, *The Homeric Gods: The Spiritual Significance of Greek Religion* (New York: Pantheon Books, 1954), p. 91; and Michael Senior, *Greece and Its Myths* (London: Victor Gollancz, 1978), p. 147.

6. Friedrich, *The Meaning of Aphrodite,* pp. 17–23.

7. Hesiod *Theogony;* Evelyn-White, trans., *Hesiod, the Homeric Hymns and Homerica,* p. 93.

8. Friedrich, *The Meaning of Aphrodite,* pp. 198–99.

9. See, for example, *Iliad* 5:297–448.

10. Deborah Dickmann Boedeker, *Aphrodite's Entry into Greek Epic* (Leiden: E. J. Brill, 1974), pp. 12–17; Friedrich, *The Meaning of Aphrodite,* pp. 44–45.

11. Farnell, *The Cults of the Greek States,* vol. 2, pp. 657–64.

12. Robert Graves, *Greek Myths* (4th ed.; London: Cassell, 1965), p. 50.

13. Martin P. Nilsson, *The Minoan-Mycenaean Religion and Its Survival in Greek Religion* (Lund: C. W. K. Gleerup, 1968), pp. 336, 397; Jane Ellen Harrison, *Prolegomena to the Study of Greek Relgion* (Cambridge: Cambridge University Press, 1908), p. 308.

14. Friedrich, *The Meaning of Aphrodite,* pp. 9–54, suggests other historical roots that may have influenced the formation of Aphrodite.

15. O. Seemann, *The Mythology of Greece and Rome* (New York: American Book Co., 1875), p. 65.

16. Hesiod *Theogony;* Evelyn-White, trans., *Hesiod, the Homeric Hymns, and Homerica,* p. 93.

17. Homer *Iliad* 14.346–53; *The Iliad of Homer,* trans. Richard Lattimore (Chicago: University of Chicago Press, 1951), p. 303.

18. Otto, *The Homeric Gods,* p. 95.

19. Farnell, *The Cults of the Greek States,* vol. 2, p. 642; Friedrich, *The Meaning of Aphrodite,* p. 75.

20. Otto, *The Homeric Gods,* p. 94.

21. Friedrich, *The Meaning of Aphrodite,* p. 75.

22. Euripides *Medea* 835ff.; cited in Otto, *The Homeric Gods,* p. 94.

23. Otto, *The Homeric Gods,* p. 94.

24. Ibid.

25. Friedrich, *The Meaning of Aphrodite,* p. 75.

26. Grigson, *The Goddess of Love,* p. 193; Friedrich, *The Meaning of Aphrodite,* p. 75.

27. Friedrich, *The Meaning of Aphrodite,* p. 75.

28. Grigson, *The Goddess of Love,* p. 191.

29. Ibid., pp. 190–98; Friedrich, *The Meaning of Aphrodite,* p. 75.

30. Farnell, *The Cults of the Greek States,* vol. 2, pp. 697–98.

31. Friedrich, *The Meaning of Aphrodite,* p. 70.

32. Cora Angier Sowa, *Traditional Themes and the Homeric Hymns* (Chicago: Bolchazy-Carducci Publishers, 1984), p. 48.

33. Ibid., pp. 79–80.

34. *Homeric Hymns* 5: "To Aphrodite"; Evelyn-White, trans., *Hesiod, the Homeric Hymns, and Homerica,* p. 411.

35. Friedrich, *The Meaning of Aphrodite,* p. 77.

36. Grigson, *The Goddess of Love,* p. 187.

37. Denys L. Page, *Sappho and Alcaeus* (Oxford: Clarendon Press, 1955), pp. 7–8; cited in Friedrich, *The Meaning of Aphrodite,* p. 77.

38. Marcel Detienne, *Les Jardins d'Adonis* (Paris: Gallimard, 1972), p. 162; cited in Friedrich, *The Meaning of Aphrodite,* p. 77; Grigson, *The Goddess of Love,* pp. 207–8.

39. Arianna Stassinopoulos and Roloff Beny, *The Gods of Greece* (London: Weidenfeld & Nicolson, 1983), p. 80.

40. Grigson, *The Goddess of Love,* p. 102.

41. Ibid., pp. 103–4.

42. Elmer G. Suhr, *Venus de Milo the Spinner* (New York: Exposition Press, 1958), p. 64.

43. Grigson, *The Goddess of Love,* p. 211.

44. Farnell, *The Cults of the Greek States,* vol. 2, p. 652.

45. Ibid.

46. Ibid.

47. Ibid., p. 653.

48. Mircea Eliade, *Patterns in Comparative Religion,* trans. Rosemary Sheed (Cleveland, Ohio: World Publishing Co., 1958), pp. 331–66.

49. Walter Burkert, *Homo Necans: An Anthropology of Ancient Greek Sacrificial Ritual and Myth,* trans. Peter Bing (Berkeley: University of California Press, 1983), pp. 68, 71, 115.

50. *Homeric Hymns* 5: "To Aphrodite"; Evelyn-White, trans., *Hesiod, the Homeric Hymns, and Homerica,* pp. 407–9.

51 Farnell, *The Cults of the Greek States,* vol. 2, p. 655.

52. Ibid., p. 656.

53. Ibid.

54. Otto, *The Homeric Gods,* p. 96.

55. *Odyssey* 20:70–74.

56. Farnell, *The Cults of the Greek States,* vol. 2, p. 657.

57. Ibid., p. 655.

58. Ibid., p. 700.

59. Ibid.

60. Friedrich, *The Meaning of Aphrodite,* p. 89.

61. Ibid.

62. Homer *Iliad* 3.395–96; trans. Lattimore, p. 110.

63. *Homeric Hymns* 5: "To Aphrodite"; Evelyn-White, trans., *Hesiod, the Homeric Hymns, and Homerica*, p. 411.

64. Homer *Odyssey* 8.362–66; *The Odyssey of Homer*, trans. Richard Lattimore (New York: Harper & Row, 1965), p. 130.

65. Homer *Odyssey* 8.339–42; trans. Lattimore, p. 130.

66. See, for example, Grigson, *The Goddess of Love*, p. 96.

67. See, for example, Kenneth Clark, *The Nude: A Study in Ideal Form* (New York: Pantheon Books, 1956), fig. 69, p. 90.

68. Sowa, *Traditional Themes and the Homeric Hymns*, p. 82.

69. Ibid.

70. Ibid., pp. 82–83.

71. Friedrich, *The Meaning of Aphrodite*, p. 78.

72. Farnell, *The Cults of the Greek States*, vol. 2, p. 624.

73. Friedrich, *The Meaning of Aphrodite*, p. 79.

74. Ibid., p. 137.

75. Clark, *The Nude*, p. 84.

76. Ibid., p. 83.

77. Otto, *The Homeric Gods*, p. 93.

78. Ibid., p. 94.

79. Ibid.; Grigson, *The Goddess of Love*, p. 196.

80. Farnell, *The Cults of the Greek States*, vol. 2, p. 690.

81. Grigson, *The Goddess of Love*, pp. 133–34.

82. Ibid., p. 134.

83. Ibid., pp. 134–38.

84. Ibid., p. 91.

85. Clark, *The Nude*, figs. 71–73, p. 92.

86. Grigson, *The Goddess of Love*, p. 92.

87. Friedrich, *The Meaning of Aphrodite*, p. 87.

88. Ibid.

89. Ibid.

90. Charles Seltman, *The Twelve Olympians and Their Guests* (London: Max Parrish, 1952), p. 79.

91. Ibid.

92. *Homeric Hymns* 5: "To Aphrodite"; Evelyn-White, trans., *Hesiod, the Homeric Hymns, and Homerica*, p. 407.

93. Grigson, *The Goddess of Love*, p. 102.

94. Whitney J. Oates and Eugene O'Neill, Jr., eds., *The Complete Greek Drama* (2 vols.; New York: Random House, 1938), vol. 1, p. 775.

95. Hesiod, *Theogony;* Evelyn-White, trans., *Hesiod, the Homeric Hymns, and Homerica*, p. 93.

96. Ibid., p. 87.

97. Oates and O'Neill, eds., *The Complete Greek Drama*, vol. 1, p. 795.

98. Grigson, *The Goddess of Love*, p. 67.

99. Otto, *The Homeric Gods*, p. 98; Seemann, *The Mythology of Greece and Rome*, p. 67.

100. Grigson, *The Goddess of Love*, pp. 74–81.

101. Ibid., p. 71.

102. Ibid., p. 72.

103. Ibid., fig. 16, p. 73.

104. Friedrich, *The Meaning of Aphrodite*, pp. 202–3.

105. Grigson, *The Goddess of Love*, p. 20.

106. Hesiod *Theogony;* Evelyn-White, trans., *Hesiod, the Homeric Hymns and Homerica*, p. 93.

107. Grigson, *The Goddess of Love*, p. 38; for images of Aphrodite emerging from a scallop shell see his figs. 5 and 6, pp. 37–38.

108. Ibid., p. 38.

109. Farnell, *The Cults of the Greek States*, vol. 2, p. 636.

110. Grigson, *The Goddess of Love*, pp. 111–24.

111. Ibid., p. 123.

112. Ibid.

113. Friedrich, *The Meaning of Aphrodite*, p. 199.

114. Hesiod *Theogony;* Evelyn-White, trans., *Hesiod, the Homeric Hymns, and Homerica*, p. 95.

115. Sowa, *Traditional Themes and the Homeric Hymns*, p. 76.

116. Homer *Iliad* 14.215–20; trans. Lattimore, pp. 297–98.

117. Graves, *Greek Myths*, pp. 633–34.

118. *Homeric Hymns* 5: "To Aphrodite"; Evelyn-White, trans., *Hesiod, the Homeric Hymns, and Homerica*, p. 415.

119. Ibid., pp. 411–19.

120. Farnell, *The Cults of the Greek States*, vol. 2, pp. 664–65.

121. Grigson, *The Goddess of Love*, p. 95.

122. Farnell, *The Cults of the Greek States*, vol. 2, p. 665.

123. Ibid., p. 680.

124. Stassinopoulos and Beny, *The Gods of Greece*, p. 85.

125. Otto, *The Homeric Gods*, p. 96.

126. Ibid., p. 98.

127. *Homeric Hymns* 5: "To Aphrodite"; Evelyn-White, trans., *Hesiod, The Homeric Hymns, and Homerica*, p. 417.

128. Ibid., p. 411.

129. Graves, *Greek Myths*, pp. 356–58.

130. Otto, *The Homeric Gods*, p. 99.

131. Jean Shinoda Bolen, *Goddesses in Everywoman: A New Psychology of Women* (San Francisco: Harper & Row, 1984), pp. 236–37.

132. Grigson, *The Goddess of Love*, p. 200.

133. Ibid., p. 70.

134. See, for example, Friedrich, *The Meaning of Aphrodite*, p. 124.

135. Ibid., p. 112.
136. Ibid., pp. 116–17.
137. Harrison, *Prolegomena to the Study of Greek Religion*, p. 314.
138. Bolen, *Goddesses in Everywoman*, p. 242.
139. Ibid., p. 242.
140. Artemis is the virgin goddess of the hunt in Greek mythology.
141. Hera is the wife of Zeus, king of the Greek pantheon. Hera is strongly associated with marriage.
142. Demeter is associated with the growth of crops and plays an important role as the mother of Persephone in Greek mythology.
143. Hestia is the virgin goddess of the hearth and home in Greek mythology.
144. *Homeric Hymns* 5: "To Aphrodite"; Evelyn-White, trans., *Hesiod, the Homeric Hymns, and Homerica*, pp. 407–9.
145. Bolen, *Goddesses in Everywoman*, p. 243.
146. Ibid., p. 254.
147. Christine Downing, *The Goddess: Mythological Images of the Feminine* (New York: Crossroad, 1981), p. 189.
148. Ibid.
149. Ibid., p. 191.
150. Ibid., p. 193.
151. Ibid., p. 201.

Chapter 10

1. English translation of the Salve Regina from John A. Hardon, *Modern Catholic Dictionary* (Garden City, N.Y.: Doubleday & Co., 1980), p. 486.
2. Translations of the Bible are from the *The Holy Bible: Revised Standard Version* (New York: Thomas Nelson & Sons, 1946, 1952).
3. *The Apocryphal New Testament*, trans. Montague Rhodes James (rev. ed.; Oxford: Clarendon Press, 1953), pp. 38–41.
4. Ibid., pp. 42–45.
5. Ibid., pp. 45–47.
6. Ibid., pp. 47–49.
7. Ibid., p. 215.
8. Ibid., p. 217.
9. Ibid., pp. 207–8.
10. Ibid., p. 208.
11. Marina Warner, *Alone of All Her Sex: The Myth and the Cult of the Virgin Mary* (London: Weidenfeld & Nicolson, 1976), pp. 64–66. For an excellent discussion of the theological, sociological, and political implications of virginity in the early church, see Peter Brown, "The Notion of Virginity in the Early Church," in Bernard McGinn, John Meyendorff, and Jean Leclercq, eds., *Christian Spirituality, Origins to the Twelfth Century* (New York: Crossroad, 1985), pp. 427–43. Brown notes that within the early

church taking a vow of celibacy was a dramatic way of declaring that one had a new allegiance to an ideal order or society that was radically different from the old society, in which marriage and family alliances were central. For a Freudian interpretation of Mary's virginity, see Michael P. Carroll, *The Cult of the Virgin Mary: Psychological Origins* (Princeton, N.J.: Princeton University Press, 1986). Carroll argues that Marian devotion became most popular in areas (notably southern Italy and Spain) where "father ineffective" families produced males who developed strong but repressed sexual desire for their mothers. Mary represents the mother to these males. Her complete disassociation from sex represents the male's repression of sexual desire for his mother, who at the conscious level becomes asexual. Carroll's theory, no matter what we may think of Freudian interpretive categories, seems peculiarly weak in that it neglects almost entirely the fact that Marian devotion has been extremely popular among women.

12. Warner, *Alone of All Her Sex*, pp. 51–52.

13. Ibid., p. 54.

14. Hilda Graef, *Mary: A History of Doctrine and Devotion* (2 vols.; New York: Sheed & Ward, 1963, 1965), vol. 1, pp. 80–81.

15. Warner, *Alone of All Her Sex*, p. 73.

16. Ibid.

17. The virginity of Jesus is not clear in the Bible but has been assumed since very early times in Christian tradition.

18. Warner, *Alone of All Her Sex*, pp. 198–99.

19. Ibid., pp. 197–98.

20. Ibid., p. 213.

21. Ibid., p. 218.

22. An example of such is an image found at the church and monastery at Mariastein in Switzerland; P. Lukas Schenker, *Mariastein, Führer durch Wallfahrt und Kloster* (Einsiedeln: Josef Eberle, 1982), p. 9.

23. Warner, *Alone of All Her Sex*, p. 218.

24. Anthony Petti and Geoffrey Laycock, eds., *New Catholic Hymnal* (London: Faber Music Ltd., 1971), p. 14.

25. See Warner, *Alone of All Her Sex*, pl. 8 (opposite p. 197), and pp. 326–28.

26. Ibid., p. 280.

27. Ibid., pp. 280–81.

28. Ibid., p. 281.

29. Ibid.

30. Ibid., pp. 274–75.

31. Ibid., p. 278. In some cases Mary acts very much like local non-Christian goddesses who control fertility and local well-being. In many parts of the world, towns, villages, cities, and regions know a patron goddess who, among other things, influences or controls the crops and diseases. A small village shrine to Mary in rural Italy is mentioned in Ignazio Silone's novel *Bread and Wine* (trans. Gwenda David and Eric Mosbacher [New York: New American Library, 1961], p. 42). A villager explains that one year roses bloomed, cherries ripened, and sheep lambed in January and a cholera outbreak struck the village in the summer; the chapel was built "to keep our Lady quiet." Another example in this vein concerns Mary's appearance in 1846 to two children who were tending sheep. The Virgin of La Salette, as she came to be known, warned the

children that she had come to the end of her patience at the sinful actions of humankind and could withhold her son's anger no longer. She demanded that people repent and threatened poor harvests if she was not obeyed (Graef, *Mary,* vol. 2, p. 101).

32. Warner, *Alone of All Her Sex,* p. 283.

33. Leonard W. Moss and Stephen C. Cappannari, "In Quest of the Black Virgin: She Is Black because She Is Black," in James J. Preston, ed., *Mother Worship: Theme and Variations* (Chapel Hill: University of North Carolina Press, 1982), p. 63.

34. Ibid.

35. Ibid., p. 65. See also Ean Begg, *The Cult of the Black Virgin* (London: Routledge & Kegan Paul, 1986). For the relationship of Mary to earlier goddesses in the ancient world, see Ethelbert Stauffer, "Antike Madonnenreligion," in Hildegard Temporini and Wolfgang Haase, eds., *Aufstieg und Niedergang der Römischen Welt* (Berlin: Walter De Gruyter, 1984), vol. 17, pt. 3, pp. 1426–99.

36. Warner, *Alone of All Her Sex,* p. 319.

37. Graef, *Mary,* vol. 1, p. 171.

38. Warner, *Alone of All Her Sex,* p. 324.

39. Graef, *Mary,* vol. 1, p. 309.

40. Ibid.

41. Ibid., pp. 238–39.

42. The image is used by Theophanes of Nicaea (d. 1381) (ibid., p. 337) and Robert Bellarmine (d. 1621) (ibid., vol. 2, p. 25), for example.

43. Ibid., vol. 2, p. 39.

44. Ibid., p. 40.

45. Ibid., p. 75.

46. Ibid.

47. Warner, *Alone of All Her Sex,* p. 293.

48. Ibid., p. 326.

49. Ibid., p. 325.

50. *The Apocryphal New Testament,* pp. 563–64.

51. Gregory Alastruey, *The Blessed Virgin Mary,* trans. Sister M. Janet La Giglia (2 vols; St. Louis: B. Herder Book Co., 1964), vol. 2, pp. 274–75.

52. Piero Bianconi, *Ex voto del Ticino* (Locarno: Armando Dado Editore, 1980).

53. Jacques Le Graff, *The Birth of Purgatory,* trans. Arthur Goldhammer (Chicago: University of Chicago Press, 1984), p. 178.

54. Graef, *Mary,* vol. 1, p. 38.

55. Ibid., p. 39. Tertullian (160–245) makes the same parallel (ibid.).

56. Ibid., pp. 40–47.

57. The evidence that Jesus was a virgin is not overwhelming.

58. Graef, *Mary,* vol. 2, p. 27.

59. Ibid.

60. Ibid., p. 81. Images showing Mary stepping or standing on a serpent are very common throughout the Christian world.

61. Warner, *Alone of All Her Sex,* p. 107; see also fig. 12 (following p. 100).

62. Ibid., p. 130.

63. Ibid., figs. 16 and 17 (following p. 100).
64. See, for example, ibid., pl. 4, fig. 6 (following p. 196).
65. As an example, see the version of this theme by Velasquez (ibid., fig. 18 [following p. 100]).
66. Graef, *Mary,* vol. 2, p. 27.
67. Ibid, p. 28.
68. Ibid.
69. Ibid., p. 36.
70. Ibid., p. 39.
71. Warner, *Alone of All Her Sex,* fig. 24 (following p. 100) and fig. 45 (following p. 292).
72. Ibid., p. 7, fig. 9 (following p. 196).
73. Henry Adams, *Mont-Saint-Michel and Chartres* (Boston: Houghton Mifflin Co., 1933), p. 95.
74. Ibid., p. 93.
75. Ibid., p. 147.
76. Ibid., p. 92.
77. Warner, *Alone of All Her Sex,* p. 304.
78. Jacques Lafaye, *Quetzalcoatl and Guadalupe: The Formation of Mexican National Consciousness, 1531–1813,* trans. Benjamin Keen (Chicago: University of Chicago Press, 1976), p. 226.
79. The traditional date of this apparition is December 9, 1531, but there is some debate concerning it. See ibid., pp. 248–49.
80. Ibid., p. 232.
81. Ena Campbell, "The Virgin of Guadalupe and the Female Self-Image: A Mexican Case History," in Preston, ed., *Mother Worship,* pp. 12–13.
82. Ibid., p. 17.
83. Lafaye, *Quetzalcoatl and Guadalupe,* p. xix.
84. Campbell, "The Virgin of Guadalupe," p. 9.
85. Lafaye, *Quetzalcoatl and Guadalupe,* p. 3.
86. Campbell, "The Virgin of Guadalupe," p. 10.
87. Eric Wolf, "The Virgin of Guadalupe: A Mexican National Symbol," *Journal of American Folklore,* vol. 71 (1958), pp. 34–39.
88. Campbell, "The Virgin of Guadalupe," p. 9.
89. Lafaye, *Quetzalcoatl and Guadalupe,* p. 300.
90. Warner, *Alone of All Her Sex,* p. 313. The recent appearances of Mary to teenagers in Medjugorje, Yugoslavia, is interpreted by political authorities as having anti-Communist implications and inspiration. "A cartoon in a national paper shows the Blessed Virgin dressed as a terrorist, a large knife held between her teeth, appearing to some children. The caption reads: 'The true face of the Blessed Mother' " (Lucy Rooney and Robert Faricy, *Mary, Queen of Peace: Is the Mother of God Appearing in Medjugorje?* [New York: Alba House, 1984], p. 10).
91. Lafaye, *Quetzalcoatl and Guadalupe,* pp. 227–28.
92. Katharine Moore, *She for God: Aspects of Women and Christianity* (London: Allison & Busby, 1978), p. 69.

93. Warner, *Alone of All Her Sex*, p. 158.

94. Ibid., pp. 156–57.

95. Ruth Cranston, *The Miracle of Lourdes* (New York: McGraw-Hill, 1957).

96. Warner, *Alone of All Her Sex*, pp. 330–31.

97. E. Ann Matter, "The Virgin Mary: A Goddess?," in Carl Olsen, ed., *The Book of the Goddess, Past and Present* (New York: Crossroad, 1983), p. 91. In the Montreal suburb of Ste-Marthe-sur-le-Lac, a small image of Mary on the domestic altar of Maurice Girouard was reported to shed tears and blood and to be attracting many pilgrims. One devotee claimed that "God is telling us to change our war mentality," while another said that the Virgin cried and bled because of child abuse and divorce (Toronto *Globe and Mail*, January 11, 1986, pp. 1, 12). This was subsequently proven a fraud.

98. See, for example, Mary Daly, *The Church and the Second Sex* (New York: Harper & Row, 1968), pp. 156–65; Mary Daly, *Pure Lust: Elemental Feminist Philosophy* (Boston: Beacon Press, 1984), pp. 91–116; and John A. Phillips, *Eve: The History of an Idea* (San Francisco: Harper & Row, 1984), pp. 145–47.

99. Andrew M. Greeley, *The Mary Myth: On the Femininity of God* (New York: Seabury Press, 1977), p. 13.

100. See also Maria Kassel, "Mary and the Human Psyche Considered in the Light of Depth Psychology," in Hans Küng and Jürgen Moltmann, eds., *Mary in the Churches* (New York: Seabury Press, 1983), pp. 74–82.

101. Greeley, *The Mary Myth*, p. 15 n.

102. Greeley, *The Mary Myth*, p. 12, quoting Charles Dickson, "Mariology: A Protestant Reconsideration," *American Ecclesiastical Review* (May 1974), pp. 306–7.

103. Mary Daly, *Beyond God the Father: Toward a Philosophy of Women's Liberation* (Boston: Beacon Press, 1973), pp. 84–85.

104. Ibid., p. 87.

105. Ibid., p. 89.

106. Rosemary Radford Ruether, *Mary—the Feminine Face of the Church* (Philadelphia: Westminster Press, 1977), pp. 78–80.

107. Rosemary Radford Ruether, *New Woman, New Earth: Sexist Ideologies and Human Liberation* (New York: Seabury Press, 1975), p. 58.

108. Virgil Elizondo, "Mary and the Poor: A Model of Evangelising Ecumenism," in Küng and Moltmann, eds., *Mary in the Churches*, p. 63.

109. Karl-Josef Kuschel, "Mary and Literature," in Küng and Moltmann, eds., *Mary in the Churches*, pp. 88–89.

Conclusion

1. The problems associated with referring to Kuan-yin and Mary as goddesses are taken up in the respective chapters concerned with these two superbeings.

2. For an attempt to trace female imagery of the divine in the Bible, see Virginia Ramey Mollenkott, *The Divine Feminine: The Biblical Imagery of God as Female* (New York: Crossroad, 1983). For an attempt to trace female imagery in the third person of the Christian Trinity, see Donald L. Gelpi, *The Divine Mother: A Trinitarian Theology of the Holy Spirit* (Lanham, Md.: University Press of America, 1984).

WORKS CITED

Adams, Henry. *Mont-Saint-Michel and Chartres*. Boston: Houghton Mifflin Co., 1933.

Alastruey, Gregory. *The Blessed Virgin Mary*. Translated by Sister M. Janet La Giglia. 2 vols. St. Louis: B. Herder Book Co., 1964.

The Apocryphal New Testament. Translated by Montague Rhodes James. Rev. ed. Oxford: Clarendon Press, 1953.

[Apuleius]. *The Golden Ass of Apuleius*. Translated by Robert Graves. New York: Pocket Library, 1954.

Arthur, Marylin. "'Liberated' Women: The Classical Era." In Renate Bridenthal and Claudia Koonz, eds. *Becoming Visible: Women in European History*. Boston: Houghton Mifflin Co., 1977. Pp. 60–89.

Babb, Laurence A. *The Divine Hierarchy: Popular Hinduism in Central India*. New York: Columbia University Press, 1975.

Babineau, Edmour. "The Interaction of Love of God and Social Duty in the Rāmcaritmānas." Ph.D. diss., McMaster University, Hamilton, Ont., 1975.

Bachofen, J. J. *Myth, Religion, and Mother Right*. Translated by Ralph Manheim. Bollingen Series, vol. 84. Princeton, N.J.: Princeton University Press, 1967.

Bamberger, Joan. "The Myth of Matriarchy: Why Men Rule in Primitive Society." In Michelle Zimbalist Rosaldo and Louise Lamphere, eds. *Women, Culture, and Society.* Stanford, Calif.: Stanford University Press, 1974. Pp. 263–80.

Banerjea, Jitendra Nath. *The Development of Hindu Iconography.* 2d ed. Calcutta: University of Calcutta, 1956.

Barstow, Anne L. "The Prehistoric Goddess." In Carl Olson, ed., *The Book of the Goddess Past and Present: An Introduction to Her Religion*. New York: Crossroad, 1983. Pp. 7–15.

Begg, Ean. *The Cult of the Black Virgin*. London: Routledge & Kegan Paul, 1986.

Behera, K. S. "Laksṃī in Orissan Literature and Art." In D. C. Sircar, ed. *Foreigners in Ancient India and Lakṣmī and Sarasvatī in Art and Literature*. Calcutta: University of Calcutta, 1970. Pp. 91–105.

Bellah, Robert N. *Tokugawa Religion*. Boston: Beacon Press, 1957.

Berger, Pamela. *The Goddess Obscured: Transformation of the Grain Protectress from Goddess to Saint*. Boston: Beacon Press, 1985.

Bhandarkar, R. G. *Vaiṣṇavism, Śaivism and Minor Religious Systems*. Strassburg: K. J. Trübner, 1913.

Bhattacharyya, Narendra Nath. *History of Śākta Religion*. New Delhi: Munshiram Manoharlal Publishers, 1974.

Bianconi, Piero. *Ex voto del Ticino*. Locarno: Armando Dado Editore, 1980.

Binford, Sally. "Myths and Matriarchies." *Anthropology*. Vols. 81/82, no. 1 (1981), pp. 150–53.

Blofeld, John. *Bodhisattva of Compassion: The Mystical Tradition of Kuan Yin*. Boulder, Colo.: Shambhala, 1978.

Boedeker, Deborah Dickman. *Aphrodite's Entry into Greek Epic*. Leiden: E. J. Brill, 1974.

Bolen, Jean Shinoda. *Goddesses in Everywoman: A New Psychology of Women*. San Francisco: Harper & Row, 1984.

Bosch, F. D. K. *The Golden Germ*. 's-Gravenhage: Mouton & Co., 1960.

Boulding, Elise. *The Underside of History: A View of Women through Time*. Boulder, Colo.: Westview Press, 1976.

Bridenthal, Renate, and Claudia Koonz, eds. *Becoming Visible: Women in European History.* Boston: Houghton Mifflin Co., 1977.

Briffault, Robert. *The Mothers*. Abridged ed. London: George Allen & Unwin, 1959. Originally published in 1927.

Brown, Peter. "The Notion of Virginity in the Early Church." In Bernard McGinn, John Meyendorff, and Jean Leclerq, eds. *Christian Spirituality, Origins to the Twelfth Century*. New York: Crossroad, 1985. Pp. 427–43.

Bruhl, Odette. "Japanese Mythology." In Robert Graves, ed. *Larousse Encyclopedia of Mythology*. New York: Prometheus Press, 1960.

Burkert, Walter. *Homo Necans: The Anthropology of Ancient Greek Sacrifical Ritual and Myth*. Translated by Peter Bing. Berkeley: University of California Press, 1983.

Campbell, Ena. "The Virgin of Guadalupe and the Female Self-Image: A Mexican Case History." In James J. Preston, ed. *Mother Worship: Theme and Variations*. Chapel Hill: University of North Carolina Press, 1982. Pp. 5–24.

Campbell, Joseph. *The Masks of God: Primitive Mythology*. New York: Viking Press, 1959.

Campbell, Lewis. *Religion in Greek Literature*. Freeport, N.Y.: Books for Libraries Press, 1971.

Carman, John. *The Theology of Rāmānuja*. New Haven, Conn.: Yale University Press, 1974.

Carroll, Michael P. *The Cult of the Virgin Mary: Psychological Origins*. Princeton, N.J.: Princeton University Press, 1986.

Chamberlayne, John H. "The Development of Kuan Yin: Chinese Goddess of Mercy." *Numen*. Vol. 9 (January 1962), pp. 45–52.

Ch'en, Kenneth. *Buddhism in China: A Historical Survey*. Princeton, N.J.: Princeton University Press, 1964.

Chikafusa, Kitabatake. *A Chronicle of Gods and Sovereigns: Jinnō Shōtōki*. Translated by H. Paul Varley. New York: Columbia University Press, 1980.

Clark, Kenneth. *The Nude: A Study in Ideal Form*. New York: Pantheon Books, 1956.

Coomaraswamy, Ananda. "On the Loathly Bride." *Speculum: A Journal of Medieval Studies*. Vol. 20, no. 4 (1945), pp. 391–404.

———. *Yaksas*. Delhi: Munshiram Manoharlal, 1971.

Cranston, Ruth. *The Miracle of Lourdes*. New York: McGraw-Hill, 1957.

Creemers, Wilhelmus H. M. *Shrine Shinto after World War II*. Leiden: E. J. Brill, 1968.

Daly, Mary. *Beyond God the Father: Toward a Philosophy of Women's Liberation*. Boston: Beacon Press, 1973.

———. *The Church and the Second Sex*. New York: Harper & Row, 1968.

———. *Gyn/Ecology: The Metaethics of Radical Feminism*. Boston: Beacon Press, 1978.

———. *Pure Lust: Elemental Feminist Philosophy*. Boston: Beacon Press, 1984.

[*Devī-māhātmya*]. *The Glorification of the Great Goddess*. Edited and translated by Vasudeva S. Agrawala. Varanasi: All-India Kashiraj Trust, 1963.

Dhal, Upendra Nath. *Goddess Laksmi: Origin and Development*. New Delhi: Oriental Publishers, 1978.

Dimmitt, Cornelia. "Sītā: Mother Goddess and *Śakti*." in John Stratton Hawley and Donna Marie Wulff, eds. *The Divine Consort: Rādhā and the Goddesses of India*. Berkeley: Berkeley Religious Studies Series, 1982. Pp. 210–23.

Dore, Henry. *Researches into Chinese Superstitions*. Translated by M. Kennelly. Vol. 6. Taipei: Ch'eng-wen Publishing Co., 1920.

Downing, Christine. *The Goddess: Mythological Images of the Feminine*. New York: Crossroad, 1981.

———. "The Mother Goddess among the Greeks." In Carl Olson, ed. *The Book of the Goddess Past and Present: An Introduction to Her Religion*. New York: Crossroad, 1983. Pp. 49–59.

Dubois, Abbé J. A. *Hindu Manners, Customs and Ceremonies*. Translated by Henry K. Beauchamp. 3d ed. Oxford: Clarendon Press, 1906.

Dudbridge, Glen. *The Legend of Miao-shan*. London: Ithaca Press, 1978.

Dunand, Françoise. *Le Culte d'Isis dans le bassin oriental de la Mediterranée*. 3 vols. Leiden: E. J. Brill, 1973.

Eliade, Mircea. *Patterns in Comparative Religion*. Translated by Rosemary Sheed. Cleveland, Ohio: World Publishing Co., 1958.

Elizondo, Virgil. "Mary and the Poor: A Model of Evangelising Ecumenism." In Hans Küng and Jürgen Moltmann, eds., *Mary in the Churches*. New York: Seabury Press, 1983. Pp. 59–65.

Ellwood, Robert S. "Patriarchal Revolution in Ancient Japan: Episodes from the *Nihonshoki Sūjin Chronicle*." *Journal of Feminist Studies in Religion*. Vol. 2, no. 2 (Fall 1986), pp. 23–38.

———. "The Saigū: Princess and Priestess." *History of Religions*. Vol. 7, no. 1 (August 1967), pp. 35–60.

Evelyn-White, Hugh G., trans. *Hesiod, the Homeric Hymns, and Homerica*. New York: G. P. Putnam's Sons, 1920.

Farnell, Lewis Richard. *The Cults of the Greek States*. 3 vols. Oxford: Clarendon Press, 1896.

Ferguson, John P. "The Great Goddess Today in Burma and Thailand: An Exploration of Her Symbolic Relevance to Monastic and Female Roles." In James J. Preston, ed. *Mother Worship: Theme and Variations*. Chapel Hill: University of North Carolina Press, 1982. Pp. 283–303.

Fluehr-Lobban, Carolyn. "A Marxist Reappraisal of the Matriarchate." *Current Anthropology*. Vol. 20 (June 1979), pp. 341–60.

Forbes, Alexander Kinloch. *Rās-Mālā: Hindu Annals of Western India*. New Delhi: Heritage Publishers, 1973.

Friedrich, Paul. *The Meaning of Aphrodite*. Chicago: University of Chicago Press, 1978.

Gelpi, Donald L. *The Divine Mother: A Trinitarian Theology of the Holy Spirit*. Lanham, Md.: University Press of America, 1984.

Getty, Alice. *The Gods of Northern Buddhism*. Translated by J. Deniker. Rutland, Vt.: Charles E. Tuttle Co., 1962.

Ghosh, Niranjan. *Concept and Iconography of the Goddess of Abundance and Fortune in Three Religions of India*. Burdwan: University of Burdwan, 1979.

Ghosha, Pratāpachandra. *Durga Puja: With Notes and Illustrations*. Calcutta: Hindoo Patriot Press, 1871.

Gilgamesh. Translated by John Gardner and John Maier. New York: Alfred A. Knopf, 1984.

Gimbutas, Marija. *The Goddesses and Gods of Old Europe: Myths and Cult Images*. Berkeley: University of California Press, 1982.

———. "Women and Culture in Goddess-Oriented Old Europe." In Charlene Spretnak, ed. *The Politics of Women's Spirituality: Essays on the*

Rise of Spiritual Power within the Feminist Movement. New York: Doubleday & Co., 1982. Pp. 22–31.

Gode, P. K. "Hari Kavi's Contribution to the Problem of the Bhavāni Sword of Shivaji the Great." *New Indian Antiquary*. Vol. 3 (1940–41).

Gonda, Jan. *Ancient Indian Kingship from the Religious Point of View*. Leiden: E. J. Brill, 1969.

———. *Aspects of Early Viṣṇuism*. Delhi: Motilal Banarsidass, 1966.

Graef, Hilda. *Mary: A History of Doctrine and Devotion*. 2 vols. New York: Sheed & Ward, 1963, 1965.

Graves, Robert. *Greek Myths*. 4th ed. London: Cassell, 1965.

———, ed. *Larousse Encyclopedia of Mythology*. New York: Prometheus Press, 1960.

Greeley, Andrew M. *The Mary Myth: On the Feminity of God*. New York: Seabury Press, 1977.

Grigson, Geoffrey. *The Goddess of Love: The Birth, Triumph, Death and Return of Aphrodite*. London: Constable & Co., 1976.

Gupta, Shankar Sen. *A Study of Women in Bengal*. Calcutta: Indian Publications, 1970.

Guthrie, W. K. C. *The Greeks and Their Gods*. Boston: Beacon Press, 1950.

Hallo, William W., and J. J. A. Van Dijk. *The Exaltation of Inanna*. New Haven, Conn.: Yale University Press, 1968.

Hammond, Dorothy, and Alta Jablow. *Women in Cultures of the World*. Menlo Park, Calif.: Cummings Publishing Co., 1976.

Handiqui, Krishna Kanta. *Yaśastilaka and Indian Culture*. Sholapur: Jaina Saṁskṛiti Saṃrakshaka Sangha, 1949.

Hardon, John A. *Modern Catholic Dictionary*. Garden City, N.Y.: Doubleday & Co., 1980.

Harrison, Jane Ellen. *Prolegomena to the Study of Greek Religion*. Cambridge: Cambridge University Press, 1908.

Hawley, John Stratton, and Donna Marie Wulff, eds. *The Divine Consort: Rādhā and the Goddesses of India*. Berkeley: Berkeley Religious Studies Series, 1982.

Heesterman, J. C. *The Ancient Indian Royal Consecration*. The Hague: Mouton, 1957.

Hein, Norvin. "The Rām Līlā." In Milton Singer, ed. *Traditional India: Structure and Change*. Philadelphia: American Folklore Society, 1959. Pp. 73–98.

Herbert, Jean. *Shinto: At the Fountain-head of Japan*. New York: Stein & Day Publishers, 1967.

Herington, C. J. *Athena Parthenos and Athena Polias: A Study of the Religion of Periclean Athens*. Manchester: Manchester University Press, 1955.

Herman, Phyllis Kaplan. "Ideal Kingship and the Feminine Power: A Study of the Depiction of 'Rāmrājya' in the Vālmīki Rāmāyaṇa." Ph.D. diss., University of California, Los Angeles, 1979.

Heyob, Sharon Kelly. *The Cult of Isis among Women in the Graeco-Roman World*. Leiden: E. J. Brill, 1975.

Hillman, James. "On the Necessity of Abnormal Psychology: Ananke and Athene." In James Hillman, ed. *Facing the Gods*. Irving, Tex.: Spring Publications, 1980. Pp. 1–38.

Hiltebeitel, Alf. *The Ritual of Battle*. Ithaca, N.Y.: Cornell University Press, 1976.

Holtom, D. C. *The National Faith of Japan: A Study in Modern Shinto*. New York: Paragon Book Reprint Corp., 1965.

The Holy Bible: Revised Standard Version. New York: Thomas Nelson & Sons, 1946, 1952.

[Homer]. *The Iliad of Homer.* Translated by Andrew Lang, Walter Leaf, and Ernest Myers. New York: Random House, n.d.

———. *The Iliad of Homer.* Translated by Richard Lattimore. Chicago: University of Chicago Press, 1951.

———. *The Odyssey of Homer.* Translated by Richard Lattimore. New York: Harper & Row, 1965.

The Hymns of the Ṛgveda. Translated by Ralph T. M. Griffith. 2 vols. 4th ed. Banaras: Chowkhamba Sanskrit Series Office, 1963.

Jacobsen, Thorkild. *The Treasures of Darkness: A History of Mesopotamian Religion*. New Haven, Conn.: Yale University Press, 1976.

Jayne, Walter. *The Healing Gods of Ancient Civilization*. New Haven, Conn.: Yale University Press, 1925.

The Journey to the West. Translated and edited by Anthony C. Yu. 4 vols. Chicago: University of Chicago Press, 1977–83.

Kakar, Sudhir. *The Inner World: A Psycho-analytic Study of Childhood and Society in India*. Oxford: Oxford University Press, 1978.

Kane, Pandurang V. *History of Dharmaśāstra*. Poona: Bhandarkar Oriental Institute, 1930–62.

Kassel, Maria. "Mary and the Human Psyche Considered in the Light of Depth Psychology." In Hans Küng and Jürgen Moltmann, eds. *Mary in the Churches*. New York: Seabury Press, 1983. Pp. 74–82.

Kayal, Akshaykumar. "Women in Folk-Sayings of West Bengal." In Sankar Sen Gupta, ed. *A Study of Women in Bengal*. Calcutta: Indian Publications, 1970. Pp. ix-xxxii.

Kerényi, Karl. *Athene: Virgin and Mother: A Study of Pallas Athene*. Translated by Murray Stein. Zürich: Spring Publications, 1978.

Kessler, Evelyn. *Women, An Anthropological View*. New York: Holt, Rinehart & Winston, 1976.

Kinsley, David. *The Divine Player—a Study of Kṛṣṇa Līlā*. Delhi: Motilal Banarsidass, 1979.

———. *Hindu Goddesses: Visions of the Divine Feminine in the Hindu Religious Tradition*. Berkeley: University of California Press, 1986.

———. "The Image of the Divine and the Status of Women in the *Devībhāgavata-purāna*." *Anima*. Vol. 9, no. 1 (Fall 1982), pp. 50–56.

———. "The Portrait of the Goddess in the Devī-māhātmya." *Journal of the American Academy of Religion*. Vol. 46, no. 4 (December 1978), pp. 489–506.

Kirk, G. S. *The Nature of Greek Myths*. New York: Penguin Books, 1974.

Kojiki. Translated by Donald L. Phillippi. Princeton, N.J.: Princeton University Press, 1969.

Kramer, Samuel Noah. *From the Poetry of Sumer: Creation, Glorification, Adoration*. Berkeley: University of California Press, 1979.

———. *The Sacred Marriage Rite: Aspects of Faith, Myth and Ritual in Ancient Sumer.* Bloomington: Indiana University Press, 1969.

Küng, Hans, and Jürgen Moltmann, eds. *Mary in the Churches*. New York: Seabury Press, 1983.

Kuschel, Karl-Josef. "Mary and Literature." In Hans Küng and Jürgen Moltmann, eds. *Mary in the Churches*. New York: Seabury Press, 1983. Pp. 83–91.

Laderman, Carol. "Giving Birth in a Malay Village." In Margarita A. Kay, ed. *Anthropology of Human Birth*. Philadelphia: F. A. Davis Co., 1982.

Lafaye, Jacques. *Quetzalcoatl and Guadalupe: The Formation of Mexican National Consciousness, 1531–1813*. Translated by Benjamin Keen. Chicago: University of Chicago Press, 1976.

Lakṣmī Tantra: A Pāñcarātra Text. Translated by Sanjukta Gupta. Leiden: E. J. Brill, 1972.

The Laws of Manu. Translated by G. Bühler. Delhi: Motilal Banarsidass, 1975.

Leacock, Eleanor. "Women in Egalitarian Societies." In Renate Bridenthal and Claudia Koonz, eds. *Becoming Visible: Women in European History*. Boston: Houghton Mifflin Co., 1977. Pp. 11–35.

Le Corsu, France. *Isis, mythe et mystères*. Paris: Société d'Edition "Les Belles Lettres," 1977.

Le Goff, Jacques. *The Birth of Purgatory*. Translated by Arthur Goldhammer. Chicago: University of Chicago Press, 1984.

Lerner, Gerda. *The Creation of Patriarchy*. New York: Oxford University Press, 1986.

Li shen-hua. "Kuan-shih-yin p'u-sa chih yen-chiu" ("A Study of the Bodhisattva Kuan-shih-yin"). *Chung-shan-ta-hsüeh min-su chou-k'an* (September 1929), pp. 5–23.

Maspero, Henri. "The Mythology of Modern China." In J. Hackin et al., eds. *Asiatic Mythology: A Detailed Description and Explanation of the Mythologies of All the Great Nations of Asia*." New York: Thomas Y. Crowell, n.d. Pp. 252–384.

Matter, E. Ann. "The Virgin Mary: A Goddess?" In Carl Olson, ed. *The Book of the Goddess Past and Present: An Introduction to Her Religion*. New York: Crossroad, 1983. Pp. 80–96.

Maury, Curt. *Folk Origins of Indian Art*. New York: Columbia University Press, 1969.

Mollenkott, Virginia Ramey. *The Divine Feminine: The Biblical Imagery of God as Female*. New York: Crossroad, 1983.

Moore, Katharine. *She for God: Aspects of Women and Christianity*. London: Allison & Busby, 1978.

Moss, Leonard W., and Stephen C. Cappannari. "In Quest of the Black Virgin: She Is Black because She Is Black." In James J. Preston, ed. *Mother Wor-*

ship: Theme and Variations. Chapel Hill: University of North Carolina Press, 1982. Pp. 53–74.

Mukerji, Abhay Charan. *Hindu Feasts and Fasts*. Allahabad: Indian Press, 1916.

Nakamura, Kyoko Motomochi. "The Significance of Amaterasu in Japanese Religious History." In Carl Olson, ed. *The Book of the Goddess Past and Present: An Introduction to Her Religion*. New York: Crossroad, 1983. Pp. 176–89.

Nārāyaṇaṉ, Vasudā. "The Goddess Śrī: The Blossoming Lotus and Breast Jewel of Viṣṇu." In John Stratton Hawley and Donna Marie Wulff, eds. *The Divine Consort: Rādhā and the Goddesses of India*. Berkeley: Berkeley Religious Studies Series, 1982. Pp. 224–37.

———. "*Karma* and *Kṛpā*. Human Bondage and Divine Grace: The Teṅkalai Śrī Vaiṣṇava Position." Unpublished paper, DePaul University, Chicago, n.d.

Nihongi. Translated by W. G. Aston. London: George Allen & Unwin, 1956.

Nilsson, Martin P. *The Minoan-Mycenaean Religion and Its Survival in Greek Religion*. Lund: C. W. K. Gleerup, 1968.

Oates, Whitney J., and Eugene O'Neill, Jr., eds. *The Complete Greek Drama*. 2 vols. New York: Random House, 1938.

Ochshorn, Judith. *The Female Experience and the Nature of the Divine*. Bloomington: Indiana University Press, 1981.

O'Flaherty, Wendy. *Asceticism and Eroticism in the Mythology of Śiva*. London: Oxford University Press, 1973.

Olson, Carl, ed. *The Book of the Goddess Past and Present: An Introduction to Her Religion*. New York: Crossroad, 1983.

Öster, Ákos. *The Play of the Gods*. Chicago: University of Chicago Press, 1980.

Ostroff, Pearl. "The Demon-slaying Devī: A Study of Her Purāṇic Myths." M.A. thesis, McMaster University, Hamilton, Ont., 1978.

Otto, Walter F. *The Homeric Gods: The Spiritual Significance of Greek Religion*. Translated by Moses Hadas. New York: Pantheon Books, 1954.

Overmyer, Daniel L. "Attitudes toward the Ruler and State in Chinese Popular Religious Literature: Sixteenth and Seventeenth Century *Pao-chüan*." *Harvard Journal of Asiatic Studies*. Vol. 44, no. 2 (December 1984), pp. 347–79.

Paul, Diana. "Kuan-yin: Savior and Savioress in Chinese Pure Land Buddhism. In Carl Olson, ed. *The Book of the Goddess Past and Present: An Introduction to Her Religion*. New York: Crossroad, 1983. Pp. 161–75.

———. *Women in Buddhism: Images of the Feminine in Mahāyāna Tradition*. Berkeley: University of California Press, 1985.

Perera, Sylvia Brinton. *Descent of the Goddess: A Way of Initiation for Women*. Toronto: Inner City Books, 1981.

Petti, Anthony, and Geoffrey Laycock, eds. *New Catholic Hymnal*. London: Faber Music Ltd., 1971.

Phillips, John A. *Eve: The History of an Idea*. San Francisco: Harper & Row, 1984.

Picken, Stuart D. B. *Shinto: Japan's Spiritual Roots*. Tokyo: Kodansha, 1980.

Plutarch's De Iside et Osiride. Edited and translated by J. Gwyn Griffiths. N.p.: University of Wales Press, 1970.

Pomeroy, Sarah B. "A Classical Scholar's Perspective on Matriarchy." In Berenice A. Carroll, ed. *Liberating Women's History: Theoretical and Critical Essays*. Urbana: University of Illinois press, 1976. Pp. 217–23.

———. *Goddesses, Whores, Wives, and Slaves: Women in Classical Antiquity*. New York: Schocken Books, 1975.

Powell, Benjamin. *Athenian Mythology: Erichthonius and the Three Daughters of Cecrops*. Chicago: Ares Publishing, 1976.

Preston, James J., ed. *Mother Worship: Theme and Variations*. Chapel Hill: University of North Carolina Press, 1982.

Pritchard, James B., ed. *Ancient Near Eastern Texts Relating to the Old Testament*. 3d ed. Princeton, N.J.: Princeton University Press, 1969.

The Ramayaṇa of Valmiki. Translated by Hari Prasad Shastri. 3 vols. London: Shantisadan, 1957–62.

Rich, Adrienne. "Prepatriarchal Female/Goddess Images." In Charlene Spretnak, ed. *The Politics of Women's Spirituality: Essays on the Rise of Spiritual Power within the Feminist Movement*. New York: Doubleday & Co., 1982. Pp. 32–38.

Rohrlich-Leavitt, Ruby. "Women in Transition: Crete and Sumer." In Renate Bridenthal and Claudia Koonz, eds. *Becoming Visible: Women in European History*. Boston: Houghton Mifflin Co., 1977. Pp. 36–59.

Rooney, Lucy, and Robert Faricy. *Mary, Queen of Peace: Is the Mother of God Appearing in Medjugorje?* New York: Alba House, 1984.

Rosaldo, Michelle Zimbalist, and Louise Lamphere. "Introduction." In Michelle Zimbalist Rosaldo and Louise Lamphere, eds. *Women, Culture, and Society*. Stanford, Calif.: Stanford University Press, 1974.

———. eds. *Women, Culture, and Society*. Stanford, Calif.: Stanford University Press, 1974.

Rose, H. J. *A Handbook of Greek Mythology*. London: Methuen & Co., 1958.

Ross, Floyd Hiatt. *Shinto: The Way of Japan*. Boston: Beacon Press, 1965.

Ruether, Rosemary Radford. "The Future of Feminist Theology in the Academy." *Journal of the American Academy of Religion*. Vol. 53, no. 4 (December 1985), pp. 703–13.

———. *Mary—the Feminine Face of the Church*. Philadelphia: Westminster Press, 1977.

———. *New Woman, New Earth: Sexist Ideologies and Human Liberation*. New York: Seabury Press, 1975.

The Saddharma-puṇḍarīka or the Lotus of the True Law. Translated by H. Kern. New Delhi: Motilal Banarsidass, 1965.

Saraswati, Bandana. "The History of the Worship of Srī in North India to cir. A.D. 550." Ph.D. diss., University of London, 1971.

Schenker, P. Lukas. *Mariastein, Führer durch Wallfahrt und Kloster*. Einsiedeln: Josef Eberle, 1982.

Schrader, F. Otto. *Introduction to the Pāncarātra and the Ahirbudhnya Saṃhitā*. Madras: Adyar Library, 1916.

Schüssler-Fiorenza, Elizabeth. *In Memory of Her: A Feminist Theological Reconstruction of Christian Origins*. New York: Crossroad Publishing Co., 1986.

Seckel, Dietrich. *The Art of Buddhism*. New York: Crown Publishers, 1964.

Seeman, O. *The Mythology of Greece and Rome*. New York: American Book Co., 1875.

Seltman, Charles. *The Twelve Olympians and Their Guests*. London: Max Parrish, 1952.

Senior, Michael. *Greece and Its Myths*. London; Victor Gollancz, 1978.

Shulman, David Dean. *Tamil Temple Myths: Sacrifice and Divine Marriage in the South Indian Saiva Tradition*. Princeton, N.J.: Princeton University Press, 1980.

Silone, Ignazio. *Bread and Wine*. Translated by Gwenda David and Eric Mosbacher. New York: New American Library, 1961.

Singer, Milton, ed. *Traditional India: Structure and Change*. Philadelphia: American Folklore Society, 1959.

Sircar, D. C. "Ardhanārī-Nārayaṇa." In D. C. Sircar, ed. *Foreigners in Ancient India and Lakṣmī and Sarasvatī in Art and Literature*. Calcutta: University of Calcutta, 1970. Pp. 132–41.

———, ed. *Foreigners in Ancient India and Lakṣmī and Sarasvatī in Art and Literature*. Calcutta: University of Calcutta, 1970.

Smith, Robert J. *Ancestor Worship in Contemporary Japan*. Stanford, Calif.: Stanford University Press, 1974.

Solmsen, Friedrich. *Isis among the Greeks and Romans*. Cambridge, Mass.: Harvard University Press, 1979.

Sowa, Cora Angier. *Traditional Themes and the Homeric Hymns*. Chicago: Bolchazy-Carducci Publishers, 1984.

Spretnak, Charlene, ed. *The Politics of Women's Spirituality: Essays on the Rise of Spiritual Power within the Feminist Movement*. New York: Doubleday & Co., 1982.

Srinivas, M. N. *Marriage and Family in Mysore*. Bombay: New Book Co., 1942.

Srivastava, Balram. *Iconography of Śakti: A Study Based on Srītattvanidhi*. Delhi: Chaukhambha Orientalia, 1978.

Srivastava, M. C. P. *Mother Goddess in Indian Art, Archaeology and Literature*. Delhi: Agam Kala Prakashan, 1979.

Stassinopoulos, Arianna, and Roloff Beny. *The Gods of Greece*. London: Weidenfeld & Nicholson, 1983.

Stauffer, Ethelbert. "Antike Madonnenreligion." In Hildegard Temporini and Wolfgang Haase, eds. *Aufstieg und Niedergang der Römischen Welt*. Vol. 17, pt. 3. Berlin: Walter De Gruyter, 1984. Pp. 1425–99.

Stone, Merlin. *When God Was a Woman*. New York: Harcourt Brace Jovanovich, 1976.

Suhr, Elmer G. *Venus de Milo the Spinner*. New York: Exposition Press, 1958.

Tay, C. N. "Kuan-yin: The Cult of Half Asia." *History of Religions*. Vol. 16, no. 2 (November 1976), pp. 147–77.

Thaplyal, Kiran. "Gajalakṣmī on Seals." In D. C. Sircar, ed. *Foreigners in Ancient India and Lakṣmī and Sarasvatī in Art and Literature*. Calcutta: University of Calcutta, 1970. Pp. 112–25.

Thomas, Paul. *Hindu Religion, Customs and Manners*. Bombay: Taraporevala, n.d.

Thompson, Edward J., and Arthur Marshman Spencer, trans. *Bengali Religious Lyrics, Śākta*. Calcutta: Association Press, 1923.

Thompson, Laurence G. *The Chinese Way in Religion*. Belmont, Calif.: Dickenson Publishing Co., 1973.

Thompson, William Irwin. *The Time Falling Bodies Take to Light: Mythology, Sexuality, and the Origins of Culture*. New York: St. Martin's Press, 1981.

Tod, James. *Annals and Antiquities of Rajast'han*. New Delhi: M. N. Publishers, 1978.

Tran tam Tinh. "Sarapis and Isis." In Ben F. Meyer and E. P. Sanders, eds. *Jewish and Christian Self-Definition*. Vol. 3: *Self-Definition in the Greco-Roman World*. Philadelphia: Fortress Press, 1982. Pp. 101–17.

Tsunetsugu, Muraoka. *Studies in Shinto Thought*. Translated by Delmar M. Brown and James T. Araki. Ministry of Education, Japan, 1964.

Tsunoda, Ryusaku, et al. *Sources of Japanese Tradition*. Vol. 2. New York: Columbia University Press, 1968.

Tulsī Dās. *Kavitāvalī*. Translated by F. R. Allchin. London: George Allen & Unwin, 1964.

———. *The Petition to Rām*. Translated by F. R. Allchin. London: George Allen & Unwin, 1966.

———. *The Rāmāyaṇa of Tulasīdāsa*. Translated by F. S. Growse. Edited and revised by R. C. Prasad. Delhi: Motilal Banarsidass, 1978.

———. *The Ramayana of Tulsidas*. Translated by A. C. Atkins. New Delhi: Hindustan Times, n.d.

Turner, Victor. *Drama, Fields, and Metaphors: Symbolic Action in Human Society*. Ithaca, N.Y.: Cornell University Press, 1974.

———. *The Ritual Process: Structure and Anti-structure*. Ithaca, N.Y.: Cornell University Press, 1977.

Vākpatirāja's Gauḍavaho. Translated by N. G. Suru. Ahmedabad: Prakrit Text Society, 1975.

Vanderlip, Vera Frederika. *The Four Greek Hymns of Isidorus and the Cult of Isis*. Toronto: A. M. Hakkert Ltd., 1972.

Wakeman, Mary. "Ancient Sumer and the Women's Movement: The Process of Reaching Behind, Encompassing and Going Beyond." *Journal of Feminist Studies in Religion*. Vol. 1, no. 2 (Fall 1985), pp. 7–26.

Warner, Marina. *Alone of All Her Sex: The Myth and the Cult of the Virgin Mary*. London: Weidenfeld & Nicholson, 1976.

Watterson, Barbara. *The Gods of Ancient Egypt*. London: B. T. Batsford Ltd., 1984.

Welch, Holmes. *The Practice of Chinese Buddhism, 1900–1950*. Cambridge, Mass.: Harvard University Press, 1967.

Whitmont, Edward C. *Return of the Goddess*. New York: Crossroad, 1982.

Whyte, Martin King. *The Status of Women in Preindustrial Societies*. Princeton, N.J.: Princeton University Press, 1978.

Witt, R. E. *Isis in the Graeco-Roman World*. London: Thames & Hudson, 1971.

Wolf, Eric. "The Virgin of Guadalupe: A Mexican National Symbol." *Journal of American Folklore*. Vol. 71 (1958), pp. 34–39.

Wolkstein, Diane, and Samuel Noah Kramer. *Inanna: Queen of Heaven and Earth*. New York: Harper & Row, 1983.

Worship of the Goddess according to the Kālikāpurāṇa. Translated by K. R. Van Kooij. Leiden: E. J. Brill, 1972.

Yoshida, Atsuhiko. *Nihon-shinwa no Gemryu*. Tokyo: Kodansha, 1976.

Yoshida, I. A. "Japanese Mythology and the Indo-European Trifunctional System." *Diogenes*. Vol. 98 (1977), pp. 93–116.

Zimmer, Heinrich. *The Art of Indian Asia*. New York: Pantheon Books, 1955.

———. *Myths and Symbols of Indian Art and Civilization*. Edited by Joseph Campbell. New York: Harper & Row, 1962.

INDEX